SE 4 '12

W9-CGX-761

Wauconda Area Library
801 N. Main Street
Wauconda, IL 60084

DISCARD
GIVE AWAY

Key West on the Edge

The Florida History and Culture Series

University Press of Florida

Florida A&M University, Tallahassee
Florida Atlantic University, Boca Raton
Florida Gulf Coast University, Ft. Myers
Florida International University, Miami
Florida State University, Tallahassee
New College of Florida, Sarasota
University of Central Florida, Orlando
University of Florida, Gainesville
University of North Florida, Jacksonville
University of South Florida, Tampa
University of West Florida, Pensacola

Key West

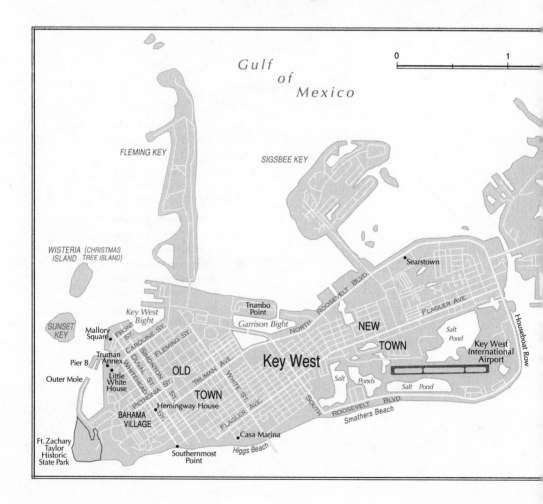

Gulf
of
Mexico

0   1

FLEMING KEY

SIGSBEE KEY

WISTERIA (CHRISTMAS
ISLAND TREE ISLAND)

• Searstown

Trumbo
Point

Garrison Bight

Key West
Bight

SUNSET
KEY

Mallory
Square

FRONT ST.

CAROLINE ST.

SIMONTON ST.

FLEMING ST.

NEW

TOWN

NORTH ROOSEVELT BLVD.

FLAGLER AVE.

Salt
Pond

Houseboat Row

Key West
International
Airport

Truman
Annex

Pier B

DUVAL ST.

WHITEHEAD ST.

Key West

TRUMAN AVE.

WHITE ST.

Little
White
House

Outer Mole

OLD

PETRONIA ST.

TOWN

Hemingway House

Salt   Ponds

Salt   Pond

BAHAMA
VILLAGE

FLAGLER AVE.

SOUTH

ROOSEVELT BLVD.

Smathers Beach

Ft. Zachary
Taylor
Historic
State Park

• Casa Marina

Southernmost
Point

Higgs Beach

Wauconda Area Library
801 N. Main Street
Wauconda, IL 60084

on the Edge

Inventing the Conch Republic

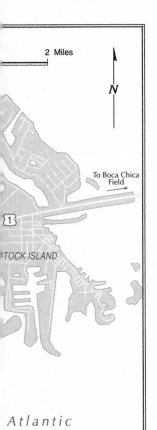

ROBERT KERSTEIN

Foreword by Raymond Arsenault and Gary R. Mormino

University Press of Florida

Gainesville · Tallahassee · Tampa · Boca Raton

Pensacola · Orlando · Miami · Jacksonville · Ft. Myers · Sarasota

Copyright 2012 by Robert Kerstein
Printed in the United States of America on recycled, acid-free paper.
All rights reserved.

17 16 15 14 13 12   6 5 4 3 2 1

A record of cataloging-in-publication data is available from the Library of Congress.
ISBN 978-0-8130-3805-6

The University Press of Florida is the scholarly publishing agency for the State University
System of Florida, comprising Florida A&M University, Florida Atlantic University, Florida
Gulf Coast University, Florida International University, Florida State University, New College
of Florida, University of Central Florida, University of Florida, University of North Florida,
University of South Florida, and University of West Florida.

University Press of Florida
15 Northwest 15th Street
Gainesville, FL 32611-2079
http://www.upf.com

CONTENTS

Foreword vii

Introduction 1

1. Key West's First Hundred Years: Wrecking, the Military,
   Cigar Making, and a Few Tourists 12

2. The Not-So-Roaring Twenties 32

3. The Depression and War Years: Tourism Dreams Give Way
   to Military Realities 44

4. Key West 1945–1970: Not a Clean Well-Lighted Place . . . 77

5. Postwar Tourism 96

6. Island of Intrigue: Key West in the 1970s 114

7. Key West in Transition 139

8. The Gay Community and the Transformation of Key West . . 158

9. Key West in the 1980s and 1990s: Bringing in the Tourists . . 174

10. The Politics of Tourism and Development 197

11. Shelter for the Labor Force? 227

12. Island Tensions in the Twenty-First Century: Mass Tourism and
    Rising Real Estate Values in a "Unique" Community . . . 247

13. One Human Family? 268

    Conclusion 285

    Acknowledgments 293

    Appendix. 297

    Notes 301

    Bibliography 343

    Index. 360

FOREWORD

Key West on the Edge: Inventing the Conch Republic is the latest volume in a series devoted to the study of Florida history and culture. During the past half-century, Florida's burgeoning population and increased national and international visibility have sparked a great deal of popular interest in the state's past, present, and future. As the favorite destination of countless tourists and as the new home of millions of retirees and transplants, modern Florida has become a demographic, political, and cultural bellwether. Florida has also emerged as a popular subject and setting for scholars and writers. The Florida History and Culture Series offers an attractive and accessible format for Florida-related books. From killer hurricanes to disputed elections, from tales of the Everglades to profiles of Sunbelt cities, the topics covered by the more than forty books published so far represent a broad spectrum of regional history and culture.

The University Press of Florida is committed to creating an eclectic but carefully crafted set of books that will provide the field of Florida studies with a new focus and encourage Florida researchers and writers to consider the broader implications and context of their work. The series includes standard academic monographs as well as works of synthesis, memoirs, and anthologies. And while the series features books of historical interest, authors researching Florida's environment, politics, literature, and popular or material culture also are encouraged to submit their manuscripts. While each book has a distinct personality and voice, the ultimate goal of the series is to foster a sense of community and collaboration among Florida scholars.

In *Key West on the Edge*, Robert Kerstein examines the cultural evolution of one of the nation's most celebrated tourist towns. Once a gritty fishing village best known for its remote southerly location, its shipwrecks, and its marauding, opportunistic inhabitants, today Key West is the self-proclaimed capital of the "Conch Republic," a whimsical, myth-laden creation that lures hundreds of thousands of tourists to its shores, shops, bars, hotels, and guesthouses. In a richly textured narrative, Kerstein traces the town's festive atmosphere and lively sense of place to a sustained community-wide effort to remake the city's image. Beginning with the 1979 Fantasy Fest—the city's first annual Halloween-themed "Bacchanal"—Key West's makeover has drawn ideas and enthusiasm from virtually every sector of the island's population, from workers to corporate and civic leaders to small-business owners to representatives of the city's expanding local gay community.

A professor of government at the University of Tampa, Kerstein pays close attention to the institutional structures related to tourism development, namely, to the economic and political logistics that have transformed life and labor in Key West. At the same time, he explores the tensions between old and new ways, and between traditional local mores and the forces of commercialization and globalization. By placing the new Key West in historical and geographical context, he presents a vivid portrait of a town on the make, revealing the challenge of retaining cultural authenticity and balance in an increasingly materialistic world. *Key West on the Edge*, like the Conch Republic itself, beckons to us all. So whatever your status—visitor or resident—pull up a deck chair, put on your tinted reading glasses, and join Professor Kerstein's fascinating historical tour of Florida's southernmost city.

Raymond Arsenault and Gary R. Mormino, Series Editors

Introduction

ON APRIL 23, 1982, the island city of Key West seceded from the Union. Mayor Dennis Wardlow proclaimed Key West "The Conch Republic" (pronounced "konk"). He surrendered a few minutes later and asked for $1 billion in foreign aid from the United Nations, but not before the Conch Republic's Minister of Defense hit a U.S. Navy officer with a loaf of Cuban bread, his version of having "fired a volley."[1]

Key West, the southernmost city in the continental United States, initiated the mock secession to protest a U.S. Border Patrol roadblock near Florida City on U.S. Route 1 that ostensibly had been established to search for illegal aliens, but that also searched for drugs in cars driving north on the only road connecting Key West with the mainland. The motivation for the "secession" was that the roadblock was hurting the island's tourism business. Tourists were unlikely to drive to Key West knowing they would face long delays driving home. The fact that Key Westers chose this strategy to express disdain for the federal action indicated that Key West was not a typical town. Although the island's protest strategy was unique, the rationale for the protest was one increasingly pursued by many communities, namely, to increase tourism.

Not everyone in the community agreed with the secession. More generally, some argued against attempts to revitalize the economy, which had suffered since the Navy closed its largest facility in Key West in 1974, primarily by increasing tourism. Conflicts over the essence of Key West were not new to the community, which in its time has been many different things to many different people. Situated on a small island, only two miles wide and four miles long, and bounded by the Gulf of Mexico and the Atlantic Ocean, it was once the largest city in Florida; at another time one of the wealthiest cities, per capita, in the United States; and at yet another time one of the poorest. Blessed with its beautiful setting and tropical climate, Key West has, like many attractive tourist destinations, undergone a mighty struggle over its identity. Buffeted over the years by economic forces and national cultural changes, not to mention the occasional hurricane, Key West has long been one of America's most unique and intriguing places. In the 1980s, it elected the first openly gay mayor in the United States, and later a mayor who, as described by the *Washington Post*, "had been a bootlegger, gambler, gunrunner, saloonkeeper, fishing boat captain, ladies' man and peerless raconteur."[2] But where Key West is going is hardly clear.

Ever since Key West first attracted large numbers of tourists in the mid-1930s, some Conchs (i.e., Key West natives) and visitors have argued that a wave of mass tourism would threaten Key West's uniqueness. Such a wave would consign the island's cultural heritage to the history books and dramatically change its look and feel as tourists grew to outnumber natives and as more businesses, increasingly multinational tourism and retail enterprises, entered town.

These tensions between local uniqueness and global uniformity have been treated more widely by scholars of tourism, who have suggested, "The globalization of mass tourism leads to an odd paradox; whereas the appeal of tourism is the opportunity to see something different, cities that are remade to attract tourists seem more and more alike." The redevelopment of Times Square during the 1990s has come to symbolize "the decay of the particular in the merciless glare of globalization." In a similar vein, an analysis of mass tourism concluded that a tourist destination often becomes "a small monotonous world."[3]

Some aspects of contemporary Key West affirm this interpretation. Duval Street, downtown's main drag, which stretches from the Gulf to the Atlantic, now includes many upscale chain retail stores, such as Coach, and less upscale chains, such as Burger King. Duval Street also features T-shirt shops galore. In addition, Key West includes the typical array of hotels owned and managed by global corporations. For example, the Casa Marina, Key West's first luxury hotel, was owned by a partnership of primarily local residents when it reopened for business in 1979 after being closed for several years. Decades later the Blackstone Group, an international private equity firm, purchased the hotel, and by 2009 the Casa Marina was managed by Hilton as one of its luxury Waldorf Astoria Hotels and Resorts. In 2000, one of Key West's top real estate firms affiliated with Christie's Great Estates, a subsidiary of Christie's auction house. On most days of the week, cruise ship passengers crowd the Gulf end of Duval Street, an increasingly worldwide phenomenon in coastal tourist destinations. Passengers walking off the ships at one of the island's docks are greeted with the following salutation: "The Westin Key West Resort & Marina and Pepsi-Cola Welcome you to Paradise," a greeting that might dampen any expectations of visiting a unique destination.

Tourism, however, does not inevitably drive destinations to converge; indeed, many still retain their uniqueness. A recent study of New Orleans, for example, concluded that tourism, to a significant extent, had preserved the city's cultural distinctiveness.[4] Variations in local culture and a community's conscious efforts to retain some degree of uniqueness are among the forces that differentiate one tourist place from another.[5] In addition, as analysts of tourism have suggested, "because the tourist experience is produced by the tourist as well as by the service provider, the character of the interaction between the two is more open . . . and in some ways compared to the relationship between artist and viewer."[6]

Much in Key West still resists the pull of globalization. Many of Key West's locally owned guesthouses distinguish themselves by catering to different groups and interests; some specialize in gay tourism, while others highlight literary and historic themes. The many independent restaurants and entertainment establishments, as well as other aspects of the island city, including its architecture, vegetation, pedestrian friendliness, and balmy winter weather, ensure that tourists experience something out of the ordinary. Few towns boast thousands of chickens roaming around to the amusement, or frustration, of tourists and residents. Six-toed cats in Ernest Hemingway's former home, now a tourist site, also defy the generic label, despite their being introduced to the house only after Hemingway's departure.

Moreover, Key West's culture has been characterized as "live and let live." Certainly this sentiment has come and gone, sometimes for the better, other times for the worse, but it has nevertheless allowed for the widespread acceptance of a diversity of lifestyles.[7] And even after the area began to attract wealthier visitors and second-home residents, Key West retained its unpretentiousness and represented, in the eyes of many, the "anti-Hamptons."

The argument that the tourist experience emerges from the interaction between the tourist and the place certainly rings true in Key West. The reaction of a visitor from Wilton Manors, a largely gay community near Ft. Lauderdale, to a drag show at Aqua on Duval Street is likely to differ dramatically from that of a straight, recent graduate of Liberty University upon venturing into the same establishment. The range of visitors' responses to the community is also, no doubt, evident in the reactions of tourism industry workers who relocate to Key West.[8]

Tourism's marketers cannot precisely predict or control what will attract or repel tourists, just as they can only nudge tourists' responses. During the 1930s, the federal government spent significant amounts of money on reinventing Key West as a tourist destination by increasing advertising and rehabilitating accommodations. The major reason many tourists traveled to Key West in late 1940, however, had little to do with these efforts; rather, they were lured by publicity regarding the bizarre relationship between Count Carl von Cosel and Elena Milagro Hoyos.

Von Cosel, the name adopted by George Karl Tanzler, arrived in Key West in 1926. The German-born x-ray technician was employed in the Marine Hospital at Key West, which treated both military and civilian patients. In 1930, Elena Milagro Hoyos, a twenty-one-year-old Key Wester whose parents had moved to the island from Cuba, arrived in the hospital for tests. Von Cosel fell in love with her and was certain Elena was the woman he had dreamt about several years before she was born. She was destined to be his wife and partner for the rest of his life. The fact that Elena died of tuberculosis in October 1931 did not end his dream. Instead, he secretly removed her body from the mausoleum in the Key West cemetery, tried to restore it with wax, plaster of paris, and glass eyeballs, and slept next to it in his home from 1933 until it was discovered in 1940. His efforts to bring Elena back to life and fly off in an airplane, which at the time still lacked wings, had failed.

Although authorities eventually decided not to press charges against von Cosel for stealing the body—the statute of limitations had expired—the national newspaper accounts of the public hearing to determine whether charges should be filed and the public viewing of Elena's body at the funeral home drew many tourists to Key West, most of whom sympathized with von Cosel. He also found a way to make money from his sudden fame by charging visitors 25 cents to visit his house and hear his story. Although some suggested that Elena's body be placed in a glass case to add to Key West's as yet limited array of tourist attractions, authorities decided to rebury her body, this time in a secret place to ensure it would not again be disturbed. This "love story" is a perfect example of the kinds of eccentricity that has enabled Key West to resist the leveling of mass tourism.[9]

This book examines Key West's transition to a tourist town. It does so, however, within a broader analysis of continuity and change in Key West. As one author points out, "place matters in the study of tourism because an analysis of why and how tourism develops will need to take into account where and when it develops." One can only understand and evaluate Key West's shift toward tourism and the consequences of this shift by examining both in the context of the city's history, including its culture, demographics, economy, and political and policy conflicts, and by taking into account national, and sometimes international, factors.[10]

Key West before Mass Tourism

Popular tourist destinations do not "just happen," but are created and promoted. Tourism boosters advertise the community, re-create its use of space to appeal to and accommodate tourists, and package the destination as a "vehicle for experiences" to be consumed by the visitors. This characterization certainly fits Key West during the last decades of the twentieth century and into the twenty-first. Public officials and organizations, as well as businesses that relied on tourism, sought to transform Key West into a tourism mecca. The seeds of the island's attraction to visitors, however, had been sown earlier.[11]

As America became interconnected via railroads in the late nineteenth century and cars in the early twentieth, Key West remained relatively isolated. The railroad would not reach it until 1912 and a continuous road from the mainland not until 1938. For decades after the American Civil War, Key West was in many senses closer to Cuba and the Caribbean than to the mainland United States, both in terms of miles and also its economy. Tobacco shipped from Cuba roughly ninety miles away served the town's thriving cigar industry, which primarily employed Cuban immigrants. Bahamians, both white and black, also arrived in large numbers before and after the Civil War.

Many who visited the island in the post-Civil War nineteenth century and the early decades of the twentieth praised Key West, describing it as different, exotic, and unique. Its weather, ambience, flora, isolation, diverse population, and relative tolerance contrasted with most other communities in the United States. And, of course, it was an island, which attracted those who enjoyed fishing and boating.

These attributes of Key West attracted numerous writers. Ernest Hemingway, who lived in the community during most of the 1930s, is the author most associated with the island, but others, including Tennessee Williams and Elizabeth Bishop, two of the most notable U.S. writers of the twentieth century, also lived and worked there. Bishop moved to Key West in the 1930s and stayed for several years. Williams bought a house in Key West in 1950 and remained a resident until he died in 1983.

Writers also moved to Key West during the 1960s and 1970s, and Jimmy Buffett, both a musician and a writer, arrived in 1971. Many others in the arts visited Key West frequently, and some were inspired by what they experienced. For example, after visiting Key West in 1941, Leonard Bernstein started writing a ballet to be called "Conch Town," influenced by the Cuban music he heard on the island. Although he never finished the ballet, he later included two of its songs, one of them being "America," in his classic musical "West Side Story."[12]

A Tourist Town

During the 1960s and 1970s, many U.S. cities, suffering from the suburbanization of their middle and upper classes and the loss of manufacturing jobs, were busy devising strategies to revitalize their economies. Their strategies generally included building a downtown replete with cultural institutions, middle-class housing, financial-service institutions, and tourist accommodations and attractions. In Key West, the primary impetus for revitalization was the significant downsizing of the military presence on the island during the 1970s, and the city adopted tourism as its primary strategy. Many in the Key West business and professional community, both Conchs and newcomers, as well as elected officials coalesced in support of tourism.[13]

Ultimately, however, it was not the promotional efforts of the community's tourism boosters so much as the initiatives of a new population that set Key West's modern course during the 1970s. A gay population had discovered Key West. While they faced some antagonism and harassment, they were drawn to the town that had attracted gay and lesbian writers, such as Williams and Bishop, and that was not dominated by Anita Bryant and her supporters, who drove antigay activities in the Miami area. The closure of Key West's primary Navy installation and the relocation of Navy personnel and civilians employed on the base left many homes and apartments available for purchase at modest prices in the Old Town historic neighborhood near Duval Street. Many of these newcomers opened guesthouses and other businesses that relied on tourism.

The inaugural Fantasy Fest, held in 1979, symbolized the changing demography, economy, and culture of Key West. Duval Street had long been the site of community festivities and parades. For decades, from the early twentieth century into the 1960s, Key West's Cuban population had on Halloween and other occasions organized a comparsa, or dance line, down Duval Street. Supporters of the victor in a political campaign often carried a mock coffin, symbolizing the loser, down Duval Street prior to burning it or throwing it into the water. This was, by and large, a homegrown activity, performed by Key Westers for Key Westers.[14]

Fantasy Fest was different. It was organized not by comparsa enthusiasts or by those rooted in the traditional politics of the island, but by gay migrants who had arrived in Key West only recently during the 1960s and 1970s. Fantasy Fest culminated in a parade held on the Saturday night before Halloween. While the parade provided entertainment for the locals, it was initially aimed at tourists, who its organizers hoped to draw to Key West. Over time, Key West's version of Mardi Gras came to attract tens of thousands to the island.

Key West had never been a puritanical community—far from it. Nevertheless, many were outraged when in 1934 Julius Stone Jr., the federal government's top official in Key West, wore Bermuda shorts, not considered proper attire on the island, to symbolize Key West's ambition to become a tourist destination like Bermuda. Decades later, at Fantasy Fest, shorts were common among viewers and participants, but many, more dramatically, "wore" only body paint. Key West had changed. Fantasy Fest was an important component of the community's early reinvention, and it became an instant tradition on the island.[15]

In 1981 tourism's boosters succeeded in adopting a tourist tax to finance a new institution, the Tourist Development Council (TDC), whose revenues would be used to attract more tourists. Advertising celebrated the community's uniqueness and openness to diverse lifestyles, urging tourists to visit "America's favorite Caribbean Island," to drive to "Key West . . . (and) Go all the Way," and to "Just Let Go." Beginning in 1986, tourists were invited to "Come as You Are," and in 2010, advertisements invited visitors to a destination that was "Close to Perfect—Far From Normal." The TDC, whose jurisdiction eventually expanded to encompass all of Monroe County, and Key West's tourism boosters did far more than simply project these images of Key West to potential visitors. They promoted attractions and festivals to provide visitors with reasons to visit Key West and created brochures and advertising that emphasized "markers" that tourists should see.[16]

During the late 1970s and the 1980s, Key West became increasingly reliant on tourism. New residents moved in, and many Conchs left. The town, however, did not change overnight. The lives of many Conchs continued as before, with large numbers working for local public agencies, such as the electric and water companies, the school system, and city government. Still, the push toward tourism changed the character of Key West and challenged different aspects of its uniqueness during the 1980s and especially in the 1990s and beyond as it attracted more tourists and owners of second homes. Several sections of Key West transformed to accommodate the new economy. For example, the Key West Bight, once home to shrimp boats and other commercial fishing vessels, became the "Historic Seaport," the new name sanctioned by the city, featuring charter fishing and sightseeing boats that catered to tourists. On Caroline Street, across from the bight, rough-and-tumble bars gave way to boutiques and mainstream restaurants. Duval Street grew to cater to tourists' desires, gaining restaurants and entertainment venues, as well as T-shirt shops and art galleries, in place of the neighborhood-based businesses that served residents.

Several of the writers who lived in Key West during these decades complained that the qualities that had initially attracted them to the island were disappearing. For example, in 1987 Philip Caputo, then a resident of Key West, wrote a far-reaching criticism of the changes in the community. He reminisced about the diverse population of Key West in the mid-1970s, including Conchs, shrimpers, lobstermen, charter captains, renegade drug smugglers, and "social outlaws." According to Caputo, by the mid-1980s that atmosphere had all but vanished: "The Boat Bar, which had been a favorite hangout of shrimpers, had been replaced by a hair salon." Developers, he emphasized, had built condominiums and resort hotels for vacation-home purchasers and short-term tourists, thereby changing the nature of Key West. For many, Key West today is a "victim of its own success" and has willingly or inadvertently negotiated a "devil's bargain" in its transformation into a tourist town.[17]

The tension between tourism and the community's culture and uniqueness, however, existed well before mass tourism engulfed Key West in the 1980s and beyond. During the influx of tourism in the mid-1930s, some Conchs, visitors, and new residents, including Hemingway, criticized efforts to reinvent Key West as a tourist destination and lamented the changed nature of the island since its "being discovered." Still, others praised these efforts, and many continued to applaud the island's transformation seventy years later. Large numbers of tourists return regularly and rave about the island's unique aura, opportunities for water activities, fine restaurants, interesting architecture, historic sites, cultural activities, drag shows, bar scene, and more. Some claim that it remains a place well suited to relaxing and losing track of time and view it as a welcome alternative to Florida's numerous theme parks and overbuilt beach communities.

The Upscaling of Key West

Regardless of people's different impressions of the community, none can deny that the Key West of 2000 was a far different town from the Key West of 1975, and by 2005 it was different again. Real estate investment rivaled tourism promotion and local color as a shaping force of the community. The island increasingly attracted wealthy purchasers of homes and condominiums. It had become "fashionable (and comfortable) rather than bohemian" to move to Key West, if only for a few months of the year. Gentrification had begun in Old Town as early as the late 1970s, but housing prices soon skyrocketed in virtually every neighborhood. By the mid-1990s, Key West ranked among the most expensive single-family housing markets in the country.[18] Rising housing prices made it impossible for many who might otherwise have been attracted to the southernmost city to move there. Those who could still afford to move to the island might well have been attracted to its "anti-Hamptons" ethos, but they were wealthy nonetheless.

Many of the seasonal and year-round wealthy newcomers who purchased homes in Key West, along with some well-off Conchs, helped organize and finance new cultural venues. They organized a symphony and an opera company, along with other organizations that the Conch community never could have supported on their own. These, in turn, led others to purchase seasonal homes in Key West. Many, however, including creative younger people attracted to the town's history and ambience, were unable to become residents due to Key West's high costs and limited opportunities for economic mobility.

Elmer Davis's article published in the January 1929 issue of *Harper's Magazine* prophesized about Key West: "Once tourists come in numbers, land will be worth more, rents will be higher. . . . That narrow gap which separates the possible enjoyments of the poorest man in Key West from those of the richest man will broaden and broaden . . ." The poet Richard Wilbur, then a Key West resident, remarked in an interview after winning his second Pulitzer Prize for poetry in 1989, "I hope it [Key West] always remains a place where you can live without being rich." Increasingly, Davis's prediction has been realized, and Wilbur's hope for Key West dashed. By the early twenty-first century, real estate was trumping tourism, as owners converted hotels into condo hotels and apartments into condominiums, and as speculators purchased homes and condos and then resold them to make a quick profit.[19]

Economic realities, along with other factors, drove many adult Conchs to move out of Key West and their sons and daughters to live elsewhere. Key West changed so dramatically that more Conchs could be found at annual reunions in the Tampa Bay area and at other Florida locations than in Key West. Some benefited economically from the move, cashing in their homes for huge profits and living mortgage free elsewhere. Others who had not purchased a home in Key West found it impossible to do so as prices rose, so they left, unable to find a job that offered upward mobility in a town so heavily reliant upon tourism.

Has Key West moved from a "unique" community to a "generic" tourist town? The answer is no, but no community, including Key West, was, is, or will be unique in every respect. Julius Stone Jr. suggested in 1934 that in some ways Key West was like other small towns, offering "a fair cross-section of the sociological and economic problems facing the country." On the other hand, its climate and indigenous architecture were unique. In 1935, Davis noted, "the homes of the more prosperous citizens look like the more prosperous homes in any small town anywhere, except for the tropic gardens around them." Still, Key West was unique in many ways, including being "a small town on an island miles away from anywhere—a town which in climate and vegetation, in population and culture, is neither Florida nor Cuba, neither American nor Caribbean but simply Key West."[20]

One can examine other eras in the town's history for characteristics many locals and visitors considered unique and for others more typical of small-town America. Today Key West is in some ways still unique, but its uniqueness lies within a vastly different context than before its transition to a tourism and vacation-home community. The Key West of today is, to a large extent, a reinvented community. It is by no means the Key West of the cigarmakers and their descendants, of Hemingway, or of Buffett, but it has managed to maintain a sense of place. This place, however, due to economic trends and public policy failures, is open to a far smaller cross-section of the population than was the case in earlier decades. The tensions between mass tourism, outside money, and a local culture that evolves with the influx of newcomers, continues. The island provides a welcome environment for many residents and visitors. Others, however, including past and present residents, both Conchs and transplants, as well as visitors to the city in earlier decades, bemoan the Key West that is gone.

1

Key West's First Hundred Years

Wrecking, the Military, Cigar Making, and a Few Tourists

DURING THE FIRST DECADES of the nineteenth century, tourism in the United States was primarily engaged in by the wealthy. Some were in search of "sacred places" where they might realize a type of religious experience. It is unlikely, however, that tourists sought such an experience in Key West. Others, suffering from various ailments, sought destinations that might help them to restore or enhance their health. They journeyed to the seashore, to a spa, or simply to a warmer climate. Still others were relatively healthy but nevertheless desired the invigorating effects of water or warm weather. Before the American Civil War, most of the winter visitors to Florida were invalids, many of whom suffered from tuberculosis. After Key West was settled in the early 1820s, some of these early Florida tourists reached the island.[1]

One of these visitors, identifying himself simply as "an invalid," stayed in Key West for two weeks in March 1838, when it was a town of just under 700 people. He had already visited Trinidad, Cuba, and other Caribbean locations in search for the most desirable environment for

. . . lived in open concubinage with a black woman from Nassau . . . who left him in consequence of continued brutal treatment, during his fits of intoxication, which occur every afternoon."

One can safely conclude that Key West, on the whole, was not given to a puritanical ethos. Jefferson Browne's history of the city, published in 1912, relates a list of grievances that a grand jury presented in 1834, a list that suggests the "invalid" who visited in 1838 missed some of the opportunities available for countering the "dullness" of the island. The grand jury noted, for example, "that grog shops, coffee houses, billiard rooms and other places were kept open on the Sabbath." Also, "the officials whose duty it was to keep persons charged with offences, suffered them to go at large when they ought to have been confined."[18]

Reverend Simon Peter Richardson, a minister of the Methodist Episcopal Church South who had just arrived in Key West in 1845, reached conclusions compatible with those of the grand jury a decade earlier. He noted that his predecessor had informed him that there were thirty-two "grog-shops" on the island, and that these shops had made his life rather difficult: "The whiskey men had threatened to wash him, which meant to tie a rope around his waist and shoulders and from the wharf to cast him into the water and then haul him in and then cast him out again."[19]

Still, Richardson reported that his arrival in Key West was met with a hospitable reception. A description of the community in 1852 claimed, "There is not a more quiet, orderly town in the United States." The same writer reported that many of the young men belonged to a "large and prosperous" temperance association. Another observer characterized the "general tone" of the island's society as "refined and polished." In 1849 a woman who lived in Key West suggested that, in a few years, Key West would likely "stand a fair competition for refinement and intelligence with any of our older southern towns."[20]

These perspectives suggest that Key West's eclecticism started early in its history. By no means a homogeneous small town, it was diverse from the beginning and became more so with each passing decade. By 1850, most of the island's immigrants had been born in the Bahamas, many to families who had been British sympathizers during the American Revolution and then fled to the Bahamas when the war did not go their way. Smaller numbers of immigrants to Key West hailed from England, Ireland, Germany, the Canary Islands and mainland Spain, Sweden, and Cuba. While the majority of U.S. Key Westers had been born in Florida, the island was also home to migrants from New England and the Mid-Atlantic States, especially New York and Connecticut, as well as to a lesser degree from the South.[21]

One author declared early in the twentieth century that "Key West has long been the most remote and incongruous city detained by an American state." In addition to being geographically unique, it was culturally unique, at least within Florida and most of the American South. The historian Charlton Tebeau concluded that during the decades before the Civil War Key West could be best "understood as a cosmopolitan, even international island of economic, social and cultural activity, unlike any other in Florida and having little contact with it."[22]

Key West's Industrial Era (Late 1860s–Early Twentieth Century)

In 1838, a lawyer in Key West wrote in a letter to his relatives, "You will naturally enquire how we live, and the reply is very simple, in, by, and through wrecks—if we are not directly interested in the business, our support wholly comes from it. Stop that and we cease to live." In fact, the wrecking business peaked just before the Civil War. After the war, the number of wrecks steadily declined and by the end of the century had fallen dramatically. A number of factors contributed to this decline, including ships' access to more accurate charts, additional lighthouses, an increase in steam-powered ships, and an expanded railroad system that reduced the number of ships transporting cargo. Rather than ceasing to exist as our lawyer predicted, however, Key West grew; by 1880, it had become the largest city in Florida. The city's population almost doubled over the next decade, from 9,890 in 1880 to 18,080 in 1890, and it remained the state's largest city until Jacksonville and Pensacola overtook it by the turn of the twentieth century (see appendix).[23]

The military once again played a significant role at certain points during this period. Before the start of the Spanish-American War, nearly the entire U.S. Atlantic Fleet arrived in Key West for winter training and to prepare for a possible war against Spain. Before the United States's entry into World War I in 1917, the military again expanded its presence in Key West. The Navy expanded the Key West Naval Station, which became the headquarters of the Seventh Naval District. The Navy also built a Naval Air Station, commissioned in December 1917, on land formed by dredge-and-fill operations at Trumbo Point on Key West's north shore. The base served both seaplanes and dirigibles. By the time an armistice was reached in 1918, more than 1,000 service personnel were based in Key West. After the war, however, activities at the Naval Station subsided significantly, and the Naval Air Station was soon deactivated.[24]

Commercial fishing in Key West continued to be an important part of the island's economy. According to the U.S. Bureau of Fisheries, the variety of fish sold on the island likely exceeded that of any other city in the United States. Conchs, shellfish readily available in Key West's shallow waters, averaged one pound in weight and were peddled for about five cents each. According to the U.S. Bureau of Fisheries, a conch "requires several hours' cooking to render it palatable," but locals consumed them in large quantities. Moreover, the term *Conch* signified far more than the shellfish. *Conch* initially designated those British loyalists who had fled the colonies before and during the American Revolution to live in the British Bahamas, only to later migrate to Key West.[25] Over time, however, native Key Westers, regardless of their ancestors' country of origin, became known as Conchs.

The sponge fleet operating out of Key West expanded considerably, employing over 1,200 men at its peak, most of them Bahamian immigrants. Key West had a virtual monopoly on the sponge trade in the United States until 1891, when Greek spongers based in Tarpon Springs, in the Tampa Bay area, began to compete with them. In 1905, the Greek spongers began using the technique of hard-hat diving, which enabled them to fish deeper sponge beds, and Tarpon Springs supplanted Key West as the center of the sponging industry.[26]

Key West also benefited from the turtle industry, which by 1890 had become an important source of revenue throughout much of Florida, particularly in Monroe (Key West) and Levy (Cedar Key) counties. Initially, the turtles brought to the kraals (underwater pens) on the docks in Key West were captured in the Keys, but by 1920 the majority were imported, primarily from the waters around Costa Rica and Nicaragua. The Thompson Company, based in Key West, shipped some of them to northern markets, sold turtle steaks to families and restaurants in Key West, and distributed turtle soup worldwide. The kraals became a well-known component of the businesses around the Key West Bight, and even after their importance to Key West's economy had diminished, they retained their importance as a tourist attraction.[27]

Key West's primary economic engine during the later decades of the century, however, was the cigar industry. Although a few cigar factories did operate in Key West before the Civil War, they represented an insignificant part of the island's economy. It was not until Sam Seidenberg, the first large-scale cigar manufacturer in Key West, built his cigar factory on the island in 1867 and constructed homes for his cigar workers that the industry took off. Other manufacturers, including Eduardo Gato and Vicente Martínez Ybor, soon followed. By the early 1880s, the industry that specialized in hand-rolled, clear Havana cigars was booming, and real estate values were keeping pace. Key West's port thrived as manufacturers imported Cuban tobacco and shipped the handmade cigars on steamers to markets in New York, Galveston, Baltimore, and elsewhere.

According to the census of 1885, 42 percent of the total work force in Key West worked in the cigar industry, which in the 1870s and 1880s was the primary contributor to the growth of Key West's population. Likewise, the losses in population that the island suffered during the 1890s and again between 1910 and 1920 were partially due to the declining fortunes of the cigar industry, as factories left the city in response to a major fire in 1886, frequent labor unrest, economic inducements from Tampa and other communities, unreliable steamship service, severe hurricanes in 1909, 1910, and 1919, and the increased prominence of machine-made, rather than hand-rolled, cigars throughout the United States by the 1920s.[28]

Key West's Diverse Population

While the island's population remained diverse, its composition changed. After the Civil War, more Bahamians than ever arrived in Key West. From the 1870s into the early twentieth century, white and black Bahamians left their country, primarily to escape its declining economy. Until around 1905, most of them migrated to Key West. As Key West's economy began to decline, Miami and other nearby communities became the more common destinations, and some Bahamians in Key West also moved to the Miami area.[29]

Spaniards, including several families from the Canary Islands, also moved to Key West, drawn primarily by the cigar industry. It was, however, the Cuban population that, due in large part to the growth of this industry, surpassed Bahamians as Key West's dominant immigrant group. Cubans began moving to Key West after the start in 1868 of the unsuccessful Ten Years' War for Cuban independence from Spain. By 1885, Cuban immigrants constituted approximately one-third of Key West's total population, compared to about 24 percent for Bahamian immigrants.[30]

Cuban neighborhoods flourished on the island, with cigarworkers and their families often living in homes rented or sold to them by the cigar manufacturers. The Cuban population engaged in an active civic life. In 1871, they dedicated the San Carlos Institute, named for Carlos Manuel de Céspedes who on October 10, 1868, had issued the call for Cubans to begin the revolution against Spain, known as the *Grito de Yara*. In 1900, Key West's Cubans formed the Cuban Club on Duval Street, which served as a social club and entertainment venue and whose members received medical care at St. Joseph Hospital after it opened in 1919.[31] Cubans in Key West also organized several clubs dedicated to raising funds for another revolution, and Spanish-language newspapers supported Cuba's drive, begun in 1895, for independence from Spain.[32]

Several Jewish families, many of them Romanian immigrants, moved to Key West in the decades following the Civil War, further adding to the town's diversity. In the late 1880s, Jewish peddlers went from house to house selling dry goods and other merchandise. In 1891, Key West's established storeowners persuaded the city to require the peddlers to purchase a license for a fee of $1,000, hoping to drive them out of business. Instead, the peddlers opened retail stores on Duval Street. Many of the Jewish merchants learned Spanish, which contributed to the success of their businesses in Key West's Cuban and Spanish communities.[33]

Key West's black residents constituted about 30 percent of the city's population in 1880, 1890, and 1900, but this percentage decreased in the first two decades of the twentieth century. Most of Key West's black immigrants came from the Bahamas, but some were Afro-Cuban. Almost all of Key West's black inhabitants lived on Whitehead Street and to its west, as well as near the city cemetery. Not long after the end of Reconstruction in 1877, Key West's African American residents, like those throughout Florida, underwent segregation in schools and public accommodations. Several churches, including St. Peter's Episcopal and AME Zion, served the black population. The Key West Cornet Band, organized in 1874, was another noteworthy institution in the black community. The band, which transitioned into the Welters Cornet Band, continued its tradition of marching alongside funeral processions from the church to the cemetery into the twenty-first century.[34]

The historian Canter Brown Jr. noted the complexity of the relationships among the different ethnic and racial groups in Key West: "The cosmopolitan population mix often produced public brawls, but it also created and fostered relatively tolerant patterns of race relations." On Election Day in 1874, local laborers attacked black Bahamian immigrants, one of several conflicts taking place during 1873 and 1874. In 1888, however, the *New York Age*, an African American newspaper, concluded that Key West was "the freest town in the South, not even Washington excepted. There are no attempts at bulldozing and intimidation during campaigns and at elections here. No Negroes are murdered here in cold blood, and there are no gross miscarriages of justice against them as is so frequently seen throughout the South." In 1895, a reporter for Florida's most widely distributed African American newspaper wrote, "we know of no other city in the United States where the Negro enjoys his liberty to a greater extent than in Key West."[35]

Key West's blacks and Cubans sometimes formed electoral alliances that were successful in electing Cubans and blacks to public office. The electoral success of African Americans prompted the state legislature to pass legislation during its 1889 session that eliminated local elections for several years in Key West. At least two blacks were elected to the Key West city council after local elections were restored, but 1907, the final year of Robert Gabriel's term, would be the last time a black served on the city council until 1971.[36]

The Built Environment

After the Civil War, new homes were built to house the growing population. While the fire of 1886 and the hurricanes that followed razed many of Key West's businesses and homes, the designs of new and rebuilt homes generally were similar to those that had been demolished. Most were made of wood and featured one or one-and-a-half stories and front porches. The formal style that most influenced builders was classic revival, which had several variations. The vast majority of houses, however, were built in the frame vernacular style. These homes were constructed by builders and carpenters who were largely self-taught and influenced more by the design of existing Key West buildings than by formal architectural styles. Differences among the vernacular styles derived from the various influences of the city's diverse population, including Bahamians, Southerners, New Englanders, and Cubans. The small dwellings cigar manufacturers built for their workers displayed the vernacular style of industrial architecture, borrowed, in part, from styles featured in design books.[37]

Although most residences were modest in size, several of Key West's wealthiest families, including the children of William and Euphemia Curry, built substantial homes. William had emigrated to Key West from the Bahamas in the 1830s. He accumulated great wealth from his business interests and his success in the stock market and became Florida's first millionaire. The building that later housed the Key West Woman's Club at 319 Duval Street was initially built around 1892 by William Curry's daughter Eleanor Curry and her husband, Captain Martin L. Hellings. In 1899, Curry's youngest daughter, Florida E. Curry, and her husband, the lawyer and judge Vining Harris Jr., built what is now known as the Southernmost House, located at the Atlantic end of Duval Street. Some of the cigar manufacturers, as well as several Bahamian immigrants and New England migrants, also built substantial homes. Almost a century later, some of these structures, both modest and substantial, were among the "Old Town" homes that attracted purchasers and visitors to the island.[38]

Some of the public buildings that were constructed also remain part of Key West's architectural heritage. The Customs House on Front Street is the most noteworthy example. Built in 1833, the Customs House building was sold and relocated to Duval Street in 1889. A new brick Customs House was then constructed on Front Street. More than a century later, this building would house the Key West Museum of Art and History, a popular destination for some of Key West's visitors.[39]

Tourists' Views of Key West

Although a visitor to Key West in 1871 contended that the construction of tourist accommodations in Key West "would be a godsend to the many who seek health or pleasure" in the Florida Keys, few of the structures built during the remainder of the nineteenth century or early in the twentieth were designed to attract or accommodate tourists. Florida's tourism increased significantly during this era, but relatively few made it to this still relatively hard-to-reach island. The primary means of reaching Key West was by steamship. In 1873, the Mallory Steamship Company initiated service between Galveston, New York, and Key West. Then, in 1886, the Plant Investment Company, headed by Henry Plant, operated the *Mascotte* steamship on a Tampa–Key West–Havana route two or three times a week, and the following year the company added the *Olivette* steamship to the same route. The ships on the Plant system, however, primarily utilized Key West as a stop on the way to and from Havana, and passengers generally spent only an hour or two in Key West.[40]

With the inauguration of service between Miami and Key West in 1896, Henry Flagler's Florida East Coast Railway (FEC) Steamship Company provided visitors with the opportunity to spend some time in Key West. In 1900, the year after Henry Plant died, his heirs and the Flagler interests merged the two steamship lines to form the Peninsular and Occidental (P&O) Steamship Company, which was controlled by Flagler and continued service to Key West.[41]

Still, for those who chose to stay overnight in Key West, accommodations were scarce. Daniel G. Brinton, in a guidebook based on his trip through Florida during the winter of 1856–57, noted the existence of only two hotels and three boarding houses. In 1891, tourists still had few choices. They could stay at the Russell House on Duval Street near the Gulf or at the Duval House (or Hotel Duval), run by "a French woman of distinguished bearing and exquisite charm," near the pier across from the Russell House. Martin Herrera's Hotel Monroe, on the corner of Division (later Truman) and Whitehead Streets, served more as a refuge for Cubans passing through Key West and as a meeting place for Cubans to discuss their plans for a revolution against Spain than as a tourist hotel. In 1912, a travel guide to Florida reported that Key West offered tourists only five overnight facilities.[42]

Indeed, some visitors were unimpressed by the island city. In 1867, the steamer *San Francisco* stopped in Key West. One of its passengers was Mark Twain, and he subsequently wrote about his visit in a San Francisco newspaper. It is unlikely that Twain's report would entice many to visit Key West. He liked the harbor and the local cigars, which he judged superior to what was available in San Francisco. He was less enamored, however, with the built environment, noting, "There are few handsome or elegant dwellings in the place—none, I might say," and although the town looked attractive and whitewashed from a distance, "a closer inspection discovers that the whitewash is dingy, and that the whole concern hath about it a melancholy air of decay." He also criticized the food. After eating at a restaurant, he complained, "We left good fare on the vessel to go and eat such a villainous mess as that. If they keep on in that way, a Key Wester will be a curiosity in Heaven here after."[43]

A reporter from New York who stayed briefly at the Russell House in March 1884 while waiting to board a schooner to Nassau and is identified only as W. D., also criticized the town. He complained that Key West's citizens all knew him to be a stranger and gave him "a critical examination" as they walked by. He also was not impressed with the cigar factories. Instead of the four- and five-story buildings he had envisioned, they were "unpretending board buildings, painted generally in a sort of gray, and carry little outward sign of the large business done within." The weather was also not to his liking: "I never felt a heat that goes through a man and breaks him up like this Key West heat" (and this was March). He concluded that after a day or two in Key West, one would find it "tiresome."[44]

The Northern writer Charles Richards Dodge traveled via steamer from Tampa to Key West in 1894, planning to board a yacht that would take him up the Keys toward Biscayne Bay. Even after his visit, Dodge's knowledge of the city was obviously limited. He concluded, for example, that fewer than 1,000 of Key West's white residents spoke English, a serious underestimation. His conclusion regarding Key Westers' spoken language was apparently based on his memory of having to ask four (presumably white) locals for directions to the post office before he received a response in English. While Dodge admired the quality of the fish available at the markets, he otherwise had little to say that was positive. Key West was a "dusty old town," the only "imposing" structures were Fort Taylor and the "government buildings," and he concluded, "There is very little of interest here to hold the tourist."[45]

A guide to Florida published in 1912 by Harrison Rhodes and Mary Wolfe Dumont was also generally critical of Key West. They observed: "The town itself is not attractive. The streets are practically unpaved except in the business portion. There is no public supply of water, a few scattered wells and cisterns of rainwater meeting the demand. There is no sewerage system. . . . The houses are principally of wood, and are not built with a special regard to architectural effect."[46] Rhodes and Dumont did note some of the community's positive aspects, such as the "unique flora" and the "picturesque" boats employed for fishing, turtling, and sponging. Still, they concluded, "A visit to the cigar factories, to the docks and to the Government Reservation, and to La Brisa, a beach pleasure resort (on the Atlantic), exhausts the attractions of the town and the island."[47]

Those who were attracted to Key West, however, appreciated it for its diversity and difference from mainstream U.S. culture. George Barbour, a former correspondent for the *Chicago Times*, traveled throughout Florida in 1880 and 1881 and stayed for a short time at the Russell House. He was intrigued by the unique, thriving locale, writing, "everything in and about Key West is strange, foreign and interesting." Barbour further noted that everything about the community, including the buildings, flowers, vegetation, and "the appearance of the people," was "so un-American and suggestive of a foreign clime" that it was "difficult indeed to realize it as one of the busy, enterprising cities of our United States." And although business was thriving, he noted that it was not the "intensely active, Chicago sort of business." Rather, it was "steady, easygoing and quiet."[48]

James Henshall, who authored a guide to fishing and camping in Florida in 1884, also was intrigued with Key West. Henshall called it a "quaint and charming city, full of oddities and incongruities." He noted the diversity that Dodge had criticized but evaluated it much differently. Henshall wrote approvingly, "Americans, Englishmen, Frenchmen, Germans, Spaniards, Cubans, Bahamians, Italians, and Negroes" and "every shade of complexion from white to yellow, brown to black, cosmopolitan all," populated the island. The homes were also diverse: "Mansions, huts, and hovels—balconies, canopies, and porches . . . are mingled in endless confusion," but they were "harmonized by arabesques of fruit and foliage . . . and shady bowers of palm and palmetto, almond and tamarind, lime and lemon, orange and banana." He and his friends clearly enjoyed their visit to Key West, and one was pleased that he had "learned to drink beer in seven languages."[49]

In 1888, Jacksonville's *Florida Times-Union* echoed Henshall's sentiments: "Nowhere within the boundaries of the United States can be found a place resembling [Key West], with its rows of frame buildings, its hundreds of cigar factories, its cosmopolitan population, and its thousand and one other peculiarities which claim the attention of the stranger." A woman visiting Key West in 1886 also emphasized its uniqueness, calling it "an odd and novel place, and the more interesting on that account. There are peculiarities here that strike a stranger very forcibly. Key West is intensely unlike any other place in the Union."[50]

The Flagler Railroad and Boosterism

Many expected that the Key West these visitors experienced would change dramatically in 1912, the year Henry Flagler's Florida East Coast Railway reached Key West. The event was much anticipated by the Key West business community and closely watched by many throughout the state who believed the city would be positioned at a turning point regarding commerce and tourism. The *Florida Times-Union* suggested, "Today marks the dawn of a new era. The Old Key West—one of the most unique of the world's historic little cities—is shaking off its lethargy and from today the spirit of progress and development will be greater than ever." Flagler had built his railroad from Jacksonville to West Palm Beach, extending it to Miami in 1896, and constructed hotels along the way. In 1904, Flagler began the Key West extension, slated to cross more than 128 miles of water. Several thousand workers struggled to complete the track, and approximately 700 paid for the project with their lives.[51]

On January 22, 1912, the day the Florida East Coast Railway reached Key West, the FEC distributed a publication highlighting the anticipated completion of the Panama Canal, which would open in August 1914, as an important motivating factor in Flagler's expansion of the Florida East Coast Railway to Key West: "Since the genius of our Government has made the Panama Canal a fact in the world's commerce, Key West has assumed new and great importance." Flagler planned to construct twelve piers at Trumbo Point, the terminus of the railroad, to handle freighters and passenger ships that would soon be traveling to and from the Panama Canal. At the banquet held to honor Flagler after the "OverSeas Railway" arrived in Key West, Flagler predicted that Key West's population would reach 50,000 within a decade.[52]

According to the Key West Board of Trade, the city would experience "a rapid growth in population, a tremendous expansion in business, a vast development of industrial enterprise, [and] a great influx of new men, new money, new interests." A Navy commodore pronounced that

Key West's strategic position, which the railroad had only enhanced, justified locating a major Naval base in the city. Key West, he argued, repeating Commodore David Porter's statement in 1829, should be the American Gibraltar.[53]

Those who had criticized Key West likely would have welcomed these changes, but not all were impressed with the prospect of significant growth. One writer struck a note that would be sounded frequently in later decades. He feared that "the whistle of the locomotive will be heard in the land and another queer corner of the earth will be put on the civilized map."[54] In other words, Key West would lose its uniqueness and grow to look like every other place. His concerns, however, were premature.

Although the railroad did build cargo facilities at Trumbo Point, the major piers it had planned were never constructed. During the 1914–15 winter, a newly organized company associated with the FEC railway, the Florida East Coast Car Ferry Company, began a ferry service between Key West and Cuba. The ferries carried railroad cars filled with cargo between the two cities so that goods did not have to be transferred between ship and rail. Ultimately, the commercial impact of the train reaching Key West was nowhere near what Flagler and others had expected.[55]

Tourism to Key West increased only modestly after the railroad reached the community. Some tourists spent a few nights at Long Key Fishing Camp, constructed by the FEC Railway in 1908, and then made the trip of about 65 miles to Key West. More tourist accommodations opened. For example, a residence on William Street added a third story and became the Island City House Hotel in 1912. By 1914, tourists also could stay at the Oversea Hotel on Fleming Street, which advertised itself as the nearest hotel to the railroad and the steamboat station, or at the Panama Hotel at the corner of Eaton and Elizabeth Streets.[56]

The island offered visitors a variety of activities. Tourists could, of course, go fishing. They could also enjoy bars and dance halls, cockfights, gambling houses, and "houses of ill fame." Newspapers reported after the hurricane of 1909 that the "red light" district was "encroaching on the respectable portions of the city," and that various forms of gambling were readily available from "5 a.m. until late at night . . . not even respecting Sunday."[57]

Tourism, however, remained limited, and Key West's major industries were suffering. The railroad failed to rescue Key West from the economic downswing that followed the decline of its cigar industry, and contrary to Flagler's prediction, in the decade the train reached Key West, the city's population decreased by approximately 6 percent, from 19,945 to 18,749. What would become Key West's source of profit, jobs, and public revenues? The answer was not entirely clear, but Key West's officials and business-sector members clearly felt the need to attract tourists and tourist facilities to the community.

2

The Not-So-Roaring Twenties

DURING THE FIRST HALF of the 1920s, Fort Lauderdale, Miami, Palm Beach, and nearby communities in South Florida tripled their population and more. Key West, however, moved in the opposite direction, attracting fewer immigrants and witnessing the departure of many of its residents. Key West's population dropped dramatically during the decade, from 18,749 in 1920 to 12,831, a drop that marked an acceleration of the trend in the previous decade. Many who left Key West moved to the growing Miami area.

As had been the case in the 1910s, the decline was especially dramatic among Key West's black population.[1] Key West's reputation for relatively civil race relations was not always borne out in practice, a factor that might have contributed to the departure of blacks from Key West. In June 1920, Monroe County officials had to request assistance from naval officers to head off the efforts of a "well organized" Key West mob to remove a black man charged with attempted rape of a white woman from the county jail and lynch him.[2]

In December 1921, members of the Ku Klux Klan whipped and tarred and feathered Manuel Cabeza, known as Isleno, an immigrant from the Canary Islands, for living with a mulatto woman. During the attack, Isleno pulled his assailants' hoods off and recognized several of them. The next day, Isleno shot and killed William Decker, who was reputed to be head of the Klan and who also, according to some, had had an affair with the same woman. Isleno was apprehended and arrested. Sheriff Roland Curry initially requested that the Marines guard the jail to prevent Klan members from attacking Isleno, but Curry released the Marines from this duty later in the evening. Hours later, early on Christmas Day, several KKK members stormed the jail, killed Isleno, tied his body to the bumper of a car, and dragged him to the outskirts of town where they hung him from a tree. No one was charged with the crime.[3]

The primary reason, however, for the departure of residents, white and black, from Key West was the island's weak economy. While the city derived some economic benefits during the 1920s from the Flagler railroad and from the train car ferry to and from Cuba, except for some perishable goods that needed to be shipped rapidly, it remained more economically viable to transport goods via ship than rail. The Florida East Coast Railway's extension into Key West was never profitable, and the "sea train" inaugurated from New Orleans to Havana and the steamship service that connected Havana to New York further threatened its business. The revenue the railroad earned from carrying freight decreased dramatically between 1926 and 1931.[4]

The cigar industry and military presence in Key West were also in decline. By the end of the 1920s, most of the cigar-making establishments could best be characterized as "small shops" rather than as factories. Although the Seventh Naval District remained headquartered in Key West, few sailors were stationed at the Navy base. Also, the Naval Air Station on Trumbo Point that was deactivated in 1920 remained closed throughout the decade.[5]

Tourism

Tourists could still travel to Key West by railroad and steamship. The P&O Steamship Company carried passengers daily between Key West and Havana and also provided service between Port Tampa and Key West. The Mallory Line from New York City and Galveston also reached

Key West. At the beginning of the decade, however, the city still offered relatively few accommodations for overnight tourists, and none were upscale. Tourism in southeast Florida flourished during the early and mid-1920s, and some in Key West wanted to follow a similar path. The opening of the city's first luxury hotel promised to expand tourism and attract a wealthier clientele.[6]

Henry Flagler had intended to build a hotel in Key West after his railroad reached the city in 1912. Flagler's death in 1913, however, delayed this plan, which was delayed again by the First World War. In 1918, the Flagler System decided to proceed with the project. On Saturday, January 1, 1921, the 250-room Casa Marina Hotel opened for business, having hosted a New Year's Eve ball the night before. Shortly after it opened, President Warren Harding was a guest at the Casa, and during the 1920s many affluent visitors to Key West stayed at the hotel.[7]

Buoyed by the opening of this luxury facility, Key West's city government and business community supported promotional efforts to boost tourism and development. In 1921, some members of the city's business community organized the Good Government League to nominate in the November election candidates for mayor and council who shared this perspective. Among the league's members was State Representative Frank H. Ladd, who successfully ran for mayor. During both of Ladd's two-year terms, and during the rest of the decade under Mayor Leslie Curry (1925–33), the city government worked with the business community to promote Key West to tourists and outside investors.[8]

The Key West Chamber of Commerce received public funds to publicize Key West via newspaper advertisements and widely distributed brochures. Visitors were promised an exotic and unique destination. The advertisements heralded the island's natural and built environment, its beautiful weather, and the character of its population, as well as the majesty of the OverSeas Railway that transported people down the Florida Keys. A 1923 publication distributed by the Chamber included the following description of the city, beginning with the initial approach by train.

> The view from the car windows begs description. The opalescent waters, . . . the varicolored seaweeds showing through the water, the deep-blue sky and the wonderful cloud effects, make a picture

long-to-be-remembered and never-to-be-forgotten by all those who are so fortunate as to make this trip.

The scenery on the island is semitropical and most interesting for the tourist and visitor.

The architecture of the houses, low and solidly built, gives an old-world charm and foreign atmosphere to Key West. From behind lightly closed shutters, down the long streets, one almost listens for the tinkle of a guitar or strains of La Paloma.

The place has as much personality as New Orleans, an atmosphere intangible and indefinable, and its code of living, like that of all islands, is autocratic, easy unto itself.

The pretty Spanish and Cuban girls as well as the lovely American maidens, and navy men in flawless white uniforms, the trim marines . . . from the barracks all form a picturesque pageant on a Key West promenade.

The coffee shops, the fish markets, the 'turtle crawls' and the street vendors crying their wares, form a marvelous medley of sound and color.

Spend your winter vacation in Key West, the only FROST-FREE city in the United States.[9]

Shortly before his hotel opened for the season on December 29, 1923, the manager of the Casa Marina expressed confidence that the winter tourist season of 1924 would surpass all previous seasons. The manager of the Oversea Hotel made a similar prediction and reported that the number of tourists in his hotel already exceeded that of the previous year at the height of the tourist season. In February 1924, tourists were unable to find overnight accommodations on certain nights. The Exchange Club had compiled a listing of apartments and rooms that were available to tourists, but the number fell far short of their goal of 1,000.[10] The *Key West Citizen*, the island's primary newspaper, saw this as an opportunity.

"The condition that now prevails in the large tourist traffic to this city bears out what was said at the beginning of the season: there is a good opportunity now to build bungalows, apartments and hotels . . . for next winter. Thousands of persons from all over the country are learning more about Key West this winter than ever before."[11]

Not all visitors to Key West were welcome, however. A headline in a December 1923 issue of the *Citizen*, "Hoboe Fraternity Much in Evidence Now on Streets," emphasized local concern about "snowbirds," which were going home to home begging for food and other handouts. The article emphasized that the panhandlers often were carefully watching homes to determine the best time to burglarize them. Shortly afterward, however, the *Citizen* proudly announced that its campaign "against the 'boes, or snowbirds, or whatever one wishes to call them, was so successful that not one of them has been seen in Key West in more than three weeks."[12]

The town that promised to be different from Palm Beach or Miami, both of which offered many more activities and amusements than Key West did, also attracted many "welcome" visitors. For example, the author Katherine Doris Sharp stayed in Key West during the 1926 winter season. She had spent the previous winter in Miami, but found it "too noisy." Many tourists were attracted primarily by fishing in the tropical climate. By 1923, one could choose from among at least three charter boats to hire for a day of fishing, and as tourism increased more became available at the Porter Docks at the Gulf end of Duval Street, at the Gulf Oil Dock nearby, and at the Thompson Fish Docks at the Key West Bight.[13]

Bootlegged liquor was readily available to tourists and residents. The Coast Guard expanded its presence in Key West during the decade, but the limited number of prohibition agents, and of law enforcement in general, contributed to its being a wide-open town, with alcohol and gambling enterprises such as bolita, slot machines, and cock fighting readily available. Much of the liquor transported to Key West arrived in small boats from Cuba and the Bahamas. According to Ernest Hemingway, the first liquor brought into Key West from Cuba was transported by Joe Russell, who would become the owner of Sloppy Joe's bar. Others hid liquor on the railroad car ferries that ran between Havana and Key West.[14]

It is likely that most of Key West's population sided with the smugglers rather than with the law enforcement officers, who themselves were reputedly not overzealous in arresting suspected bootleggers. Indeed, some law enforcement officials in Key West sided with suspected bootleggers against other law enforcement agents. In April 1926, prohibition agents from Miami raided several Key West establishments, confiscating liquor and arresting the proprietors. At the same time that the agents were appearing before a U.S. commissioner to provide information against those they had apprehended, others who had been raided persuaded a Monroe County justice of the peace to issue warrants charging these agents with larceny, the destruction of private property, and other crimes. Monroe County Sheriff Roland Curry urged the Dade County Sheriff to arrest one of the prohibition agents for theft and to return him to Key West to stand trial. After some negotiations, charges were dropped against both the agents and those the agents had arrested.[15]

Even when Key West citizens were found guilty of violating prohibition and gambling laws, the penalties were often rather lenient. For example, Raul Vasquez operated the Florence Club, which availed customers of both liquor and gambling. He was arrested and sentenced to jail, but the jailer provided him with a key so he could come and go as he chose and continue to run his business.[16]

Although lax law enforcement during prohibition was certainly not unique to Key West, many perceived other aspects of the island city as different from those of the South Florida boomtowns. In his essay "America's Island of Felicity," the explorer and science fiction writer George Allan England described Key West as "different from all other cities, filled with beauty and with curious, unique pictures." He added that Key West was "somewhat a state of mind, unique and unapproachable save by those who love and understand the tropics, and yield gladly to their enchanted wooing. Key West, to understanding hearts and souls, is more than can be written down in words."[17]

Elmer Davis, in an article published in the *New Yorker* in 1926, emphasized that at the Casa Marina one did not see "the overdressed overanxiety" that one observes at the Poinciana Hotel in Miami. The Casa Marina was "too quiet to be in favor with the earnest spenders and the serious drinkers and the younger set." In fact, he observed that after the train arrived three nights a week, the hotel was full, but after breakfast the next morning the "money-bees" would once again "swarm to the Havana boat." The Casa Marina would then stand virtually empty for thirty-six hours.

Davis also asked, more generally, "What does one do in Key West?" His answer: "Let the news serve as enticement to the elect and warning to the general—one does nothing in Key West." He added that one might swim, play golf, or fish, but noted "for the true hound of spring it is enough to lie shirtless on the sand . . . or lie motionless in a rocking chair on the porch, smoking a Key West cigar . . ." Three years later, Davis had not changed his opinion: "There is nothing to 'do' in Key West except swim and fish and play golf and drink the excellent Bacardi rum and Tropical beer with which Cuba pays its debt to its liberators; and after the first three hours there is nothing to see, in the sense in which that verb is used by tourists."[18]

The writer John Dos Passos voiced similar sentiments during his visit to Key West in March 1929. On his way to the island in 1928, Dos Passos had written to a friend, "At this moment I'm in a little jerkwater boat full of seasick passengers being conveyed (I hardly know why) to Key West." During his 1929 visit, however, he cast the island in a much more positive light: "life is agreeable, calm and gently colored with Bacardi—the swimming is magnificent and you catch all sorts of iris colored finnies on the adjacent reefs, you broil them, basting them with a substance known as Old Sour and eat mightily well." Dos Passos concluded, "apart from that there's absolutely nothing to do, which is a blessing."[19]

Davis warned, however, that Key West might well be spoiled, as Palm Beach and Miami had. A bad omen was the highway being built through the Keys that would connect the islands to the mainland. When it was completed, Davis lamented, the town's boosters would strive to build more accommodations and provide more amenities for the tourists driving to Key West. Key West would no longer be different and exotic. In fact, according to Davis, one seeking quiet would have to dive into the water, which, he emphasized, would be safe because "the realty business will have absorbed all the sharks." Davis's fear that Key West would be sold to the highest bidder would be echoed frequently later in the century.[20]

The Overseas Highway

Key West's boosters sought just what Davis dreaded: better access to the island. The railroad service to Key West was unreliable. Trains from New York to Key West often arrived considerably behind schedule, and it was not uncommon for the trip down the Keys to Key West to take seven hours rather than the four-and-a-half specified in the railroad's schedules. To address this problem, city officials and business leaders focused on building an Overseas Highway that would connect Key West with the mainland and accommodate the increasing number of American tourists who owned cars. Real estate interests were strong advocates of the highway. As William Herren of the National Real Estate Association stated at a Key West Realty Board dinner, "The Overseas highway would never have been spoken about if it had not been for real estate." Key West's civic boosters hoped that increasing numbers of travelers would drive to Key West and that real estate values would increase as developers sought land to build accommodations for tourists and homes for seasonal residents.[21]

In 1923, voters in Monroe County approved a $300,000 bond issue to connect Key Largo, the northernmost island of the Florida Keys, to the mainland and to build the highway from Key Largo to Lower Matecumbe in the Middle Keys. In 1924, voters approved another bond issue, this time to finance bridges and roads to connect Key West to the Middle Keys. In an editorial in early January 1924, the *Citizen* declared, "Key West is on the brink of becoming a great tourist center." Two years later, as the highway was being constructed, the New York businessman and journalist Clarence W. Barron confidently predicted, "The success [of the Overseas Highway] will be greater than ever came from the Flagler's Florida East Coast Railway. It will be unparalleled in the history of the world."[22]

In August 1926, Monroe County's voters passed a referendum granting a franchise and a guaranteed return on investment to the C.A.P. Turner Company of Minneapolis to construct three toll bridges that would connect major sections of the highway and provide an uninterrupted road to Key West. The Board of County Commissioners initiated the referendum and campaigned for its passage. In Key West, Mayor Leslie Curry, the Key West Realty Board, several businesses, the Carpenters' Union, and the *Citizen* actively backed the referendum.[23]

Ultimately, however, fiscal realities dictated that, instead of financing the bridges, Monroe County paid for the operation of ferryboats to convey motorists along the forty-mile gap in the road between No Name Key (about 25 miles from Key West) and Lower Matecumbe. On January 25, 1928, the Overseas Highway connecting Key West and Miami officially opened. Despite the fact that the trip took longer than originally planned because the toll bridges were replaced with ferries, the *Citizen* still predicted that Key West would take "her place as one of the leading industrial and resort cities of the state."[24]

Anticipating that the automobile would become the dominant means of transportation for visitors to reach Key West, the city built a boulevard along several miles of the city's waterfront. The road, primarily constructed by dredge and fill, was named Ocean View Boulevard, later renamed North and South Roosevelt Boulevard. Also in response to the new emphasis on auto travel, Key West replaced its electric streetcar system with buses in 1926. The *Citizen* spoke approvingly of this change, noting, "There could be no more convincing evidence that Key West is absolutely up-to-date in every way than the fact that a modern and complete bus service has entirely replaced the old trolley car which is now so rapidly becoming obsolete."[25]

Tourism Dreams

In January 1924, the *Citizen* carried an article, including a letter from a winter visitor, under the headline, "Island City's Climate is Worth Thousand Dollars a Square Inch." The author of this letter noted that he had been "coming to Florida several years" before discovering "what a superb climate" it had. He continued, "And one of these days, and it won't be long either, so many tourists will want to spend the winter here that accommodations must be provided for them, and many of them will build themselves, resulting in a boom that will send realty values sky high in Key West. It's coming; nothing can stop it, but its coming should be hastened, and it is up to your people to do that."[26]

The next year, Malcolm Meacham, a wealthy businessman from New York who had been involved in development in the Palm Beach area, appeared to confirm the letter writer's prediction. Meacham had been one of the most vocal supporters of the Overseas Highway. In 1925, at the peak of the Florida real estate boom, he bought 1,000 acres on the east side of Key West, including the Salt Ponds, for $500,000.[27]

Meacham paid $200,000 of the $500,000 purchase price and gave a $300,000 mortgage to the Key West Realty Company, which had owned the property when Flagler's railroad reached Key West in 1912. William R. Porter, a leading Key West businessman and politician, was the president of Key West Realty and an avid promoter of tourism and development on the island. Porter had been the first president of the Commercial Club, which was organized in 1907 and later merged with the Chamber of Commerce. In 1924, he was appointed president of the First National Bank, in which capacity he served until 1944. Porter was also a member of the Board of County Commissioners, which in 1926 approved the contract for the construction of the bridges to complete the Overseas Highway.[28]

Meacham planned to build hotels, yacht basins, and new housing on his property, which he predicted would attract more tourists to the island. A reporter for the *Citizen* suggested that after Meacham's project was completed a winter visitor would find "all the advantages of Venice." The Chamber of Commerce's advertising campaign for the 1925–26 tourist season—on which the advertising committee spent approximately $30,000, more than it had on any other season—reinforced Meacham's plans. The *Citizen* emphasized the success of this effort, claiming that thousands had visited Key West for the first time and that many of them had subsequently invested in the community, thus benefiting Key West far into the future. Further, the *Citizen* predicted, many of these tourists would likely become permanent residents of Key West.[29]

By the mid-1920s, in addition to the Casa Marina, tourists in search of upscale accommodations could stay at the Hotel La Concha on Duval Street, which celebrated its grand opening in January 1926. John Wanamaker of New York designed its interior, and its six stories made it the tallest building in Key West. The new luxury hotel's Rainbow Room regularly hosted dances with live orchestras. Many well-off visitors stayed there, and when Pan American Airways began passenger flights in 1928 between Key West and Havana, it located its office in the new hotel.[30]

In the meantime, Meacham formed the Key West Foundation Company, establishing himself as its president. In February 1926, Meacham announced that New York Title & Mortgage Company had issued a $1 million policy insuring the title of all of the Foundation Company's property in Key West. As such, any buyers of the property could forgo the time and expense of paying for an examination of the title abstract, and their legal right to title would be guaranteed. Meacham emphasized that the imminent completion of the Overseas Highway would ensure the value of their investment. "Now is the time to buy!" he exclaimed. "Motor-connection with the Mainland is IN SIGHT."[31]

A publication sponsored by the Key West Chamber of Commerce, "Key West 'The Island City,'" praised Meacham's plans. It boasted that he would "erect a winter-resort . . . upon this area, a paradise of winter homes, yacht basins, scenic waterways and bathing casinos." This type of development would not be unique to Key West; in fact, it would be "representative of similar developments effected elsewhere along the East Coast of Florida." Still, its beauty and architecture would surpass many of the others.[32]

The same publication praised the "Martello Towers" residential development that would encompass about thirteen acres near the Casa Marina. Burbank Realty Company owned the property and was developing it with homes designed to appeal to winter residents. Initially, in July 1925, the company established a minimum price of $10,000 for the lots. After lots sold quickly, investors started asking between $14,000 and $25,000 per lot.

In addition, C. S. Baxter, one of the partners with the Burbank Realty Company, announced that he would build a bathing casino and hotel on the oceanfront property he owned adjacent to the proposed development. The Martello Towers project, in conjunction with the plans for Baxter's property, "call[ed] for an elaborate program of macadamized streets, white ways, Roman baths, bathing casino, hotel and residence lots prepared for actual building." Once completed, the project would "become linked with Malcolm Meacham's development as one continuity of beautiful winter homes and recreational centers."[33]

Dreams on Hold

Ultimately, however, little development resulted from these announced ventures, in part because Florida's land boom ended shortly after Meacham's purchase. Instead of filling large areas of the Salt Ponds, Meacham merely sold some building lots on dry land on Flagler Avenue (then called County Road) and on Eagle Avenue (then called Avenue "E"). No homes were constructed in the Martello Towers subdivision, and the plans for the Baxter property next to the subdivision also came to naught. Some speculators had made money buying land and then selling it to new buyers. Others undoubtedly lost money. In the end, development of the property would have to wait several decades. After the stock market crash of 1929, plans for filling the Salt Ponds were put on hold, and Meacham's land reverted to the Key West Realty Company.[34]

Meacham had leased some of his land to Pan American Airways, and in 1927 Pan Am built what became known as Meacham Field. Pan Am began mail service between Key West and Havana in October 1927 and initiated passenger service in January 1928. Pan Am, however, operated from Key West for only a short period, and no other airline replaced it.[35]

The impact of the Overseas Highway was also far less than its supporters had anticipated. The need to take the car ferry over the water gap certainly discouraged some potential visitors. From Miami, tourists could drive to Lower Matecumbe, about 70 miles northeast of Key West, but they then had to pay a toll to drive onto a ferry for a roughly four-hour, forty-mile trip to No Name Key and then drive another twenty-five miles to Key West. In all, the trip took about eight hours, which was no faster than the train. In January 1930, additional road building created two water gaps, rather than one, between Lower Matecumbe and No Name Key, which together totaled fewer miles than the single forty-mile gap. Still, the shortage of ferries usually necessitated that cars be transported in one trip over the entire forty miles. Ultimately, however, what ensured Key West's decline was that by the time the highway opened, the depression had already impacted Florida, even before the onset of the Great Depression nationally. During the early years of the next decade, the island's economy weakened further: tourists were few, poverty was widespread, and the town was virtually bankrupt. During the Great Depression, even more so than during the 1920s, enhanced tourism was viewed as the answer to the island's problems.[36]

3

The Depression and War Years

Tourism Dreams Give Way to Military Realities

The New Deal Comes to Key West

By the early years of the Great Depression, Key West's economic base had been decimated. During the first half of the 1930s, Key West's population declined from 12,831 to 12,317, continuing its trend of population loss in the 1920s. Both Key West and Monroe County lacked the revenue to pay their workers and provide services to their population. Faced with the impossible task of raising enough funds to finance its debt and operating costs, the Key West City Council and the Monroe County Board of County Commissioners (BOCC) on July 2, 1934 abdicated the operation of government in Key West to the state of Florida.[1]

Florida's state government, however, was also in no position to assist the financially plagued community. Instead, Governor David Sholtz asked Julius Stone Jr., the head of the Florida operations of the Federal Emergency Relief Administration (FERA), to act as the governor's agent. Stone recognized the severity of Key West's situation. He reported that a significant portion of the city's population was already on relief and that the "means of support" were weakening. Further, the citizens had not had access to medical care for the previous three years, and their diets consisted almost entirely of fish, except for the songbirds they managed to shoot or the coconuts they managed to steal.[2]

What might get Key West through the tough times was the question. Stone's answer was to expand on the efforts made in the 1920s to convert Key West's economy to tourism. He noted, "We must make Key West so attractive that the world will beat a path to its door. Why not make it 'the Bermuda of Florida.'" To symbolize this goal, Stone began wearing Bermuda shorts around town. He created the Key West Administration (KWA) to plan the program to attract tourists, as well as to implement the relief program for Key West's poverty-stricken residents. Stone pronounced that the KWA would construct new buildings and renovate existing ones so as to "accentuate the charm of the city," adding, "When we have a real quaint town we shall resort to extensive advertising to draw the tourists."[3]

Although the city and county governments had agreed to abdicate decision-making responsibility, they continued to function. In 1935, Dr. Harry Galey defeated William H. Malone, the incumbent mayor, and served until 1937. The locally elected officials were not entirely devoid of authority. For example, in August 1935, a circuit judge ruled that Mayor Malone could suspend city employees for due cause. During the two years that the Key West Administration operated in Key West, however, the city council and county commission generally deferred to its policies.[4]

Stone and the KWA faced a formidable task in transforming Key West into a tourist paradise. By the fall of 1934, the Casa Marina had been closed for two years, so only the Gibson and the Oversea Hotels, both on Fleming Street, and the Colonial Hotel (formerly La Concha) offered accommodations to guests. The KWA organized relief recipients and other Key Westers into the Key West Volunteer Corps, and in this capacity they renovated and painted houses, demolished other houses, and cleared debris and garbage from the streets. The KWA also brought artists to the community to entice tourists to visit. The paintings of the artists of the Key West Arts Project, which included Avery Johnson, F. Townsend Morgan, Eric Johan Smith, Stanley Woods, and others, were initially displayed during the 1934–35 tourist season at the Colonial Hotel and then were shown and sold at a new gallery in the renovated Caroline Lowe house at Duval and Caroline Streets. The artists also painted murals on several buildings, including two well-known restaurants, Delmonico's and Ramonin's.[5]

Some of the artists' paintings were reproduced on postcards and in brochures and distributed widely. Included in one brochure, for example, was a painting of Rest Beach on the Atlantic, which was "ideal for children as well as grown-ups" and offered "palm-thatched cabanas and umbrellas" and "small sailing boats and glassbottomed boats." Also included was a painting, titled "Deep Sea Fishing," showing Key West as "the fisherman's paradise . . . whose waters contain more than six hundred varieties of edible fish." The "Key West Golf Club" was an ideal place for the "wan and haggard lawyers, doctors and executives" who arrive in Key West to forget "the cares of city life, its endless hurry and complexity." Semitropical Key West, the Island City that has always been frost-free, was described as the perfect vacation spot for "The tired business man, the sportsman, the lover of the outdoors, the artist, the writer—in short any one seeking a change from the normal routine." Tourists were also enticed, by words and pictures, to visit Key West to experience its natural vegetation and to admire its architecture.[6]

As during the 1920s, the brochures invited tourists to appreciate the rhythm of the community and its people, which they claimed constituted a unique environment.

> In the afternoons the town is quiet, and the little houses seem asleep; their shutters are closed against the sun, and the citizens take their siesta. But with the coming of evening, after the splendid fires of sunset grow pale, the town stirs and comes to life. . . . Dozens of little native cafes are bright with life, and for blocks the central street of town is crowded with sociable people out to parade and admire each other. . . . The young Cuban blades stand on the edges of the sidewalk, the handsome girls parade up and down; Key West has lost all resemblance to a United States town, and has become Spanish again.[7]

Some newspaper reports also emphasized Key West's uniqueness. The *Miami Herald* called attention to its physical environment and flora, noting "Visitors in Key West say that they could go into many other tourist cities blindfolded, and having had their blindfolds removed, would be unable to tell what city it was; while if they went through the same test in Key West, they would recognize immediately the island city—by its houses, its strange little naturally floral decorated lanes, or by some other 'something' which makes the city Key West."[8]

The KWA was not content, however, to emphasize Key West's unique population and environment. In December 1934, it published an elaborate booklet, "Key West in Transition, A Guide Book for Visitors," that enumerated forty-six "points of interest" in Key West, along with a map that pinpointed where each was located. Included among the points of interest were the sponge docks, turtle kraals, fish market, and Fort Taylor. The booklet also highlighted an upcoming attraction, the open-air aquarium that was approved for funding by the federal Civil Works Administration (CWA) in late 1933 and opened in February 1935. The booklet further appealed to tourists' wilder aspirations, encouraging them to go to the Havana Madrid Club, which offered visitors "an opportunity to enjoy some 'night club' life in Key West," and Pena's "Garden of Roses," where tourists could dance and "never leave unhappy." Also, Raul Vasquez's Club Miramar on Roosevelt Boulevard was "not to be missed by the person liking gaiety."[9]

These efforts to attract more tourists succeeded. During the tourist season of 1934–35, which lasted from November to February, more than 30,000 visitors arrived in Key West, and the number of guests staying in hotels increased by 85 percent over the 1933–34 season. Key West's efforts to move toward a tourism-based economy garnered nationwide attention. Most of the commentary was positive. For example, the New York Times praised the FERA program for changing the city into a "clean and shining tourist haven." The Palatka Daily News noted, "It would not occasion surprise if the devout Latins, who constitute the bulk of the population should nominate him (Julius Stone) as their Saint Julius and should erect a shrine in his honor." Some locals also voiced their appreciation for the federal efforts. One wrote to Eleanor Roosevelt in October 1934, "I am going to have little Eleanor Ann Baptized who has been named after you and want you and the president to be little Eleanor Ann's God parent . . . I will send you a picture of her next month."[10]

Not all of the commentary, however, was glowing. A wire service reporter called Stone authoritarian, characterizing him as "the king of a tight little empire." And not all Key Westers reacted positively to Stone's initiatives. Elmer Davis, who had previously visited and written about Key West during the 1920s, noted, "It has been quite a strain on the inhabitants, all this hullabaloo—greatest strain of all, perhaps, the impact of new ideas: for while Key West in many ways is unique, in some ways it is like any other small town."[11] For example, not everyone welcomed Stone's decision to have New Deal-hired artists paint murals on the walls of some of the local restaurants and nightspots: "Mr. Antonio Pena Morales, whose bar is to Key West what the Brevoort is to Greenwich Village, agreed to accept some murals on the supposition that they would be little ones; when one morning the government sent him a whole truckload of art he went into eruption and sent it back, not without the hearty applause of some of the oldtimers who felt that, however good those paintings may have been, Pena's overlaid with art was no longer Pena's."[12]

Many in the community found Stone's favorite attire, designed to make tourists feel comfortable in the "new Key West," difficult to accept. Davis noted, "Julius Stone, observing that shorts were the most sensible and comfortable costume in that climate, issued . . . a request that all administration employees should wear them. . . . Shorts never had been worn in Key West; they were not part of the traditional atmosphere; to any habitual visitor—still more to any native—they look out of place, even though they might seem perfectly natural in Miami or on Long Island. But next year, in all likelihood, Key West will be wearing shorts; and so will be a little less like Key West."[13]

Some disagreed more with Stone's strategy than with his style, arguing that he was relying too heavily on tourism to revitalize Key West. Mayor Malone, for example, proposed that Key West petition Congress for authorization as a foreign trade zone, which he contended would increase job opportunities in the community. Stone blocked this proposal. Key West should be "a tourist town or nothing," Stone maintained. "It would be a mistake to attempt to make it anything except a resort city. If you brought in one or two industries, they would drive away the tourists. The industries would not support it, and then it would be neither fish nor fowl."[14]

Key West was, for now, committed to the tourism strategy. Its economy had relied most heavily on wrecking until the Civil War. Then, the cigar industry had dominated the city's economy. Now tourism would take over.

After the tourist season of 1934–35, M. E. Gilfond, who was appointed the administrator of the KWA in December 1934, announced the new projects that were to be undertaken in Key West to attract more tourists. These included the construction of an outdoor swimming pool and a bridle path along the Atlantic, as well as a general plan for beautification. In order to attract tourists for the 1935–36 season, Gilfond and several Key West citizens, including the banker William R. Porter and Jack Golden, the manager of the Colonial Hotel, agreed to finance an advertising campaign in Northern publications.[15]

Then Mother Nature intervened, as it had periodically throughout Key West's history. A hurricane hit the Keys on Labor Day, 1935, killing almost 500 people. A majority of the dead were war veterans, most of the First World War and the remainder of the Spanish-American War. They had been hired by the Veterans Work Program, primarily administered by FERA and financed by both the federal government and the state of Florida, to build bridges for the Overseas Highway on Lower Matecumbe Key and nearby locations in the Middle Keys. The hurricane left Key West with little damage, but destroyed enough of the railroad bridges that the Florida East Coast Railway, which was already in receivership, was unable to resume its operations, thereby ending rail service to Key West. The train ferries that had shipped cargo between Key West and Cuba were moved to Port Everglades in Broward County.[16]

Inevitably, this disaster hurt Key West's tourism during the 1935–36 season. In February and March 1935, over 5,000 people had arrived in Key West via the railroad. The highway connecting Key West to the mainland that remained interrupted by two water gaps was also damaged by the storm but reopened in November. Still, the number of people driving to Key West was 15 to 20 percent lower in each month of the 1935–36 tourist season than in the previous year. The P&O steamships also brought fewer tourists to the island. There was an overall decline in the number of guests staying in hotels and motels and renting rooms in Key Westers' homes. In spite of this decline, however, considerably more tourists arrived during the 1935–36 season than had visited Key West two winters earlier. The fact that tourism had increased dramatically during the winter of 1935 and remained high, relative to earlier in the decade, during the 1935–36 tourist season led many to believe Key West could continue to expand its tourism business.[17]

From FERA to WPA

One major rationale for Stone's tourism initiative was to provide jobs for Key West's citizens. The improvement in the tourism business during the 1934–35 season contributed to a drop in the relief rolls, but a significant number of Key Westers nevertheless remained on the rolls. Key West's movement toward a tourism-based economy had failed to generate enough jobs in the private sector to get most of the city's unemployed back to work, so federal programs continued to fund projects and hire workers. Even before the hurricane hit the Keys that Labor Day, the Works Progress Administration (WPA) had begun operating in Key West, and gradually it succeeded FERA in assuming responsibility for much of the federal activity in the city. While FERA continued to operate through mid-July 1936, much of the transition to the WPA took place in July and August 1935.[18]

In August 1935, the first WPA projects for Key West were approved, offering employment to over 300 people. After the hurricane, in October 1935, the federal government approved a grant for the construction of a sewage and water distribution system for Key West. The island would still have no fresh water supply, but the pipes would be installed in preparation for a possible future project in which water would be pumped from the mainland to Key West. Through this and other projects, by the end of November the WPA had put 1,400 men and women, virtually all of whom had been on relief, back to work.[19]

Some of the WPA projects were directly related to the tourist strategy of the Key West Administration. For example, the WPA created botanical gardens on Stock Island, located just east of Key West, that opened in February 1936 during Key West's second "La Semana Alegre" (The Week of Joy). This weeklong festival, financed and organized primarily by FERA in 1935 and by the WPA in 1936, was initiated to attract more tourists to Key West, but it also celebrated Key West's Cuban heritage and the Cuban fight for independence from Spain. The festival incorporated the celebration of El Grito de Baire, the start of Cuba's second revolution against Spain on February 24, 1895, in the town of Baire. Cuban gunboats arrived to help celebrate the event and were greeted by representatives of the San Carlos Institute and the Cuban Club.[20]

Cubans in Key West had not only organized to support Cuba's independence from Spain but had also formed unions in the cigar industry that periodically went on strike to secure benefits for the workers. Labor strife also impacted WPA programs. Stone's tourism strategy might have brought more visitors to Key West, but it did not create docile workers eager to conform to their representation in KWA's tourist brochures as exotic, content islanders.[21]

In early December 1935, about 1,300 WPA workers in Key West went on strike, protesting their salary of $6.05 a week for four days of work. Florida's WPA administrator, E. A. Pynchon, responded by suspending work on all the city's WPA projects, with the exception of the sewing project, which employed women, and emphasized that none of the workers would be paid until they returned to work. The workers voted to continue the strike, prompting about thirty "robed and hooded men," some carrying guns, to "guarantee protection to any workman who desires to return to work." Many of the WPA workers then signed petitions asking WPA officials to resume the projects. Louis Avila, the head of the strike committee, agreed, citing the possibility of bloodshed should the strike continue. The strike ended about a week after it had started. Workers were informed that their wages would increase to $7.50 for five days of work, the offer that the strikers had rejected just a few days earlier.[22]

In August 1936, about 500 WPA workers again went on strike. This time, although he hoped that the issues could be resolved peacefully, Avila promised that should any of the masked men from the last strike reappear, he would "shoot into them with his double-barreled shotgun." Herbert F. R. Reck, who had been appointed the new director of the WPA in Monroe County, responded by firing Avila and the other WPA workers who supported the strike, and the strikers returned to their jobs.[23]

Reck also emphasized to Key West's public officials that the federal presence was weakening. Key West's city government and the government of Monroe County regained their governing authority from the KWA that summer. Still, local officials continued to pursue tourism, and federal money played a significant role in their endeavors. Willard Albury succeeded Henry Galey as mayor in 1937 and served until his resignation in 1945. However, Florida State Representative Bernard ("Bernie")

Papy, who was initially elected in 1934 and served until his defeat in the 1962 Democratic primary, was soon recognized as the "king of the Keys" and was the most prominent political actor in Monroe County. Papy was in many ways a machine-style politician, delivering jobs, contracts, and other benefits to some of his constituents in exchange for political support. He also became a successful businessman, due in part to his political connections and influence. Papy's close-knit group of political allies were members of the "courthouse gang" that held important public positions in Monroe County. In addition, Papy was influential in Key West's politics, in part because of his ability to sponsor or reject in the state legislature "local" bills that impacted the community.[24]

The Overseas Highway

After the hurricane of 1935 destroyed the railroad, it was clear that the future of land travel between the mainland and Key West rested with the highway. Papy played an important role in the reconstruction of the highway through the Keys. The state legislature had created the Overseas Road and Toll Bridge Commission in 1933, granting it the authority to sell bonds to support the completion of a toll road between Lower Matecumbe and Big Pine Key that would provide for the first time a direct road connection between Key West and the mainland. Although it was Florida's governor who appointed the members of the commission, once Papy was elected to the legislature he exerted a strong influence on the governor's decisions. Work on extending the Overseas Highway had started in 1934, but the section of the road that had been completed was destroyed by the hurricane. The highway project now became Key West's top priority, in hopes of drawing more tourists to the island. The federal Public Works Administration (PWA) approved a $3,600,000 loan to the commission in June 1936 to finance the construction of highway bridges over the water gaps. While the Overseas Highway was under construction in 1937 and 1938, Howard E. Wilson, a Papy ally, served as chair of the commission.[25]

In April 1938, the first travelers to drive by car directly from Miami to Key West entered the island city. The entire trip took approximately four hours, several hours shorter than the route that required a ferry trip across the water gaps. Key Westers celebrated the official opening of the highway on July 4, 1938. The completion of the Overseas Highway, which connected Key West to the mainland, compensated in part for the loss of the train connection, and many forecast that Key West would become a thriving tourist destination. Florida Congressman J. Mark Wilcox, for example, predicted that Key West would become "one of the busiest cities in Florida," with "visitors . . . the year round."[26]

The New Monte Carlo?

Just as federal and local promoters of tourism didn't publicize the labor unrest in Key West, they also didn't advertise a major pastime of the Conch community—gambling, long popular and widespread on the island. However, around the time that construction of the highway was commencing, speculation surfaced that to attract tourists the island city would be transformed into "the new Monte Carlo." According to some, this transformation was a logical one for the community, given Key Westers' penchant for gambling and the city government's generally tolerant policy toward this activity.

On June 21, 1936, an article in the *Miami Daily News* described the pervasiveness of gambling in Key West and the hope some had that the city could be transformed into a tourist destination that offered gambling as its major draw—a rather different enticement from those featured in the KWA's brochures. The article noted:

> Much has been said about Key West becoming a second St. Petersburg [Florida] if and when the Overseas highway becomes a reality, but many of the southernmost city's residents have different ideas. Pointing to the fact the island city is run on a 'wide open' policy, many residents hope to see the place turned into an American Monte Carlo. If the city is turned into the gambling capital of the nation it shouldn't be any great shock to the residents in view of the fact that even now there is hardly a bar in the downtown area without a gambling room. Bolita, however, is the city's favorite sport, with tremendous interest concentrated on the game.

One of Tennessee Williams's earliest recollections of Key West dates to his first visit, in 1941. A friend had to leave town because he owed money to professional gamblers who had threatened to kill him. Williams concluded that Key West was "as wide open as a frontier town in those days."[27]

A draft of the *Key West Guide*, published by the Writers Program of the WPA, described the excitement that bolita generated in the community: "Tuesdays and Saturdays are Key West bolita days. Bets are on numbers from one to one hundred, placed in any one of the many houses. . . . A grapevine telegraph now comes into play. Over back fences may be heard, 'Que numero tire al Al?' and the answer 'Cincuenta y cuatro.' (What number did the Alley throw? Fifty-four.) . . . Nearly all Key Westers and many visitors play it." Placing bets on the Cuban National Lottery generated similar excitement.[28]

In September 1937, speculation surfaced once again that Key West was soon to merge its gambling and tourism sectors and be transformed into the "Monte Carlo" of the western hemisphere. Rumors circulated that a "Great Gambling Syndicate" and Lloyds of London were negotiating to invest about $40,000,000 in the transformation of Key West. The plans were said to include a modern race track, beach accommodations, casinos, and hotels, together constituting "the most complete resort facilities to be found anywhere in the world."[29]

Why the investment was not forthcoming and whether it was, in fact, a serious possibility remains unclear. Although some in Key West would have welcomed such a transformation, others, including Mayor Albury and several activists in the business community, presented a different vision for the island city. A booklet released by the Key West Chamber of Commerce in 1939 urging tourists to come to Key West emphasized the usual drawing points: the weather, the "healing power" of Key West's sunlight, the several hundred types of fish to be found in its waters, and attractions such as Fort Taylor. In addition, it declared, "Key West is Different" and supported the characterization of Key West, in a recent advertisement financed by the Monroe County Commissioners, as "a friendly, hospitable, joy-loving island city, devoid of Monte Carlo sensational stuff." "And we are determined to keep it so," the advertisement concluded. The booklet went on to establish what was at stake: "The problem before us is, 'Shall Key West be a shining example of a city rightly governed which offers in addition to its unsurpassed natural advantages an abode of peace and safety for the American family; or, shall it accept the wages of prostitution, and for a false and transient show of money, harbor underworld exploiters, great and small?'"[30]

Although the mayor and other community activists maintained that they were protecting their community from unseemly interests, it is just as likely that at least some of them wanted to protect local gamblers from outside competition. The journalist Ernie Pyle noted that when "outsiders" became involved in the gambling business in Key West, they increased the price of roulette chips from five to twenty-five cents. Key Westers stopped playing roulette at these gambling houses in protest, and their business suffered. Conchs likely opposed additional challengers to their gambling enterprises.[31]

Regardless of the mayor and others' motivation for publicly rejecting a "Monte Carlo" in Key West, the city remained a relatively "open community." In August 1941, a naval intelligence officer stationed at the Naval Station offered these observations about vice in Key West in a letter to Governor Spessard Holland: "'Juke' joints . . . open prostitution, with solicitation on the street, and narcotic selling are rampant here as in Miami." He also mentioned that since he had arrived in Key West twenty-one months earlier, four murders had been committed and no indictments had been issued. He concluded that "The local police are either incapable or do not wish to enforce the laws and clean up the city."[32]

At the time the mayor declared that his administration would reject the "wages of prostitution," several houses of prostitution operated in Key West. Mom's, Key West's best-known house, located on the west side of the island in the African American part of town Key Westers called "colored town" or "jungle town," did a lively business. During the war, Mom's moved to Stock Island and renamed itself Mom's Tea Room, not because of actions taken by the city's government, but because the military forced it to close its operations in Key West. Other brothels included Alice Reid's, Big Annie's, The Yellow House, and The Square Roof. In addition, as the naval intelligence officer suggested in his letter to the governor, some women apparently worked freelance.[33]

Literary and Artistic Landscape

While the island's tourism promoters declined to publicize gambling and prostitution as part of their efforts to attract visitors, they did boast about the writers and artists who lived in or visited Key West during the depression years. Some tourists, they reasoned, might want to visit a place whose qualities attracted creative figures, and these personalities were welcomed and publicized.

Number eighteen on the KWA guidebook's list of places for tourists to visit in 1934 was the home located on the corner of Olivia and White-head Streets, owned and occupied by Ernest Hemingway, "author and sportsman." Hemingway, tourists were told, purchased the home because he could not resist the "magnetic charm of the Island City." One of the KWA's brochures, distributed during the same period as the "Guide," noted, "A town which shelters in one season three writers of international importance is no ordinary town." Clearly, those trying to attract visitors to the community hoped that invoking its "literary landscape" might be appealing. The brochure continued to reason that since "in the same season (1934–35) Key West numbers among its guests such interesting people as dukes, dancers, playwrights, artists, explorers, you must come to the conclusion that life on this little island has a flavor all its own." Thus, the KWA promoters of tourism suggested that Key West was an island whose exotic appeal derived not only from its indigenous population but also from some of its visitors.[34] Ironically, Hemingway and other of these visitors criticized changes to the community that were the direct result of the KWA's efforts to increase tourism.

Ernest Hemingway was the best-known author to live in Key West during the late 1920s and 1930s. Initially fascinated with Key West, Hemingway lowered his opinion of the island as more visitors showed up. He and his second wife, Pauline Pfeiffer, first arrived in Key West in April 1928 on a P&O steamship from Havana. Their trip had begun in Paris, where Hemingway spent much of the 1920s. They had married in May 1927, and Pauline's pregnancy contributed to their decision to move back to the United States. They intended to stay in Key West for only a short time and then drive to the Pfeiffer family home in Arkansas in a Ford that Pauline's uncle had purchased for them and arranged to have transported to Key West. The automobile, however, was late in arriving and Hemingway quickly decided that he liked the place. He reported to a friend, "It's the best place I've ever been anytime, anywhere, flowers, tamarind trees, guava trees, coconut palms. . . . Got tight last night on absinthe and did knife tricks." Hemingway became friends with several Key Westers, including Charlie Thompson, a member of one of Key West's most prominent families, who shared his love for fishing and hunting. Hemingway also invited several friends to visit him in Key West during his initial short stay there.[35]

Although Hemingway left Key West in late May (the Ford did arrive) to join Pauline, who had traveled to Arkansas by train, he returned to Key West that November, staying until mid-March to work on revisions of what would become *A Farewell to Arms*. He and Pauline, with their baby, Patrick, returned to the island in February 1930 and rented a house through June, where Hemingway worked on *Death in the Afternoon*. The Hemingways returned to Key West again in January 1931. They initially rented a place to stay but in late April purchased a house that had been built in the mid-nineteenth century for the businessman Asa Tift. Hemingway lived in Key West until he moved to Cuba in 1939. Although he spent much of the decade elsewhere in the United States and overseas, Hemingway worked on several titles in Key West. In addition to *A Farewell to Arms* and *Death in the Afternoon*, these include *Green Hills of Africa* and "The Snows of Kilimanjaro."[36]

Hemingway wrote in the morning and had ample interests to occupy him for the rest of the day and evening. He refereed boxing matches and sparred with local boxers. Hemingway also got the best of the poet Wallace Stevens in a short fight, after Stevens had distressed Hemingway's sister by making insulting comments about Hemingway at a party. Hemingway also enjoyed watching the cockfights held not far from his home on Whitehead Street. Fishing, however, was his favorite pastime. Hemingway and his friends often went on fishing trips and spent much time on his boat, *Pilar*, which he purchased in 1934.[37]

Hemingway also spent a considerable amount of time in his favorite bar, owned by Joe Russell. Russell owned a speakeasy on Front Street during prohibition. After prohibition ended in late 1933, he opened a bar on Greene Street. Legend has it that it was Hemingway who suggested to Russell that he name his establishment Sloppy Joe's, based on the name of a club in Havana. Hemingway's notoriety brought many customers hoping to catch a glimpse of him into the bar, and in return Russell rewarded him generously with cases of liquor.[38] In May 1937, upset with his landlord, Isaac Wolkowsky, for raising his rent, Russell moved Sloppy Joe's half a block away to the building on the corner of Duval and Greene Streets, and Hemingway resumed his drinking at the new location.

It was in Sloppy Joe's on Greene Street, in December 1936, that Hemingway met writer Martha Gellhorn, who, with her brother and mother, had gone to vacation in Miami and then taken a bus to Key

West. The next year, he and Martha had an affair in Spain, where both were covering the Spanish Civil War. They moved to Cuba in 1939 and married the next year after his divorce from Pauline.[39]

Hemingway was critical of Stone and the Key West Administration and was upset when the KWA's guidebook listed his house as a place tourists should see. In *To Have and Have Not*, which is set in Key West, Hemingway used Stone as the basis for a character who claimed to be "one of the three most important men in the United States today." After the hurricane in 1935, Hemingway published an article in the *New Masses*, a leftist magazine that severely criticized the federal programs.[40]

Michael Reynolds, a Hemingway biographer, has argued that Hemingway would have left Key West even if he had not met Gellhorn: "Hemingway always resented what Roosevelt's program had done to Key West. The quiet fishing village which was Ernest's haven . . . was transformed into a tourist resort . . . and soon overrun with gawking mainlanders looking for a glimpse of Ernest Hemingway." He left Key West just as the tourists started to arrive "looking for characters out of *To Have and Have Not*."[41]

Katy Dos Passos, wife of the writer John Dos Passos, shared some of Hemingway's misgivings about the Key West Administration. She wrote to a friend,

> Don't be surprised when you see the town—There's been changes. The New Dealers are here . . . and Key West is now a Greenwich Village Nightmare . . . they're painting murals on the café walls, and weaving baskets, and cutting down plants and trees, and renting all the homes (with Washington money) and arranging sight-seeing tours, and building apartments for tourists so they can observe the poor Hemingways . . . and all the dreary international smart-alecs are turning up as they always do about six years later, 'discovering' the place. . . . There is even a band of fake Cubans with velvet pants and red sashes that meets the train every day.[42]

Wallace Stevens and Robert Frost also criticized Key West, based in part on an aversion to the town being recreated and "discovered," but their impressions of the island apparently changed over time. Stevens proclaimed in 1935 that "Key West is no longer quite the delightful affection it once was" because it attracted too many visitors. His concern in 1941 had shifted to its being too dominated by the Navy. More than a decade later, in a letter written in 1953, he remembered Key West not as too overrun with tourists or the Navy, but as "the most old-fashioned place in the world."[43]

Frost first visited Key West with his wife, Elinor, in December 1934, ten years after he had won his first Pulitzer Prize for poetry. At the urging of Elinor's doctor, they spent the winter in the community, a visit that the FERA made a point to publicize. Shortly after arriving on the island, Frost complained, "Neither of us likes it very much yet." He observed, "It is tropical all right but it is rather unsanitary and shabby." When Frost left in March 1935, however, he expressed a different, albeit still negative, view and suggested he would not return to Key West. He wrote to his daughter, "To Santa Fe, Carmel, Greenwich Village, Montmartre, and Peterboro, add Key West. Arty Bohemias! I have stayed away from the others. The Lord delivered me into this one to punish my fastidiousness."[44]

So Frost criticized the poverty-stricken Key West because it was shabby and was no more satisfied with Stone's efforts to rehabilitate the community and attract tourists. One might have expected that he would leave and never return. Frost, however, did return to Key West, this time for an extended winter stay at the Casa Marina in February 1940 to recuperate from an operation. In 1941, Frost hired a builder to construct a winter home in Miami, and he spent winters there from 1942 until his death in 1963. During these years, he often visited Key West and stayed in the cottage next to the home of his friend Jessie Porter, the daughter of the businessman William R. Porter. Although he now regretted that "progress" was changing the island, as long as its narrow lanes and byways remained, the city would still have charm to him.[45]

Several writers who visited Key West praised it unequivocally, although the reasons for their affection varied. In 1937, a writer for *Collier's* magazine complimented its unique physical environment, the liveliness of Duval Street in the evenings, the Spanish restaurants, and the friendly people. Martha Gellhorn appreciated the climate and also romanticized the island's poverty and blight. In a letter to Eleanor Roosevelt in January 1937, Gellhorn spoke positively of the author she had just met at Sloppy Joe's, but even more approvingly of the city. "I'm in Key West: to date it's the best thing I've found in America. It's hot and falling to pieces and people seem happy. Nothing much goes on, languidly a sponge or a turtle gets fished, people live on relief cosily, steal coconuts off the municipal streets, amble out and catch a foul local fish called the grunt, gossip, maunder, sunburn and wait for the lazy easy years to pass. Me, I think all that is very fine indeed and if all the world were sunny I daresay there'd be much less trouble as well as much less of that deplorable thing called officially progress."[46]

Tennessee Williams also praised Key West, whose appeal for him lay in its uniqueness. He first visited the island in 1941 when he was thirty years old, renting a small cabin behind the Trade Winds boarding house on the corner of Caroline and Duval Streets. Williams later described Key West as "a mecca for painters and writers," but he also emphasized other of the town's attractive attributes. In a letter to a friend in New York City, Williams wrote: "I got all my stuff packed in about 15 minutes Wednesday night. . . . Friday morning I was in Miami and Saturday night I was in Sloppy Joe's bar in Key West. This is the most fantastic place that I have been yet in America. It is even more colorful than Frisco, New Orleans or Santa Fe. There are comparatively few tourists and the town is real stuff. It still belongs to the natives who are known as 'conks' . . ." Several years later, Williams moved to Key West.[47]

Critics consider Williams to be one of the best, if not *the* best, American playwrights of the twentieth century. Hemingway is likewise one of the century's best novelists. Elizabeth Bishop, who also lived in Key West for several years, enjoys a similar reputation among poets. In late 1936, on her first trip to Florida, Bishop traveled by train from Jacksonville to a fishing camp in Naples on Florida's southwest coast and then visited Key West. In 1938, she moved to Key West, buying a house on White Street with her partner, Louise Crane, a classmate from Vassar College. After their relationship ended, Bishop, in the spring of 1941, moved a few blocks west to a house at 623 Margaret Street to live with Marjorie Carr Stevens.[48]

Bishop moved away from Key West in 1946, but she returned periodically. For a time in 1947, she lived in Pauline Hemingway's home on Whitehead Street while Pauline was away, and then lived for a short time in an apartment on the island loaned to her by the philosopher John Dewey. And as late as December 1948, she rented an apartment on Frances Street, living in Key West for several months. According to one interpreter of her work, "Key West's community of artists, exiles and outsiders made her feel more at home than she had for years."[49]

brought freshwater to Key West from Florida City, located just south of Miami. Congress appropriated financing for the water supply system, and in March 1941 the Department of the Navy and the Florida Keys Aqueduct Commission (FKAC) signed a contract authorizing the FKAC to issue $1 million in bonds to finance one-third of the cost of its construction. The pipeline was completed in 1942. Initially, the water was unsuitable for human consumption because it was too hard and contained much "suspended matter." By the end of the war, however, the system had been improved by the addition of a treatment plant and Key West's households and businesses no longer had to rely exclusively upon rainwater and cisterns for their drinking water.[57]

The military also impacted the community by necessitating the construction of new housing for war workers and their families. In fact, housing for the general population was scarce, with many local business owners building rooms behind their businesses to house their employees. The Casa Marina exclusively served military officers and their families during 1942, and from 1943–45 the U.S. Navy took over the hotel to accommodate Navy personnel. By mid-1942, the Navy had constructed housing, including the Gato dormitory, for male workers. In January 1944, the Navy Low Cost Housing Project on Palm Avenue became available to married enlisted personnel and their families. The Key West Housing Authority built its first public housing projects during the war years, which primarily housed service personnel and their families, as well as civilians employed by the military.[58]

In addition, in 1942, the Key West Housing Authority built the Fort Village Apartments to provide housing for some of the African Americans who had been displaced when the Navy took over their residences to expand the Navy Base. Key West's black population, the vast majority of whom lived in the neighborhood west of Whitehead Street that would be absorbed by the Navy Base, suffered not only displacement from their homes but also other losses. Before the war, Key West had provided the black neighborhood with a baseball field, and the residents in the neighborhood had also contributed funds for a community center. During the war, however, the land containing the ball field and the community building became part of the military property, and the city did not provide the black community with replacement facilities.[59]

In a letter to President Roosevelt in 1935, Reverend Arthur B. Dimmick, a minister at St. Paul's Episcopal Church on Duval Street, criticized several aspects of the KWA's tourist initiative. He predicted that Key West was unlikely to succeed in attracting large numbers of winter tourists because it could not offer them adequate "amusement and recreation." In the later decades of the twentieth century, Dimmick's prediction would be proved incorrect, but the reverend made other points that recurred in various forms, even as tourism increased. One was that tourism was a "fickle" business and should not be relied on as the community's primary source of revenue. Another was that tourism was unlikely to provide "useful profitable employment and occupation for the good bulk of the population." Rather, holders of real estate would derive the most benefit from increased tourism.[60]

In 1937, the *New York Times* reporter Meyer Berger predicted that increased tourism would bring to Key West "modern hotels, apartments and bungalows," as well as nightclubs and theaters. He added, "It will probably be very lovely and fill the pockets of Key Westers and investors from the outside, but what, then, will become of the Old Key West?" Berger suggested that some Key Westers were asking the same question and that a "whooping family war" might break out over the desirability of tourism and development in the area.[61]

The residents of Key West would return often to the questions Berger and Dimmick raised about how tourism would impact Old Key West and continued to struggle with issues related to their community's identity, economy, and future.

The expansion of Key West's military facilities during the war, however, temporarily made tourism less of a presence, and the concerns Dimmick and Berger raised less pressing. From the end of the war through the early 1970s, the military remained a more significant presence in Key West than tourism, although Key West was by no means just a "military town." It was an island community that remained true to its early years—diverse and, in several respects, unique.

AIDS MEMORIAL

The AIDS Memorial where
White Street meets the Atlantic
Ocean was dedicated on World
AIDS Day, December 1, 1997. By
2004, it bore the names of over
a thousand Key Westers who
had died of AIDS. Courtesy of
Scott Keeter.

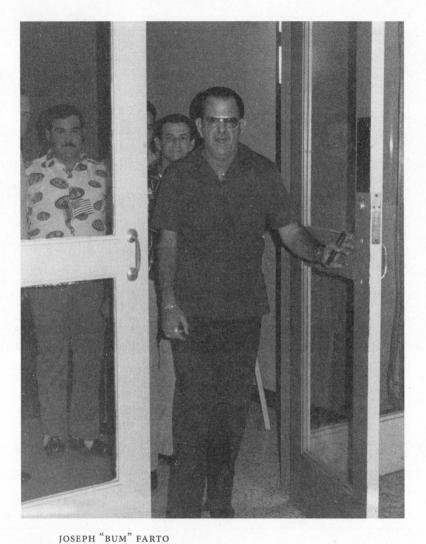

JOSEPH "BUM" FARTO

Joseph "Bum" Farto was the
Key West Fire Chief who was
convicted of drug trafficking in
1976. Before his sentencing, he
disappeared, never to be seen
again. Courtesy of Monroe
County Public Library system.

CAPTAIN TONY TARRACINO

Right: Captain Tony Tarracino moved to Key West from New Jersey in 1948. He worked on a shrimp boat, was a charter boat captain, and opened a popular bar. He also served as mayor of Key West from 1989 to 1991. Photo from "So Long Captain Tony," by David Hoekstra, *Chicago Sun-Times.*

CAPTAIN TONY'S SALOON

Below: Captain Tony Tarracino opened his bar on Greene Street in the mid-1960s. It soon became popular with Conchs, new residents of the island, sailors, and tourists. Sloppy Joe's had once graced this site, and in the early 1960s Morgan Bird operated "The Oldest Bar" there. Although Bird's bar closed after about a year, it was a popular spot for Key West's still relatively small gay population. Courtesy of Stuart Newman Associates.

CHRISTMAS TREE (WISTERIA)
ISLAND

Christmas Tree (a.k.a. Wisteria)
Island is an undeveloped island
near the Key West Bight (a.k.a.
Historic Seaport). In 2007,
citizens successfully mobilized
against an effort to develop the
island. Courtesy of Monroe
County Public Library system.

JACK CHURCH, BILL BUTLER,
BOB GRAHAM, HARRY
CHIPCHASE, AND
COFFEE BUTLER

Jack Church, the head of the
Key West Art and Historical
Society, the musician Bill Butler, Governor Bob Graham, and
the musicians Harry Chipchase
and Coffee Butler. Courtesy of
Monroe County Public Library
system.

CLIFF ROBERTSON AND
MEL FISHER

Cliff Robertson, an actor, and
Mel Fisher, a treasure hunter.
Robertson played Fisher in
the 1986 TV movie, *Dreams
of Gold*. Courtesy of Monroe
County Public Library system.

CONCH TOUR TRAIN IN
FRONT OF SLOPPY JOE'S

Above: The Conch Tour Train ride is a popular way for citizens to see the island. Here, it is stopped in front of Sloppy Joe's on the corner of Greene and Duval Streets. The bar's owner, Joe Russell, moved Sloppy Joe's to this location from the present home of Captain Tony's Saloon in May 1937. Ernest Hemingway was a frequent visitor to the bar. Courtesy of Stuart Newman Associates.

CONCH REPUBLIC FLAG

Right: The flag of the Conch Republic was raised as Key West declared independence on April 23, 1982. Author's collection.

COUNT CARL VON COSEL

Right: Count Carl von Cosel removed the body of Elena Milagro Hoyos from her mausoleum in the Key West cemetery in 1933 and slept next to it in his house until it was discovered in 1940. The hearings held to determine whether he would stand trial attracted numerous tourists to Key West. Courtesy of Monroe County Public Library system.

CRUISE SHIP AT PIER B WESTIN HOTEL

Below: This cruise ship docked at Pier B at the Westin Hotel in 2011 was one of the many ships that bring hundreds of thousands of day tourists to Key West each year. Author's collection.

ENTRANCE TO BAHAMA VILLAGE

Top: The "entrance" to the historic black neighborhood that in 1981 was designated by the city as "Bahama Village." Author's collection.

DEPRESSION-ERA HOUSE

Above: One of the homes inhabited by a poverty-stricken Key Wester during the Great Depression. Courtesy of Monroe County Public Library system.

FANTASY FEST REVELERS

Above: Fantasy Fest revelers "dressed" in body paint during the weeklong celebration first organized in 1979. Courtesy of Tony Gregory.

FLAGLER TRAIN AND P&O STEAMSHIP

Top: After the Flagler railroad reached Key West in 1912, visitors could board the Flagler company's P&O Steamship to travel the roughly ninety miles to Cuba. Courtesy of Monroe County Public Library system.

FLATS FISHING

Fishing has long attracted
visitors to the Florida Keys
and Key West. Flats fishing
for permit, tarpon, and other
fish provides an alternative to
deep-water fishing and appeals
to many Conchs and tourists.
Courtesy of Stuart Newman
Associates.

HEMINGWAY LOOK-ALIKE CONTESTANTS

Above: Contestants have participated in the Hemingway Look-alike contest each year since the festival known as Hemingway Days was organized in 1981. Courtesy of Stuart Newman Associates.

HEMINGWAY HOUSE AND CAT

Right: The former home of Ernest Hemingway and Pauline Pfeiffer on Whitehead Street has been open to tourists since 1964. Courtesy of Stuart Newman Associates.

4

Key West 1945–1970

Not a Clean Well-Lighted Place

AFTER THE SECOND WORLD WAR, the focus of Key West's public and private activists was not on promoting tourism as the key component of the island's economy. While many of them encouraged tourism, Key West was by no means a tourist town nor was it expected to become one. In fact, as a town, Key West was hard to characterize because it was different from most. Although relatively small, it boasted the economic and social diversity of larger cities. The Bahamian, Cuban, Spanish, and black populations remained vibrant, and the community continued to attract notable writers and others involved with the arts. A small number of gay men also regularly visited Key West, and some chose to move there permanently. Dorothy Raymer, a newspaper columnist for the *Citizen* during this era, described the culture of Key West as "laissez-faire." This "live-and-let-live" culture contributed to widespread illegal gambling and political corruption, as well as to attracting creative newcomers who valued a community where, they believed, "anything goes."[1]

During the 1950s, Key West's population increased from 26,433 to 33,956, only to drop to 29,312 in 1970.[2] During the 1950s, Key West was a moderate-income community, with less economic disparity than most of Florida's cities. By the end of the 1960s, however, Key West's income spectrum had shifted downward relative to other cities in the state. For example, in 1959, only 8.5 percent of Key West's families earned $10,000 or more, the lowest percentage of the 22 Florida cities with a population of at least 25,000. Key West's median family income of $4,736, however, fell roughly in the middle among these cities. Its poverty rate, although significant, was lower than that of most of them. By 1969, while still a small percentage of Key West families were included in the higher income categories, its median family income was lower, and the percentage of families earning less than $3,000 higher, than in most of Florida's cities with populations over 25,000. Housing costs in Key West were lower than in most Florida cities in both 1959 and 1969.[3]

As had been the case for generations, Conchs commonly addressed each other using nicknames, such as Bad Heart, Baby Face, Bubba Light, and Smokey Joe, as well as the generic Bubba. Conchs and newcomers whose children attended Key West High School were fervent followers of their sports teams. High school stars such as George Mira and Boog Powell, who later played professional football and Major League Baseball, respectively, led the baseball team to several state championships.[4]

Music and dance played a prominent role in the Conch community. Although he lived in Tampa for several years in the 1950s and 1960s, Buddy Chavez remained one of the most popular and talented musicians in Key West. He played with several bands at venues including the Cuban Club, the center of the social life of Key West's Cuban population during the 1950s. The club celebrated Halloween with a big party, and many regularly participated in the comparsas whose conga lines danced from one end of Duval Street to the other.

The black Welters Cornet Band, which had originated as the Key West Cornet Band, continued to accompany Key West funerals, New Orleans–style. Coffee Butler, a Conch of black Bahamian origin, was one of Key West's most popular entertainers. One of his bands, Coffee and his Cups, played at several local clubs.[5]

Conchs, as well as some newcomers, belonged to several civic organizations, and politicians running for office regularly sought their support. The Chamber of Commerce was the most significant business organization. Active clubs, including the Lions, Rotary, and Elks, as well as several Masonic Lodges, provided social venues for their members and also engaged in charitable activities. The Key West Woman's Club housed and ran a public library in its building on Duval Street. The Woman's Club then organized a drive that, in 1959, would fund the construction of the Monroe County Public Library on Fleming Street.

Members of several Conch families were prominent in the community's economic and political hierarchy. Many Conchs, predominantly whites, procured jobs in city government, the school system, the city electric company, and in other public-sector positions. A bubba system prevailed whereby governmental positions generally went to locals connected with State Representative Bernard Papy (until his defeat in 1962) and other insiders. The military also provided jobs for Conch civilians, as did the shrimping industry and its related enterprises.[6]

Although many Cubans arrived in Key West during the 1960s, after Castro's revolution in 1959, most of Key West's Cubans and Spaniards had arrived earlier or were descendants of those who had migrated to Key West in the late 1800s. Prior to Castro's takeover, it was common even for Key Westers not of Cuban or Spanish descent to travel to Havana by boat or the inexpensive airline, Aerovías Q, for shopping, medical care, and entertainment. Indeed, it was not unheard of for male high school students to skip school and fly to Havana for the day, where they drank alcohol and visited houses of ill repute. Although ferries and passenger ships had long been carrying passengers between Key West and Havana, the inauguration of the car ferry, City of Havana, in the mid-1950s enhanced this travel, transporting hundreds of passengers and over one hundred cars three times a week from its Stock Island terminal.[7]

The revolution in Cuba shut down both the ferry and the airline service, ending travel between Key West and Cuba for locals and tourists alike. The ferry sailed to Havana in January 1959 to evacuate U.S. citizens who wanted to return to the United States after Castro's forces entered Havana, and on its final trip in October 1960 it brought back embassy staff. After the U.S. government banned tourism to Cuba in January 1961, Aerovías Q stopped its flights between Cuba and Key West.[8]

In both 1950 and 1970, black Key Westers constituted approximately 11 percent of the island's population. Key West during these decades did not experience the intense racial conflict that plagued many Southern cities. Indeed, on some occasions, the city commission supported the interests of Key West's black population. For example, in 1953, after the city eliminated rent controls, the Navy asked the Key West Housing Authority to transfer to it two of its public housing projects, including the black-occupied Fort Village housing, to serve Navy personnel. The city commission unanimously opposed the transfer, and one commissioner voiced concern that blacks would be unable to afford rents in the private market. The Housing Authority agreed with the city commission, and Fort Village remained public housing.[9]

Still, as in other Florida communities, segregation prevailed until the passage of federal legislation in 1964. Before this legislation, in the Monroe movie theater blacks were restricted to the balcony, and in the Strand, the other movie theater on Duval Street, they were not allowed to attend the movies. The Lincoln Theater on Emma Street opened shortly after the Second World War to serve Key West's black population. Even after the 1964 Civil Rights Act, however, blacks sometimes faced discrimination from business owners. In April 1968, approximately forty African Americans demonstrated in front of the Southernmost Skating Rink to protest the owner's refusal to admit them. The owner conceded and allowed them to skate. Monroe County schools were partially desegregated in the fall of 1964, earlier than most districts in Florida, and fully desegregated in 1965. The African American Douglass High School was transformed into an integrated grammar school, and African Americans attended an integrated Key West High School.[10]

Some blacks benefited from procuring civil-service jobs in Key West's military facilities. A relatively small number of black Key Westers worked as shrimpers and in jobs generated by the shrimping industry. As a whole, however, Key West's black population remained disproportionately poor and held relatively little political influence. None served on the city commission or held other elective positions. At the end of the 1960s, representatives of the NAACP met with Chamber of Commerce officials to discuss the lack of job opportunities for African Americans in Key West. NAACP president Charles Major noted that the City Electric System employed only ten blacks and the Southern Bell Telephone Company employed none. A spokesperson complained that when qualified applicants applied for jobs, they were "told the application was lost. Or there has been a delay." He added, "We get the run-around. Nothing happens! Yet we regard this as a good community with good relationships." The Chamber's Board responded by passing a motion to adopt a policy that all businesspeople hire on the basis of an applicant's qualifications, regardless of color, a policy that was, of course, already required by federal law.[11]

The Military

Most of the Army's limited facilities in Key West were transferred to the Navy in 1947, and the Navy continued to be the most significant contributor to Key West's economy during the 1950s and 1960s. The primary Navy facilities remained the Boca Chica Naval Air Station, the Naval Air Station at Trumbo Point, and the Naval Station on the west end of the island (later renamed Truman Annex), which included one of the largest submarine bases in the Navy and where radar, or sonar, work was conducted. In 1960, approximately 57 percent of the male labor force in Key West was in the military. The Cuban Missile Crisis in October 1962 led to a short-term build up of Key West's military facilities. The Army returned to Key West and signed a lease with the Casa Marina to house its personnel there. It took over Smathers Beach, on the Atlantic Ocean near the airport, and also occupied the Wickers Field municipal ballpark. Tourists and residents gawked at the Army's antiaircraft Hawk missiles and radar installations, which necessitated filling a section of the Salt Ponds. Marines also arrived in Key West during the crisis, with many staying at the Town House Motor Inn (formerly, and later, La Concha).[12]

In the words of the author of a book on the crisis, published in 2008, "Key West, on the tip of the Florida Keys, suddenly found itself on the front line of the Cold War, like Berlin or the demilitarized zone between the two Koreas. . . . The Navy ran reconnaissance and code breaking operations out of the naval air station; the CIA established safe houses on neighboring islands . . . Marines set up machine-gun nests on the beach, surrounded by rolls of concertina wire."[13]

Some of the military personnel stationed in Key West during the 1950s and 1960s lived in private housing, primarily in Key West and on Stock Island and other areas outside of the city. Most of the military personnel and their families, however, lived in military housing. Many of the military dependents were employed by businesses in Key West, as well as by the school system and other public employers. Therefore, the military, in effect, provided affordable housing for many in the Key West labor force.[14]

Commercial Fishing

Commercial fishing had long been a component of Key West's economy, but in 1949 its importance surged. The Salvadore brothers, fishermen from St. Augustine, had found "jumbo" shrimp in their nets. Word traveled quickly, and the shrimp, fondly called "pink gold," attracted many shrimpers to Key West during the prime winter fishing months. The *Tampa Sunday Tribune* noted in February 1950 that the "rush for pink gold in shrimp beds brought all the excitement of a Klondike gold strike to this southernmost city in the United States." The shrimpers, unlike the military, were primarily seasonal visitors, and most slept on their boats when they weren't out at sea. Still, they made a significant mark on the community.[15]

By February 1951, the shrimping industry was generating as much as $500,000 a week and was second only to the Navy as a generator of income in the city. In the mid-1960s, about 25 to 30 year-round shrimp boats were housed at the Key West Bight, where additional commercial fishing boats also docked. During the shrimping season in the winter, more than 250 shrimp boats, many of them from Texas and North Carolina, docked at the bight. The Thompson Enterprises' businesses on the Key West Bight played a key role in the city's shrimping business. They unloaded the shrimp from the trawlers, kept the shrimp in cold storage until they were trucked to the markets, and supplied the trawlers with fuel and ice so they could resume their fishing. After Norberg Thompson died in 1951, most of his business continued under the leadership of A. Maitland Adams, who had been with Thompson Enterprises for decades and had served as Key West's mayor from 1946–49.[16]

Drinking and Gambling

There was no shortage of bars on the island for shrimpers, Navy personnel, tourists, Conchs, and new residents to enjoy. According to a 1945 census, Key West included 53 "liquor vending establishments" (presumably bars), five package stores, and 48 retail liquor stores. A state law passed in 1947 limited the number of bars a community could have based on its population, which in Key West would have forced quite a few establishments to shut their doors. Fortunately for those who enjoyed visiting these establishments, as well as for the owners, existing bars were allowed to continue operating.[17]

Across from the shrimp docks, on Caroline Street and nearby, were several rough and tumble bars. One of the most notorious had a succession of names, including the Red Doors Inn, but was most commonly known as "the bucket of blood," due to the frequent fights on its premises. An informally run house of prostitution was located on the second floor, adding to the recreational opportunities available to the shrimpers. Nearby were the Mascot Lounge, the Midget, and the Swinging Doors, where country and western music was a welcome sound to the primarily Southern shrimpers. Shrimpers also frequented the West Key Bar at 506 Fleming Street, which featured topless dancers. According to the author Tom Corcoran, this establishment "asked the musical question, 'Can this really be a strip club if the women are all sitting down and the men are too drunk to care?'" It went out of business after a dancer, upset with her boss, set it on fire.[18]

The police sometimes raided clubs, but whether the raids were actual attempts at enforcing the law or were related to police payoffs remains uncertain. In August 1945, the manager of the Havana Madrid nightclub on Duval Street was found guilty by a city court judge of operating a "disorderly house." The judge imposed a light sentence, citing evidence that police officers had been visiting the club for months without making an arrest. A witness asserted during the trial that the raid was conducted because the police captain, who was taking bribes from the club owner, was not paying the patrolmen their share.[19]

In fact, former and present police officers were themselves sometimes arrested. For example, several former city and county law enforcement officers were arrested for stealing six slot machines from the Elks Club. Sam Cagnina, a policeman, was suspended after being investigated for committing an armed robbery of Ringside Billiard Parlor on Truman Avenue. Other police officers broke the law with impunity. A summer employee with the Key West Police Department during the mid-1960s observed that officers often sold marijuana from the police station.[20]

Many bars offered various gambling devices in the backrooms of their establishments. Slot machines, nicknamed "one armed bandits," had been legalized in Florida in the 1920s, but the law was repealed in 1937. Still, slot machines operated in several Duval Street establishments in the late 1940s. The writer Benedict Thielen observed that many tourists were "not shocked by the click of dice or the whirl of the roulette wheel which comes from the back rooms of most of the city's . . . bars."[21]

In 1948, city commission members declared their support for a "liberal" application of the city's laws regarding gambling. Commissioner Louis Carbonell noted, for example, "I want to state that I am for liberal interpretation of the existing laws." Commissioners John Carbonell (unrelated to Louis) and Fred J. Dion agreed.[22] Commissioner Hunter Harden presented a slightly different take on the matter, suggesting, "There is no such thing as a liberal interpretation. I believe in enactment of liberal laws." The commission practiced what it preached by refusing to support the city attorney's request that an ordinance be passed granting the municipal judge the authority to destroy all devices related to local gambling activities, such as "bolita, wheel, cards, dice, slot machines, and the like."[23]

A discussion of law enforcement during a commission meeting provides an interesting window on the character of Key West during the years after the Second World War. City Manager Ralph Spalding, in response to Dion's concerns about the lack of adequate police enforcement in the city, noted, "We have several names available from the civil service board of whom I am not satisfied. We have appointed several special police. Frankly, I am not inclined to fill the police force too quickly. I would rather go short handed than accept some of the men recommended to me for the positions."[24]

Mayor A. Maitland Adams agreed with Spalding's hesitancy in hiring new officers from the existing pool. He suggested, "We are better off with a small police force than with the type of officers that we have just gotten rid of (for corruption). We have had better law enforcement in the last couple of weeks than we had in the past with a larger force." Spalding further reported, "Some men whom I have appointed as special police have been threatened. Their wives have been threatened. Some of these men's lives have been threatened between the time I appointed them and their arrival at home." The special police officers refused to say who had threatened them, leading Spalding to conclude: "That's the trouble with Key West. I can't get any information."[25]

State Representative Bernard Papy supported Key West's gambling industry. His brother, Whitney, owned Whitney's, an establishment on Simonton Street one block from the police station. It offered the "umbrella game" (i.e., roulette) from 11 p.m. to 7 a.m., in spite of the city's ordinance that established 2 a.m. as the closing time for bars. Representative Papy devoted a great deal of effort during the 1947 state legislative session to defeat the "anti-bookie wire service bill." In fact, he was indicted for trying to bribe two other legislators to join him in voting against it. Papy was found not guilty and was reelected in 1948.[26]

In the early 1950s, public officials were relatively more reluctant to admit to the presence of widespread gambling than they had been in the second half of the 1940s. After an article appeared in the *Miami Herald* documenting the wide-open gambling in Key West, officials feigned incredulity. Sheriff Berlin A. Sawyer emphasized, "There's no gambling in this town—on Saturday night or any other night." The Key West city manager, Dave King, offered a similar line, declaring, "I can say on my word of honor that I know of no place where a man can bet a nickel."[27] The Navy, however, expressed a contrary view, estimating that sailors lost about $150,000 a month, or about 10 percent of their monthly payroll, to the bolita peddlers, dice tables, roulette wheels, and other gambling games. The Navy emphasized that it was up to local officials to enforce the laws, but noted that in the past it had declared establishments that "pander to sexual perverts" off-limits and that shore patrolmen encouraged Navy personnel to abide by Key West's 2 a.m. closing time for liquor sales, an ordinance bar owners often ignored.[28]

Sheriff Sawyer chose not to run for reelection in 1952. Instead, he endorsed John Spottswood, whom he had defeated in the Democratic Party primary runoff election in 1948. Spottswood was elected, and yet the tenor of the community concerning gambling seemed to change very little. In January 1955, the Undersecretary of the United States Navy complained that sailors often gambled in the "floating games" in Key West and were victimized by "b girls," who he described as prostitutes who worked with taxi drivers to procure customers. In addition, the Navy alleged police brutality against sailors and even threatened to downsize its presence in Key West if these activities continued.[29]

Cockfights brought more opportunities for gamblers. Although cock fighting was illegal in Florida, because it involved gambling as well as the injury of "dumb creatures," it was practiced widely in Key West and elsewhere in the Florida Keys in the decades following the war. The major cock-fighting pit during the 1940s, and into the next decade, was located behind the Cuban Club on Duval Street. Patrons bet on the fights, through which the more successful roosters earned names such as "The White Rooster" and "La Cucaracha."[30]

Bolita, the numbers game with a long history in Key West, continued to be popular. In 1951, a sheriff's deputy estimated that 100 bolita houses were operating in Key West under the control of three major bankers, including the brother of a former city official. Each evening at 8 p.m. balls were drawn in a room behind a bar at 925 Truman Avenue. Among the runners who sold bolita tickets was Milton A. Parrot, who had nearly won a city commission seat in the 1949 election. Key West's primary bolita kingpins were local and did not welcome outside interference. According to an officer in the Key West Police Department, at one point "the syndicate" tried to take over the bolita trade and sent in three "enforcers." They were unsuccessful. One "was found in the public swimming pool . . . with his hands tied behind his back and a line running around his neck and feet, and was weighted down with old time window weights. One of the others was found on Stock Island lying on the ground shot, and the other was found on South Beach also shot." No guns were found near the bodies on Stock Island or South Beach. Still, the Justice of the Peace, an elected official, declared that the deaths were suicides.[31]

The *Citizen* contended that bolita activity slowed in Key West in the late 1950s, but by 1960 it undoubtedly had returned. That year, the *Citizen*'s editorial page referenced reports that at least one county and several city officials were involved with the bolita trade. In 1961, state investigators from Governor Farris Bryant's office, along with officers of the State Attorney General's Office and the Monroe County Sheriff's Department, raided several locations and arrested Louis "Blackie" Fernandez and a number of others. Raids such as these periodically drove bolita dealers underground, but they continued to operate. An editorial published in the *Citizen* in 1966 noted that bolita "tickets can be bought openly on the streets of Key West." The fines imposed on those convicted were generally small and did little to discourage people from joining or remaining in the business.[32]

In fact, many in the trade enjoyed a cozy relationship with certain elected justices of the peace and others in the criminal justice system, who sometimes offered the bolita players wise advice. For example, Tom Caro, judge of the criminal court, after learning from a man on trial for bolita gambling that his banker refused to pay off on his winning tickets, counseled, "That'll teach you, don't buy from him; he's got a bad reputation." Artemio (Artie) Crespo, himself a bolita banker, perhaps best summarized the role of bolita in the community. Crespo, testifying in a U.S. District Court, noted, "Judge, bolita is a way of life in Key West."[33]

The City Electric Scandal

Bolita was sometimes rigged in favor of certain "insiders." It appears that a different type of game was also rigged—a real estate game linking the electric company with land deals. In 1943, the Key West City Council authorized the creation of a municipal electric utility named the City Electric Company, approving the purchase of the utility from an affiliate of the Stone and Webster Company based in New England. For decades, State Representative Bernard Papy controlled most of the appointments to the Utility Board, which included the mayor and four other members. The City Electric Company was providing service to Key West only when, in 1952, the county requested that City Electric expand its service to unincorporated Monroe County. The company then extended its service area to the Lower Keys, initially by constructing a transmission line to Big Pine Key. Between mid-1952, when the contract to build the transmission line was awarded, and March 1953, when the line was completed, developers planned several subdivisions and real estate values in the Lower Keys climbed rapidly.[34]

Papy was defeated in his bid for reelection in 1962 by Hilario Charles (Charlie) Ramos Jr., who was from a politically influential Key West family. His father, Hilario Ramos, came to Key West in 1917 from the Asturias province in Spain. After working on steamships for many years, Hilario was hired to manage Delmonico's Restaurant on Duval Street, owned by the Lopez family, which also owned a significant amount of downtown real estate. He married Placeres Lopez, the owner's daughter, in 1931 and shortly afterward was named president of Lopez Wholesale Liquors, Inc., which held the franchise to the Budweiser beer distributorship in Key West. Hilario never ran for political office, but he was politically active and influential. He hosted many political figures at his home on the Atlantic end of Duval Street, which many referred to as the "Southernmost House."[35]

Charlie Ramos's successful race against Papy in 1962 was sometimes referred to as the "battle of the beers," because Papy held the Schlitz beer distributorship in Key West and Ramos the Budweiser distributorship. Ramos served only one term in Tallahassee and chose not to seek reelection. In 1964, Papy was elected once again to his seat in the Florida House but died shortly after the election. His son, Bernard Papy Jr., was elected to the seat and served until he was defeated in the Democratic primary in 1968.[36] In 1967, while Papy Jr. still served in the legislature, the Utility Board purchased from him and his partners 6.06 acres of property at Cudjoe Key, about twenty miles from Key West, for a greatly inflated price. The Utility Board planned to locate facilities on the property that would service the growing area. After the newspapers drew attention to the sale, the deed was suddenly "corrected" to read 62 acres, but the transaction remained quite profitable for Papy.[37]

A grand jury investigation resulted in an indictment in September 1968 against Papy Jr. Also indicted were Paul Sawyer, an attorney and Papy's cousin, Merville Rosam, the manager of City Electric, and J. Willard Saunders, who had been head of the Utility Board at the time of the transaction. Governor Claude Kirk suspended three Utility Board members and appointed three new board members to replace them.[38]

Neither Papy Jr. nor the others indicted were convicted of any crimes connected to the land deal. Criminal Court Judge John Ferris threw out all of the indictments in October 1969 on a variety of procedural grounds. Still, as a result of this scandal, the legislature in 1969 approved the special act proposed by State Representative William G. Roberts from Key West that changed the structure of the Utility Board such that it was autonomous from the city and that called for each of the board's members to be elected directly by the citizens.[39]

The prevalence of private and public corruption in Key West did not deter prominent writers and artists from moving to and visiting Key West. In fact, the same laissez-faire culture that fostered drinking, gambling, and corruption translated into a general tolerance of differences. Many sought a community they perceived as relatively accepting, or at least tolerant, of "eccentrics" and of those whose lifestyles might have led them to be ostracized in most American communities, and certainly in other small towns. Some were gay males, and although most were not open about their sexual preferences, Key West offered a less hostile atmosphere than most other environments. A city whose culture was relatively "laissez-faire" was clearly preferable to one invested in "traditional" values.

In the late 1940s and into the 1950s, McCarthyism influenced American politics. In Florida, the state legislature authorized the Johns Committee in 1956 to investigate the influence of communists and the presence of gays in the state universities. As a result of the Johns Committee's "investigation," a state committee published pamphlets "to prepare . . . children to meet the temptation of homosexuality lurking today in the vicinity of nearly every institution of learning." Included in Key West's diverse population were those who would feel comfortable in most "mainstream" small towns in America and were likely sympathetic to McCarthy and the Johns Committee, and the actions of public officials at times reinforced this fact. These attitudes, however, did not dominate the island's public forums or culture.[40]

Tennessee (Thomas Lanier) Williams, the most prominent writer to live in Key West during this time, certainly would not have felt comfortable in most American cities. He was outgoing, gay, and by no means "in the closet." First visiting Key West in 1941, he returned in 1947 with his grandfather, Dakin. By then, his play "The Glass Menagerie" (1944) had been widely acclaimed. During their stay at La Concha hotel, Williams finished writing "A Streetcar Named Desire."[41]

Williams purchased a house at 1431 Duncan Street in 1950, shortly after "A Streetcar Named Desire" won a Pulitzer Prize. He did not view Key West as a utopian paradise. For example, in several letters to friends written in March and April 1950 he expressed concern that a sailor had killed a New York "queen" who was visiting Key West, and that the response of the police was to arrest all the "Bohemians" in town for vagrancy, giving them twelve hours to leave the island. Still, Williams remained in Key West until his death in 1983. His fascination with the island on his first visit did not quickly ebb. He enjoyed swimming and liked that the island's climate allowed him to swim year-round. Williams liked Key West for other reasons, too. Once, when asked what he found attractive about Key West, he responded, "The Navy." More explicitly, he wrote to a friend "that the town is literally swarming with men in uniform, mostly sailors in very white pants. . . . It is extremely interesting!"[42]

Williams and Frank Merlo, his longtime partner, would often swim and then go to Logan's Lobster House on the Atlantic end of Simonton Street. Nearby was the Papillon Bar, popular with Key West's small gay population. They would also sometimes visit the Trade Winds at the corner of Duval and Caroline Streets, the boarding house where Williams had stayed during his first visit to Key West and that had since been transformed into a nightclub. Many of Williams's literary friends visited him in Key West, including Carson McCullers, Truman Capote (before he and Williams had a falling out), Gore Vidal, and the English director Peter Hall.[43]

In addition to "Streetcar," Williams worked in Key West on other of his major plays, including "Cat on a Hot Tin Roof," which won the Pulitzer Prize for Drama in 1955, "Suddenly Last Summer" (1958), and "Night of the Iguana" (1961). Although Williams did not set any of his plays in Key West, he noted that "The Gnädiges Fräulein," which ran only briefly in 1966, had a "vaguely 'conch' atmosphere." And in 1955 part of the film adaptation of his play "The Rose Tattoo" was filmed in Key West.[44]

Although today most people associate Hemingway more closely with Key West than they do Williams, this was perhaps not always the case. In 1970, Dorothy Raymer wrote that Williams was "second only to former President Harry S. Truman in being responsible for fine, consistent, international publicity for Key West. . . . Celebrities from around the globe have visited Key West due to his influence."[45]

In an article he wrote in 1973, Williams referred to his friend James Leo Herlihy, the author of *Midnight Cowboy* (1965), as Key West's "preeminent writer." Herlihy grew up in Detroit and, after serving in the Navy, attended Black Mountain College in North Carolina. He explained, "I chose Black Mountain College because I don't like to live by rules, and the only one they have there is the forbidding of possession of firearms on the campus."[46]

Herlihy first came to Key West in 1957 to meet with the producer of his play "Crazy October." Not surprisingly, as someone who "didn't like to live by rules" Herlihy found Key West attractive, and he lived there until 1972. Herlihy wrote the following about his first visit to the island:

> The town excited me too much. I spent all my time exploring, walking the streets. The place was mysterious, funky, indescribably exotic. It had much of the charm of a foreign country, but you had the post office and the A&P and the phone worked, so life was easy
>
> . . .
>
> I loved the houses with the big porches, high ceilings, and shuttered windows. Many of them hadn't been painted in decades. The town had the kind of beauty that did not know about itself: it just was . . .
>
> We used to say Key West was the last outpost in the U.S., the end of the line, there was no place left to run to. Everything around the island suited me right down to the ground.[47]

In 1969, Herlihy noted: "There is still a haunting mystique about the Keys, the mixture of the young and the old, the Establishment and the carefree souls like the fishermen and hippies. For the writer or the artist, it's a simple, pressure-free existence, touched with beauty."[48]

Although the travel writer Hanns Ebensten did not move to Key West until the 1970s, he later recalled that two images of the community, both written in the early 1960s, had attracted him to the island. One was written by James Morris, a transgender British author who later became Jan Morris. In *Coast to Coast*, published in 1956, Morris characterized Key West as "the most cheerfully un-American city in the United States." Ebensten was attracted by Morris's description of the southernmost city: "everywhere men are lazing about with no shirts on. It is a little city dedicated to easy living. At night, along Duval Street, a colorful crowd saunters and sips and gossips. In little cafes you can wile away the hours listening to music and eating pungent Cuban sandwiches. Patio restaurants, in the courtyards of old houses, offer immensely long and varied meals. You can sip good wines and talk to artists, profane seamen, idlers, scientists and collectors of shells." The second image appeared in an article in the *New York Times*, which offered a similar assessment of Key West as "a tropical resort that attracts a live-and-let-live breed for its blend of sun, salt, salubrity and a soupçon of sin."[49]

Several artists also made Key West their home, at least for part of the year. Henry Faulkner was one of Key West's best-known artists. He first visited Key West during a hitchhiking trip in the 1940s. He visited again briefly in 1957 and met Herlihy, who was to become one of his best friends. Faulkner returned to Key West in 1965 and bought a house. Originally from Kentucky, he continued to spend time there, as well as in Sicily, but he lived in Key West during the winter at his home on Peacon Lane.[50]

Faulkner's lifestyle was uniquely suited to the community, and he became widely recognized around town. One Key Wester recalled seeing Faulkner often on his bicycle, loudly singing Bessie Smith songs as he pedaled down Duval Street. His pet goat, Alice, was his frequent companion, often accompanying him to parties. In 1980, the year before he died in a car accident, Faulkner articulated what he liked about Key West: "I love the poetic lanes and alleys, the expressive architecture. Key West has always been right for me because I am able to blend with the Conch lifestyle without ever harming or compromising my own."[51]

A few galleries opened where Key West's artists could show their work. The Key West Art & Historical Society, organized in 1949, opened a gallery for a short time at the West Martello Tower near the Casa Marina but then moved it to the East Martello Tower, adjacent to the airport. In December 1962, Marion Stevens opened what was to become Key West's most popular local gallery. Her gallery, Artists Unlimited, initially occupied the former John Dewey house on Greene Street and then moved to a location on lower Duval. Among the artists she featured were her husband, Paul Stevens, and Jack Baron, who became a prominent local artist. Suzie dePoo, who moved to Key West from New York City in the mid-1950s, opened her dePoo's Island Gallery in 1967.[52]

New Town

These writers and artists lived and spent their days in Key West on the same streets Hemingway and Bishop had frequented during their time on the island. They created books, plays, and paintings, and perhaps altered states of consciousness. During this period, however, another type of creation also occurred—land development. Malcolm Meacham in the 1920s had purchased the majority of the eastern section of Key West with the intent of developing homes and resort hotels. Although his plans came to naught, after the war much of the property he had purchased was developed into an area that became known as New Town, which included residential, commercial, and tourist facilities.

Meacham had sold much of the property to the Key West Realty Company, headed by William R. Porter. Porter, in 1949, sold his entire tract for $200,000 to the Key West Improvement Company. Abraham Golan, a lawyer from Chicago then living in Miami, organized the company with two partners from Chicago, Vincent Conley and Charles Helberg. Their purchase included the Salt Ponds and the Meacham Field airport site, which the county leased from Key West Realty after the war.[53]

The Chicago team focused much of their initial energies on the airport property. They initially leased the airport to the county, but in 1950 Conley, Golan, and Helberg asked the county to discontinue the operation of Meacham Field so that they could begin developing residences and hotels there and on nearby property. The county initially favored building another airport outside of Key West, which would have likely made Meacham Field and the surrounding property available for development. Key West's city commission, however, opposed this proposal, and in 1952, the Key West Improvement Company agreed to sell Meacham Field and surrounding property to the county for $150,000. In November 1952, Monroe County assumed ownership of what was now known as Meacham Airport. After the sale, the airport began a major expansion of its facilities, including a new runway and terminal building, and the new Key West International Airport was dedicated on July 4, 1957.[54]

Even before the Key West Improvement Company sold the Meacham Airport property, both Conchs and newcomers were developing some of its property, and development continued afterward. In 1960, many of the new homes were on the market for under $15,000, and several others were available for under $21,000. For example, NU AGE Construction Company, which was selling homes in a development near North Roosevelt Boulevard, emphasized in its advertisements that FHA financing would be available for the two- and three-bedroom homes for sale between $16,400 and $21,000. Buyers would pay mortgages of approximately $86 a month for a two-bedroom home and $107 a month for one of the most expensive three-bedroom homes.[55]

Some Key West families moved to these new homes from what became known as Old Town, which was primarily the neighborhood west of White Street. Some of those who moved converted their Old Town homes to apartments and rented them, often to Navy personnel, to provide themselves with monthly income. Others who purchased homes in New Town were the grown children of Conch families who had stayed in Key West or returned to their community. Many retired military personnel and their families who had been stationed in Key West or elsewhere in Florida also elected to reside in the city and purchase homes in New Town. In addition, a significant number of active-duty Navy officers purchased New Town homes. Other buyers were associated with enterprises connected to the thriving shrimping business.

Much of this area was underwater and therefore had to be filled with marl from the bay bottom before it could be developed. At the time, the state of Florida was encouraging developers to buy bay bottom and then fill it, with the goal of generating tax revenue. Golan and his partners, along with those who purchased "land" from them, were willing to comply. Charley Toppino & Sons, Inc. was the main firm with which developers contracted to dredge and fill, and smaller companies gained some of the business.[56]

Key West adopted its first zoning code in 1952 and its first subdivision regulations in 1962, but these laws placed few limits on development. The city commission complied with the property owners' desire to zone much of the property for commercial development, which allowed for either residential or commercial use, and, according to one person who was active in land development and real estate transactions during this period, some public officials willingly took bribes to grease the wheels.[57]

The few regulations on development that did exist were loosely applied. Years later, the builder Jerry Ellis emphasized the "flexibility" of Key West's building regulations. Once, when Ellis presented plans to a building official, the official said he could not approve them because they violated the regulations. After some conversation, Ellis asked the official what he would do were he in Ellis's position. He responded, "I'd build it and tell you to go to hell." Ellis willingly complied. Ellis also described practices of dynamiting at night to complete canals that had not yet been approved. And even after state laws prohibited most dredging, "midnight" dredging operations were not unusual.[58]

The primary commercial development in New Town was called Searstown. Abraham Golan announced in 1960 that the Searstown shopping center, anchored by a new Sears and Roebuck department store, was being developed on land he owned along North Roosevelt Boulevard. Golan emphasized that the center would attract many national chain stores, as well as other retail establishments owned by Key West merchants. Much of the area was swampland, but that would present no problem. The area would be filled, the buildings constructed, and shoppers who now had to go to Miami to satisfy their consumer needs would be able to stay in Key West. Searstown opened in 1965, and the mall was successful in drawing many shoppers, which contributed to weakening the business of the retail stores on Duval Street.[59]

The partners in the Key West Improvement Company bet on the fact that Key West would draw more tourists, just as Meacham had decades earlier. Helberg and a partner built the Key Wester Hotel, which in December 1951 opened as the first hotel on South Roosevelt Blvd., along the Atlantic Ocean. It offered tourists hotel rooms, cottages, and efficiency apartments and attracted major attention in 1964 when the Beatles stayed there for a short vacation. Abraham Golan built the Key Ambassador Motel near the Key Wester, which opened around the same time. Later, other tourist facilities were built in New Town. Sam Golan, Abe's brother, and Sam's wife, Margo Golan, opened the Holiday Inn in May 1960 on the "mangrove studded bay bottom" at the entrance to Key West from Stock Island.[60]

Although these new hotels offered visitors accommodations in New Town, the majority of tourist facilities in Key West were in Old Town, and efforts to encourage tourism during this era were focused on the Old Town historic area of Key West. Earlier efforts to encourage tourism in Key West had often emphasized the island's "uniqueness," exotic flavor, interesting architecture, and fascinating lanes and narrow streets. New Town, while it offered affordable housing, mall shopping, and a few hotels, had little that could be considered unique or exotic. Still, the fact that the city now offered new hotels with water views encouraged tourism's boosters.

Postwar Tourism

IN THE INITIAL POSTWAR YEARS and the 1950s and 1960s, tourism in Key West grew only modestly. An article published in 1949 suggested that not all Key Westers sought or welcomed even this modest amount of growth. The writer Benedict Thielen, a seasonal resident of Key West, noted: "So far, no proud signs WATCH US GROW have been erected to greet the entering motorist. No very drastic steps have been taken to correct the town clock, which every now and then, after the proper number of strokes, takes it into its head just to go on striking for a while anyway. No one gets very excited about the proposed new ferry to Cuba, except to point out that all those cars that would come pouring in would really clutter up Duval Street." Thielen went on to comment about a local drugstore that he thought had gone out of business. He discovered instead that the druggist had moved it out of the center of town because "there was too darn much going on down there." He clearly preferred the two people now seated at his counter to the crowds at the city center.[1]

Not everyone, however, shared the druggist's desire for peace and quiet. Although the military and commercial fishing brought increased consumer spending and jobs to the island, many in the business community saw tourism as an essential component of a new economy. Tourism in Florida increased dramatically during these decades, doubling during the 1950s and again by 1967, and some in Key West hoped to lure more visitors to Florida's southernmost city.[2]

Even before the war ended in September 1944, Stephen Singleton, the manager of the Key West Chamber of Commerce, argued that the time had almost arrived for Key West to begin an advertising campaign to attract tourists, and he stressed that other communities in Florida were planning to do the same. He emphasized, "Florida cities are making ready to cash in on the visits as soon as conditions change, and Key West faces . . . competition for this business which is more important to us than it is to cities with industrial and agricultural back country areas."[3]

A tourist brochure published by the Chamber after the war emphasized the uniqueness of the island and praised some of the same community assets as the prewar advertising had. The fishing was superb and the climate was beautiful and brought relief from sinus problems, arthritis, and jittery nerves. Visitors would enjoy Key West's historic architecture and "picturesque structures." Further, "The island attracts interesting people, permanent residents and visitors—writers, painters, sportsmen, scientists, sophisticated travelers . . . because it has so much that is 'off the beaten track' and out of the usual resort routine."

The brochure emphasized that the island was not a tourist trap nor were tourists channeled to particular attractions or events created to lure them to Key West. Rather, "Most of the facilities the visitor enjoys were not created for tourists, but for the residents." And most of the activities were free; "Key West does not 'nickel and dime you': the municipal beach is free, the whole island is a free 'botanical garden,' the waterfront an 'aviary,' each fishing spot a fascinating 'aquarium' of beautiful tropical specimens." The brochure also noted that the military installations added a "colorful background" to the island.[4]

Some soon realized that the presence of the Navy was a potential draw for more tourists due to the many visits made by President Harry Truman, who spent a significant amount of time in what became known as the "Little White House" on the grounds of the Naval Station. Key West's public officials expressed their gratitude to Truman in 1949 by renaming

Division Street, one of the city's major east-west thoroughfares, Truman Avenue, which, appropriately, turns into North Roosevelt Boulevard, the name given to Ocean View Boulevard in 1934.[5]

Truman in Key West

Truman visited Key West eleven times between November 1946 and March 1952 on "working vacations." Truman first visited the island in November 1946 after his physician urged him to take a vacation in a warm climate and get much-needed rest. He stayed at Quarters A, the former residence of the base commander. In the speech Truman delivered in December 1947 at the dedication of the Everglades National Park, he noted, "I have a White House down in Key West," which led to Quarters A being nicknamed the Little White House.[6]

Truman enjoyed his visits to the island. He wrote to his wife in March 1949, "I've a notion to move the Capital to Key West and just stay." And Key Westers had affection for the president. He became close friends with the civic activist John Spottswood, who was elected sheriff in 1952 and later state senator, but Truman also exchanged smiles and chatter with thousands of Key Westers. On his visit in November 1948, an estimated 25,000 people viewed his motorcade as it drove the length of the island from Boca Chica Field to the Naval Station.[7]

The newspaper reporters and broadcasters that accompanied Truman on his trips made certain that Key West would receive national attention. During his first trip to Key West, reporters from the Associated Press, International News Service, the New York Times, the Chicago Tribune, and several other papers covered his visit. Radio correspondents from NBC, CBS, ABC, and the Mutual Broadcasting System were also in Key West with Truman, as were photographers and a motion picture pool. On later visits, representatives from the major television stations joined them. Dignitaries, such as Supreme Court Chief Justice Fred Vinson, visited with Truman at the Little White House, garnering much attention in the national press.[8]

Those trying to promote tourism in Key West were well aware that the publicity accompanying Truman's trips to the island attracted visitors. The Citizen, for example, noted in November 1948, shortly after his victory over Thomas Dewey, that Truman's visits to Key West encouraged more tourists to vacation on the island. Proprietors of Key West's two best-known hotels, the Casa Marina and La Concha, agreed that Truman's visits often meant more "heads in beds," as latter-day tourist officials would put it.[9]

Tourist Promotion

The owners and managers of tourist facilities, along with public office holders, Chamber officials, the *Citizen*, activists in a preservation group, and others, tried to attract tourists in hopes that they would fill the motels and hotels and spend their money around town. Tourism by no means dominated Key West's economy, labor market, or street life, but it was part of Key West's mix, and its promoters closely observed its growth or stagnation. For example, an editorial published in the *Citizen* in 1960 noted, "With recent cutbacks in the number of Navy personnel here, and problems in the shrimp industry, our tourist trade takes on an increasing importance as a source of income that we simply cannot do without." As it turned out, the military's cutback was merely temporary, and the shrimp industry would remain strong for the next decade, but this focus on tourism prompted by concern about the weakening of other sectors of the economy foreshadowed the intensified effort to increase tourism in the 1970s after a significant military downsizing.[10]

During the Cuban Missile Crisis in October 1962, which led to a military buildup in Key West, public officials expressed concern about its short-term negative impact on tourism. When President John F. Kennedy visited Key West that November, Mayor C. B. Harvey presented him with a gold key to the city that differed from the keys usually presented to visiting dignitaries. Harvey noted that the key symbolized the "strain which the Cuban crisis has put on the Key West economy" due to the drop in tourism. In late October, the Chamber of Commerce arranged for "Miss Florida" to visit the community, where she was treated to a fishing trip and visits to Key West's nightspots in hopes of showing potential tourists that Key West was available for their vacations. In the longer term, the city's tourism boosters saw that making Cuba off limits to U.S. citizens could enhance tourism in Key West.[11]

Once again, advertising praised various aspects of Key West's historic heritage, natural environment, and demographic mix, and highlighted the island's exotic uniqueness. One brochure from the early 1960s included a reference to a "Pelican Path" that visitors could follow to visit the "quaint older section of our city and learn more about the buildings and their history." The brochure also referred to the diverse heritage of Key West's citizens, including Cubans and Bahamians. It emphasized, "One forgets this is the United States, as Spanish is heard drifting from porch to porch, and Conchs, the natives of English strain, tell in cockney accent stories of anything from marlin to mermaids." And, of course, it pointed to the "perfect" climate that was "almost pollen-free."[12]

Key West's tourism boosters continued to try to parlay Key West's appeal to literary and artistic figures for the purpose of attracting more visitors. For example, the *Citizen*, in discussing the city's efforts to promote tourism, reminded readers, "Ernest Hemingway, Tennessee Williams, Gloria Swanson, Sally Rand, Robert Frost, John Dos Passos and John Dewey are among the varied personage who have lived here, or made the city their winter home."[13]

Organized Tourist Attractions

Some boosters emphasized the importance of adding activities and attractions that, they argued, would draw more tourists to the community. In 1960, Marcia Fitch, a Key Wester interested in promoting the arts, complained about the dearth of activities available for tourists. She recognized that charter fishing boats did an active business, with many of them operating out of the Garrison Bight along North Roosevelt Boulevard. Still, Fitch observed, most visitors stayed for a relatively short time, in part due to the lack of amusements available to the "fishing widow" whose husband spent his vacation fishing. According to Fitch, the "widow," out of boredom, would urge her husband to cut the vacation short.[14]

A limited number of attractions were added during the 1960s, the most significant being the Hemingway House, which became a major lure for visitors. After Hemingway committed suicide in his home in Ketchum, Idaho, in July 1961, family members inherited the Key West house and sold it to Jack and Bernice Dickson Daniel, who had formerly rented the property. The couple parted ways, and Bernice transformed the house into a tourist attraction. It opened in January 1964, and visitors could pay $1.00 to tour the Ernest Hemingway Home and Museum. Soon after it opened, advertisements for Key West highlighted the Ernest

Hemingway Home and Museum as a reason to visit the community. In 1966, the Key West Art & Historical Society opened the lighthouse museum across the street from the Hemingway House.[15]

The Conch Train, started by Bill Kroll, a citizen of Key West who once leased and operated the city's aquarium and gift shop, became a significant component of Key West's tourism. After taking a train tour in Helena, Montana, Kroll decided to start a "Conch Train" in Key West. He began operations in 1958 using a jeep he covered with sheet metal to resemble a locomotive and pulling passengers seated in flatbed trailers. A ride on the Conch Train enabled tourists to see the island and be provided a selective sketch of some of its history, architecture, and attractions. About 37,000 passengers rode the Conch Train in its first year.[16]

Kroll's initial operation was quite limited. He was one of the Conch Train's original drivers, along with his niece and Rex Brumgart, who lived in Key West during the winter months. Brumgart had first spent time in Key West in 1942 while he was serving in the Navy. After the war, he returned to Chicago but soon settled in Key West, where he lived in a small house behind the "oldest house" on Duval Street. One of the relatively small number of gay men to move to Key West after the war, Brumgart was not known for sticking to any formal script when giving his Conch Train tours. Lee Dodez, an artist and writer who became the head of the Key West Art & Historical Society, provided the following description of one of Brumgart's digressions, "A very masculine man was caught in the middle of a block on Duval without a store front or alley in which to hide. Rex announced over his microphone 'Key West is known for its many transsexuals. What may look like a man to you, the guy on the other side of the street is really Miss Betty Jones. Good morning, Betty Jones.'"[17]

In 1960, the city commission awarded Kroll a twenty-year franchise for the operation of his train. Others then saw the potential to enter the tour business. After the city commission assigned a second franchise to a competing company, the Town House Tours, in 1963, Kroll organized a petition drive to overturn the ordinance that granted the franchise. His campaign, "The Committee to Save Our Conch Tour Train," collected the signatures of 40 percent of Key West's registered voters. Then, in the referendum election in November 1963, a majority voted in favor of voiding the second franchise, leaving Kroll's company with a monopoly on a significant component of Key West's small but growing tourism in-dustry. Kroll's business grew during the 1960s, and in 1971 approximately 300,000 passengers paid for rides on the company's nine trains.[18]

Historic Preservation

A historic preservation movement that sought to maintain and show-case Key West's historic buildings also focused on enhancing tourism. Preservationists in Charleston, Savannah, and several other southern cities had embraced this strategy, and Key West followed suit. The forma-tion in 1960 of the Old Island Restoration Foundation (OIRF), motivated in part by the unsuccessful effort in 1956 to save the historic Caroline Lowe House from being razed after it suffered fire damage, served as the foundation of the renewed renovation and preservation movement.[19]

Mitchell Wolfson, a businessman who was born in Key West and later made a fortune in Miami's motion picture theater business, helped spur this movement. His Mitchell Wolfson Foundation purchased and reno-vated the historic Audubon House, constructed in the mid-nineteenth century on the corner of Whitehead and Greene Streets. The building had been the home of the wrecker and salvager Capt. John Geiger, whom the ornithologist John James Audubon had visited during his trip to Key West in May 1832. Despite the fact that the home likely had not even been constructed at the time of Audubon's visit, it became known as the Audubon House. The Wolfson Foundation dedicated the renovated building to the state of Florida, and it reopened as a historical museum in 1960.[20]

In honor of Wolfson's effort, Jessie Porter and other Key Westers founded Old Island Days on March 18 and 19 to commemorate Key West's heritage. The activities were organized by the Lions Club and by a "women's committee," chaired by Rita Sawyer, who had been instrumen-tal in forming the Old Island organization shortly before. Several of the women also served as hostesses for the tours of the seven homes open to visitors.[21]

The activities garnered publicity for Key West. For example, "ASTA Travel News," the publication of the American Society of Travel Agents, carried an article on Old Island Days that noted Key West's "Old World charm." It also called attention to the bars along Duval Street and re-minded travel agents that, thanks to the Navy base, "handsome gobs are everywhere," a fact agents might share with their "young lady customers."[22]

The *Citizen* emphasized that Key West should "realize the value of our own individual island charm: Our wooden-shuttered dwellings, palm and Poinciana shaded lanes; our picturesque appeal of bygone years." Its editorial noted, "it was this charm that first brought tourists to Key West and gave rise to their affection for it." Key West's historic neighborhoods, it emphasized, were appealing to both visitors and native Conchs. Further, it warned, as had others earlier, "attempts to turn Key West into a flashy 'junior Miami' are a great, big, sad mistake. Good motels, good restaurants, and good bars we should have . . . but they can be found almost anywhere. The town which wants to stay a tourist town must have something more to offer."[23]

Shortly after the Old Island Days, the Old Island Committee invited to Key West Richard Howland, the president of the National Trust for Historic Preservation, who emphasized that the Old Island Committee would benefit from joining his organization. Among his reasons was the fact that historic renovation would entice more visitors to Key West, who would spend money that would, in turn, stimulate the economy. Following Howland's presentation, the Old Island Committee incorporated and became known as the Old Island Restoration Foundation, Inc. (OIRF), joining the National Trust soon after. OIRF's chair, Rita Sawyer, and its other leaders began planning for a two-week Old Island Days festival to be held in March 1961. Recognizing the importance of Key West's Cuban heritage, they emphasized that it would include a Latin American "Noche Alegre (Happy Night)"[24]

OIRF's articles of incorporation listed several goals. One was "To restore and or maintain the tangible and intangible atmosphere of 'Old Island' history and lore by proper zoning and other pertinent measures, requiring new buildings within any area, zoned or otherwise, to conform to the traditional architecture of Key West, Florida." Therefore, regulations governing property owners in Old Town would be necessary to accomplish OIRF's goals, which included luring more visitors to Key West.[25]

In August 1960, at OIRF's request, the Key West Board of Public Works, created by the state legislature, passed a resolution creating a district "to be known as 'Section A,'" as well as a Board of Architectural Review in the City of Key West Building Department to oversee renovation within the district, with the goal of encouraging restoration and preservation "of the unique architectural designs" there. Any property owner seeking a building permit to repair, construct, or restore a building in the district would have to appear before the new board for approval. The board could urge the applicant to make changes but could impose no sanctions if the applicant refused. In 1965, the state legislature adopted a bill that granted the city commission the authority to create an Old Island Restoration Commission (OIRC), whose goal it was to ensure "the preservation of historic buildings . . . in the Old Section of Key West." The city commission created the OIRC in 1966 to take the place of the Board of Architectural Review, but its role likewise remained only advisory.[26]

In spite of such recognition of the importance of Key West's historic heritage, the historic Convent of Mary Immaculate on Truman Street was demolished in the late 1960s. The Sisters of the Holy Names of Jesus and Mary had built the convent in 1886, eighteen years after their arrival in Key West for the purpose of establishing a school. During the 1960s, preservationists strove to save and restore the deteriorating building, but St. Mary's Sister Theodora Therese concluded, "Our job is to educate children, not to restore antiques." After the school's demolition, preservationists in Key West frequently cited this loss as evidence of the need for stronger regulations in Key West's historic district. In 1969, the state legislature passed new legislation governing the "Old Section" that for the first time provided penalties for those who violated the statute. Although this statute by no means guaranteed more stringent regulations in the historic district, it was directed at strengthening the process.[27]

Mallory Square

In addition to its focus on the architectural style and renovation of homes in Old Town, the OIRF encouraged the city to refurbish Mallory Square on the Gulf near Duval Street and to work with Key West's artistic and theatric groups to renovate buildings there. The city aquarium was already drawing some tourists to the area; now there was a potential to draw more. The *Citizen* supported this general plan and noted that the city had been unsuccessful in attracting businesses dependent on shipping goods to the dock area. Now, the *Citizen* suggested, the tourist strategy had promise. The mandate of the Old Mallory Square Committee, created by the city to advise it on future uses of the property, reaffirmed the goal of transforming Mallory Square into a tourist magnet. The committee was "empowered to see that the area is maintained as a place . . . to be used for the pleasure of the tourists."[28]

Promoters of renovating the buildings on Mallory Square encountered the obstacles anyone urging the expenditure of public money would face. The city manager Victor Lang's warning in 1963 that the city was operating under an "austere budget with a bleak future" was typical during this era. The government often had to borrow funds to continue operating until the next fiscal year. The city's fiscal situation was not enhanced by the fact that its leases of city-owned land to private organizations, such as the Key West Yacht Club, often benefited the lessee and provided little revenue to the city.[29]

For tax purposes, many of Key West's properties were assessed considerably below their market value, which only compounded the city's financial troubles. More than half of Key West's homeowners paid no property taxes, because their assessments were lower than the $5,000 homestead exemption that state law mandated. In addition, there was a wide disparity in the dollar value of assessments on comparable property. A 1960 study by the Monroe County Taxpayers Association reported that the tax assessments in the city ranged from 4.5 to 63.3 percent of the value of the property, a disparity that likely derived in part from the "bubba system" that brought favorable assessments to political insiders and their friends.[30]

Still, the Old Island Restoration Foundation's initiative did realize some success, due in large part to the efforts and financial support of the city and private organizations, including some in the arts. Major improvements included the transformation of abandoned buildings into an art gallery, a theater, a hospitality center, and a small convention building. Cement piers also were added to Mallory Dock, enabling its use as a cruise ship dock.[31]

The Key West Art Center made a significant contribution to the Old Island Restoration Foundation's initiative by restoring a Mallory Square building without public financing. The original Art Center had formed during the 1930s, next to the aquarium on Front Street. It eventually disbanded, but by 1960 another group of artists had organized and adopted the Key West Art Center name for their gallery on Duval Street. The Art Center's activists encouraged the city to lease them the original building on Front Street, now known as the Red Cross Building, a proposal that the OIRF supported. Although the city-owned building had been condemned, the Key West Art Center began a drive to raise money in hopes of renovating it as an art museum, and the city commission assisted their efforts by awarding them a ten-year lease for $1 a year. In June 1961, The Key West Art Center opened in the original building, which was designated as a historic landmark. Promoters of tourism hoped the restoration would encourage those interested in the arts to visit, and perhaps relocate, to the community.[32]

During the same period that the Key West Art Center was arranging to open its facility on Front Street, the Key West Players theater group began negotiations with the city to lease a building that had been the Monsalvage warehouse on Mallory Square. The city leased what was now known as the Waterfront Playhouse to the theater group, which financed rehabilitation of the warehouse. The Key West Players began performing at the Waterfront Playhouse in the 1961–62 season, vacating their former space in the Barn Theater, located behind the Woman's Club on Duval Street.[33]

Other renovations in the Mallory Square area complemented these endeavors. In 1961, Jimmy Russell, Peter Pell, Bill Johnson, and Walter Starcke opened Key West Hand Print Fabrics, which made and sold fine fabrics and remained a thriving business in Key West for decades. These men were not Key West natives; they came from different locations, but all had ties to the New York theater industry. Starcke in particular became active in the Old Island Restoration Foundation. In line with their interest in preservation, the owners of Key West Hand Print Fabrics located their business on Front Street, near the Key West Art Center, in the "Historic Harbor House," which had originally housed Key West's first bank.[34]

The Rejection of Urban Renewal

Although the activities of Key West's public sector were limited in scope during this era, several office holders promoted urban renewal, an activist public policy that had the potential to dramatically transform the neighborhood on the west side of the island, just blocks from Duval Street. Rather than preserving and renovating buildings in this area, urban renewal would raze most of the homes to make way for redevelopment.

They targeted an area where the vast majority of the city's African American population lived. Clearly, many Key Westers who wanted to enhance their town's potential as a tourist destination viewed the black neighborhood, traditionally called colored town by Conchs, as a deterrent to tourism rather than as a neighborhood whose heritage might be highlighted to attract tourists.[35]

Mayor Kermit Lewin, accompanied by other public officials and civic-group leaders, went to Tampa to examine that city's plans for urban renewal. They left having resolved to support a referendum to initiate urban renewal. The referendum they placed on the ballot in 1963 did not call for targeting a specific neighborhood for urban renewal but for endorsing Key West's participation in the federal program. Still, it was clear that officials intended to target the black neighborhood west of Duval Street.

The *Citizen* and the Key West Rotary Club supported the referendum, but others urged the citizens to "vote against dictatorship," noting that if voters passed the referendum, the city commission would appoint seven persons to a board endowed with the authority to condemn and demolish property in Key West, issue city bonds, and levy taxes. Opponents also argued that urban renewal would ultimately lead to the razing of a large number of older houses in "Conch Town," in addition to those in the black section. Voters rejected the proposal by a majority of four to one.[36]

The legacy of urban renewal in other communities suggests that Key West's rejection of the referendum spared it from suffering a similar decrease in affordable housing. And many in Key West's black population who would have been displaced by urban renewal undoubtedly benefited from Key West's decision not to implement the program. Blacks, however, would find that in the next decades they benefited little, and in many cases suffered, from Key West's increasing popularity as a tourist and second-home community.

David Wolkowsky

Key West's rejection of urban renewal reinforced the fact that during this era it was primarily private individuals and organizations, and not the public sector, that spearheaded renovation and activity related to tourism. David Wolkowsky, a third-generation Key Wester, played key roles both in the renovation of existing structures and in new construction in Old Town, especially in the area close to Mallory Square. Wolkowsky's family had acquired a significant amount of real estate on the island, including the building on Greene Street that had housed the original Sloppy Joe's. In fact, it was Wolkowsky's father, Isaac, who had raised the rent for the building, thereby provoking Joe Russell to move.[37]

David was born in Key West in 1919, but when he was four years old his family moved to Miami. After graduating from the University of Pennsylvania, Wolkowsky became involved with development projects in Philadelphia. He moved back to Key West in 1962, after his father died and left him his property near Mallory Square. Wolkowsky renovated several houses in Old Town, and he moved older buildings from other sections of town, including Navy houses from Trumbo Point, to the Greene Street vicinity. He also opened Café La Brisa, along with several other businesses, on an alley off Greene Street, which became known as Pirate's Alley.[38]

Wolkowsky renovated the Greene Street building that had once housed Sloppy Joe's, and in 1963 he rented the building to Morgan Bird, who opened "The Oldest Bar." Although it remained in business for only about a year, the opening of The Oldest Bar signified the growth of what was then a small gay population in Key West that included such literary and artistic figures as Tennessee Williams, as well as Brumgart, Wolkowsky, and Bird.[39]

Bird had been raised in a wealthy family in Pennsylvania and attended Harvard University. After visiting Key West in 1959, he decided that it was the place for him. Bird moved into the former home of the philosopher John Dewey, which was located near the shrimp boats that docked at the Key West Bight. Tennessee Williams and Frank Merlo, the building designer Dan Stirrup, Wolkowsky, the French artist Marie de Marsan, who arrived at the New Year's Eve party at The Oldest Bar on horseback, service personnel, and others in Key West's diverse population frequented The Oldest Bar.[40] Its renovation as a bar included the transformation of the huge cistern into what was first known as The Prize Room, and later as the "cistern and brethren," where the patrons could engage in "highly intimate" activities.[41]

Wolkowsky's primary contribution to tourism was the Pier House hotel, which he constructed on waterfront property on Front Street, between Duval Street and a city-owned strip of property bordering

Simonton Street, purchased from the Gulf Oil Company. Wolkowsky opened the fifty-room Pier House in 1968, an impressive structure designed by Miami architect and planner Yiannis Antoniadis and landscaped by Key Wester Frank Fontis. Wolkowsky also moved the Gulf Oil office, which once housed the ticket office for the P&O Steamship Company, to the end of a 300-foot-long pier. Initially leasing it to a company that operated a restaurant there, he eventually opened his own restaurant in the historic building. Wolkowsky had close ties with newspaper writers in Miami and the Northeast, and he was successful in garnering significant publicity for the new hotel and for Key West in general. Wolkowsky also was friends with many writers and artists, and the Pier House became the place to stay when they visited Key West. Writer William Wright and others who initially stayed at the Pier House purchased homes on the island.[42]

Tourism Trends

In spite of the efforts to attract more visitors to Key West, the increase in the number of tourists arriving during the 1950s was limited. *Newsweek* magazine estimated that approximately 190,000 tourists arrived in Key West in 1950. A decade later, the Florida Development Commission reported that in 1960 approximately 177,000 tourists visited by car, the means of travel for the vast majority of the island's visitors. Overall, tourism remained relatively stable during most of the 1950s, although it almost certainly rose and fell to some extent during these years. The number of tourists driving to Key West rose by about one-third during the 1960s, reaching 234,000 in 1969, which was actually a decrease from the nearly 263,000 that visited during the peak year of 1967.[43] Still, Key West was by no means a primary tourist destination for those vacationing in Florida. In 1965, Key West ranked fourteenth among communities in the state for attracting visitors, a drop from its ranking of twelfth in 1960. Although the *Citizen* and some businesspeople predicted that the renovation of the Mallory Docks would attract the cruise-ship business to Key West, cruise ships sailed to Key West only intermittently.[44]

Although new hotels and motels were built, the increase in the number of rooms available to tourists after the Key Wester and Key Ambassador were completed in New Town in 1951 was small. The number of tourist accommodations (including hotels, motels, or tourist courts) rose from 60 in 1955 to 65 in 1966, and the number of rooms in these accommodations increased from 1,050 in 1955 to 1,239 in 1966. Often the city's hotels and motels had difficulty attracting customers. In 1960, representatives of the Motel Owners Association complained that their competitors engaged in "street hawking" to entice visitors into their hotels, and they asked the city commission to repeal the ordinance that allowed "street solicitation within 100 feet of the entrance to one's own property."[45]

The fortunes of the Casa Marina and La Concha, Key West's two major hotels dating from the 1920s, illustrate the limited amount of tourism during this era. While the Casa Marina remained the primary destination for Key West's wealthiest visitors during the 1950s, it suffered financial difficulties throughout the decade. In the mid-1950s, the hotel's corporate owner, the Emmeff Corporation, headed by Max Marmorstein, sold the hotel. Shortly afterward, however, the corporation that had purchased the hotel defaulted on its payments, and the court appointed Marmorstein as the receiver of the hotel, making him responsible for its operation during the litigation proceedings. Marmorstein then repurchased the Casa Marina at a foreclosure sale in 1959 for a considerably lower price than he had sold it for in 1956. Several months after Marmorstein died in May 1961, his wife sold the hotel to Sam Hyman, who was associated with James Hoffa's Teamsters Union, which invested money from its pension fund in the hotel. Hyman, however, closed the Casa Marina after it failed to attract enough tourists and then leased it to the Army from the Cuban Missile Crisis in October 1962 until the end of 1965.[46]

Hyman was indicted on charges of fraud and conspiracy related to the use of the union's pension fund, found guilty in 1964, and sentenced to a fine and a year and a day in prison in the same trial in which Hoffa was convicted and sentenced to jail. State Senator John Spottswood purchased the Casa Marina from Hyman in 1966. Spottswood continued to hold office until 1967, when he decided not to seek reelection. By then, real estate had become his primary focus. Having purchased the Casa Marina and procuring additional property in its vicinity, Spottswood initially planned to significantly renovate the hotel. Instead, he leased the Casa Marina to the Westinghouse Corporation for use as a dormitory and training facility for Peace Corps volunteers. The hotel closed once again after the Peace Corps left the facility in late 1966.[47]

The success of La Concha Hotel, named the Town House Motor Inn during most of this period, was no better. The Jacksonville banker Ed Ball had purchased the hotel in the 1930s. In 1960, Ball still was the primary owner of Jacksonville Properties, the hotel's owner, which was a subsidiary of the DuPont interests in Florida. Ball closed the hotel in 1961 and donated his majority interest in La Concha to the Roman Catholic Diocese of Miami. Hyman, on behalf of the Teamsters, then purchased La Concha from the church. Although the U.S. Marines who arrived in Key West during the Cuban Missile Crisis stayed at the hotel for a short period, it remained closed to the general public. Spottswood purchased the hotel in 1966, restored its name to La Concha, and located the office of his businesses, WKWF and Cable Vision, Inc., there. With the exception of its popular bar, however, the hotel remained closed.[48]

Key West at the End of the 1960s

In 1953, the author and Key Wester Colin Jameson noted that some Key West residents and visitors fit into the "Abandon-Ye-All-Hope" group. Jameson wrote that according to them, "Key West has gone to Hell and soon won't be distinguishable from Miami Beach and I hate it." He continued, "They greet each modernistic improvement with I-told-you-so's, and then start muttering about the Virgin Islands and the Isle of Pines."[49]

The Key Wester Esther Chambers surely belonged to this group. In March 1950, she wrote a letter to her friend, Charles Olson, a poet who had spent the 1944–45 winter in Key West. She complained, "The old island is sure not what it used to be due to Harry [Truman] I think, damn him. Motels are sprouting up all over the place, new beaches pop up where there was only a small sand pile." Almost two decades later, others interpreted the changes in Key West as evidence that it was losing its uniqueness and becoming too mainstream and touristy. For example, the novelist and playwright Jose Yglesias visited Key West in 1969 and described the changes based on what he had heard from others about the old Key West: "Front Street, once all gambling or bawdy houses, is today the focus of a committee that is restoring the old island: it has become a nucleus of tourist shops, restaurants, marine exhibits, and bars with coyly designed atmosphere—the place where visitors, who usually come to spend only two or three days, gather to catch the Conch Train for a two hour tour of the island." When he described the scene to a friend who had lived in Key West for a few years after the Second World War, the friend was not surprised: "When the madams started moving their houses over to Stock Island, I knew it was all beginning to go."[50]

Although Mallory Square and some of the area around Front and Greene Streets had been renovated by the late 1960s, and the Pier House was becoming a popular spot for tourists, the restoration of and increase in tourist accommodations were only a small step in a much longer stride. True, Hemingway's House was now being promoted as an attraction, and one could pay to visit the lighthouse or East Martello Gallery. The Conch Train was now a popular vehicle for visitors to tour the island. Still, Key West's attraction for tourists derived more from its exotic and eccentric community than from its boutique-style shops. And many of the activities tourists engaged in while visiting Key West were more spontaneous than scripted by tourism's entrepreneurs.

For example, the now famous Sunset Celebration held on Mallory Square was then still a relatively small, occasional gathering. Visitors might find themselves there at sunset, but they would not specifically plan to be there based on advertisements in tourist brochures. Rex Brumgart, whose ad-lib style on Conch Train tours had already made him a local character, is also credited with initiating some of the first sunset celebrations at Mallory Square. Not everyone tells exactly the same story about the origin of the Sunset Celebration, but the writer Bud Jacobson captured its flavor. Brumgart, one Sunday evening in the mid-1950s, was bored, so he packed a martini shaker, some brie, and a bit of caviar and walked down to Mallory Square with a fold-up table and a beach chair. He settled on a location at the end of the dock, near the warehouse owned by Champion Seafood, mixed a pitcher of martinis, got drunk, and watched the sunset, shouting "Bravo" at the spectacular view. He later raved about his experience to several of his friends, and they began to join Brumgart on the docks to watch the sunset. Among these friends were Earle S. Johnson, the owner of the "Oldest House"; the jazz pianist Lyle Weaver; Liz Lear, who worked with Key West Hand Print Fabrics; Morgan Bird; and Jacobson.[51] Tennessee Williams also sometimes joined the group and is said to have clapped and yelled "author, author," as the sun went down.[52]

At the end of the 1960s, Key West was still primarily a military town, and commercial fishing was an important component of its economy. Military personnel and their dependents, shrimpers, and Conchs of various backgrounds constituted the major segments of the community. Tourists and tourism were noticeable in Key West, but for most the island city was still an out-of-the-way place. Airline service brought some visitors, but the numbers arriving by plane were relatively few. And driving down the narrow U.S. Route 1 was an experience many chose to avoid, even after the elimination of the toll in 1954. In the 1970s, Key West would enter a new phase of tourism, one that served as a prelude to the tourism industry's more rapid growth during the last two decades of the twentieth century. During the 1970s, however, Key West was by no means defined by its quest for or the presence of tourism.[53]

6

Island of Intrigue

Key West in the 1970s

IN THE 1970S, Key West hosted a variety of newcomers. Some took their places alongside the Conch population and those who had earlier moved to the city. Others purchased the homes of Conchs who relocated to other Florida communities. Gays, hippies, writers, artists, other "celebrities," shrimpers, military personnel, Conchs, and various combinations thereof inhabited this diverse community. The island also attracted more visitors than in previous decades. The military presence continued but by the middle of the decade had become less significant. Those desiring a community that offered a variety of lifestyles could find nothing similar to Key West. Greenwich Village, San Francisco, and other neighborhoods and cities might have been similar in certain respects, but they were more "sophisticated" and offered a greater variety of restaurants, bookstores, and other amenities. The island of Key West exuded a culture that blended several qualities into a unique, and sometimes uneasy, mix.

Demographic and Economic Trends

In the decades after the Second World War, many of America's cities underwent deindustrialization, and their economies shrank dramatically as factories closed or relocated and manufacturing jobs disappeared. Key West had suffered the loss of its cigar industry long before. The decline of the military presence on the island in the 1970s, then, was Key West's version of a second deindustrialization. The island's overall population decreased from 29,312 to 24,292, primarily due to the downsizing of its military facilities.[1]

Even before the Naval Station, renamed Truman Annex in 1972 in honor of the former president, closed in 1974, Key West's economy exhibited serious problems. The city's unemployment rate was higher than that of the state of Florida, and family incomes were relatively low. In 1970, Key West's unemployment rate was 5.7 percent, compared with 4.3 percent in Monroe County and 3.7 percent for the state, and its median family income was $6,918, which was lower than those of Monroe County ($7,334) and Florida ($8,267). In the first half of the 1970s, commercial construction in Key West also slowed.[2]

Although it had initiated some cutbacks in 1969, the military was still a significant presence in Key West at the beginning of the decade. A report prepared by a local bank in 1970 estimated that the military generated over $56 million in revenue for Key West's economy. Furthermore, the economic health of local utilities and businesses depended on the military. For example, approximately 36 percent of the City Electric System's gross sales were to military facilities. In addition, in the late 1960s, the Florida Keys Aqueduct Commission had constructed a $4,500,000 desalination plant on Stock Island, necessitated in large part by the military's demand for fresh water. Many of the dependents of military and civil service personnel were employed by Key West businesses.[3]

So in the early 1970s, when the Navy announced a major downsizing in Key West, the community was alarmed. The number of military personnel and civilians employed by the Navy fell dramatically when the Navy closed its Truman Annex Naval Station. Although some of the civilian personnel were transferred to the Boca Chica Naval Air Station, most of them had to seek employment elsewhere.[4]

Commercial fishing, primarily shrimping, was still an important industry in Monroe County in the 1970s, with the boats primarily operating out of the Key West Bight and from Stock Island. The shrimping fleet was also a "spectator sport" for tourists. In the early 1970s, the industry employed about 1,400 people in Key West during its peak winter season, but by the end of the decade its contribution to Key West's economy had weakened, and its future was uncertain.[5]

Drugs: Where is Bum Farto?

A more lucrative business, also connected to the sea, proved far more profitable than fishing for some shrimp boat owners and enriched many others in Key West—drugs. Drug trafficking is arguably the industry that kept Key West's economy alive as the military and commercial fishing declined. It was not uncommon in those years for certain Key Westers to pay for a car or boat in cash, money they had earned from the drug trade. During several decades in the nineteenth century, Key Westers had waited for ships to wreck on the reef and then raced to reach their frequently lucrative cargos. In the 1970s, it was not uncommon for bales of marijuana, or "square grouper," to drift onto Key West shores. Witnesses to these "beachings" might not have amassed the fortunes of some of the wreckers of bygone days, but they likely procured enough to satisfy their own appetites, at least for a while, and also earn some cash. Those who inhaled sometimes complained that the weed tasted somewhat soggy due to its watery journey, but the high was generally deemed good enough.

The trade in marijuana, cocaine, and other drugs was common knowledge. Two popular T-shirts declared "Save the Bales" and "Smoke Key West Seafood." Another advertised "Square Grouper—$30 an Ounce," while yet another noted, "If Marijuana is Legalized, I'll be on Welfare." The author Jim Harrison recollected how men would openly test a bale of marijuana on Simonton Street in broad daylight. "They'd put a handful in a small paper bag, light the bottom of the bag, take a deep drag, toss the burning bag into the street, become contemplative for a few minutes, then make a judgment."[6]

This openness would have been impossible without a police department and sheriff's office whose staff included officers who supplemented their own salaries through involvement in the drug trade. Early in January 1976, Sheriff Bobby Brown reported that three sacks containing 150 pounds of marijuana had disappeared from the police compound where 97 water-soaked sacks of dope were drying out. Events such as this did not inspire confidence in the integrity or competence of the sheriff's office. Some Key West police officers went to jail. In September 1978, for example, four officers were arrested and convicted of being paid lookouts for smugglers unloading marijuana at the dock of a seafood company on Stock Island.[7]

The Florida Department of Criminal Law Enforcement, the U.S. Drug Enforcement Administration, and the Dade County Organized Crime Bureau organized "Operation Conch" to investigate the drug trade. Most Key West and Monroe County law enforcement officials were not informed of the investigation, given that they were among the suspects. In September 1975, nineteen alleged drug traffickers were arrested, including several city officials.[8]

Among those arrested was Manuel James, the adopted son of the Key West Police Chief Winston James and a close friend of State Attorney Ed Worton. James was arrested while in a car with Mae Arnold, a convicted bolita dealer. Another person arrested for dope trafficking was Artemio Crespo, a major figure in the bolita rackets in Key West, which suggests that some of the island's gambling kingpins had diversified into the drug business. James had been appointed the Key West city attorney in January 1974 and still held this position at the time of his arrest. Previously, he had been a prominent defense attorney with a reputation for successfully defending citizens accused of drug dealing, often securing their release before formal charges were filed. James was an outstanding example of why the newspaper reporter and author Carl Hiaasen described Florida as "a great place to live if you're a novelist or columnist or a criminal defense attorney."[9]

James escaped prosecution on the charges related to selling cocaine because prosecutors concluded that a paid informant had lied. Initially suspended, James was reinstated as city attorney when the charges were dropped. However, in late 1977, he was fired from his city position for having been a key member of the defense team that succeeded in gaining acquittals for, or getting charges dropped against, 23 defendants in drug smuggling cases in Monroe County. He left Key West in late 1980 as an investigation mounted evidence against him and others concerning their involvement in a major statewide marijuana smuggling ring. James was convicted in March 1982 and sentenced to five years in prison.[10]

Another Key West official fled when confronted with prison. Joseph "Bum" Farto, the Key West Fire Chief, was arrested and indicted for his involvement in the marijuana and cocaine drug trade, which included selling drugs from fire stations. Farto was found guilty in February 1976 and faced a long prison term. Before his sentencing, Farto rented a car and told his wife that he was going on a business trip to Miami for the day. He never returned to Key West, and the next month police found his rental car parked on a Miami street. Rumors abounded; one claimed he had escaped to Brazil while another maintained he was living in Costa Rica. Some concluded that Farto was killed by his associates in the drug trade, who feared he would provide information to law enforcement officials. After his disappearance, "Where is Bum Farto?" T-shirts became a popular item in Key West stores. Another big seller featured the words "El Jefe" ("the chief") in red lettering on a white background, in reference to the lettering on his license plate, as well as the rose-tinted glasses that Farto wore and his red sports jacket.[11]

Some Key Westers sought lucrative drug profits far from home. For example, Carl Rongo, a developer who had profited from federal funds awarded to Key West for Duval Street projects, pled guilty in 1981 to smuggling several tons of marijuana into South Carolina. In 1985, the former City Commissioner Johnny Hernandez was convicted in Mobile for smuggling fifteen tons of pot into Alabama on the shrimp boat *The Crimson Tide*.[12]

Most Key Westers involved in the drug trade, however, found ample opportunities to do business closer to home. In 1980, the *Miami Herald* ran a series on the Key West drug trade, entitled "Smugglers' Island," that was based on extensive interviews and analyses of police and court records. The stories highlighted the involvement of public employees and detailed a culture that allowed drug smuggling to flourish. The articles also emphasized the drug use of the Monroe County State Attorney, Jefferson Davis Gautier, whom they accused of prosecuting smugglers leniently. Bob Graham, the governor at the time, removed Gautier from office in November 1980 for using quaaludes and marijuana, although no criminal charges were filed against him.[13]

The rampant drug trade motivated some in law enforcement to expand their efforts. Many viewed the election of Billy Freeman to the office of Monroe County Sheriff in 1976 as a step toward stronger and more reputable law enforcement. After his election as Monroe County State

Attorney in 1980, Kirk Zuelch appointed J. Allison DeFoor II to direct a Narcotics Task force, which operated from 1980 to 1982. Drug raids became more common. One of the most publicized raids was the "Big Pine 29" bust of 1980, which resulted in the arrest of 29 people for possessing and intending to distribute marijuana. Four law enforcement agencies seized 31,000 pounds of marijuana at Big Pine Key, several miles from Key West. Twenty-two of the 29 dealers lived in the Keys, several of them in Key West. The majority of those who stood trial were convicted the next year.[14]

The task force was credited with confiscating drugs valued at $30 million in Monroe County, leading to the convictions of 100 accused drug smugglers. The much-publicized efforts of this task force contributed to DeFoor's election as county judge in November 1982, and then as Monroe County Sheriff in 1988, after Freeman decided not to run for another term. The activity of DeFoor's task force, however, by no means eliminated Key West's drug activities; the drug trade continued to flourish during the 1980s, and once again public employees played a prominent role.[15]

In the "Bubba Bust trial" of mid-1985, Raymond "Tito" Casamayor, Key West's Chief of Detectives and Deputy Police Chief, was tried in U.S. District Court, along with thirteen other defendants, for racketeering related to a cocaine smuggling operation based out of the Key West Police Department.

The prosecutors emphasized that the police department was awash with "graft and corruption" and labeled Police Chief Larry Rodriguez as an "unindicted co-conspirator." A convicted drug dealer testified during the trial that he had delivered cocaine, hidden in containers from Burger King and Chicken Unlimited, to Casamayor at the police station. The verdict determined that under federal law the Key West Police Department was a "continuing criminal enterprise," and Casamayor, along with two other members of the Key West Police Department and nine codefendants, was convicted. Casamayor was sentenced to thirty years in prison, and the two police detectives were each sentenced to fifteen years.[16]

Also arrested in the Bubba Bust trial were the prominent Key West lawyer Michael Cates and his wife, Janet Hill Cates. A former Key West High School football star and Monroe County Attorney, Cates had defended several clients accused of involvement in the drug business. He also had been the attorney for Historic Tours of America, which operated several of the community's tourist enterprises, including the Conch Train. Edwin Swift III, one of its owners, testified in Cates's defense. Swift said of Cates, his "word can be trusted; he's honest, and he obeys the law." Witnesses for the prosecution, however, testified that one of the drop-off points for their weekly cocaine deliveries in Key West was at the Cates's law office, and the jury found both husband and wife guilty. Michael Cates was sentenced to fifteen years on three felony charges, including his function as the legal adviser to a major cocaine operation, and Janet received ten years for selling cocaine. After Cates was released from prison, an experience he and his friends referred to as attending "graduate school," he worked as a consultant for Swift's company, which prospered as Key West attracted more tourists.[17]

One might think Key West's tourism boosters would have feared that the publicity around the drug busts would tarnish the island's image and decrease its appeal for tourists. David Wolkowsky, however, offered a different theory. He suggested, instead, that the scandals might actually help, noting, "Intrigue, you know, is what Key West is about."[18]

Jimmy Buffett, Mel Fisher, and Captain Tony

One of those attracted to the intrigue of Key West was Jimmy Buffett, who arrived on the island in late 1971. He and his friend, musician Jerry Jeff Walker, drove to Key West from Miami, and Buffett recalls that he "just got on the back of a conch train and got blitzed out of my mind." In 1980, Buffett recalled his early days in the town. "I was just footloose and fancy free and going crazy," he said. "We didn't have much money and didn't know much about cocaine so we stayed drunk a whole lot. Key West was the most wonderful, wonderful place I'd ever seen in my life. That's why I wrote about it, and that's the way I still feel about it." Although "Margaritaville" (1977) is his best-known song from the 1970s, several of his other songs explicitly celebrate Key West. In "I Have Found Me a Home" (1973), Buffett celebrated the Key West culture he found so enticing. "A Pirate Looks at Forty," on his "A1A" album (1974), tells the story of Buffett's Key West friend, Phil Clark, whose life revolved largely around drug smuggling, seafaring, and women.[19]

Although Cubans constituted a smaller portion of the population than in earlier decades, Duval Street still boasted several Cuban restaurants and coffeehouses. For example, El Cacique, a Cuban café, specialized in meals such as turtle steak, arroz con pollo, black bean soup, and flan. In Buffett's autobiography, *A Pirate Looks at Fifty* (1998), he explains, "living in Key West in the early seventies was not like living in America," adding "you could not live in Key West without being exposed to Cuban culture." Buffett celebrated other elements of Key West's mix as well, including the writers and musicians, Conchs, rowdy shrimpers, and drug smugglers. He was glad the gay community benefited from the fact that the "Puritans had never made it this far south."[20]

That this diverse population lived and worked in such close proximity contributed to the island city's unique culture. Lee Dodez began visiting Key West as a young gay man in 1959 and moved there in the mid-1960s. He later captured the essence of Key West's wild life in the 1970s, calling it "not only a place" but "also an attitude": "You can walk or stagger to the bars and restaurants, always meeting people you know or know about. . . . These people do crazy and wonderful acts and say wild and funny things. Maybe every city has a section like Old Town. The difference may be that everyone here knows everything about everyone, and no one gives a damn."[21]

Buffett and his friends enjoyed a choice of hangouts in the Key West of the 1970s. An early favorite was the Old Anchor Inn on Duval Street. Victor Lathum, a bar owner in Key West and a friend of Buffett in New Orleans in the 1960s, described the Anchor as "just as bizarre as it could be. It was the kind of place that one bartender would open the beer cooler to get a beer out and find the other bartender curled up asleep on top of the beer, because it wasn't air conditioned in there and the beer coolers were cool. It was just total insanity." A longer-lasting hangout for writers, musicians, and smugglers was the Chart Room Bar in the Pier House. It became well-known for the politicos that used it to make deals "out of the sunshine." Another spot was Louie's Backyard, which basically served as Buffett's backyard, being located behind his house on Waddell Street. The Full Moon Saloon on United Street, owned by Latham and two partners, was also a frequent stop.[22]

Buffett often encountered Mel Fisher in Key West. At about the age of forty, Fisher drove with his wife and four kids from California, where he had been operating a dive shop, to Florida to become a treasure hunter. He had some luck and moved his business, Treasure Salvors, Inc., from Fort Pierce to Key West in the early 1970s to search for the sunken ship, *Nuestra Señora de Atocha*, a Spanish galleon carrying a massive amount of gold, silver, and other valuables that sank near the Keys in a fierce storm in 1622.[23]

Fisher set up his headquarters, the Galleon, near the shrimp fleet on the Key West Bight and became a notable character around town as he continually searched for investors in his project. Fisher was the eternal optimist; "today's the day," he would tell his divers as they headed out to search for treasure. Still, Fisher was constantly living on the edge, having to borrow money and entice new investors into his enterprise. And he had to deal with the tragic deaths of his son Dirk and Dirk's wife, Angel, when the salvage ship on which they were working sank during the night.[24]

Fisher and Buffett appeared in Key West early in the decade, trying to make it in a town that was receptive to unconventional characters. As Eugene Lyon, the historian responsible for pointing Fisher to the *Atocha's* underwater location, noted, Key West in the 1970s was "Mel Fisher's kind of town." It was a "natural gathering place for eccentrics of every kind. To those it extends an easy tolerance."[25]

Another well-known Key West character during the 1970s was Tony Tarracino, or Captain Tony, a charter boat captain who had moved to Key West from Elizabeth, New Jersey, in 1948 to, he later claimed, flee the mafia, who were after him for his gambling debts. In the mid-1960s, he opened his bar, Captain Tony's Saloon, in the same building on Greene Street that had once housed Sloppy Joe's and The Oldest Bar. His establishment was popular with different segments of Key West's community, and Tony fit in well with Key West's non-Puritanical culture, as Buffett had described it. At one point, Tony credited his success in the world (especially with women) to his "healthy sex drive" and "strong ego." He married several times and fathered numerous children with his wives and other women. Fittingly, Captain Tony was a friend of both Fisher and Buffett, and Buffett paid tribute to him in his song "Last Mango In Paris" (1985).[26]

Art, Theater, and Writers

Key West continued to attract artists and those interested in the arts. The closure of the Naval Station at the Truman Annex enabled some artists to rent a studio inexpensively in the abandoned buildings of the station. For example, the sculptor John Martini moved to Key West in 1977 and rented a large studio there, as did the painter Stephanie Sanchez and the photographer Adolph Gucinski.[27]

Several art galleries operated on and near Duval Street. Marion Stevens' Artists Unlimited gallery, located next to John Brown's Bar, continued to be popular. Stevens and Brown sometimes spiced up lower Duval with their shouting matches over one issue or another. The Key West Art Center on Front Street still showcased the art of local and other artists, and by the end of the decade the Guild Hall art gallery had opened on Duval Street. Richard Heyman and Lee Dodez established the Gingerbread Square Gallery in 1974, which displayed the work of many of Key West's gay painters. One of the most prominent was John Kiraly, who moved to Key West with Heyman.[28]

Conchs and newcomers admired the work of Mario Sanchez. Although he sometimes lived in Tampa, Sanchez was generally known as Key West's greatest artist. Known for his painted woodcarvings, he created distinctive works that highlighted the flavor of the Key West of his younger years. Mario's father was a lector (reader) in cigar factories in Key West, and Mario, born in 1908, grew up in Gatoville, a Cuban neighborhood of cigarmakers' homes and small stores. His artwork featured cigar rollers, fishermen, and street vendors. In a city replete with newcomers, many of whom were unaware of Key West's history, Sanchez's work stood out. In 1996, the magazine "Folk Art" named Sanchez as the century's most important Cuban-American folk artist.[29]

Theater companies contributed to the island's cultural life. In addition to the Key West Players, who still performed at the Waterfront Playhouse at Mallory Square, a new theater company, the Greene Street Theatre, appeared, organized by Peter Pell, the president of Key West Hand Print Fabrics, Jay Drury, an actor and director who had worked in New York and Boston, and Roderick Brown, who with Rita Buckner and several other young graduates of Virginia Commonwealth University in Richmond moved to Key West in 1974 and 1975. The group renovated an old building across from Sloppy Joe's as a playhouse and in 1976 performed their first play, Tennessee Williams's "Suddenly Last Summer." Williams became friends with Brown and others in the group, assisted them in their rehearsals, and rewrote the play's final scene for their performance.[30]

After the Tennessee Williams Fine Arts Center at the Florida Keys Community College opened in 1979, the Greene Street Theatre became its company in residence. Although Greene Street disbanded in the early 1980s, some of its members had already organized another company. They renovated the building at the back of the Woman's Club on Duval Street, where the Key West Players had performed, before relocating to the Waterfront Playhouse. The new company was initially known as the Red Barn Actors Studio and evolved into the Red Barn Theatre, which thirty years later continues to thrive.[31]

Key West also continued to attract writers. Some spent significant time in the city but never became permanent residents, while others chose to call Key West home. They did not arrive in Key West to live in luxury. Most lived in modest houses, and several were associated with a writers' compound of small cottages on Windsor Lane, near the cemetery.[32]

Richard Wilbur, the United States's second poet laureate and two-time winner of the Pulitzer Prize for poetry, lived in the compound. Wilbur and his wife, Charlee, began spending winters in Key West in the mid-1960s at the suggestion of a friend at Wesleyan University. The friend told Wilbur that if he liked the movie *Bonnie and Clyde*, he would also like Key West, which is "both beautiful and tacky." Wilbur "fell in love with the town immediately." Among his first observations of Key West was its spirit of "amused tolerance." Also, the dilapidated houses and cracked sidewalks brought back memories of his childhood during the Depression. In the mid-1980s, he told a reporter, you experienced "bohemian energy" on the island and a "constantly changing population of artists, writers, conchs and drifters."[33]

The Wilburs' friends, John and Barbara Hersey, moved to the Windsor Lane compound in 1976. Both couples shared the lifestyle common to most of Key West's writers, living in Key West during much of the year, but leaving for the summer. Although John Hersey is best known for his Pulitzer Prize–winning novel *A Bell for Adano* (1944) and for *Hiroshima* (1947), he also wrote *Key West Tales*, a series of short stories set in Key West, which was published in 1993, the year Hersey died. John Ciardi also moved to the Windsor Lane compound. Ciardi and Wilbur, who had taught together at Harvard, had known each other for decades. A writer of poetry and prose, as well as a noted translator who was frequently heard on National Public Radio, Ciardi, with his wife, Judith, first became a winter resident of Key West in the 1970s, and the couple returned annually until Ciardi's death in 1986.[34]

Wilbur also was friends with John Malcolm Brinnin, who wrote poetry and biography among other genres, from their days as students at Harvard University and encouraged him to move to Key West. Brinnin had visited Key West briefly in 1944 and did not immediately fall in love with the island. He wrote in his journal that he took a Trailways bus to Key West from Miami and had to stand up for the entire trip because all the seats were "occupied by booze-sodden sailors returning to base." La Concha was full, but he was allowed to sleep on a sofa in the lobby. The next day, he took a walk and noted the dilapidated condition of the city, including "dead trees on ruptured sidewalks" that a local told him stemmed from the hurricane "fifteen, maybe twenty years back." Brinnin then went to the ocean, took off his shoes, and began to "feel out the contours of a buried mound of something directly below" until he could see it was "the swollen belly of a dead dog." He returned to the hotel, picked up his bag, and took the next bus out of Key West.[35]

He did not return until 1975, when he stayed at the Pier House and spent time with Truman Capote, a frequent visitor to the community. Brinnin continued visiting Key West, and by 1980 he was a regular winter resident. For Brinnin, the city was a "perpetual carnival" that one could participate in whenever one chose.[36]

Ciardi, Wilbur, and Brinnin were also friends with Philip Burton, the foster father of the actor Richard Burton. An actor, director, and Shakespearian scholar, Philip Burton was born in Wales in 1904, worked and lived in London, and then moved to the United States, becoming an American citizen in 1964. He first visited Key West in the 1960s during a lecture tour. After suffering a heart attack in 1970, he began spending his winters on the island. Years later, Burton recalled his early years in Key West fondly. The city, he said, "was much more simple. . . . There was something about the atmosphere of this place—not only the climate but the people. There was such friendliness here, such as I had never really felt before."[37]

Not all writers reacted positively to Key West. Ralph Ellison, the author of *Invisible Man* (1952), and his wife, Fanny, purchased one of the cottages on Windsor Lane in 1975, at the urging of the Wilburs. Ellison, however, was not attracted to the island, and he and Fanny spent little time there. They sold their house in 1993 and rented it to others during most of the time they owned it. The Ellisons, however, were the exception rather than the rule.[38]

In addition to those who lived in the Windsor Lane compound, and the friends they managed to entice to the island, several other writers lived in Key West during much or all of the decade. James Kirkwood Jr., the co-author of the play, "A Chorus Line," for which he won the Pulitzer Prize in 1976, first spent time in Key West in 1963 at the suggestion of James Leo Herlihy, who told him that it was "an ideal place 'to create,'" and that it also offered tennis and swimming. In the early 1970s, Kirkwood was one of the first homeowners in the Conch Grove Compound in Old Town, and he became a frequent winter resident of the city until his death in 1989. He suggested that the island was "not Florida, maybe not even America, but a country and a state of mind. It's the end of the line, even the world." Kirkwood, one of Key West's several gay writers, also emphasized Key West's tolerance: "There was never a stigma attached to anything you did in your private life. Key West has always had a great attraction for people who are a little tilted, a little crazy . . . a little off-center, even kinky."[39]

Tom McGuane fit Kirkwood's description of those in Key West who were "a little crazy." His first novel, *The Sporting Club*, was published in 1968, and he moved to Key West the next year with his wife, Becky, and their young child. The family began spending their winters in Key West, summering on their ranch in Montana. As he noted in 1974, McGuane was drawn to Key West for the fishing and to satisfy his desire to "get out on the most scrambled edge of this one [culture]." McGuane later described one of his novels, *Panama* (1978), as a "very personal book about the process of going completely crazy in Key West."[40]

The best known of his novels set in Key West, *Ninety-Two in the Shade*, was made into a movie and filmed on the island in 1974. McGuane served as its director, and its stars included Elizabeth Ashley, Margot Kidder, and Peter Fonda. McGuane and Fonda spent considerable time frequenting Key West's drinking establishments, including the Full Moon Saloon and the Chart Room. Dennis Hopper, Fonda's co-star in *Easy Rider*, came down to join the party. As a result of the festivities surrounding the making of the movie, McGuane had an affair with Elizabeth Ashley, divorced his wife, Becky, and married Margot Kidder, although this marriage also ended in divorce. Becky, in the meantime, married Peter Fonda. Later, McGuane married Fonda's former wife, Laurie Buffett, who also happened to be Jimmy Buffet's sister. In 1984, when he and Laurie were spending most of their time in Montana and only occasionally visiting Key West, McGuane recalled his years in Key West as being "very explosive."[41]

One of McGuane's friends was the author Jim Harrison, who spent much time in Key West and in the Keys during the 1970s and 1980s. He raved in his book, *Off to the Side* (2002), about the flats fishing and the bird and marine life in the Keys, as well as the "peculiar combinations of a first-rate sporting life in the closest proximity with a sprawling colony of writers and musicians." He experienced "an island totally devoid of rules of behavior, a tropical island fueled by sunlight, dope and booze, as far from Kansas as you could get in America."[42]

Harrison, McGuane, and several others organized an informal social club that McGuane dubbed Club Mandible. "There were about twenty or thirty members and they had shirts and they had their different club names," one member recollected. "They had Lieutenant Barko, and there was General Chaos, and Private Parts. We'd always go out en masse and boogie." Harrison recalled that Club Mandible "spearheaded our efforts toward unconsciousness, or a rather punishing form of consciousness," a state easily realized due to the ready availability of drugs. When the comedian John Belushi died of a drug overdose in 1982, Harrison remarked that he "didn't seem all that crazy by Key West standards."[43]

The gonzo journalist Hunter Thompson also visited Key West, staying in Buffett's apartment for a period when Buffett was on tour. Buffett introduced him to Harrison and McGuane, with whom Thompson had a natural affinity. In Buffett's words, "Hunter loved Key West because in those days there was such a crazy end-of-the-world mentality down there."[44]

Among the most versatile writers to move to Key West in the 1970s was Shel Silverstein. He also spent considerable time on Martha's Vineyard and in Sausalito, California, but he lived in his home on William Street in Key West until he died in 1999. An accomplished author of short stories, poems, and songs, Silverstein wrote for children as well as for *Playboy Magazine*. One of his best-known songs was "A Boy Named Sue," a title suited to the Key West community, which was made famous by Johnny Cash. Among his other songs was "The Great Conch Train Robbery," about a shrimper who tries to rob the conch train but is shot and killed by a tourist "redneck of respect" from Muscle Shoals who was riding the train. Its lyrics capture the flavor of the island: "'Twas sunset down in old Key West / the locals all were high. / The tourists snapped their photographs / and munched their Key Lime pie. / And meanwhile down at Sloppy Joe's / the drinks were standin' tall / with Buffett on the jukebox / and Hemingway on the wall."[45]

The Pulitzer Prize–winning author Alison Lurie arrived in Key West at the end of the decade, and she later underscored the attractiveness of the island to writers. She found Key West "a good place to be in those years," where writers worked (or "pretended to") during the day and joined dinners and parties at night. She characterized Key West as a "little-known, cut-rate paradise," that was "full of small shops and sagging ginger bread cottages, unpaved streets and untrimmed bushes and trees."[46]

Lurie also observed that at that time, "The package tourists and cruise ships had not yet discovered it, and the streets were not jammed with traffic." Many who arrived in Key West during the 1970s and earlier, as well as many Conchs, valued this environment. Others, however, envisioned an island bustling with tourists and commerce.

HOMELESS MAN AND HIS DOG

"Jack Jr." rests near his owner,
Michael Sanier, also known
as Captain Gypsy. Sanier, a
member of Key West's homeless
population when this picture
was taken in 2004, tried to raise
money by persuading tourists
to pay to take a picture of him
and Jack Jr. *Tampa Tribune*
archives.

HOUSEBOAT ROW

Houseboat Row was established
along Roosevelt Blvd. during
the 1960s. For decades, residents of this boat community
fought efforts to displace them
from this location. Courtesy of
Monroe County Public Library
system.

**HOUSEBOAT ROW AFTER
HURRICANE**

Hurricane Georges devastated
Houseboat Row in 1998. The
last houseboat vacated the area
in 2002. Courtesy of Monroe
County Public Library system.

JAMES LEO HERLIHY

James Leo Herlihy, the author of *Midnight Cowboy* (1965), first visited Key West in 1957 and lived there until 1972. Herlihy was close friends with Tennessee Williams and others in Key West's literary community. Courtesy of Monroe County Public Library system.

**JIMMY BUFFETT AND
BETTY WILLIAMS**

Jimmy Buffett and Betty Williams, a reporter for the *Key
West Citizen*. Buffett moved
to Key West in 1971. His hit
song, "Margaritaville" (1977),
undoubtedly attracted tourists
to the island city. Courtesy of
Monroe County Public Library
system.

JOHN SPOTTSWOOD AND
HARRY S. TRUMAN

State Senator John Spottswood
with Harry S. Truman during
one of Truman's visits to Key
West after he left the presiden-
cy. Courtesy of Monroe County
Public Library system.

KEY WEST CHICKEN

Right: One of the many chickens that inhabitant the island, to the joy of some and the consternation of others. Courtesy of Michael X. Delli Carpini.

KEY WEST CORNET BAND

Below: In 1874, some of Key West's black residents organized the Key West Cornet Band, which became the Welters Cornet Band. The band was well known in town into the twenty-first century for marching with funeral processions. Courtesy of Monroe County Public Library system.

KEY WEST LIGHTHOUSE

The Key West Lighthouse on
Whitehead Street was built in
1847 and deactivated in 1969.
The Key West Art & Historical
Society now operates the Key
West Lighthouse & Keep-
ers Quarters Museum on the
site, which is a popular tourist
attraction. Courtesy of Stuart
Newman Associates.

LITTLE WHITE HOUSE

President Harry Truman spent
several "working vacations" in
Key West. He stayed at "Quarters A" in the Naval Station,
which soon became known as
the Little White House. It was
opened to the public in 1991.
Courtesy of Stuart Newman
Associates.

MALLORY SQUARE AERIAL
VIEW

Above: An aerial view of Mallory
Square, the scene of large crowds
of people who gather at sunset
to look at performers and at
each other. Courtesy of Monroe
County Public Library system.

MALLORY SQUARE SUNSET
PERFORMER

Right: One of the many perform-
ers at the sunset celebration at
Mallory Square. Courtesy of
Stuart Newman Associates.

7
Key West in Transition

ALTHOUGH BUFFETT AND MANY OTHERS valued Key West for its diversity, eccentricity, and uniqueness, many other newcomers and Conchs focused on the investment potential of Old Town homes, on the possibilities of downtown revitalization, and on bringing more tourists to the island and providing them with accommodations. By the late 1970s, many of the homes in Old Town were being rehabilitated, primarily by gay newcomers to Key West, and a trend toward gentrification was underway, bringing with it higher housing prices. Commercial buildings on several blocks of Duval Street were renovated, and additional guesthouses and other accommodations were made available to the increasing number of tourists who visited the community. Developers proposed additional projects in New Town, primarily designed to meet the needs of seasonal residents and tourists. Although many welcomed these trends, others resisted them, and conflicts erupted over various aspects of tourism and development.[1]

The Mallory Docks and some of the surrounding areas had been reno-vated during the 1960s, but many of the homes in Old Town, as well as commercial property, continued to deteriorate. A study conducted by the planning consultant Milo Smith in 1967 documented the blight on sev-eral blocks around Duval Street. It concluded that almost 40 percent of the residential structures and 36 percent of the non-residential buildings west of White Street, which constituted the boundary of the Historic District, were in substandard condition. Smith advocated a major reha-bilitation program for the "Old Section."[2]

Over the next decade, gentrifiers renovated homes in the historic dis-trict, a trend many lauded. A study conducted in 1978 noted, "In many ways, history is Key West's leading product, and anything that may dis-courage the present trend of private and public preservation can seri-ously damage the island's economy." An article on historic preservation in the Keys concluded, "In the Florida Keys, rich in history unique in the nation, historic preservation has become an economic imperative."[3]

The Key West Historic District, established by state statute in 1965, was in 1971 listed in the National Register of Historic Places, which en-abled those who renovated buildings in Old Town to benefit from federal tax credits. In 1972, the state legislature created the Historic Key West Preservation Board, which was granted the authority to recommend to the city commission changes to the boundaries of the historic district and to the design standards within it. The board was also involved in a number of other preservation activities in Old Town, including the res-toration of the San Carlos Institute on Duval Street.[4]

State regulatory policies that restricted new development also rein-forced the renovation activity in Old Town. In 1972 the Florida Pollution Control Board imposed a moratorium on dredge and fill operations, pro-hibiting the legal creation of new land in the New Town area. In addi-tion, to protect the Keys' already inadequate water supply from saltwater intrusion and contamination, likely results of increasing demand from a growing residential and tourist population in the Keys, the state in 1974 imposed a moratorium on new water hookups.[5]

Renovators could purchase homes inexpensively in the Old Town neighborhood they found appealing. George Born, a historic preserva-tionist, described in 2004 some of the features of Old Town that had attracted newcomers to the island. These included mixed-use zoning, which ensured that homes, entertainment venues, and businesses in Old Town were close to each other and to the street. Also attractive were the yards whose lush landscaping made walking inviting, the front porches, the reasonable building heights, and the diverse architectural styles.[6]

The interior designer Angelo Donghia was one of the prominent gay men involved in the restoration movement. Ranked as the most noteworthy interior designer in the country, Donghia had designed homes for celebrities such as Diana Ross and Joel Grey, as well as New York New York, the trendy Manhattan disco. In 1974, he purchased a house built in 1894 at 712 Eaton Street in Old Town. Donghia spent two years and more than $200,000 renovating it.[7]

What attracted Donghia to Key West? He found it "visually appealing" and "cosmopolitan," describing it as a "cross between Nantucket and Papeete, in Tahiti": "It's not a prissy resort, like Nantucket, but there's some of Nantucket's old elegance mixed with Key West raunchiness. And like Papeete, it's a tropical port full of transients and traders." Donghia owned a townhouse in Manhattan, but he valued fleeing "to the anonymity of Key West." His nationwide prominence and large circle of friends and business acquaintances added to the city's popularity for gay men and others in the arts. By the time he moved away from Key West in 1981, selling his home to the designer Calvin Klein, Old Town property was becoming a hot commodity in a global real estate market.[8]

While restoration efforts were changing the character of Old Town, Mayor Sonny McCoy and several businessmen were focusing their efforts on renovating downtown storefronts and promoting business development on Duval Street. The closing of the Truman Annex Naval Station just a few blocks from Duval hurt the downtown's consumer base. The opening of Searstown shopping center in New Town in 1965, as well as other commercial developments along North Roosevelt Blvd., had also contributed to the decline of the downtown retail market. McCoy was a third- or fourth-generation Conch of Irish and Spanish descent. He had graduated from Key West High School and earned architectural degrees from the University of Florida and the University of Michigan. McCoy was in office for nearly the entire 1970s, winning his first two-year term in 1971 and reelection to four more two-year terms.[9]

When McCoy took office, Key West's government had only limited financial reserves to aid the restoration of downtown Key West, but

McCoy successfully sought federal money to aid the effort. Beginning in 1975, the U.S. Department of Housing and Urban Development (HUD) provided Key West with approximately $200,000 each year for several years in the form of Community Development Block Grant funds, to be used for downtown improvements. HUD also allocated the city additional money for downtown projects. The city channeled many of the funds into two blocks of Duval Street, which benefited from updated streetlights and overhead wires, as well as new trees and other beautification projects.[10]

Edwin Swift III, Gerald "Moe" Mosher, and Christopher Belland, who had formed Old Town Key West Development, Ltd. in 1973, were the primary businessmen involved in redeveloping buildings on Duval Street. Swift's family had moved to Key West from Marathon when he was ten years old, and his father owned a camera shop and a greeting-card store on Duval Street. Mosher came to Key West with the Navy in the early 1950s and opened a barbershop on Duval. Belland grew up in Miami, graduated from the University of Pennsylvania Wharton Business School, returned to Miami for a short period, and then moved to Key West in 1973. The decline in the downtown business district struck these businessmen as an opportunity to invest in a potentially revitalizing area. In the mid-1970s, their company purchased and renovated several properties on Duval Street, primarily in the 600 block, about halfway between the Gulf and the Atlantic.[11]

Tourism

As the Old Island Restoration Foundation (OIRF) had anticipated in the 1960s, this renovation activity reinforced tourism. In 1978, McCoy waterskied from Key West to Cuba, where he was met with a hero's welcome. His feat earned Key West national press, which many in the community sought as its economy transformed into one based primarily on tourism. In 1971, Walt Disney World opened in Orlando. Some promoters of tourism in Key West reasoned that tourists in search of a different kind of destination might, instead, choose their southernmost city. By the mid-1970s, after the military had significantly downsized in Key West, tourism had become the city's most important, legal, income-producing industry. The Key West Chamber of Commerce estimated that in 1970 268,800 tourists arrived, only slightly more than the peak year of 1967, but that in 1973 the number of visitors increased to 402,000 before decreasing during the 1974–75 recession. After the recession, however, the number of visitors again increased. Although one study reported that over one million tourists reached Key West in both 1978 and 1979, no precise count of tourists during this decade exists. The estimate of over one million visitors is almost certainly higher than the actual figures, but it is likely that the number of visitors to the island at least doubled during the 1970s.[12]

Tourism in Key West remained seasonal. Just as many of the city's authors and artists lived on the island only during the winter, most of the tourists chose the winter months to visit. Some entrepreneurs, however, bet on the fact that tourists would continue to arrive in increasing numbers, a wager evident in the rising number of rooms available in tourist accommodations. The 1,239 rooms available in 1966 had become 2,088 by 1978, and 2,380 by 1980, primarily owing to the conversion of homes and apartment buildings in Old Town to guesthouses and the reopening of the Casa Marina.[13]

In 1974, several of the staff of the Chart Room Bar at the Pier House left it to reopen the Birdcage Lounge at the Casa Marina, but the hotel remained closed to guests. Then, in 1977, Cayo Hueso, Ltd., a company composed largely of longtime Key West residents, purchased the property from Mary Spottswood, John's widow. They added a small convention center and 150 additional rooms and reopened the facility in May 1979, as Marriott's Casa Marina Inn. The reopening of the Casa Marina was a symbolic boost to Key West's image as a tourist town and suggests that many business interests both in and outside of Key West expected the town to attract its share of wealthy tourists who would want to stay in fancier accommodations.[14]

The sale of the Pier House also reflected the general belief that the island would attract upscale visitors. The Pier House thrived during the 1970s, and in December 1977, Clancy Dupepe, a New Orleans hotel developer who owned a home in Key West, announced that he and his business partner were about to conclude a deal to purchase the Pier House from David Wolkowsky. Ed Knight, the realtor whose firm handled the transaction, reported that the $4.6 million sales price was the highest yet in Key West. Wolkowsky had already expanded the original Pier House, and Dupepe announced that he would add more rooms in addition to other improvements.[15]

Not all who visited Key West relied on hotels or motels for a place to stay. Some came by boat to fish or simply relax and slept on their boats. They could dock at the Garrison Bight Municipal Marina, which included about 100 slips. In addition, the new King's Point Yacht Club and Marina, later renamed the Oceanside Marina, on Stock Island contained about 90 slips. In the mid-1970s the U.S. Customs Service reported that about 150 yachts from other countries visited Key West each year. The island city clearly had become popular with many well-heeled tourists, not all of whom were attracted by Key West's diverse population or those characteristics that had drawn Kirkwood, McGuane, and so many other writers and artists.[16]

Alice Turner, in an article that appeared in *New York* magazine in 1978, observed, "Key West is our winter Hamptons." She noted regretfully that Lillian Hellman and Diane Keaton both had to cancel their reservations at the Pier House, which was the "chic place to stay" and the "permanent floating salon for decorators and the literati," but Pete Hamill, Dustin Hoffman, Calvin Klein, and Kurt Vonnegut Jr., all made the trip, as did writers from the *New Yorker* and the *Village Voice*. Turner also was impressed that Donghia and a host of literary luminaries, including Tennessee Williams and John Hersey, had homes in Key West.[17]

Why, in Turner's estimation, did she and the other New Yorkers visit Key West? Well, the food was good, but there wasn't much to do besides eating, drinking, and talking. The beaches were not noteworthy, the aquarium was "pathetic," and the turtle kraals were "depressing." She was impressed with a few local nightspots, including the Monster, where one could observe or participate in "effete decadence." Her conclusion as to why New Yorkers came to Key West? To be with, well, other New Yorkers. It was "the place we go to continue the conversation we started at Elaine's.... Given the choice between mingling with the outside world and with each other, we almost invariably opt for each other."[18]

Still, an article published in the *New York Times* at roughly the same time as Turner's article appeared in *New York* magazine interpreted the attraction of Key West differently, pointing to some of the same characteristics Buffett and others had praised. Key West was, it emphasized, "a community of minorities, a heterogeneous mix of whites and blacks and Cubans, artists and writers and hippies, homosexuals and fishermen—a richly ragtag assortment of diverse people who manage somehow to get along together—well. There is also an atmosphere of lush laziness, of sunlit decadence, and there's that live-and-let-live ambiance that lures and fascinates a special breed." So, according to this analysis, Key West was unique; and its allure differed from that of the majority of tourist destinations.[19]

Sunset at Mallory Square

Just as tourists visited Key West for different reasons, Key Westers were divided in their reaction to some of these visitors, divisions that represented competing visions about what Key West was and should be and that defied the simple "let-and-let-live" characterization of island culture. During the 1970s, Mallory Square at sunset became the place to be. In the beginning of the decade, relatively few journeyed there to view the sunsets. The numbers sometimes reached forty or fifty, but often were smaller. Increasingly, however, the daily sundown festival at Mallory Square became the destination for Key West's tourists and residents, gays and straights, street people and the well-heeled, both continuing and transforming the practice Brumgart and others had initiated over a decade earlier. Everyone would flock to the old dock area, which still was riddled with cracked sidewalks and potholes despite the improvements made during the 1960s. Jugglers, musicians, the Iguana Man, who walked around with three lizards on his shoulders, and others would spontaneously perform for all who gathered at Mallory Square.[20]

Indeed, word spread about the sunset gathering at Mallory Square to such an extent that some visited Key West primarily to participate in the celebration. Jack Lange, a native Californian and a frequent visitor to Key West from his home in Delray Beach on the east coast of Florida, noted that Key West was the reason his friends from California wanted to return to Florida: "It's that ceremonial gathering on the dock where the sun is lowering, that mixing of native and tourist, young and old and in-between; kids, dogs, parrots, monkeys, iguanas; jugglers, flutist, rock combo, belly dancer, bongo player—the 'people happening' that takes its only orchestration from the burning star on the water. That, sir is a reverence in action."[21]

Not everyone, however, reacted as favorably to the Mallory Square scene. City Commissioner Mary Lee Graham, for example, complained about the hippies and street people who had found their way to Key West in spite of the anti-hitchhiking law Monroe County had adopted.

These unwelcome newcomers were, she emphasized, regulars at Mallory Square, where they often panhandled and then slept on the street. The chairman of the Mallory Square Advisory Committee to the city commission declared that he would never visit Mallory Square late at night, because he could never be sure of what might happen. In January 1973, two of the most prestigious groups in the city, the Key West Woman's Club and the Key West Garden Club, called for a "ban" on "hippies," claiming that they were responsible for the increase in crime and for the decision of many downtown merchants to close early.[22]

Key West's Chamber of Commerce did not want to be identified with the nightly celebration. A spokesperson for the Chamber emphasized in 1977, "We do not have a brochure on the sunset. And if people come in to ask what is to be seen here, that is not one of the things we tell them to do." Joe Pinder, a banker and influential member of Key West's business establishment, agreed with this sentiment, emphasizing that the "vagrants" should be arrested and sent to jail and then used to clean the streets or parks, as, he suggested, was the case in "the old days." He complained, "You can't do that today." Occasionally some were thrown in jail for at least a few hours for violating a somewhat obscure law that banned two or more musicians from performing in the city without a permit. Still, this did little to deter the sunset activities.[23]

Others, however, presented a different perspective. For example, the director of the Old Key West Civic Association emphasized that his organization was formed to beautify Old Town, as well as to foster an environment wherein tourists could feel safe. "Longhairs," he argued, were not to be blamed for the problems of indecent exposure, panhandling, and profanity in the area. City Manager Ron Stack commented, "You can't stereotype the elements that break our laws and commit crime. Our records show arrests of local civilians, transients and the military. It's unjust to single out any particular group."

The *Citizen* surveyed downtown businesses and found that none cited the hippies' presence as a reason for closing early. Its editorial disagreed with the "serious-minded Chamber of Commerce members" and urged people to view the sunset from Mallory Square. It emphasized "more than the glories of the universe in this eternal display of brilliant color and fabulous design, is the mad wonder of the wild collection of our young hippie community who make sunsets at the Mallory Docks a ritual experience."[24]

For many promoting tourism in Key West, however, whose percep-
tions of the hippies and the sunset celebration were more accurate was
not necessarily all that important. The key point for them was that not
enough tourists were attracted to the community, especially tourists
with disposable income. More efforts were needed to bring visitors to
the island.

Organized Attractions

The city gained very few tourist attractions in the 1970s. The historic
Watlington house, known as Key West's oldest house, was added to the
city's inventory of attractions. Although it never became a major tourist
draw, it, along with the Hemingway House, the lighthouse, the Audubon House, and a few other sites, represented the effort to build on Key
West's historic heritage. In 1832, Captain Francis Watlington, a federal
employee and part-time wrecker, purchased the house, which had been
built around 1825 on Whitehead Street, and moved it to 322 Duval Street.
For a period in the 1940s and early 1950s, Mary Watlington Douglass,
a Watlington family member who had married a naval officer, owned
it and opened it to the public as a family museum. The house was later
closed to the public, but in 1974 a new owner donated the house to the
Historic Key West Preservation Board, which arranged with the Old Island Restoration Foundation to maintain the building and reopen it as
a museum.[25]

By the end of the decade, however, Key West had lost the turtle kraals
that had been a leading tourist attraction. The turtle schooners owned by
Thompson Enterprises had stocked the kraals until 1968, when Thompson sold its holdings to Sea Farms, a shrimp mariculture firm. Sea Farms
continued to stock the kraals until 1971, when Florida adopted a regulation that was the beginning of the end of the commercial trade in green
sea turtles and, therefore, of Key West's turtle kraals. The regulation
stipulated a minimum size limit of 41 inches on all green turtles held in
Florida, regardless of their origin. As a result, the kraals could not be re-
plenished. Nevertheless, the kraals remained open throughout the 1970s,
in part because some green turtles exceeded the legal size and in part because the kraals also held other species of sea turtles. By the late 1970s,
however, the kraals held only a few turtles and were less of an attraction
for tourists. In early 1982, concerns about deteriorating conditions at the

kraals prompted the National Oceanic and Atmospheric Administration (NOAA) to direct Ed Little, a NOAA fisheries service biologist, to remove the last of the turtles from the kraals and ship them to the Theater of the Sea marine animal park in Islamorada.[26]

Fantasy Fest

Fantasy Fest was designed to put Key West on the map for tourists in search of an experience comparable to New Orleans's Mardi Gras. And there was no better time for this activity than October, when Key West's tourism business was especially slow. The origin of Fantasy Fest in 1979 also signified the importance of gay businessmen to the stimulation of tourism. There is some disagreement about who first conceived of the idea of the festival, but it is clear that it grew out of discussions that began at a luncheon at the Pier House attended by the hotel's manager, Peter Henry; Peter Pell and Jimmy Russell, owners of Key West Hand Print Fabrics; Frank Romano and Joe Liszka, the owners of Key West Aloe; Fast Buck Freddie's owners, Tony Falcone and Bill Conkle; a representative of the Conch Train; and a few others. Their discussions led to the formation of the Tourist Development Association (TDA) to plan for the first event.[27]

The activities began on Friday evening, October 26, with the arrival of the "Mistress of Madness" at Mallory Square, who invoked "the spirit world to terrorize the Fantasy festivities." Later in the evening, the Casa Marina hosted the Masked Fantasy Ball. Saturday afternoon featured a party and "water creatures contest" at the Pier House beach. The Grand Parade on Saturday evening included about seventeen floats showcasing themes such as "Fear House," "Rocky Horror Show," and "Night Train." The parade also featured a woman known as "Sister," dressed only in gold body paint, who posed as a hood ornament on the front of a Lincoln Continental. At midnight, judges, including Tennessee Williams and the gallery owner Marion Stevens, chose the best costume. Several "hangover brunches" were held on Sunday. Finally, on Sunday evening, the East Martello Gallery and Museum hosted the Benefit Masquerade Ball. Although several thousand watched the parade, it did not attract a significant number of tourists. Gay guesthouses were fully occupied, but the hotels and motels still had vacant rooms. And shop owners on Duval Street reported little change in their business over the weekend. Still, the organizers anticipated that an expanded Fantasy Fest would attract more visitors in the future.[28]

The most vocal naysayers were those associated with a Christian group that criticized what they considered to be the open display of raucous behavior. This parade would not be the last Fantasy Fest about which they expressed their concerns. Others were critical not of Fantasy Fest per se, but of the fact that it represented increased efforts to attract tourists to the island. For example, one city official worried that Key West would become a "Disneyland South" and proclaimed that the city should "bulldoze all the new stuff off the island and start over again using rainwater and cisterns." Some citizens protested and initiated legal proceedings after Air Florida started flying larger planes into the airport to accommodate more tourists. Even more telling was the defeat in 1980 of a referendum for a new tax to finance more advertising to potential tourists, a defeat that suggested many in the community were wary of a massive new effort to promote a tourism-based economy.[29]

A Tourist Tax?

In 1977, the Florida legislature authorized local governments throughout the state to impose a "local option tourist development tax" on those who rented accommodations for six months or less. Under this act, a county's governing board had to pass an ordinance approving either a 1 or 2 percent tax, after which the tax had to win, in a referendum, the approval of voters in the jurisdiction where the tax was to be imposed. The Monroe County Board of County Commissioners (BOCC), however, defeated a proposal to create a Tourist Development Council, which would offer recommendations to the county concerning the merits of adopting a resort tax. Margo Golan, an influential businesswoman and owner of the Holiday Inn in New Town, was among the strongest opponents of the tax, because, she contended, it was unfair for only tourist accommodations to be responsible for collecting the tax. The Key West attorney David Paul Horan, the banker Joe Pinder, and others opposed the tax, because the state legislation confined the uses of its revenues too narrowly; the revenues were to be used for the advertisement and financing of festivals and other activities designed to attract more tourists. They argued that these revenues should also be available to finance improvements to infrastructure and basic services.[30] The issue continued to be debated into 1978, with some in the accommodations industry supporting the tax and others opposing it. The *Citizen* in July 1978 contended that a tax to raise more money for advertising was unnecessary. Key West, it pointed out, was garnering much free attention from the national and international media. In addition, the county's advertising commission was already successfully promoting the Florida Keys and Key West. Still, the *Citizen* urged a public debate on the merits of the tax and advocated that the county commission place the referendum on the ballot. The BOCC, however, decided against placing the tourism tax referendum on the November 1978 ballot.[31]

A difference of opinion within the Chamber of Commerce regarding the tourist tax was an important contributing factor to the chamber's split. Pinder, Golan, Horan, and others critical of the tourist tax and what they perceived to be the chamber's increasingly single-minded emphasis on tourism formed their own chamber in November 1978, which they incorporated as the Southernmost Chamber of Commerce. In their "open letter to the business community of Greater Key West," they argued that while tourism was important to Key West's economy, the city should not rely exclusively on any one industry and the Chamber should not focus exclusively on promoting tourism.[32]

Debate about the merits of a resort tax resurfaced in 1979. The BOCC appointed a countywide Tourist Development Council (TDC) in August, composed primarily of supporters of the tourist tax. Don Schloesser, who served as the chair of both the TDC and the BOCC, argued that a countywide bed tax would benefit the taxpayers because their taxes were currently funding the roughly $136,000 budget of the Monroe County Advertising Commission, revenue that could be used in other ways. The TDC advocated holding a referendum on the tax, and the BOCC agreed to hold a series of public hearings on the issue.[33]

At these hearings, held in January 1980, many argued that the county lacked adequate infrastructure, such as water and sewers, to accommodate more tourists and that passage of the tax would not result in lower property taxes for residents. On the other side of the argument, Monroe County Advertising Commission member Frank Romano complained, "We sit by in September and watch our businesses go down the drain." More advertising, he argued, would bring in more tourists who would finance improved facilities.[34]

The BOCC agreed to place a referendum on the Tourist Development Tax on the ballot. If the measure passed, 50 percent of the revenues would finance advertising for the Keys, 20 percent would be allocated to the nine chambers of commerce in the Keys, and the remaining 30 percent would finance festivals, cultural events, boat races, and fishing tournaments that appealed to tourists. Ed Swift, Joe Liszka, and others organized the "Citizen for Tourist Development Committee" to garner support for the tax.[35]

Despite their efforts, however, voters in the March 11 referendum defeated the "bed tax" proposal by a margin of more than two to one (7,213 to 3,230). The proposal failed to win a majority in any of the county's voting precincts, and Key West voters turned it down, 2,671 to 1,462. Both proponents and opponents of the proposal agreed that one significant factor that contributed to its defeat was the water shortage the Keys were facing, a factor that led many voters to doubt whether the infrastructure in Key West and the rest of the Keys could support more tourists. More generally, however, the defeat indicated that at least some citizens were not persuaded that they would benefit from increased tourism.[36]

Growth Conflicts

Not only was there disagreement on the tourist tax and, more generally, about the extent to which Key West should focus on enhancing tourism, but conflict also surfaced over development projects in New Town that were designed to accommodate more tourists and residents. In 1973, the authors Stan Windhorn and Wright Langley suggested that Key West was not facing the same development pressures as many other communities: "No Chamber of Commerce board of directors has yet had the temerity to place at the city's limits a neon-flashing billboard proclaiming 'Watch Us Grow!'" They continued, "In all probability none ever will. Again there is that element that makes Old Key West different from all other cities. There is growth, there will be growth, but only a growth that is relevant to—and will enhance—Key West's past." In fact, developers were planning projects similar to those of other towns, and, as in other communities, citizens mobilized to oppose them.[37]

One of the major controversies surrounded a proposal advanced in 1973 by Donald Berg of Key Biscayne and his development firm to build a 750-unit condominium on North Roosevelt Boulevard. Condominiums had been gaining in popularity in southern Florida since their introduction in the 1960s, and Berg and his Key West allies wanted Key West to join the trend. The firm requested a change in the zoning classification for its property on North Roosevelt that would significantly increase the maximum density allowed. Mayor McCoy and the Key West Planning and Restoration Commission endorsed the changes, as did the Key West Chamber of Commerce. Charles Aguero, Key West's acting city manager, reported to the city commission that the City Electric System and the Florida Keys Aqueduct Authority had indicated they could supply the necessary power and water. And Aguero contended that the developer would "do what is necessary" to ensure that sewage requirements were met. The attorney for the developer, former Florida State Senator William Neblett, argued that the city would benefit from increased property tax revenues and the construction would provide jobs for residents, who were being hurt by military cutbacks. Representatives of the local carpenters' and electricians' unions reinforced this claim. Neblett also emphasized, as a former president of the OIRF, that the older, historic areas of Key West would retain their character.[38]

William Westray, the president of the Old Key West Civic Association, presented to the city commission the arguments of several local groups opposed to the development. Westray contended that the high-rise condominiums the developers sought to build would tarnish the existing character of Key West's built environment. Further, the increased traffic would detract from the island's "laid-back" climate. In fact, he argued, the condominiums would hurt Key West's effort to become a tourism-based economy, which, he agreed, was increasingly essential as the military downsized. In addition to asking the city commission to oppose the developer's request for a zoning change, Westray urged the city to limit the height of all buildings to four stories or 40 feet. Dr. Arthur Weiner, who spoke for the Florida Keys Citizens Coalition, composed of several different civic and conservation organizations, emphasized many environmentalists' concern that due to the limited carrying capacity of the Florida Keys, new development would result in a lower quality of life for everyone. A spokesperson for the owner of the Southernmost Motel, who claimed to speak for most motel owners, also questioned the "scale" of the project relative to the rest of the island.[39]

This opposition did not sway the city commission. In July 1973, it voted unanimously to approve the zoning and density changes the developer had requested. Opponents of the high-rise development, however, did not give up the fight. Westray and Gene Skaggs became the spokesperson and president, respectively, of a new organization, the Greater Key West Citizens Association, which filed a suit challenging the city's zoning ordinance. Westray summarized the organization's views as follows: "We already have water and sewer problems, overcrowded schools, and an increasing crime rate, and yet the local government is rubber-stamping a lot of high-density projects that will destroy the whole character of Key West."[40]

The association also initiated a referenda petition drive that apparently garnered enough signatures to place two issues on the ballot: the first called for the city to repeal its approval of the condominiums and the second for the city to adopt a policy to limit the height of multiple family units to four stories. Proponents of the petitions displayed yellow bumper stickers on their cars proclaiming "No High Rises on the Keys." City Attorney Manuel James, before his indictment on drug smuggling charges the following year, ruled in May 1974 that the petitions, which almost one-third of Key West's registered citizens had signed, were not legally adequate. Circuit Court Judge M. Ignatius Lester, however, overturned James's ruling. Recognizing that the citizens would vote for both referenda, the city commission in November 1974 passed ordinances that accomplished the referenda's goals.[41]

Later in the decade, other development proposals likewise divided the community. *Solares Hill*, a newly organized "alternative" newspaper named for the "highest point of Key West, literally and spiritually," represented the views of many environmentalists and other opponents of rampant development and focused attention on these conflicts. William Huckel, its editor, had found his way to Key West in the 1960s. He became known as "Dancing Bill" and "the king of the hippies," at least to some Key Westers. Huckel recalled in 1970, when he was 32 years old, how he had earned the nickname "Dancing Bill": "when I first got here I felt so released, free, happy that I danced all the time, in the bars and in the streets." He noted, "I can communicate with the kids. . . . It's the establishment I can't communicate with." Huckel's newspaper became his vehicle for "communicating" with the establishment.[42]

Conflicts related to development were not always confined to the city commission chambers, the courtroom, or the ballot. After a successful effort by Westray and others in 1978 to block a proposed development, Westray's car had acid poured over it and its tires slashed, and tar was poured over his house. Westray, a former military officer, readied himself for a recurrence by keeping several loaded pistols and rifles in his house. Key West's famed laid-back, live-and-let-live attitude was apparently not universal, especially when the opportunity to make significant profits was at stake.[43]

The Cost of Gentrification?

Key Westers' successful mobilization against rampant development likely enhanced Key West's allure for visitors and purchasers of vacation homes. The renovation and gentrification of Old Town also increased Key West's tourist appeal, which benefited businesses associated with tourism. In the eyes of some, gentrification and enhanced tourism provided Conchs with significant benefits. Although it was primarily newcomers to Key West who purchased and renovated the Old Town houses, these projects, they argued, provided employment for many Conchs skilled in carpentry and other trades. In the words of the gentrifier Marvin Brandwen, "The natives recognized that the new homeowners and restorers, as well as the tourists they attract, give them one vital thing: more money."[44]

Many Conchs and other longtime residents of Key West worked to spur tourism and revitalization as well as benefited from it. Not all Conchs, however, benefited from the increase in home values that gentrification produced. In fact, some left the community, unable to cope with the financial stress the changing community imposed on them. After the city reassessed property values in 1978, property taxes increased dramatically for many Old Town households, making it difficult for some families to meet their expenses.[45] Some moved to New Town, while others left Key West altogther. Joe Pinder described this process: "You take a conch family that has lived in that old section of Key West all their life. Now, suddenly, some very wealthy person from New York buys a house for an inflated price of $70,000 to $80,000, and they'll put $150,000 in restoring it, fixing it up, stuff like that. . . . When they reassess this year [the Conch family is] not gonna be able to afford to live in that house. . . . This is gonna force a lot of people to put their homes on the market. They'll leave town. The conchs are being driven out." Monroe County's property appraiser agreed with Pinder's analysis, after finding, before the reassessment, that about 200 to 300 Conch homes had been purchased "by the wealthy."[46]

A City in Transition

By the end of the 1970s, Key West had been discovered, or rediscovered, by writers, celebrities, hippies, gays, yachtsmen, and many others. The writer and photographer Tom Corcoran recollects his time working as a bartender in the Chart Room Bar in the Pier House in 1974. "One day in late September I walked into the Chart Room for the 4pm to 10pm shift. . . . It was a full house. Truman Capote, Annie Leibovitz, Burgess Meredith, Margot Kidder and Warrren Oates at the bar. Peter Fonda . . . and McGuane were standing, along with a usual assortment of locals. That was the moment I knew that something had happened to our quiet little island—a change that never would be reversed." Corcoran realized that the island had "truly been 'discovered'" in spring 1977, when he noticed that large numbers of college students descended upon Key West over spring break. Many spring breakers had discovered Ft. Lauderdale and other Florida beach communities during the 1950s, a phenomenon popularized in the film *Where the Boys Are* (1960). Now they had found their way to the southernmost city. In addition to the spring breakers, other types of visitors were arriving in Key West in the late 1970s in larger numbers than at the start of the decade. They visited for a variety of reasons, but they shared the desire to experience an environment different from the world of Disney.[47]

As the vote in 1980 against the tourist tax indicated, many citizens questioned the thrust toward mass tourism, and some community studies only confirmed their doubts. An assessment of Key West's economy at the end of the 1970s concluded, "Despite the City's unquestionable attraction for tourists and its relaxed and pleasant atmosphere for residents, Key West is a troubled community." The study noted that Key West's growing reliance on tourism had several potentially negative consequences. Tourism-related industries generally provided low-paying jobs with few opportunities for advancement. The seasonal nature of the tourism-based economy attracted a significant number of transient workers who worked during the winter months for low wages and then relocated during the slow season. These workers took jobs from Key West's native populations and kept the community's wage scales low.

In addition, the report issued a warning about a potential trend in the real estate market. It noted:

> due to the perceived idyllic setting and atmosphere of Key West, the potential exists . . . [for housing to be purchased by] non-resident speculators and [subjected to] subsequent resale for high profit. While this is not unhealthy in a balanced economy, it increases real estate values for the resident population who are hampered by low wages and limited job prospects. In addition, many year-round rental units have been converted into seasonal tourist facilities, as owners can get as much from several months rental to tourists as from a year's rental to local residents. This also removes rental housing units from the year-round market and tightens the housing market in terms of both availability and costs.[48]

The report emphasized that although in 1978 housing in Key West was still cheaper than in the rest of South Florida, it was relatively more expensive for residents due to their lower incomes. Further, by 1979 housing costs were rising more rapidly in Key West than in the rest of the region. The report recommended, among other things, that Key West broaden its economic base and cultivate businesses that offered its citizens jobs with opportunity for advancement and enhanced the taxable property base on which the city depended.[49]

Some Key Westers, Conchs and newer arrivals alike, focused more on discouraging tourism than on diversifying the economy. Tennessee Williams in 1980 still was enamored with his community, observing, "Key West has the most character of any town I've ever visited—It's like being in another country." He also feared that it was changing for the worse and urged, "please don't hurry down here: the island has finally run out of coral-rock extensions into the sea. . . . And there is almost nothing at all to do but drink or swim or . . ."[50]

Of course, this description was as likely to attract newcomers as to keep them away. In fact, Key West was about to embark on a new phase bought a two-story house on Fleming Street in 1986 and restored it as both their home and the office for the advertising agency Marlowe had started. They later purchased the house next door, renovated it, and moved there in 1991. The composer Jerry Herman, well known for writing the music for several Broadway plays, including "Mame" and "Dolly," became a part-time resident of Key West in 1986. Herman had been a frequent visitor to Key West, and he and his partner, Marty Finkelstein, had formed a business that purchased and renovated Old Town homes. Among Herman's renovations were two adjacent homes on Fleming Street; one had been cut up into three apartments and the other into a rooming house. Herman transformed both into single-family homes, moved into one, and sold the other for $435,000.[6]

Although many of Key West's gay residents were financially well-off, others were not. A lower-income gay resident in Key West, who in 1986 was making ends meet by doing renovations for a wealthy gay lawyer, offered this perspective on life at the subsistence level: "'Life is a Breeze in the Florida Keys. Or as Matt likes to say—who spends his life catering to the whims of the rich, working hard to afford his piece of paradise—"On Your Hands and Knees in the Florida Keys."'"[7]

Night Life

Key West's gay population frequented the night scene on and near Duval Street. Some destinations primarily attracted gay customers, while others attracted a mix of Key West's residential and tourist populations. For many, Captain Tony's Saloon was among the "places to go." Howie's Lounge, near the Pier House on lower Duval, was also popular. Many went to see Coffee Butler play late at night, and Jimmy Buffett sometimes gave "spontaneous performances" there.[8]

When the Monster opened on Front Street in Key West in 1975, the nightclub became an instant hit with gays and straights, Key Westers and visitors, alike. The original Monster opened on Fire Island in 1970, another destination for many of Key West's gay tourists. Often, after the Monster's doors closed at 2 a.m., those inside would shed their few remaining inhibitions, partying into the early morning. Celebrities, including Devine, Eartha Kitt, Phyllis Diller, and Leonard Bernstein, frequented the Monster while visiting Key West.[9]

of tourism, one that would increasingly permeate the community. Tourism was the key to Key West's future and, although it was less obvious to most, so too was the accompanying appreciation in real estate values. Key West's growing gay population played a significant role in the island's burgeoning tourism industry and the gentrification of Old Town. Its presence, however, also reinforced the perception that the island, although changing, was still a relatively unique place.

8

The Gay Community and
the Transformation of Key West

DURING THE 1980S, the size of Key West's population changed very little, increasing 2.2 percent from 24,292 in 1980 to 24,832 in 1990. The population increased at roughly the same pace during the 1990s (2.6 percent), reaching 25,478 by 2000. During these two decades, however, the composition of the city's population changed dramatically, as many moved to and from Key West. In 1980, about 44 percent of the city's population occupied the same house as they had five years earlier. By 1990, only 38 percent of those living in Key West, compared to 44 percent of all Floridians, reported occupying the same residence as they had in 1985. The mobility only accelerated during the first half of the 1990s. By the end of the century, Key West had relatively few long-term residents.[1]

The black community's share of the population decreased from about 11.4 percent in 1980 to 10 percent in 2000. Key West's Cuban population also decreased, from 10.9 to 7.8 percent of the total population, as did the entire Hispanic population, from 20.1 to 16.5 percent. In the meantime, increasing numbers of Eastern Europeans, largely from Poland, the

Czech Republic, and Russia, immigrated to Key West durin Many such newcomers worked in the community's touri employed by hotels, motels, guesthouses, and restaurar the men also worked on construction jobs, and a number women worked in the city's adult entertainment industry.[2]

While the military remained a presence in Key West, it near as significant as before the downsizing of the 1970s the 1990s the number of military personnel further decr meantime, the number of retirees living in the city increase Conchs. Others were among those who had joined the cor ing their working years, including some military person families, and decided to stay. Yet another group had worl and then retired to Key West.[3]

The most dramatic influx of new residents to Key West who by the late 1970s constituted a significant portion population. They continued to move to the island through century, although some stayed for only a brief period. Mo Town, constituting as much as 30 percent of the neighborl tion in 1983, and were the primary drivers of its gentrifical Lesbian Atlas, based on information gathered in the U.S. C 2000 Census, concluded that Key West had the eighth high tion of gay and lesbian couples of any city in the United it was Key West's number of gay, rather than lesbian, cou the high ranking. As Manuel Castells found in his study o hoods in San Francisco, gay Key Westers created a com Town, not only by residing in that particular neighborh opening businesses, meeting in bars, inventing celebratic ing in politics.[4]

Many gay men employed in the tourism industry w summer working in Provincetown, Massachusetts, on (other locations, returning to Key West at the end of the made Key West their full-time residence. One young ga moved to Key West from upstate New York explained pa tion, "People who are gay feel like outsiders in a lot of pla it's just the opposite. You feel you are on the inside here

During the 1980s and 1990s, gay men continued to in Old Town, and property values escalated. For exampl and Del Brixey moved to Key West from Chicago in the e

Delmonico's at 218 Duval Street also became a popular bar. Delmonico's had a long history in Key West, operating at different times as a restaurant or a bar, and during prohibition as a speakeasy. Jonathan Amoral and Eleanor "Babe" Moskal of Massachusetts opened their version of Delmonico's in 1976, and emphasized that it appealed to the dominant culture in Key West, which "believes in the total freedom of the individual."[10]

In 1977, two gay men opened The Affair, a bar and restaurant on the 900 block of Duval Street. Although The Affair operated for only about a year, it gained widespread attention in January 1978 when the national gay magazine *After Dark* ran a cover story on the island. The story featured a picture of Bobby Nesbitt, a piano player and vocalist who had moved to Key West from New York City in 1976, at The Affair. The magazine also included several pictures of gay men in scanty bathing suits enjoying themselves in Key West. The article described Key West as possessing an "indefinable magnetic field, a beneficent Bermuda Triangle that drugs one into a dreamy stupor." And, it reported, "cocaine is as available as Key Lime pie."

From the late 1970s through most of the 1980s, Claire's on upper Duval, owned by Claire and Marvin Paige, was a popular restaurant and bar. According to one observer, it was, for a time, "the most popular night spot for interesting dining and a wild, social bar, the most 'in' spot since the Monster." Thursday evening was Claire's designated "girl's night" for Key West's growing lesbian population. A few lesbian bars appeared during the late 1970s, including Anabek's Bar and Twigg Bar. Lesbians also frequented Café 416 on Applerouth Lane, operated by "Stretch."[11]

The Copa, a primarily gay dance club, opened in 1981 in the building on the 600 block of Duval that had housed the Monroe Theater. Its attractions included drag shows and Wet Jockey Shorts nights, and it was traditionally the scene of a popular New Year's Eve celebration. The Copa remained a prime destination for gay residents and tourists until it burned down in 1995. The *Miami Herald* headline to its story about the fire captured the essence of The Copa: "Ten Years of Debauchery Goes up in Flames."[12]

After the fire, the owner of The Copa opened another gay venue, The Epoch, in the same building, but it was never as popular as The Copa. Joe Shroeder, a gay businessman, along with Jim Gilleran, who had been

The Copa's manager at the time of the fire, helped to revitalize the gay night-scene by creating the Bourbon St. Pub Complex. Shroeder opened the Bourbon Street Pub at 724 Duval Street in October 1995. He and Gilleran then purchased the building that had housed the 801 Bar and changed its name to the 801 Bourbon Bar, which began to offer regular drag shows upstairs at the 801 Cabaret, featuring nightly performances by the 801 girls, including Sushi, Margo, and Destray. They moved One Saloon, a "leather & Levi" gay bar, next door to the 801, and the New Orleans House guesthouse also became part of the complex. In 2002, Jill McDonald opened the Aqua night club across Duval Street from the Bourbon Street Pub. The club, which was home to Inga and other well-known Key West drag queens, became a major component of Key West's "Pink Triangle."[13]

Tourism and the Gay Community

Many gay Key Westers became directly involved in the tourism business by renovating buildings and converting them into guesthouses that attracted primarily gay tourists. The prominent gay writer Edmund White concluded in *States of Desire: Travels in Gay America* that in 1979 Key West had "more and better gay accommodations for tourists than any other resort." About fifty such accommodations had opened by mid-1982, along with a few lesbian guesthouses.[14]

Jim Camp opened Island House, one of the earliest gay guesthouses, on Fleming Street in Old Town in 1976. Two years later, Lawrence Formica started La Te Da, a guesthouse with a bar and restaurant, on Duval Street near the Atlantic. Its name derived from the building's longtime moniker La Terraza de Marti, based on the fact that in the 1890s José Martí had spoken from its balcony, urging Key West's Cubans to support Cuba's fight for independence from Spain. The building was now used for far different purposes. In the words of one realtor, the establishment was, in the early 1980s, "probably the most decadent place in Key West." Formica, who was easily recognized driving around town in his pink Cadillac convertible, admitted that an "element of voyeurism" accounted for its attraction, referring no doubt to the prevalence of topless or bottomless sunbathing at the guesthouse. Open drug use was also common, a practice that Formica said he tried to discourage, although he made "a point of not checking what my guests do." Some, in fact, claimed that it was common for guests to be "greeted in their rooms with a line of coke and a houseboy placed at their disposal." La Te Da was also well known for hosting afternoon Tea Dances, and in 1991 the Atlantic Shores motel, located nearby on South Street, joined in the festivities. Around 7 p.m., participants in the Tea Dances would leave La Te Da for Atlantic Shores, which included a popular clothing-optional deck and pool area.[15]

La Te Da gained national attention in 1980 when Elizabeth Weigand, the niece of the Missouri senator Thomas Eagleton, claimed that Eagleton was "bisexual, if not totally gay" and emphasized that he had been seen at La Te Da, "disheveled and unshaven." A U.S. District Court found both Weigand and her lawyer guilty of conspiracy and extortion for threatening to turn over "damaging information" about Eagleton to a newspaper if he refused to buy her shares in a family-owned company. Eagleton testified that he hadn't purchased the stock because he suspected that Weigand and her attorney would transfer the money to their church, the Church of Scientology.[16]

Among the other popular gay guesthouses were the Lighbourn Inn on Truman Avenue, not far from Duval Street, and Alexander's on Fleming Street. The cigar manufacturer Walter Sayers Lighbourn built the former in 1903 for his son Walter James Lighbourn. Scott Fuhriman and Kelly Summers, AKA the Bitch Sisters, later the Queens of Fantasy Fest 2000, purchased the dilapidated property in 1991, renovating and reopening it as a guesthouse in 1993. Marlowe and Brixey purchased and renovated an old boarding house on Fleming Street and opened Alexander's, a ten-room guesthouse they named after their pet canary.[17]

Gay migrants to Key West also started other types of businesses that benefited from the tourist trade. Among them were two of the original organizers of Fantasy Fest, Frank Romano and Joe Liszka. In 1971, they opened the Key West Fragrance and Cosmetic Factory, commonly known as Key West Aloe, which became a prominent perfume and cosmetics business. By 1978, their business, located on Front Street, had grown to around 85 employees and was generating $4 million annually from the sale of perfume and cosmetics, which boasted names such as Sexy Afternoon and Cayo Hueso.[18] Tony Falcone and Bill Conkle, also among the organizers of Fantasy Fest, opened the very successful Fast Buck Freddie's department store in the former Kress Building on Duval Street.[19]

Gay business owners organized to increase gay tourism to the island. Initially, the owners of two nightclubs and several gay guesthouses simply financed advertisements in national publications, publicizing Key West as a gay tourist destination. In April 1978, they formed the Key West Business Guild to promote tourism and to foster the involvement of the gay business community in civic activities. The guild also raised funds for crime prevention, an effort provoked partially by the fact that some gay tourists and residents, including Tennessee Williams, had been assaulted on the streets of Key West. In addition, the guild sponsored voter registration drives and endorsed candidates for office. Later, recognizing the importance of gay tourism, some straight business owners joined the organization. By 1982, the guild had grown to include 170 businesses, including mainstream enterprises such as Alamo Rent-A-Car.[20]

Organizing the Gay Community

Gay Key Westers formed other organizations that enabled them to meet, interact, and get involved in the community. One of the most significant of these organizations was the Metropolitan Community Church (MCC) that Gerry Franz and others organized in 1980. Initially, twelve members of MCC Key West held services at the Woman's Club on Duval Street, whose president, Wilhelmina Harvey, welcomed them. After Steven Torrence arrived from Seattle in 1985 to become the church's minister, the congregation grew, and the MCC received a sizable gift that led to a fundraising campaign for a permanent facility. MCC purchased a building on Petronia Street in Old Town, renovated it, and moved to the new location in the late 1980s. In addition to continuing as the MCC's pastor, Torrence joined the Key West Police Department in 1991 and served as its chaplain. On May 1, 2003, he became the first openly gay clergy member to lead the U.S. House of Representatives in prayer on the National Day of Prayer.[21]

Torrence, Tom Puroff, and Betty Campbell founded AIDS Help in 1986 to help members of the community cope with the devastating disease. Help Line, an affiliate of AIDS Help, provided 24-hour phone lines for people in distress. Many in the gay community organized fundraising drives for AIDS Help, including Gordon Ross and Friends, who drew large crowds at The Copa and other venues. Beginning in 1989, the funds raised by the candidates for the King and Queen of Fantasy Fest were all donated to AIDS Help, the winner of each crown being the candidate who had raised the most money. The Key West Wreckers Club, a men's organization of gays and bisexuals, also raised money for AIDS Help, Hospice, and several other organizations. Two Key West doctors, Dr. Jerome Covington and Dr. Mark Whiteside, gained a national reputation for their work with AIDS patients and their focus on AIDS prevention.[22]

Steve Smith was hired as the director of volunteers for AIDS Help after he moved to Key West in 1988. Shortly afterward, Smith organized a fundraiser to finance the construction of an AIDS residential compound. In a single evening, supporters contributed $750,000, and the Marty Finkelstein Center opened in the early 1990s to provide housing for some of those who were suffering from AIDS.[23]

Decades later, Gordon Ross recalled this period in Key West: "It was the best of times that morphed into the very worst of times. Slowly but surely people were getting ill . . . VERY ILL and dying. It affected every business and every aspect of people's daily lives here. . . . At its awful peak, it was nothing for me and others to attend three to four funerals a month (if not more) and at those funerals you'd speak to others who had just begun to be sick, fearing they would be next."[24]

Several people and organizations raised funds to establish a Key West AIDS Memorial at the end of White Street on the Atlantic Ocean, the first of its kind in the country. At the time of its dedication on World AIDS Day, December 1, 1997, the memorial included the names of 760 citizens of the Keys who had died of AIDS. By mid-2004, more than a thousand names appeared on the memorial, which was maintained by a private group, the Friends of the Key West AIDS Memorial.[25]

The Gay and Lesbian Community Center of Key West opened in 1997 to serve as a resource center for gays and lesbians, as well as to document and preserve the history of their presence in Key West. Two years later, it sponsored the first annual Pride Follies during PrideFest, which became its major fundraising effort. The center succeeded in raising enough funds to finance a permanent facility, which was completed in 2004.[26]

Many gay newcomers also joined organizations that were not specifically identified with the gay community. James McLernan was a prominent example. Born on Staten Island, he worked in Los Angeles as the head of advertising and sales for a magazine before moving to Key West in the early 1970s. McLernan was successful as a real estate investor and broker. More generally, however, he became one of the city's best-known and active citizens. McLernan was the first president of the Founders Society, which formed in 1979 to support the performing arts at the

Tennessee Williams Fine Arts Center at the Florida Keys Community College. He also served on several boards, including those of the Old Island Restoration Foundation and the Key West Art & Historical Society. McLernan was one of the leaders of the environmental organization Last Stand which was organized in the late 1980s, and he served as its president for several years.[27]

Political Mobilization: the Election of Richard Heyman

The growing number and organization of gay residents in Key West translated into political involvement. The successful candidacy of Richard Heyman, initially for a four-year term on the city commission in 1979 and then for a two-year term for mayor in 1983 and again in 1987, represented significant electoral successes for Key West's gay population and indicated that many Key Westers were willing to vote for a gay candidate for office. In winning these contests, Heyman, who had moved to Key West from Ohio in the early 1970s and opened, with Lee Dodez, the Gingerbread Square Gallery on Duval Street, became one of the first openly gay elected officials in the United States and the first openly gay mayor.[28]

Heyman and his backers believed that the growing gay population in Key West, as well as other newcomers to the community, needed a political voice on the city commission. Some Conchs who had opposed McCoy during the 1970s were also eager for political change. Heyman and many of his supporters advocated a growth management perspective on development, especially in Old Town. They were also critical of the mayor and commissioners' common practice of holding unadvertised "workshops" in the mayor's office, during which they made decisions on important issues without public input. In addition, some gay guesthouse owners in the Business Guild contended that the police department was often unresponsive when their guests faced threats.[29]

Peter Ilchuk, a gay migrant to Key West from Washington, D.C., was instrumental in persuading Heyman to run for the city commission. He closed his guesthouse temporarily to work as Heyman's campaign manager. Dennis Bitner, the owner of Club Bath, a gay bathhouse, and several others also played major roles. Partisanship had next to no role in Key West's nonpartisan elections, which did not list a candidate's party affiliation on the ballot. Rather, candidates' own organizations were vital to their securing votes. Heyman finished second out of five candidates in the initial election and then won the runoff. Heyman's victory came just two years after Harvey Milk, one of the first openly gay officeholders in the nation, was elected to the Board of Supervisors in San Francisco. And Heyman's success was especially noteworthy because he won a city-wide election, which necessitated gaining the support of many non-gay residents. Milk had unsuccessfully run in citywide races in San Francisco and won only after San Francisco changed its electoral system to district elections.[30]

Heyman was often on the losing side of votes on the city commission. For example, in April 1982, he was the only commissioner to vote in favor of urging the Florida legislature to support the national Equal Rights Amendment. Mary Lee Graham, the only woman on the city commission, voted against the measure. Commissioner James Mira, in justifying his opposition, assured the commissioners, "Most of the women I asked, believe you me, they like things the way they are."[31]

Still, in 1983, Heyman entered the race for mayor. Heyman and other gay activists were well aware that despite his victory in the 1979 election, many politically connected Key Westers resisted sharing political power with members of the gay community. For decades, Key West's mayors and other office holders had primarily been native-born Conchs. True, there were several exceptions shortly after the Second World War, when Key West's population increased significantly. C. B. Harvey, a retired military officer who was born in Louisiana, served as mayor from 1951 to 1957 and then again from 1961 to 1963. The fact that Harvey married Wilhelmina Goehring, a well-known Conch who later was elected to the Monroe County School Board and in 1980 became the first woman elected to the county commission, likely aided his political success. The four mayors after Harvey were all Key West natives, and many still characterized the political system as a "Bubba system," which provided jobs and favors to political insiders, most of whom were Conchs. While gay men now played a significant role in Key West's business community, how receptive the political system would be remained uncertain.[32]

Conch Mayor Dennis Wardlow, who had been elected mayor in 1981 after serving on the city commission from 1973 to 1977, had not hesitated to criticize newcomers to Key West. In 1982, he complained that some would "love to see the Conchs all leave town and turn this into another Fire Island or Cape Cod." If Heyman won, Wardlow warned, the city would "lose the family-oriented tourists" and the town would turn into a gay resort. He complained that the "true history of Key West" was "being lost": "We're winding up with something that some northerner thinks Key West should look like. It's not the true Key West." Wardlow also criticized the renovators' approach to restoring old Conch houses: "[they] go in there and completely gut the thing and make it something that it has never been, with big rooms and all. They call this history. Conch houses always had small rooms, like on a ship. These houses now have big rooms. The exterior has been painted and dolled up like George-town." In reality, he noted, the Conchs seldom painted their houses, and when they did they used the battleship gray paint they were able to procure from the Navy base.[33]

Even some in the tourism industry questioned the desirability of the growth of gay tourism. They contended that Key West should not go down the slippery slope of promoting itself as a gay tourist community, which, they argued, would discourage other visitors. One manager of a restaurant noted, "there are a lot more straights than gays in this world—even if you couldn't tell it from downtown Key West."[34]

This sentiment was echoed by Charlie Ramos, who had left politics in 1964 after serving one term in the state legislature to devote his time to overseeing his family's real estate holdings and beer distributorship. Ramos bemoaned the potential weakening of the Conchs' power base in Key West and complained, "Every time you go to a cocktail party the talk is, who's leaving the town next?" He advised environmentalists to "give up on Key West. This isn't an environmentally endangered island." True, Ramos did not explicitly target the island's gay population; although not "out of the closet," he himself was a gay Conch. Still, Heyman and many of his gay and straight supporters were among those outsiders that Ramos was, at least implicitly, criticizing.[35]

Wardlow opted out of running for another term for mayor in 1983. Instead, Richard Kerr, a former member of the Monroe County Commission and the Key West Utility Board, entered the race against Heyman. Kerr ran as "Richard Kerr—family man," and he associated Heyman with a gang of "morally insensitive radicals." He also emphasized that voters were choosing between a native-born Key Wester, who was "proud to be a Bubba," and a relative newcomer, who was looking to buck the Bubba system. Although the mayor of Key West did not have significantly more power than did the city commissioners in the city's commission-manager form of government, many viewed the election as symbolically important and knew that the mayor could play an active role in establishing the agenda and promoting policy. Sonny McCoy had been one such mayor during his tenure in the 1970s.[36]

Conch City Commissioner Joe Balbontin vocally supported Kerr. Balbontin, the owner of a plumbing company, had drawn some attention when he suggested during a commission debate on banning topless sunbathing that this practice was part of a Russian-inspired plot to demoralize the American people and to make the United States vulnerable to a Russian takeover. He had no immediate response when Heyman held up a matchbook cover featuring a topless woman in an advertisement for Balbontin's business. Balbontin observed during the campaign that some voters feared "if a gay got elected as mayor, then it would get in every paper in the nation and it would bring more of them down here."[37]

The city's gay population saw the election as an important measure of their ability, as relatively new residents of Key West, to translate their numbers into electoral success, and from there into policy change. They initiated a massive drive for voter registration, including at The Copa and other predominantly gay nightclubs. Although Heyman actively sought gay support, during the campaign he did not focus primarily on identity politics. Instead, Heyman's campaign slogan called for "fair laws, fairly applied." He did not challenge the city's increasing reliance on tourism. Indeed, during his term on the city commission, Heyman had supported Key West's efforts to attract tourism. For example, he advocated changing the law to allow liquor to be sold and consumed at Mallory Square with the permission of the city commission. This, he argued, would enhance the attraction of Key West to tourists, as well as provide revenue to the Tourist Development Association, which promoted Fantasy Fest.[38]

Heyman advocated greater governmental regulation of the growth pressures Key West was facing. He especially criticized the lack of proper planning for Old Town, where two time-share projects were being built, and advocated a new zoning designation for the Historic Preservation District around Duval Street. Heyman argued that the city needed tighter controls over the types of businesses that could set up shop in the high-density Duval Street area, because without tighter controls new businesses could generate loud noise and traffic in the still primarily residential area. City policy, Heyman emphasized, needed to preserve the charm and character of the island, which both attracted new people and was valued by existing residents.[39]

In addition to appealing to gay voters, preservationists, and advocates of growth management, Heyman sought the support of African American voters. As a city commissioner, he had recommended that Key West change from the at-large (citywide) system of elections to district elections, a change many African Americans also supported. Both Emery Major, the NAACP's president, and Rose Kee, the president of an African American women's organization, had threatened legal action against the city if the system was not changed. Lang Milian had been elected to the city commission in 1971, the first black to be elected since early in the twentieth century. He had lost his bid for reelection in 1975, and no other blacks had been elected to the commission since.[40]

Two candidates running for commission seats, Emma Cates, a third-generation Conch who owned a health-food store on Duval Street, and George Halloran, a general contractor who had moved to Key West several years earlier, advocated perspectives that were similar to those of Heyman. The three candidates coordinated their campaign efforts, hoping to gain office and thereby constitute a majority of the five-person city commission, which included the mayor. All were successful. Heyman defeated Kerr, gaining 52.6 percent of the vote in a high-turnout election. Heyman then endorsed both Cates and Halloran, who, failing to secure 50 percent of the votes, had to compete in runoff races for their commission seats. Both won in their runoffs.[41]

After his election, Heyman did not propose gay rights legislation. He later remarked there "was no need for gay issues in Key West," and suggested that legislation along these lines would be "superfluous." Still, not everyone was happy with Heyman's victory or some of the changes he proposed after gaining office, including his successful effort in 1984 to persuade voters to support a new city charter. Among those who opposed him were several members of the police department, who felt that the new charter would weaken the department's relative autonomy and grant the city commission and the mayor more authority over them. This conflict fueled a much-publicized incident, which occurred shortly before the charter vote. Heyman was driving downtown in his van and picked up an inebriated man, who he then drove to the Island House, a gay guesthouse in Old Town. Heyman then went to Delmonico's, where he was apprehended by a police officer who claimed that Heyman had engaged in oral sex at the corner of Truman and Simonton. The state attorney refused to press charges, concluding that no evidence existed to substantiate the accusation.[42]

Heyman did not seek reelection in 1985 for health reasons but ran again in 1987 and defeated former mayor Sonny McCoy in the runoff election. Heyman secured his biggest margin of victory in precinct 6, a downtown district comprising primarily newcomers to the city, many of them gay. Only three of the ten districts supported McCoy and not by significant margins. Heyman had succeeded in building an electoral coalition that spanned most segments of Key West's population. After his term ended in 1989, however, he chose to leave political office. Five years later, Heyman died of an AIDS-related disease.[43]

The Fight for Gay Rights

Despite the gay community's political successes, a controversy that erupted in 1995 over who could participate in a Christmas parade showed that some still viewed gay Key Westers as second-class citizens. That year, Metropolitan Community Church's application to enter a float in the Christmas parade was rejected by the parade's organizers, the Lower Keys Ministerial Association. Gary Redwine, the pastor of the Big Coppitt First Baptist Church, located several miles outside of Key West, argued that allowing the MCC to participate in the parade would be tantamount to endorsing a way of life that "we believe is not in accordance with the image of biblical morality and family that we wish to project." Redwine added, "It's not that we hate homosexuals or anything. We just don't agree with homosexuality, and we can't condone the homosexual life style." It seemed that at least some in the Keys had become no more accommodating of gays since the Baptist minister Morris Wright had urged his congregation in the late 1970s to strike out against "female impersonators and queers."[44]

Many Key Westers protested the rejection of the MCC by the parade's organizers. Ann Boese, the publisher of the *Bone Island Press*, observed, "Most people think it's stupid. The gay community is involved in everything. Then you come to a Christmas parade without a political agenda, and all of a sudden this silent, disapproving minority is able to exert power." The City of Key West responded by withdrawing its financing for the parade. In addition, Mayor Dennis Wardlow, who had been elected in 1991, Monroe County Mayor Shirley Freeman, and the city commissioners refused to march in the parade. Wardlow's perspective appeared to have changed dramatically since his first term as mayor in the early 1980s, before Heyman's election. Now he noted, "I think it is hypocritical on the part of the association. Key West is a very tolerant town. We've always had a live-and-let-live feel. We're all God's children; we're all created equally. That's what I think the Bible says." Two churches who were to have floats in the parade withdrew in protest, and St. Paul's Episcopal Church allowed Rev. Steve Torrence of the MCC to view the parade from the church on Duval Street and "offer up prayers for a tolerant and inclusive community." The city of Key West then organized its own Christmas parade in which the MCC participated.[45]

Like the controversy over the Christmas parade, other incidents indicated that discrimination against gays did exist in the community. For example, in the late 1980s members of the Key West Yacht Club blackballed a gay Key Wester who had been sponsored for membership. The Key West Historic Memorial Sculpture Garden on Mallory Square, which opened in the mid-1990s, did not include a bust of Tennessee Williams because some of those responsible for choosing the 36 Key Westers to be honored in the garden did not want to celebrate a gay person.[46]

During the late 1980s and the 1990s, gay citizens successfully pushed for gay rights legislation. Ilchuk was one of the organizers of the Key West Human Rights Committee, which was associated with the Human Rights Campaign Fund, a national group that endorsed candidates who supported gay rights. The Key West Business Guild strengthened and expanded its membership base. Both the Human Rights Committee and the Business Guild advocated antidiscrimination legislation, and the city commission responded by amending the Key West Human Rights Ordinance in 1991 to legally protect gays and lesbians from discrimination.[47]

In 1995, several gay Democrats formed the Key West chapter of the Lambda Democrats, which by early 1996 had approximately thirty members who were active in the local Democratic Party. One of the candidates the Lambda Democrats backed for the city commission was Jimmy Weekley, who was initially elected to the commission in 1985 and was reelected several times before becoming mayor in 1999. On the urging of the Lambda Democrats and other of Key West's politically active gay organizations, Weekley sponsored a domestic-partner ordinance, which the commission passed in 1998. This legislation made Key West the first city in Florida to qualify domestic partners for the same employment benefits as a spouse. The Monroe County Board of County Commissioners shortly afterward adopted similar legislation.[48]

These civil-rights ordinances clearly reflected the political influence of Key West's gay population. Most of the gay men who were active in these organizations, as well as many others who were not politically involved, held prominent places in the city's new tourism economy. Key West's business and professional activists disagreed in the late 1970s over the community's thrust toward tourism, but the adoption of the tourist tax in 1981 signified and partially financed the island's future as a tourist town. Several prominent gay newcomers and the Business Guild worked with non-gay civic activists to gain voter approval for this tax and then to expand tourism during the next two decades.

9

Key West in the 1980s and 1990s

Bringing in the Tourists

Securing the Tourist Tax

Key West's tourism industry suffered in 1980, due both to the national recession and to the attention Key West received owing to its involvement in an international event. The Mariel boatlift brought thousands of refugees from Castro's Cuba to Key West. The first boats left Mariel in April, and by the time the exodus ended in September over 125,000 persons had fled Cuba. Many Cubans living in the United States traveled to Key West and paid local boat captains to sail to Cuba and transport their family members and friends to the United States. Others drove to Key West with their boats hitched to boat trailers and made the journey to Cuba themselves. Some of the refugees from Cuba who reached Key West boarded a bus to reunite with other Cubans who had earlier immigrated to Miami. Others were transported by plane from Key West to

Wardlow made it clear before the proclamation that the secession was well justified: "The only place the Border Patrol patrols is on the border of a foreign country. . . . If the Border Patrol was that concerned with catching illegal aliens they should move their roadblock around to I-95 or I-4 to Disney World and then see what reaction they get." Wardlow announced, "We will . . . declare war, fire one shot, surrender and then ask for $1 billion in foreign aid for the damage they've caused. . . . We might also ask the U.S. to pay us for the military use of our land here." The secession and rapid surrender took place, as planned, on April 23, 1982, and while it garnered no foreign aid, it did earn Key West significant national publicity.[14]

Key Westers began to commemorate the secession with an annual "Conch Republic Days" festival. This celebration was by no means the only festival to be initiated in Key West. Businesses, not-for-profit organizations, and civic groups participated in organizing tourist-related enterprises. The TDC helped to finance many of them and to publicize them to potential visitors. Key West had long been able to entice tourists with its weather, ambiance, fishing, and boating. Other visitors were attracted to various aspects of the island's historic heritage. Old Island Days had drawn visitors since the festival began in 1960, and the powerboat races in early November also drew tourists to the island. Other visitors came to participate in Fantasy Fest. Now, the promoters of tourism had the resources to provide additional support to these activities, as well as to initiate new festivals and sporting and cultural events. A prominent scholar of tourism has stressed that communities are more likely to be successful in attracting tourists if they offer different segments of the market a variety of potential experiences, adding that doing so involves the presentation of vehicles "for experiences which are to be collected, consumed and compared." Key West's tourism boosters pursued this strategy.[15]

Bringing In the Tourists

Fantasy Fest

The inaugural Fantasy Fest, held in 1979, was a relatively limited event, but its promoters hoped it would grow to become a major draw for tourists. The executive director of the Tourist Development Association

(TDA), which had been organized to plan Fantasy Fest, reported in late October on the day before the second annual Fantasy Fest in 1980 that many of the hotels and motels were fully booked. A newspaper report after the festival concluded, "crowded streets were a welcome sight to Key West business people this weekend after the disastrous effects the Cuban Freedom Flotilla had on tourism." After the parade, the director of the TDA declared that her goal was for Fantasy Fest to someday rival Mardi Gras.[16]

Although in 1981 Fantasy Fest attracted between 10,000 and 15,000 "revelers," the *Citizen* provided considerably more coverage to the World Powerboat races to be held in Key West that November than it did to Fantasy Fest. During the 1980s and 1990s, however, Fantasy Fest drew increased attention as tourists flocked to Key West around Halloween to observe or participate in the festivities. Each year, beginning in 1983, the TDA (later renamed the Association for Tourism Development) chose a new theme that, theoretically, would guide the floats and costumes for the Saturday night parade that served as the climax to the week's activities. For example, the theme in 1986 was "Fantasy in Space," in 1988 it was "B.C.," and in 1989 it was "Future Fantasies, Key West 2089." In 1990, participants in the parade were to envision "Caribbean Fantasies," and in 1996 came the "Call of the Wild."[17]

The number of tourists who visited Key West during Fantasy Fest increased, and the parade grew dramatically. Fewer than twenty floats participated in the first parade in 1979; by 1999, the parade had grown to seventy-five floats. The parade also attracted national corporate sponsors. In fact, by 1995, the official name of the nighttime parade had become the "Coors Light Fantasy Fest Parade." By 2001, Captain Morgan, rather than Coors, had become the sponsor of what was then known as the "Captain Morgan Fantasy Fest Parade."[18]

Beginning in 1987, a King and Queen of Fantasy Fest were chosen, and the two played a significant role in the events. The prominent place gays occupied both in the community and in the Fantasy Fest activities was highlighted in 1989 when the organizers of Fantasy Fest decided to choose the King and Queen based on which contestants had raised the most funds, all of which were donated to AIDS Help. In 1990, King George Murphy and Queen Pat Green raised over $30,000 for AIDS Help. In 1993, the winners raised almost $73,000 and in 1998 the amount more than doubled to $160,000.[19]

In response to complaints about risqué activities during the inaugural parade in 1979—primarily, Sister's display on the hood of the Lincoln—the TDA assured the community that in 1980 Fantasy Fest would offer "family friendly" events, including a Fantasy Fest children's party. The parade itself, however, remained the primary draw for most visitors, and many participants followed Sister's lead, wearing body paint as their only "attire."[20]

Before the activities in 1985, the parade's organizer reminded participants, "People can still have a great time without having to dress up as a sexual organ." Not everyone shared this sentiment. Some participants, for example, interpreted "B.C.," the theme of the parade in 1988, as "before clothes." George Murphy probably best expressed the dominant perspective by proclaiming during his successful campaign for king, "I want to instigate mayhem, frivolity, stupidity, hedonism and excess. And I'm also calling for the energetic disregard of propriety, decency, common sense and good taste."[21]

After the Fantasy Fest in 1992, complaints surfaced once again. Some were offended that a pickup truck in the parade, ostensibly one of the floats, had carried a couple simulating oral sex. Others were uncomfortable with another parade participant's costume, namely, a trench coat from which he flashed a huge phallus strapped to his waist. Still others objected to the symbolism associated with the parade's prize-winning float, "The Devil's Octopussy," created by Fast Buck Freddie's.[22]

Mayor Wardlow responded to the controversy by forming a "Mayor's Advisory Committee on Fantasy Fest," which was to investigate how the parade might be tamed. Most concluded that the parade was indeed calmer in 1993, probably due to a new city order allowing outdoor drinking at only six beer gardens and to a law enforcement helicopter hovering above. Not everyone welcomed this tameness, and some tourists threatened to skip Fantasy Fest in the future, unwelcome news for the city's hotel and motel proprietors, who significantly increased their prices and profits during the week of events.[23]

At a city commission meeting before the Fantasy Fest in 1994, "a determined Christian contingent worried about the decline of society" debated "hoteliers and business people worried about dwindling dollars." The Key West Chamber of Commerce, Key West Hotel and Motel Association, Key West Business Guild, and other organizations whose members benefited from tourism urged the commission to loosen the restrictions, and the city commission agreed to establish a "Fantasy Zone," streets where revelers could stumble around with their drinks in hand. The police also promised that the helicopter would not fly west of White Street. Most Fantasy Fest visitors seemed to approve of these changes. As the headline in the *Citizen* noted, "Consensus: Happy Days are here again for Fantasy Fest." And the 1995 parade, with its theme of "Tinseltown Dreams . . . Lights, Cameras, Fantasy," drew record crowds and more participants.[24]

Some Key Westers emphasized that the conflict over Fantasy Fest represented a more general debate about the character of their city. Their resistance to efforts to restrain behavior at Fantasy Fest symbolized their desire to make sure Key West remained a community that was different, tolerant, and not "generic." As Tony Falcone emphasized, "It's about the way things used to be . . . about the laissez-faire attitudes that for decades has attracted gays, hippies and intellectuals to the continent's southernmost resort." And Bruce Amsterdam, a radio personality and guesthouse owner, added that the controversy was due to a small number of people "who don't like pluralism."[25]

Other supporters of Fantasy Fest ignored the broader issues. What mattered most to them was that the tourists continue to flock to Fantasy Fest, which would be more likely if the festival retained its image as being different from most others in the country. In her study of the connections between city festivals and tourism between 1890 and 1915, Catherine Cocks emphasized, "The more commercial the festival became, the less important it was for the communities making up the city to represent themselves. Carnival fun rather than civic or historical symbolism became the key to attracting tourists." Although Fantasy Fest was initially identified primarily with the island's gay population, over time it came to strive more generally to attract tourists.[26]

Fantasy Fest, however, only drew visitors for several days toward the end of October. Key West's tourism boosters emphasized that festivals and attractions were necessary to complement Key West's drawing power and recognized that TDC money was available to subsidize the costs. During the 1980s and 1990s, additional festivals and attractions were initiated to draw more tourists to the island.

and included Porter's home and the cottage next door where Frost stayed when he visited. This component of the island's literary heritage, however, closed to the public in 2010 after the Porter family sold the home and cottage.[40]

The same year the Heritage House Museum closed, the Tennessee Williams in Key West exhibit opened for viewers at the Gay and Lesbian Community Center. The exhibit remained open into 2011 and, in addition, Dennis Beaver, a long-time activist in the island's gay community, along with the Key West Art & Historical Society, organized a week of events to celebrate the one hundredth anniversary of Williams's March 26 birthday. They also aspired to expand the celebration into an annual festival that might attract visitors to the island.

Bringing in the Tourists: Music

Jimmy Buffett's persona and music had been drawing tourists to Key West from as early as the mid-1970s after the release of his albums "A White Sport Coat and a Pink Crustacean" and "A1A" in 1973 and 1974, respectively. His album "Changes in Latitudes, Changes in Attitudes" (1977), with its hit song "Margaritaville," certainly drew more visitors. In 1973, after returning from a tour, Buffett noticed an increase in the number of tourists driving down the Keys. He drank a margarita at the Old Anchor Inn, one of his favorite Key West bars, and was inspired to write his testament to life on the island.[41] Tourists envisioned Key West as "Margaritaville," and they were anxious to experience its lifestyle.

In the late 1990s, Key West became the site of the "Meeting of the Minds," the annual convention of Parrot Heads in Paradise Inc., comprising some of Buffett's staunchest fans, hailing from chapters in the United States, Canada, and elsewhere. The first few meetings were held in New Orleans, but in 1998 it was moved to Key West. Although the Parrot Heads organization raised significant sums of money for charities, the convention was, of course, mostly just an excuse for Parrot Heads to come to Key West in early November, after Fantasy Fest, (or to stay a few extra days recovering from Fantasy Fest), party for several days, and hope that Buffett would make an appearance. From the perspective of tourist businesses in Key West, it was a welcome add-on to the profitable days of Fantasy Fest.

In 1995, the songwriter Drew Reid from Nashville and Charlie Bauer organized what became known as the Annual Key West Songwriters'

Festival. Reid had lived in Key West during the 1970s, and Bauer was the general manager of the Hog's Breath Saloon, which opened in the late 1980s at the former location of the Monster at the corner of Duval and Front Streets. Writers and singers of country music, many of them from Nashville, performed at the inaugural and subsequent festivals.[42]

The first festival featured free performances at the Green Parrot, Bull & Whistle, and the Hog's Breath Saloon by artists such as the Nashville songwriter Mickey Newbury, who wrote "Just Dropped In to See What Condition My Condition Was in." At future festivals, performers staged concerts at the Waterfront Playhouse in addition to playing at bars. Recognizing Key West's increasing attraction to tourists, several national sponsors stepped in to help finance and expand the festivities, including Jimmy Buffet's restaurant, Margaritaville, which started in Key West and had since opened chains in several other cities; the American Society of Composers, Authors, and Publishers; and Broadcast Music, Inc.[43]

Bringing in the Tourists: Heritage Tourism

Different authors have defined heritage tourism in slightly different ways. Typically, "heritage tourism involves travel to sites that in some way represent or celebrate an area, community, or people's history, identity or inheritance." In addition to Key West's literary history, other aspects of its heritage—including its arts, maritime, and military history—also contributed to its growing tourism-based economy. The Key West Art & Historical Society played an important role in fostering Key West's heritage tourism. It had long managed the museum and gardens at the East Martello Tower near the airport and the Key West Lighthouse & Keepers Quarters Museum across from the Hemingway House. In 1999, the society opened the Key West Museum of Art and History in the Custom House on Front Street.[44]

Although Mel Fisher did not arrive in Key West until the 1970s, his treasure-hunting business soon became an essential part of the island and its maritime history. Initially, Fisher's office was located in the Key West Bight in a replica of a Spanish galleon, which also served as a small museum in which he displayed his treasures. In 1982, having achieved some success in retrieving treasure from sunken ships, he organized the Mel Fisher Maritime Heritage Society, which opened a museum in a building across the street from the Customs House. Fisher became nationally known in 1985, when his divers found the "Mother Lode," the treasure carried in the Spanish ship, *Nuestra Señora de Atocha*. The museum displayed and sold many of the treasures Fisher's divers recovered and also featured exhibits associated with the treasure hunters' expeditions.[45]

Other heritage attractions were associated with Key West's military history. The Army owned Fort Zachary Taylor until 1947, when the fort was transferred to the Navy, which used it primarily as a storage area. In 1971, Fort Taylor was placed on the National Register of Historic Places. In 1973, it was designated as a National Historic Landmark and later as a state historic site. The Florida Park Service began managing the fort in 1976 and in 1985 officially opened the Fort Zachary Taylor State Park, including the fort, a park, and a beach, to the public.[46]

The first annual Civil War Heritage Days Festival, held at the park in February 1986, featured a variety of activities, including a reenactment of Union troops' occupation of the fort. In 1995, the sculptor Jim Racchi, also a park ranger, began Sculpture Key West, meshing Key West's artistic and military heritages. Initially, the exhibition featured mostly the work of a small group of Racchi's friends. Over the years, however, Sculpture Key West grew into a major art exhibition.[47]

The Harry S. Truman "Little White House" located on Truman Annex—the naval base that had been named for the former president who had spent many "working vacations" there—was another component of Key West's military heritage that was transformed into a tourist attraction. One year after he purchased the Truman Annex property in 1986, Pritam Singh transferred the Little White House to the state of Florida, and the house was opened to the public in 1991. In 1999, Historic Tours of America (HTA), the successor to Old Town Key West Development, assumed responsibility for managing the facility, and tour guides employed by HTA provided daily tours of the historic building.[48]

Historic Tours of America

By the time the HTA began operating the Little White House, this tourist conglomerate was a dominant component of Key West's tourism industry. In 1973, Ed Swift and his partners, Chris Belland and "Moe" Mosher, had organized Old Town Key West Development and purchased and renovated buildings on Duval Street. Old Town Key West Development had also leased from the city and improved the Key West Aquarium on

Mallory Square in the late 1970s and then leased and renovated other Mallory Square properties, including the Shell Warehouse and Key West Sponge Market.

In 1980, Old Town Key West Development purchased several trolleys and offered tourists island tours on Old Town Trolley, a business in which it had purchased an interest during the late 1970s, but which did not operate during 1978 or 1979. In 1983, Old Town Key West bought the Conch Tour Train from the Mitchell Wolfson estate, thereby gaining control over the most successful sightseeing business in Key West.[49]

Swift, Belland, and Mosher organized Historic Tours of America in 1984, which assumed ownership and operation of the trolleys and trains and which would later conduct tours in several other cities. As Key West's cruise ship traffic increased during the 1990s, HTA garnered additional profits from taking many of the ships' passengers on tours of the island and from a contract with the city to pick up passengers at the cruise ship dock at the Outer Mole. In 2004 and 2005, as a result of a lawsuit brought by a sightseeing company that had operated in Key West during 1995 and 1996, the courts ruled that the city ordinance governing tour operations and the franchise agreement between the city and HTA violated Florida anti-trust law by, in effect, granting HTA a monopoly. Key West paid a settlement to the company, Duck Tours Safari, and also granted a franchise to a new company, CityView Trolley Tours of Key West, which began operating trolleys in 2010. Still, HTA remained the dominant tour provider on the island.

In addition to the Conch Train and Old Town Trolley, HTA offered water excursions on the schooner, *Western Union*, and the *Yankee Freedom* ferry, which carried passengers to the Dry Tortugas. HTA also owned several retail outlets that sold souvenirs to tourists who stopped to browse at points along the Old Town Trolley route. Old Town Key West Development, as well as another HTA-affiliated business, continued as enterprises involved in real estate development and property management.[50]

By the early 1990s, Key West had begun to attract more tourists, and Swift and his partners worried that Key West did not offer enough attractions, a deficiency that threatened the profitability of their enterprises. In response, they developed the Shipwreck Historeum Museum on Mallory Square, which opened in 1994. Tourists could climb a 65-foot lookout tower, observe actors portraying the wrecker Asa Tift and his crew, watch a film about the wrecking industry, and view some of the cargo of the *Isaac Allerton*, which was wrecked off of the Florida Keys reef in 1856.[51]

Where is the Southernmost Point?

Not every tourist attraction or festival in Key West relied on significant financing from the TDC or corporate or nonprofit sponsors, or involved major organizing efforts. For decades, the Southernmost Point at the Atlantic Ocean end of Whitehead Street was associated with Julian "Yankee" Kee, who, like his mother, "Belang" Junior, before him, sold conch and other shells to tourists from the "Kee Seashell Corner." Julian's sons, Julian Kee Jr. and Albert, were found at the Point more frequently as their father aged, and they took over the business when he died in 1993.[52]

According to Albert Kee's recollections, the city had placed a sign reading "Southernmost Point in the USA" at that location, but it was stolen, as were several replacement signs. Then, in 1983, the city installed a cement monument weighing several tons that designated the corner as the southernmost point in the continental United States. Still, problems remained. People could not resist writing whatever occurred to them on the marker, which upset other visitors. As one tourist viewing the Point noted, "It's the end of the earth and you get all that crap in the photo. Who cares that Matt loves O.B.?" The Hotel and Motel Association partnered with the city to hire someone to paint over the graffiti in 1989 one week before Fantasy Fest, an "improvement" most revelers likely did not notice.[53]

Owners of the homes adjacent to the Point grew weary of the tour buses and the Old Town Trolley, which would stop to allow their passengers to take pictures, buy shells, and, according to the homeowners, occasionally relieve themselves on their lawns. Among the protesters was Sally Lewis, a city commissioner, whose house sat at the corner of Whitehead and South Streets, subjecting her to a constant flow of tour vehicles and tourists.

In reality, the monument did not occupy the southernmost point of the continental United States. The true southernmost point fell within the U.S. Naval Station, which tourists were not permitted to enter. According to Key West's assistant city manager, whether the officially designated Southernmost Point was, in fact, more "southernmost" than two other nearby locations that were accessible to tourists wasn't entirely clear. He found a sign that had once designated one of those other locations, at the Atlantic Ocean end of Duval Street, as the southernmost point, and the city considered reestablishing it as the officially recognized "southernmost point." Ultimately, however, the city commission decided to retain the existing location, reasoning that most tourists did not give a moment's thought to the geographical "authenticity" of the "official" southernmost point; they could still write their words of wisdom and snap their pictures. The more general issue, however—namely, the opposition of some to what they saw as the undesirable consequences of tourism—took on different forms in the 1980s and 1990s.[54]

Tourism Trends

While it is impossible to know the extent to which the enhanced advertising and expanded festivals and attractions were responsible for the increase in tourism, several indicators suggest that this increase was substantial during the 1980s and 1990s. Key West was fast becoming a community that attracted "mass tourism."[55] The number of flights arriving at Key West International Airport increased in the mid-1980s, when both Piedmont and Eastern started offering flights into Key West.[56] The number of passengers, most of them tourists, increased from 104,232 in 1984 to 192,777 in 1990 and then reached 268,940 in 1999 (see appendix).

Even more significant was the increase in the number of tourists arriving via cruise ships. Between 1969 and 1984, an average of only eighteen cruise ships docked at Key West each year. Relatively few ships moored at the city's cruise ship port at Mallory Square, which could not accommodate the large vessels. During 1984 and 1985, the city improved Mallory Dock, making it a full-service cruise ship facility, and more ships began to dock there. By 1991, a few cruise ships were also regularly docking at Pier B, located adjacent to Mallory Square, which had been Navy property but then was conveyed to private owners as part of the sale of Truman Annex in 1986.

Nevertheless, in the early 1990s, the largest ships had to anchor off shore and transport their passengers by boat, because neither Mallory nor Pier B could accommodate them. In 1995, the city and Navy reached an agreement that allowed cruise ships to dock at the Navy-owned Outer Mole, which could serve the larger cruise ships. In 1997, the city financed additional improvements at Mallory Dock. Pier B came under the ownership of the Hilton Hotel, and by the end of the 1990s it had been significantly improved, which allowed the mega cruise ships to dock there.[57] Throughout the first decade of the twenty-first century, more ships docked at Pier B than at the other two ports, with the Outer Mole placing second and Mallory a distant third.

In 1986, about 46,000 cruise ship passengers disembarked in Key West, a significant increase from previous years, and by 1990, the number had increased to 132,840. By 1995, the number had increased even further to 398,370, climbing to 609,860 in 1999 (see appendix). Although these tourists only spent about six or seven hours on the island before returning to their ships and continuing on to other destinations, they had ample time to spend their money, leaving Key West with lighter pockets than when they had arrived, much to the joy of bar and shop owners on Duval Street.[58]

One indicator of the increase in tourism was the amount of revenue garnered from Key West's "bed tax," which visitors in hotels, motels, and guesthouses all paid. The revenue the tax generated increased dramatically between 1984 and 1990, from $556,614 to $2,978,499, in part because the tax was increased from 2 to 3 percent in 1986, an increase which took effect in November 1986 (see appendix). It then rose more than 90 percent between 1990 and 1999 to $5,696,390, due to both higher rates of occupancy and higher room rates. Although this increase was due in part to inflation, even in constant dollars the revenue increased about 56 percent between 1990 and 2000.[59]

By the mid-1980s, tourism had unequivocally become the "economic engine" of Key West, as well as of the rest of the Florida Keys. According to a study conducted in 1992, tourism was responsible for 71 percent of Key West's jobs, which were primarily in the lower paying sectors of retail trade and services. These two sectors provided a majority of the jobs in Key West both in 1990 and 1995, and they also secured the largest employment gains during this period.[60]

The public sector also relied on revenues from tourism. A study conducted by the Key West Hotel and Motel Association reported that the city's guesthouses, motels, and hotels paid two-thirds of the city's property taxes in 1986. Property taxes, in turn, represented about 48 percent of the city's revenue. In the mid-1990s, seven of the top ten payers of property taxes in Key West were hotels. In addition, the third largest source of city revenue was the proceeds from a one-half cent sales tax, which tourist spending played a major role in generating. Tourists also purchased tickets to ride on the Conch Tour Train and Old Town Trolley owned by HTA, which, in turn, paid franchise fees to the city. As more ships docked at Key West, the disembarkation fees paid by the cruise ship companies became a significant source of revenue for Key West's government. In 1986, these fees generated only about $190,000, but by 1999, they had increased to $3,350,862. The city estimated that tourism-related revenues generated between 35 and 38 percent of its general fund revenues for each fiscal year between 1997 and 2002.[61]

Community Change and the Sunset Celebration

The same sun set over Key West during the 1980s and 1990s as had set in previous decades, but the celebration that accompanied its setting was much changed. In 1984, the performers who gathered regularly at Mallory Square organized the Key West Cultural Preservation Society (CPS), primarily in response to their displacement from Mallory Square to an adjacent parking lot while the city constructed a cruise ship port designed to buttress its still-limited cruise ship traffic. After the port's completion in 1985, the performers returned to Mallory Square, and the CPS requested that the city grant it the authority to manage the sunset celebration.

When, after a year of negotiations, the CPS and the Key West Port and Transit Authority (PATA), which managed Mallory Square on behalf of the city, failed to reach an agreement, CPS charged that PATA had shown a lack of respect for the sunset artisans, had harassed them, and had engaged in "selective enforcement of non-existent laws." In response, CPS staged a peaceful demonstration in Mallory Square while a cruise ship was in port.[62]

This demonstration provoked the *Citizen* to attack CPS. Its editorial on the subject reminded readers that the newspaper had once supported the sunset celebration. Now, however, the *Citizen* reported, the demonstration was "succeeding in turning us against" those involved. The *Citizen* suggested that for many Key Westers the demonstration "will confirm suspicions that a majority of the sunset performers and vendors are not decent folk with reasonable demands, but instead irrational hippies eager to make a big fuss—and a big mess—at the City's expense, simply to extort for themselves their 'fifteen seconds of national fame' on TV network news." The *Citizen* captured the feeling of some Key Westers when it noted, "Old hippies never die, they just go to Key West and hang out." And it asked, "Is this the image we want to project to national and foreign tourists"?[63]

In other words, holding a peaceful demonstration on the day a cruise ship came into port might deter future cruise ships from docking in Key West. Key West depended on tourism, and those who challenged it, even peripherally, were clearly "irrational" and self-serving. In spite of the *Citizen*'s critique, however, the CPA demonstrated that it was capable of continuing to negotiate the terms of the nightly festival, which was clearly a boon to Key West's tourism. In May 1986, PATA and the CPS agreed to a lease that formalized arrangements for the celebration and granted the CPS significant authority over it.[64]

Although the conflict produced at least a partial victory for the CPS, the *Citizen* need not have worried that the performers were "anti-tourist." The "Mallory Square Program" that the CPS issued shortly after reaching its agreement with PATA emphasized that the performers at the celebration felt a kinship with Key West's tradition of attracting artists and writers, calling the celebration "an incubator for the arts and a focal point for visual and performing artists." However, the program also included advertising from several hotels, restaurants, and other businesses and confirmed that the CPS viewed the celebration as primarily a tourist attraction. In 1996, The Hilton Resort and Marina (later the Westin), a new hotel located adjacent to Mallory Square, began to stage its own sunset celebration. They hired several of the most popular entertainers on Mallory Square, including Will Soto, known for his juggling and high-wire acts, to perform for the nightly crowds.[65]

Most tourists flocked to the sunset festival, which by the 1990s, Key West's tourism boosters were warmly endorsing. Not all visitors to Key West, however, shared this enthusiasm; some, in fact, consciously avoided it. The writer and television commentator Charles Kuralt was among this group. In his book *Charles Kuralt's America* (1995) he emphasized:

I avoided Mallory Square at sunset. I suppose everybody who visits Key West should squeeze into the six-o'clock throng there once, pina colada in hand, mingle with the stilt walkers and break dancers, watch the cat jump through the flaming hoop, buy a cookie from the Cookie Lady, and applaud as the sun sinks behind all those other people on the pier. I did it once, a long time ago. The sunset can be truly melodramatic at Key West, depending on the presence of high clouds and air pollution, both of which make it better. But it is best watched in peace from anywhere but Mallory Square.[66]

The days of Rex Brumgart, Tennessee Williams, and a few of their friends drinking martinis and watching the sun set at the dock were long gone. According to Lee Dodez, one of those friends, "the Mallory Square Sunset grew from a religious ritual to a commercial sales and entertainment center." Whether the original sunset ritual was truly a religious experience is debatable, but by the 1980s and 1990s the sunset celebration had clearly become a significant component of Key West's tourism-based economy. Like Kuralt's displeasure with the sunset celebration, others criticized the island's trend toward mass tourism, more development, and gentrification. Conflict surfaced among Key Westers over various aspects of these trends, and the outcomes of these conflicts would shape the character, composition, and quality of life of the community.[67]

10

The Politics of Tourism and Development

BY THE MID-1980S, most Key Westers had realized that there were no realistic alternatives to Key West's tourism-based economy, but several aspects of the growth of tourism continued to generate significant conflict. Civic activists argued that growth interests who sought the unbridled expansion of tourism and the development of a built environment to accommodate it were leading Key West into an unsustainable future. They contended that if the public sector permitted, and even reinforced, the pursuit of private profit by tourism businesses and developers, Key West's quality of life would suffer. They felt a more activist governmental policy was necessary to regulate tourism and development in the public interest, to provide public services, and to maintain Key West's ability to accommodate citizens with different lifestyles and incomes. Wise policy, they argued, would maintain the uniqueness and diversity of Key West and would also ensure that the general public, and not just the tourism industry and development interests, benefited from enhanced tourism.[1]

The Tourist Development Council

By its own measures, the Tourist Development Council achieved great success. Its promotional activities ensured that more prospective visitors were aware of Key West. With the TDC's financial support, festivals and attractions grew. And, most important, more tourists arrived in Key West. By others' measures, however, the TDC's operations and impact fell short. Community groups and others criticized the council for engaging in conflicts of interest and misguided policy.

Critics attacked the TDC director, Sandra Higgs, for awarding the Key Advertising and Marketing Company, which she owned, a lucrative contract from the TDC, and they also criticized the TDC board for approving the contract. A grand jury report released in 1989 by the State Attorney created further problems for Higgs and the organization. It reinforced the view that the TDC was an incestuous organization, characterizing as "inappropriate and outrageous" the fact that every member of the District 1 (Key West) Advisory Committee, which played a major role in allocating the revenue generated by the third penny of the tourist tax in Key West, were appointed exclusively by the Key West Chamber of Commerce.[2]

In 1989, the BOCC awarded Higgs a new three-year contract worth $243,000, which only buttressed the argument that the TDC was a "private club funded by bed tax dollars." Not until August 1992 did the BOCC dismiss Higgs. The TDC operated without a director until April 1996, when it hired Harold Wheeler, who had held a similar position in South Padre Island, Texas. During the interim period, the TDC's focus and operation changed very little. Its board still comprised primarily tourism-industry interests, and it retained the service of the Miami-based Stuart Newman and Associates, which had been contracted to conduct TDC's public relations since the council's inception. The TDC also retained as its advertising firm Miami-based Tinsley Advertising & Marketing, Inc., which was organized in the mid-1980s by several former employees of Stuart Newman.[3]

In 1995, the BOCC amended the ordinance governing the selection of the members of the District Advisory Committees (DACs). The Chamber no longer retained the right to appoint all of the representatives to the District Advisory Committees for Key West and the four other districts in the Keys. Nevertheless, most of the DAC members remained representatives of the tourism industry.[4]

The criticisms of the TDC, however, went beyond Higgs's leadership or the council's method of choosing DAC members. Many focused their criticism on the TDC's preoccupation with increasing the number of visitors to the island. For example, the following letter, addressed to Sam Feiner, the chair of the TDC, appeared in the *Citizen* on July 24, 1994.

> I understand and agree with the need to provide jobs and a healthy economy for those of us who live here. But Mr. Feiner, do you not know of the Ocala contingent of Conchs and why they left the Keys? Do you read . . . letters pouring in from residents who are fed up with the declining quality of life here in the Keys? The overcrowding . . . the incessant noise . . . and the ceaseless air, water and noise pollution associated with welcoming unrestricted numbers of tourists who drive their cars to the Keys.
>
> Are you aware of the impending death, yes death, of our coral reef, a major factor in tourism and livelihoods here in the Keys? . . . How much TDC money have you allocated toward correcting these problems? How will you convince anyone to come here if the reef is dead and gone?
>
> The problem lies in the fact that you and the rest of the business community . . . are so out of touch with the broader, all-encompassing aspects of living in and promoting a paradise. Have you ever heard of sustainability? It is evident in the way you promote and over-develop our once unique and beautiful city that your real interests are short-term and lie simply in your own wallets.

A common criticism of the TDC was that it spent too much of the tourist tax revenues on advertising to attract more tourists and on assistance to tourist-related festivals and not enough on projects that would benefit the wider community. The TDC did not initially reallocate its spending to provide community benefits, but in 1988 the residents of Key West and the rest of the Florida Keys passed a referendum that increased the tax levy on tourists. These revenues would be spent on projects unrelated to tourism. The referendum added a 1-percent "tourist impact tax" to the existing 3-percent tourist or "bed" tax. One half of the proceeds from this tax would go directly to the county's general revenue fund. The other half would be earmarked for the Monroe County Land Authority, a new county agency established to appropriate funds to purchase environmentally sensitive land for conservation or to acquire land for affordable housing projects. Although the referendum itself was controversial, the principle that tourists should pay for governmental activities unrelated to tourism was widely accepted.[5]

A decade later, many residents of Key West and other parts of Monroe County once again urged that more of the revenues generated by the 3-percent tourist development tax be used for purposes other than attracting and serving more tourists. In Key West, an organization known as Last Stand was at the forefront of this campaign. Last Stand was organized in the late 1980s, and its membership comprised primarily those who had moved to Key West, including realtors, business owners, and retirees, rather than Conchs. Last Stand activists argued that the increasing number of tourists detracted from the quality of life in the community. They pointed to the popular tourist community, Jackson, Wyoming, as an example of a community whose citizens had voted, in 1994, to repeal the 2-percent lodging tax, the revenues of which were spent on promoting tourism. Although Last Stand did not advocate repealing the tourist tax, it called for significant portions of its revenues to be used for purposes other than advertising and sponsoring events to attract tourists, purposes that would more directly benefit Key West residents.[6]

Several national publications suggested that Key West's transition toward mass tourism detracted from the tourists' experiences, which only reinforced Last Stand's perspective. The headline to an article published in *USA Today* in 1999 read "Charm and Commercialism Sour Mix in Margaritaville." The article concluded that Key West had "become a victim of its own allure": "The droves and the development are threatening the very things that make the continental USA's southernmost island so popular: quirky charm, a laid-back pace and crystal-clear waters." *Miami Herald* columnist, Carl Hiaasen, who two decades earlier had reported on the drug business in the Keys, asserted, "The last traces of funky charm are being trampled by hordes of cruise-ship goobers whose major contribution to the economy is the purchase of $5 T-shirts. If Hemingway were alive today, he'd take a flamethrower to Duval Street." Hiassen emphasized that, unlike tourism in Orlando, tourism in Key West relied on the destination's unique atmosphere, and that atmosphere was being threatened. In mid-1998, an article in *Newsweek* concluded, "the prize for the most spoiled vacation spot in America . . . probably goes to Key West." The 1999 edition of *Fodor's* observed that Duval Street was becoming "an open-air mall of T-shirt shops and tour shills," concluding that one can still have fun in Key West, "but the best advice is to come sooner rather than later."[7]

These critiques initially failed to impact policy. In August 1999, only one county commissioner voted to allocate less of the TDC revenue to the promotion of tourism and tourist attractions. Instead, in late 1999, the BOCC voted to survey all of the county's registered voters. Approximately three-quarters of the respondents wanted the TDC to spend less on advertising and more on local projects. In 2000, the TDC finally agreed to allocate 30 percent of its bed tax revenue to capital projects, a change in policy advocated by its chair, Bill Wickers, after he attended a series of meetings in the Keys and was confronted with the high level of citizen discontent.[8] These funds, however, would not be allocated to general public services or to infrastructure, uses which the TDC determined was prohibited by the state legislation that authorized the tax. Rather, they would finance capital projects that might benefit locals, as well as tourists, such as beach improvements and the renovation of local theaters.

Tourist Accommodations

The more tourists that were beckoned to Key West, the more the businesses offering them accommodations had the opportunity to profit. Tourism entrepreneurs converted homes and apartment houses in Old Town to guesthouses. Developers also built new hotels and motels to serve the growing tourist trade, including some that offered time-share units. In 1980, Key West had about 2,380 transient units (primarily motel, hotel, and guesthouse rooms). By 1985, that figure had increased to 3,403 and by 1990 to 4,267. In 1999, Key West had a total of 4,618 transient units. In addition, many investors obtained transient licenses and rented out their houses or condos to tourists. Although the official figures indicated that the number of investor-owned transient licenses remained relatively stagnant during the 1990s, the number of "phantom" units operating without a license likely exceeded those with licenses, and these numbers increased during the 1980s and 1990s.[9]

Key West's two most historic hotels both prospered during the 1990s. La Concha was closed during most of the 1980s, but after a major remodeling it reopened in March 1987 as the Holiday Inn La Concha. The Casa Marina had already reopened in 1979 as Marriott's Casa Marina Resort, but it expanded in the 1990s and underwent changes of ownership, indicating a strong market for upscale tourist property in Key West. In 1999, the Wyndham International Corporation purchased and assumed management of the Casa Marina.[10]

Citizens of Key West opposed several new projects and expansions of existing facilities, and these conflicts often turned into legal challenges. State agencies frequently became involved in the disputes. For example, the Save Our Neighborhoods (SON) citizens' organization challenged a time-share project on the Gulf end of Duval Street, Reflections of Key West, whose architect was the former mayor Sonny McCoy. SON's lawyer, Henry Lee Morgenstern, argued that the project's density exceeded that permitted under the city's land-use regulations and that some of the property the developer claimed to own was, in fact, owned by the state. Florida's Department of Natural Resources joined the legal action against Reflections. Ultimately, a compromise was reached that kept some of the property accessible to the public.[11]

The most conflict-ridden hotel proposal called for a development on the ocean at the southern end of Simonton Street. David Wolkowsky had purchased the property toward the end of the 1970s, razing the existing Sands Restaurant & Cocktail Lounge and building the Sands Beach Club, which opened in 1980. Soon after it opened, Wolkowsky began negotiations with the New York–developer Austin Laber that led to Laber's purchase of the property. In 1983, Laber proposed the construction of a 150-unit hotel that he initially called the Sands Beach Resort, a considerably more intensive project than had previously existed on the site.[12]

SON and other citizens vocally opposed the project, claiming, among other things, that the proposal violated the city's ordinance banning projects exceeding four stories, that there was inadequate sewer capacity, that its scale was incompatible with the character of the neighborhood, and that the project had not been properly reviewed and approved by all of the required city boards.

The Florida Department of Community Affairs (DCA) soon became involved in the controversy. In early 1984, Key West had been redesignated under state law as an Area of Critical State Concern (ACSC), due to the city's weak enforcement of its land use codes, a designation that brought increased state oversight. DCA supported some of SON's contentions. The U.S. Department of Housing and Urban Development also shared some of SON's concerns and rejected the city's application for an Urban Development Action Grant (UDAG) to help finance Laber's project.

In spite of the opposition, however, the city commission, after an elaborate process involving lawsuits and revisions of the development plans, approved the project. Opponents alleged conflicts of interest on the part of some commissioners who had voted to approve the hotel. Some Key Westers especially voiced suspicions when Laber named the hotel's restaurant "Emma's," in honor of city commissioner Emma Cates. After construction began in 1985, the Old Island Restoration Commission requested that it be halted owing to several differences between what was actually being built and what the city commission had approved. The project, however, was allowed to continue and the resort, renamed The Reach and managed by Wyndham Hotels, opened in December 1985.[13]

Political Mobilization

Conflicts over development also contributed to turnover in political office. For example, in 1983, after a newly formed citizens group, Save Our Shorelines (SOS), mobilized successfully against an effort by the Pier House to purchase and expand its facility on city-owned Simonton Beach, the SOS activist George Halloran was elected to the city commission. In 1985, Jimmy Weekley, a Conch who owned Fausto's grocery store, defeated incumbent Conch James Mira, who had supported the Reach project. During his campaign, Weekley advocated a growth management perspective and proposed that the government impose a moratorium on development in order to allow the planning department to analyze the needs of the city. He also advocated for limits on the number of transient units in the city and emphasized the need for more affordable housing for Key West's workforce.[14]

In another commission race in 1985, Sally Lewis, the president of the Key West Art & Historical Society, who had moved to Key West eight years before, defeated Joe Balbontin, a Conch who had supported the Reach and other development projects. Lewis emphasized during her campaign, " I vow to end the destruction of our shoreline for the benefit of out-of-town developers. Key West will NOT be another Miami Beach." Balbontin offered a different viewpoint. In arguing against growth control legislation and a moratorium on building, he urged, "More controls on the ENVIRONMENTALISTS!" Among his contributions was a $1,000 donation from Laber. Although he gained strong support in the heavily Conch districts, Balbontin lost to Lewis in the runoff.[15]

In the 1987 elections, Harry Powell, an avid environmentalist who had lived in Key West for thirteen years, defeated Emma Cates. During his campaign, Powell was critical of many of the changes he had observed in the community. He argued that the previous commissioners often were "shortsighted" and had deferred to tourist interests and developers. Instead, Powell declared, "[I will] be a commissioner who will fight to keep our community the well balanced and viable social entity it has been for 150 years."[16]

Another candidate for office who was critical of the proposed land sale to the Pier House and of the construction of the Reach was Tony Tarracino, better known as "Captain Tony," the well-known proprietor of Captain Tony's Saloon on Greene Street. Tony, whose honorary campaign manager was Jimmy Buffett, narrowly lost his bid for mayor in the 1985 election to Tom Sawyer, a Conch bank executive. Tony lost again in 1987 to former mayor Heyman, but Tony persevered and was elected mayor in 1989 after Heyman chose not to seek another term.[17]

One reporter summarized Tony's unofficial campaign slogan, as well as his life philosophy, as "All you need is a tremendous sex drive." Tony, however, did not transfer this libertine philosophy regarding personal behavior to his perspective on development projects in Key West. The city should be open to diverse lifestyles, he argued, but it needed to regulate those seeking to profit from its attractiveness by building more hotels and condominiums.[18]

Among Tony's proposals during the mayoral race in 1985 was a three-year moratorium on development. Tony criticized the Reach, saying, "There's another beach they're taking away from us. Once they open up with cabanas and everything, forget the public. In two weeks they'll say kids are urinating in the sand, drinking beer, smoking drugs, fornicating. They'll set up a couple of phony fights and that's it. They'll put the fences up." Tony's campaign even featured a rock song, which promised,

"He'll STOP THE BIG CONSTRUCTION! And have no peace, for folks who want Key West to look like Miami Beach."[19]

Nevertheless, not once during his three election campaigns did Tony take a stand against tourism. In fact, he promised during his 1989 campaign, "If I'm elected, I'll be a tourist ambassador with class and taste." He further noted, "If I'm mayor, I'll tell you, we'll make the papers at least once a month. We'll find some way to make the shit fly. That's what brings the people here." Tony even sympathized with the college students who flocked to Key West during spring break. After the Key West Hotel and Motel Association urged the city commission to take steps to discourage the influx, he recalled fondly, "We swallowed goldfish years ago and had sex in rumble seats. Youth has to be served."[20]

During his swearing-in ceremony in 1989, Tony offered his perspective on the Key West of times past and his fears about the present, declaring, "[I have] found my Utopia and now I'm trying to save it." During his term in office, he asserted that Key West was "not your normal town in the U.S.": "People came here looking for their utopia. They're dreamers, artists, people with high IQs. Whether it's making beads or painting or fishing, they came here for their little paradise in the sun. Then look at all these big hotels. It's all built on paper. And when they stop making money, they'll pull out and leave the stake holes. These are the people who are going to tell us what the rules are, how to live here? They're strangers." Messages such as these ruffled a few feathers in the tourism industry.[21]

After his election, Tony proposed an additional 3-percent bed tax on tourists to finance basic governmental services, such as the police, the fire department, and recreation facilities. The Hotel and Motel Association successfully opposed this proposal, and in the 1991 mayoral race, it endorsed former mayor Dennis Wardlow, who defeated Captain Tony by 304 votes.[22]

Other activists and officeholders in Key West, however, shared Tony's general orientation. Although most developers ultimately succeeded in gaining approval for their projects, not all policy leaned in their direction. For example, the city retained its four-story limit on building heights, which it had adopted in the 1970s. Growth management advocates and environmentalists also significantly influenced policy regarding Key West's Salt Ponds. Citizen activists and their allies, however, failed to achieve their goal of retaining some of the Key West Bight for commercial fishing. They also achieved only limited success in the debate over cruise ships and lost in their efforts to retain the public recreation facilities at the Navy-owned Peary Court and to protect Houseboat Row.

Salt Ponds Conflicts

Conflicts raged for decades over proposed developments in and near Key West's Salt Ponds. In the mid-nineteenth century, some entrepreneurs harvested salt from the ponds, but it was never a lucrative undertaking, and the hurricane of 1876 ended the business. The part of the island that in the mid-twentieth century became officially recognized as the Salt Ponds included bodies of water that were not historically part of the Salt Ponds but were deemed important to protect by those opposed to development pressures. A report by the Key West Planning Department in 1986 estimated that the Salt Pond area encompassed over 400 acres.[23]

In 1983, the Key West Salt Ponds Committee (KWSPC), a grassroots organization, emphasized the importance of preserving the Salt Ponds:

> The Salt Ponds support valuable ecosystems . . . they are breeding and nursery areas for dozens of species of fish that depend upon the ponds for their survival into adulthood. Some species have died out due to the extreme salinity caused by lack of circulation, but new and unusual species have evolved and are thriving. The abundant marine life attracts large numbers of migratory waterfowl as well as herons and other native birds. . . . The higher ground behind the mangroves contains a dozen or more species of increasingly rare native trees . . .
>
> The narrow barrier spits and the surface area of the Salt Ponds offer important storm protection. . . . Buildings constructed on these sand bars would be extremely vulnerable to hurricanes.[24]

A small portion of the Salt Ponds was filled in the late 1970s to accommodate the lengthening of the Key West International Airport's runways. Other areas in the Salt Ponds were also filled during the 1960s and 1970s. A building department official who emphasized the desirability of filling the "mosquito breeder" and developing the property on it echoed the general sentiment of both developers and Key West's city government during this era.[25]

The city commission in the 1970s and early 1980s was not exactly known for closely scrutinizing proposed projects, especially if the project's developer was politically connected. The La Brisa condominium development on the edge of the Salt Ponds on South Roosevelt Boulevard is a good example of this kind of cronyism. Its developer, Ed Knight, had long been involved in real estate development and sales in the community. Although he and his attorney, James Hendrick, had to complete a CIAS (Comprehensive Impact Assessment Statement) that analyzed the proposed project's potential impacts, this procedure was largely symbolic. For example, one question asked whether the project was likely to have an impact on law enforcement. Hendrick responded that the impact would be minimal, based on the fact that none of the "units w[ould] be sold to drunken shrimpers." The commission approved the project.[26]

During the 1970s, the federal and state governments provided some protection for the Salt Ponds. The U.S. Army Corps of Engineers published guidelines in 1972 that called for the protection of tidal wetlands subject to its jurisdiction, which included the Salt Ponds, and the Florida Pollution Control Board imposed a moratorium on dredge and fill operations in Monroe County. Other state agencies potentially exercised regulatory authority over the Salt Ponds, and the redesignation of Key West as an Area of Critical State Concern (ACSC) in the 1980s gave environmentalists some hope that state agencies would carefully scrutinize proposed development in the Salt Ponds.[27]

The major project proposed for the Salt Ponds, however, had been approved by the city commission before any significant local, federal, or state restrictions were in place. The Miami developer Larry Marks had submitted a plan to the city in 1972 to build a large development on a piece of property he and several partners had purchased on the eastern end of the island. This project, named "Island in the Sun," was significantly larger than any other development in Key West.[28]

In March 1972, the city's Planning and Restoration Commission (PRC) supported Marks's request to rezone the property and thereby allow higher density development, and in August 1972, the PRC recommended that the city commission approve Marks's site plan for 1,120 residential units in several four-story buildings. The city commission approved the rezoning and the site plan, and in November the city issued a building permit that authorized the filling of the property. After Marks had filled some of the area, the city in February 1973 issued a permit allowing him to build foundations for 360 units, the first phase of Island in the Sun. After the completion of the foundations, however, state and federal agencies filed complaints concerning the environmental impacts of the project. By 1985, the city commission still had not granted Marks the final authority to build the Island in the Sun.[29]

One Key West resident argued, with some literary flair, that Marks's proposal was a symptom of "an epidemic . . . every bit as pernicious and debilitating as the plagues which swept across Europe in the Middle Ages . . . a disease . . . not of the body but of the mind": "It is spawned by the greed of corporate-commercial interests, nourished by developers who would sacrifice environmental and ecological concerns on the altar of financial expediency, and condoned by misled civil authorities who have monumental pressures exerted on them." Jimmy Buffett was among those who fought the development. At a city commission meeting in October 1986, he emphasized that the wetlands were a "symbol of the quality of life in Florida." Buffett also informed the commissioners that he had established a Friends of Florida Trust Fund to raise money to buy the property on which Marks and Bob Butler, who had purchased some of Marks's property, wanted to build.[30]

In November 1987, Buffett gave a concert to help raise funds for the city to purchase Marks's property. The concert undoubtedly provided many Key Westers with a good time, but raised nowhere near the money necessary to purchase the land. In February 1988, the city commission finally voted to allow Marks and Butler to build Island in the Sun. The size of the project was decreased slightly, and Marks agreed to return some of the area to natural wetlands.[31]

Ultimately, Marks sold his interest to the Argonaut Development Group, of which Butler and Paul Waldron of Washington, D.C. were partners. The project was carried out in several phases, and construction continued through 2006. The name Island in the Sun was jettisoned and replaced with condominium and apartment projects collectively known as SeaSide. A total of approximately 1,050 units were constructed on the property, along with the Grand Key Resort Hotel, another addition to Key West's tourist accommodations.[32]

Other projects were also approved and constructed along Atlantic Avenue close to the Salt Ponds, during the 1980s. Still, environmentalists were fairly successful in their battle to protect the Salt Ponds. In March 1989, Joan Borel, a citizen activist, emphasized that the remaining owners of property in the Salt Ponds would not have the same legal claims to building as Marks had enjoyed, because they had not proposed and received approvals before the new wetland regulations were adopted in the early 1970s. She also emphasized that even after one subtracted the acreage on which Island in the Sun was to be built, undeveloped land in the Salt Pond area totaled approximately 370 acres. Some of these acres had already been acquired for preservation, and many more were in the process of being acquired.[33]

Part of the reason for her optimism was the activity of the Florida Keys Land Trust, which was formed in 1978 and played a significant role in acquiring land in the Salt Ponds. Another non-profit, the Nature Conservancy, purchased several acres in the Salt Ponds and then transferred them to the city. The Monroe County Land Authority also obtained several additional Salt Pond tracts over the next decade, and the City of Key West purchased some Salt Pond property as well.[34]

By 2000, the City of Key West had acquired around 160 acres in the Salt Ponds, and Monroe County owned even more, including property owned by the Land Authority. In 2005, the city purchased the last parcel of privately owned land in the Salt Ponds, but it did not come cheap. The city commission agreed to buy the two acres near the airport from the Old Town Key West Development company. In exchange for the property, the city agreed to pay Ed Swift, the company's primary owner, several million dollars from a Salt Pond fund established expressly for the purchase of Salt Pond land. The city also granted Swift the right to build several units of market-rate housing in Key West, a venture that promised to garner large profits.[35]

The Transition of the Key West Bight

During the 1980s and 1990s, the Key West Bight transformed from a site dedicated to commercial fishing to one dedicated to tourism-related enterprises. Not only did many commercial fishermen lose their livelihoods but an important aspect of Key West's character and diversity was also lost. In 1980, the shrimp fleet and related maritime activity still dominated the Key West Bight. During the mid- and late 1980s, however, some shrimpers were leaving the Key West Bight for Stock Island and others departed from the Keys. By the end of the decade, only a handful of commercial craft were based at the bight. In 1988, Singleton Seafood, the largest wholesale seafood packing business in Key West, also moved to Stock Island.[36]

The fishing boats that once docked close together on the Key West Bight were replaced by enterprises primarily geared toward tourists. These included charter fishing boats, dive boats, and craft used for excursions. In addition, wealthier Key Westers docked their boats at the bight. The bight uplands were redeveloped, and restaurants and bars frequented by locals and tourists became prevalent. Various factors accounted for the decline of Key West's shrimping industry, including competition from foreign imports and the diminished productivity of the Tortugas shrimp beds. However, the recreational desires of Key West's more affluent residents and the city's tremendous reliance on tourism also significantly contributed to the departure of commercial fishing from the Key West Bight. Key West was fast attracting seasonal and full-time residents who were willing and able to pay handsomely to dock their boats at the bight. Moreover, charter boats and other operations that catered to tourists were often more profitable than commercial fishing, so their operators could afford to pay higher dockage fees.[37]

In the mid-1980s, commercial fishermen at the Key West Bight mounted a campaign to protect their declining industry. They proposed, with significant support from others in the community, zoning a portion of the bight exclusively for commercial fishing. The Key West City Commission considered the designation of a commercial fishing district, a proposal Mayor Heyman and Commissioners George Halloran and James Mira defended, stressing that fishing provided jobs and was a key component of the island's heritage. The proposal garnered widespread support, including from the Chamber of Commerce, the NAACP, and the Old Town Merchants Association. Captain Bill Frank, the president of the Key West Maritime Historical Society, emphasized, "There's a point at which a person's life and what he wants to do with his life can't just be measured by whether or not it's economically feasible. For God's sake, let's not move our fishing fleet out of Key West to build a few more goddamned buildings." On the other hand, owners of property in the Key West Bight and developers who spoke at the meeting contended that tourism was the key to the city's economy; according to them, preserving commercial fishing was a "useless romance."[38]

In the end, no commercial fishing district for Key West's shrimpers was maintained at the bight. By 1990, the city commission had decided that the city should buy the Key West Bight property when its current leaseholder, ConAgra, relinquished its lease the following year. Key West, however, lacked the financial resources to complete the purchase, so in July 1990, the city commission adopted a resolution requesting that The Trust for Public Land, a non-profit conservation organization, arrange for an option to buy the land until the city could obtain the financing. The city of Key West then purchased the Key West Bight property in 1993, using an $18,500,000 bond issue as financing.[39]

The Key West Bight was renamed the Historic Seaport at the Key West Bight. The new name was likely designed to attract tourists who were interested in the area's "historic heritage." In reality, little of its history was there to be found. When the city first acquired the bight, Edward Little Jr. and other members of the Key West Maritime Historical Society attempted to persuade city officials and the Key West Bight Management Board, created by the city to manage the Historic Seaport, to berth a traditional wooden lobster boat on the bight. They also recommended that the building that had once housed the turtle cannery be transformed into a "maritime commons/gallery." Their efforts were to no avail. Instead, the only pretense of history on offer at the re-imagined "Historic Seaport" was a small building, designated as the "Turtle Kraals Museum and Educational Center." Here, tourists could view pictures and descriptions of the former turtle kraals, which had actually attracted tourists in decades past, when they were still part of the working Bight. HTA opened the Flagler Station Train Historeum in 2000, a small museum that paid homage to the Florida East Coast Railway–magnate Henry Flagler. The museum, however, closed several years later.[40]

Cruise Ship Battles

Just as the Key West Bight was transformed into a tourist area, the docks at and near Mallory Square grew to accommodate more and more tourists, a transition some in the community resisted and others welcomed. The Key West Chamber of Commerce had long sought increased cruise ship traffic to Key West. In April 1984, it passed a resolution asserting, "the chamber will take all actions necessary and proper in order to promote cruise ship visitation to the island of Key West." It added that it was "unalterably" opposed to the actions of any who would discourage the growth of cruise ship visits to the community. During most of the 1990s, the city shared this perspective and encouraged cruise ship companies to increase the number of stops they made at Key West's port. Mayor Dennis Wardlow, who served as mayor for most of the decade, urged the Key West Hotel and Motel Association, whose members derived no direct economic benefits, to embrace cruise ships, noting that they would "benefit in the long run." Julio Avael, Key West's city manager from 1995 to early 2007, contended that the city benefited from the disembarkation fees the ships paid, and he often met with representatives of the cruise companies and of the Florida-Caribbean Cruise Association, an industry trade association, to encourage cruise ships to visit Key West.[41]

Businesses on and near Duval Street, including bars and the increasing number of T-shirt and souvenir shops, also became increasingly dependent on cruise ship traffic. In fact, some business owners on Duval Street contracted with cruise ship companies to recommend their businesses to passengers. HTA benefited from the increased demand for its Conch Train and Old Town Trolley tours around Key West.

Frank Romano, who had served on the Monroe County TDC, was one of the most outspoken advocates of cruise ships. He declared, "They are the cleanest source of tourist income we have. . . . They don't belch fumes, they don't impact our infrastructure, other than walking our side walks and riding the Conch Train." Romano also noted that cruise ship passengers accounted for almost 50 percent of the business of his company, Key West Aloe. According to Romano, many cruise ship passengers were visiting Key West for the first time, and many returned for extended stays, occupying tourist accommodations and spending their money at restaurants and retail stores.[42]

Spokespersons for Last Stand, however, offered another perspective and advocated for both strong limits on the number of cruise ships allowed to dock in Key West and higher disembarkation fees. Last Stand's president, Elliot Baron, suggested that the increased cruise ship traffic was changing the nature of lower Duval Street. He argued that the throngs of cruise ship passengers diminished the experience of Key West's overnight visitors, who valued a relaxed island environment. Baron also cited increased foot traffic and customers as the reasons some property owners were raising their rents, forcing some long-established local owners to close their businesses. What followed, he noted, was a proliferation of T-shirt shops and cheap jewelry stores.[43]

Reef Relief, organized in the late 1980s "to preserve and protect living coral reef ecosystems," generally shared Last Stand's perspective. Reef Relief's DeeVon Quirolo emphasized that large cruise ships stirred up contaminated sediments that damaged the coral reef and detracted from Key West's appeal to tourists. She also pointed to a report issued by the Center for Marine Conservation, which concluded that cruise ships discarded trash into the water that often ended up on Key West's beaches.[44]

The cruise ship controversy was an important component of the discussions that commenced in the mid-1990s regarding the city's acquisition of the Truman Waterfront property, adjacent to Truman Annex, which the Navy determined it no longer needed. In 1995, the city and Navy agreed to allow cruise ships to dock at the Navy-owned Outer Mole at the Truman Waterfront. Prior to this agreement, the largest cruise ships had to drop anchor and shuttle passengers to shore on boats, because both the Mallory Dock and Pier B, which the Hilton Hotel owned, were unable to accommodate these vessels. These anchored ships paid no disembarkation fees, so the Navy's leasing of the Outer Mole to the city, which permitted cruise ships to dock there, provided the city with additional revenue.[45]

Before the city acquired ownership of the Truman Waterfront, including the Outer Mole, however, Last Stand initiated an administrative challenge to the plan amendments and land-use regulations that Key West had adopted for the property, a challenge that threatened to delay the transfer of the property from the Navy to the city. After a long period of negotiation, Last Stand and the city reached a settlement agreement that the city commission ratified in May 2000. The city agreed to allow only one cruise ship berth on the Outer Mole, rather than the two it was considering, and to contract with a firm to conduct an extensive study of the cruise ship business and its environmental, social, and economic impacts. In addition, the city agreed to enforce strict limits on the number of cruise ships docking at the Outer Mole between October 1, 1999 and September 30, 2003, before the study was completed. Last Stand had been advocating for a limit on the amount of cruise ship traffic, so this agreement represented a compromise by the city.

Nevertheless, the number of cruise ship passengers arriving at Key West increased dramatically in the first years of the new century. Ironically, while those opposed to the increase in cruise ship traffic in Key

West focused their attention on the Outer Mole, the capacity of the Hilton-owned Pier B expanded during the late 1990s, and its cruise ship traffic increased dramatically, surpassing that of both the Mallory Dock and the Outer Mole during the first decade of the twenty-first century. Further, the Navy reconsidered its decision to convey the Outer Mole to the city, although cruise ships were still allowed to utilize the pier.[46]

Peary Court: Public Recreation or Military Housing?

During the late 1980s and early 1990s, a conflict over development at Peary Court, a recreation area located just east of White Street on the edge of Old Town, split the community. Unlike the cruise ships conflicts, this battle related not to tourism per se but to issues regarding the quality of life that many of Key West's community activists who were wary of increased tourism and development held dear. Involved in the dispute were community groups, city government, the Navy, other federal agencies, and the courts. Ultimately, the Navy accomplished its goal of building housing for military personnel at Peary Court, an area formerly used as military housing but then as a popular recreational area for the public. Last Stand suffered a major defeat, as did other activists who opposed the new military housing.

Shortly after World War II, the Navy constructed housing in Peary Court, but in 1976 it razed the buildings, which had significantly deteriorated. The Navy leased the twenty-nine acre area to the city, which converted it to a public park with softball fields. In the late 1980s, the Navy decided that it again wanted to use Peary Court for military housing, a move that would eliminate the ball fields used by the city's men's and women's softball leagues.[47]

Initially, in 1988, during Mayor Richard Heyman's second administration, the city commission urged the military to continue leasing Peary Court to the city and to build new housing for its personnel elsewhere. That December, the commission passed a resolution asking the city's elected representatives in Washington and Tallahassee to lobby the Navy to find an alternative site for the housing. The Key West Chamber of Commerce, the Hotel and Motel Association, and the Key West Business Guild supported this resolution. The Military Affairs Committee (MAC), a group including some of Key West's major business and professional figures, however, adopted a resolution in December 1989 that supported the Navy's position.[48]

On December 3, 1990, Molly Logan, a twenty-one-year-old who had recently moved to Key West, protested the Navy's proposal by chaining herself to a tree in Peary Court and remaining there for several days. She attracted media attention and the applause of many Key Westers. The mayor, now Captain Tony, visited and threw her a pack of Lucky Strikes. Restaurants provided her with food, and the Conch Train even changed its route so tourists could observe her act of civil disobedience. The Navy and FBI, however, failed to appreciate her verve. They cut her chain with bolt cutters, and the FBI arrested her. Although she initially faced a felony charge of trespassing on federal property, the charge was ultimately reduced to a misdemeanor.[49]

Prior to the 1991 elections, the majority of the city commissioners were sympathetic to those who opposed the Peary Court housing. Commissioner Jimmy Weekley tried to arrange a compromise by proposing to the Navy that it build the 160 housing units on only 14 acres of Peary Court, rather than on the entire 29 acres, but the Navy refused. Last Stand responded to this refusal by initiating a lawsuit asking the court to issue an injunction against the Navy forbidding it from constructing the housing until it had completed a satisfactory impact analysis.[50]

Before the case reached the court, however, the Key West city elections changed the composition of the city commission. That November, Harry Powell did not seek reelection, and newcomers Joe Pais and Harry Bethel, along with Weekley, now sat on the commission. Former mayor Dennis Wardlow replaced Captain Tony as mayor. On February 19, 1992, this new commission voted unanimously for a resolution in favor of the Navy's project. Although the project was delayed because the court ordered the Navy to complete an adequate environmental assessment of the Peary Court housing, the Navy ultimately was given the go-ahead on the project and broke ground on October 5, 1992. One last chapter, however, remained to be written.[51]

In January 1994, the former city commissioner Harry Powell moved into a trailer on the Peary Court construction site. He brought with him material that could be used to construct a bomb, including gasoline, a motorcycle battery, and ammonium nitrate. Powell, who later compared his actions to those of the Boston Tea Party, insisted that U.S. Senator

Connie Mack and the General Accounting Office review the Peary Court Housing Project. Officials agreed to his demand and his occupation lasted only a single day, after which he surrendered. After his arrest, some Key Westers wore "Free Harry Powell" T-shirts; others wore T-shirts bearing a different, though related, sentiment, "Stop the Fight, Give Harry a Light." For his actions, Powell ended up serving time in prison. Shortly after his arrest, the housing project was completed.[52]

The Demise of Houseboat Row

At the same time the Navy was building new housing at Peary Court for military families, Houseboat Row, a neighborhood that symbolized Key West's eclectic population, was on its last legs. Houseboat Row was composed of "water view homes" located on the seawall across from those sections of the Salt Ponds that were transformed into the SeaSide development during the 1990s.

The first houseboat docked at the seawall in 1957 and was owned by Morgan and Margaret Dennis. Morgan was an artist and author who had grown up in the Northeast. The primary subject of both his writing and his art was dogs, which likely inspired the name of their houseboat, "The Sea Dog."[53]

Morgan died in 1960, but over the next several decades other liveaboards joined Margaret and "The Sea Dog" along the seawall, and boats also moored in the water nearby. Public officials initially accepted the expansion of Houseboat Row, but in the early 1970s, the city charged residents of Houseboat Row with various offenses, including polluting offshore waters, constructing ramps on city property, and docking in an illegal area, and ordered them to vacate. Margaret Dennis refused to move, and she and other Houseboat Row residents fought the city in the courts, arguing that rather than force liveaboards to dock only in designated areas, as new city ordinances were attempting to do, the city should establish standards for the boats and allow Houseboat Row to remain intact. In 1980, the District Court of Appeal overturned an earlier court ruling, securing a victory for the residents of Houseboat Row.[54]

Just a few years later, however, residents of Houseboat Row again faced the possibility of being evicted. Mayor Wardlow proposed to build a new city marina at the location of Houseboat Row, and the state approved Key West's application for a permit to build the marina along the seawall over the state-owned bay bottom. Twenty-six houseboats signed leases with the city for the twenty-six available slips, but Key West was to build additional piers in the city's Garrison Bight marina within five years, at which point the vessels docked at Houseboat Row would have to move.[55]

Five years later, however, Garrison Bight had not been expanded and Houseboat Row remained in place. In March 1988, during Mayor Heyman's second administration, the city commission passed a resolution calling for a city marina at Houseboat Row. The apparent intent of the commission, however, was not to evict the houseboats but to formalize the city's relationship with Houseboat Row residents, who would pay "competitive rents" for their leaseholds to the city and be allowed to remain in place. The state agency, however, insisted that this be a temporary arrangement and continue only until space became available at Garrison Bight. After Captain Tony's election as mayor in 1989, he reconciled himself to the fact that Houseboat Row would not last forever, even as he emphasized that he "didn't want to see a rich people's marina started there by the people who own Ocean Walk [a part of SeaSide]. I promise, as long as I'm living, there won't be another marina there."[56]

In 1993, after Dennis Wardlow succeeded Captain Tony as mayor, the city completed the expansion of Garrison Bight and ordered the Houseboat Row residents to relocate. The residents refused to do so, and both the city and the state sued them. Michael Barnes, the residents' attorney, asserted that the city and the state's claim that the houseboats were polluting the waters was unfounded. Rather, he insisted, the raw sewage emanated from other sources. He also emphasized that the owners volunteered to pay for sewage connections to the city's system. In 1997, however, the Circuit Judge ruled that the state and the city could evict the inhabitants of Houseboat Row.[57]

In January 1998, citizens in Key West, by an overwhelming majority of 70 percent, voted in favor of a nonbinding referendum that would allow Houseboat Row to remain intact. The referendum called for the city to acquire or lease the bay bottomland under Houseboat Row and connect the boats to the city sewer system. Residents would pay for the sewer connection and also pay property taxes to the city. Mayor Sheila Mullins, who had succeeded Wardlow in 1997, supported an agreement along these lines, as did several of the city commissioners. The state, however, opposed them, and in April 1998, the Third District Court of

Appeal in Miami sustained the ruling of the circuit court, which held that the state owned and controlled the bay bottomland and therefore could establish policy for Houseboat Row.[58]

In July 1998, Key West appealed to the governor and Cabinet, who were meeting as the Board of Trustees of the state's Internal Improvement Trust Fund, to lease the bay bottomland to the city, so that Key West could allow Houseboat Row to remain. The state's Department of Environmental Protection opposed the city's request and ordered the boats removed within six months. Then, in September, Hurricane Georges hit Key West, destroying several of the twenty-six boats along Houseboat Row. In December, the Board of Trustees ruled against the city's request to lease the submerged land and gave the city until April 7, 1999 to propose an acceptable relocation plan and a more general plan for mooring and anchoring boats in the waters around Key West. More legal cases and other maneuverings followed, but in 2002 the last vessels left Houseboat Row.[59]

During the debates in the late 1990s, several Houseboat Row residents, along with their attorney, argued that Wardlow and others were acting out of ulterior motives, namely, to replace Houseboat Row with a marina for expensive private boats. At least one inhabitant of Houseboat Row contended that the realtor Ed Knight, a "neighbor" of Houseboat Row who lived on his own island, influenced public decision making. Ultimately, a new marina did not take the place of Houseboat Row, and, as yet, no gentrification has transformed the waterways. Still, the residents lost their struggle to preserve something valuable to them. One aspiring writer who worked as a waitress and lived on a boat articulated a perspective many in Key West shared, as they realized their vote in support of Houseboat Row had been rendered meaningless: "We are smart people who work at menial jobs because that's all we can find and still live on this crazy island. That doesn't mean we have menial mentalities. We, the creative people, the Bohemians and the whackos choose to live here. But, we're being pushed out. That's not only sad for us. That's sad for Key West." Increasingly, people of modest means found it difficult to afford housing in Key West, which was fast becoming a haven mostly for tourists and buyers of second homes.[60]

MARIEL BOATLIFT

Top: In summer 1980, thousands of refuges came to Key West from Cuba in the Mariel Boatlift. Some chose to remain in Key West, but most relocated to Miami and elsewhere. Key West's already limited summer tourist season slowed due to publicity about the refugees. Courtesy of Monroe County Public Library system.

TOM MCGUANE, TRUMAN CAPOTE, TENNESSEE WILLIAMS, AND JAMES KIRKWOOD JR.

Above: The writers McGuane, Williams, and Kirkwood all lived in Key West during the 1970s. Capote was a frequent visitor. Courtesy of Monroe County Public Library system.

RAINBOW FLAG DOWN DUVAL STREET

Above: This rainbow flag, which stretched from the Atlantic to the Gulf during PrideFest 2003, attracted national attention. Courtesy of Stuart Newman Associates.

OLD SOUTHERNMOST POINT SIGN

Right: The sign designated the supposed southernmost point in the continental United States where Whitehead Street meets the Atlantic Ocean. Several signs similar to this one were stolen, so in 1983 the city replaced them with a buoy. In reality, this is not the Southernmost Point; the true point lies on Navy grounds that are not open to the public. Courtesy of Monroe County Public Library system.

SHRIMP BOATS AT KEY WEST BIGHT

From 1949 until the 1980s, shrimp boats dominated the Key West Bight. "Pink Gold" was an important component of Key West's economy during these decades. Courtesy of Monroe County Public Library system.

SOUTHERNMOST PARROT HEAD CLUB

In communities throughout the United States, admirers of Jimmy Buffett organized Parrot Head clubs. Many of their members congregate in Key West each November for the annual "Meeting of the Minds." Courtesy of Scott Keeter.

SOUTHERNMOST POINT BUOY

Top: In 1983, the city replaced the markers at the officially designated "Southernmost Point" with this heavy buoy that could not be carried away by those looking for a Key West souvenir. It is a popular spot for taking pictures. Courtesy of Scott Keeter.

STREET PERFORMER ON DUVAL STREET

Above: Performers on Duval Street contribute to the character of the island's main drag. Periodically, the city revisits the issue of whether and to what extent their activities should be "regulated." Author's collection.

SUNSET KEY

Top: This island, just a short boat trip from Mallory Square, was developed in the 1990s to house expensive homes and the cottages of the Westin Resort, located adjacent to Mallory Square. Courtesy of Monroe County Public Library system.

SUSHI IN SHOE, NEW YEAR'S EVE

Above: New York City's Times Square is famous for its New Year's Eve Ball drop. In Key West, Sushi, a well-known drag queen, brings in the New Year in front of the Bourbon St. Pub. Courtesy of Stuart Newman Associates.

I TOLD YOU I WAS SICK

Top: A popular tombstone in the Key West cemetery. Courtesy of Scott Keeter.

SIGN AT ENTRANCE TO TRUMAN ANNEX

Above: The Truman Annex Naval Station closed in 1974. Conflict ensued for more than a decade over the future use of this prime property. Finally, Pritam Singh purchased the property in 1987. He and others developed Truman Annex during the next decade. Author's collection.

Arrival and Unloading of a Turtle Boat, Key West, Florida 24

UNLOADING GREEN TURTLES

Above: The turtle industry became important in Key West in the late 1800s. Turtles were unloaded at the Key West Bight and placed in kraals (underwater pens) until they were slaughtered in Key West or shipped elsewhere. Even after the industry had lost its importance, the turtle kraals remained a tourist attraction. They were closed in 1982. Courtesy of Monroe County Public Library system.

U.S. ROUTE 1 MILE 0 MARKER

Left: U.S. Route 1 stretches from Key West to Maine. This marker on Whitehead Street designates the beginning (or end) of the road. Courtesy of Michael X. Delli Carpini.

VIRGINIA PANICO, RICHARD HEYMAN, AND HARRY POWELL

Top: Key West City Commissioner Virginia Panico, Mayor Richard Heyman, and Commissioner Harry Powell. Heyman, the first openly gay mayor in the United States, was elected to a two-year term in 1983 and again in 1987. Courtesy of Monroe County Public Library system.

BOATS AT HISTORIC SEAPORT

Above: By the 1990s, the shrimp fleet at the Key West Bight (renamed the Historic Seaport) was gone. Instead, commercial charter fishing and sightseeing boats, as well as boats owned by the island's wealthier year-round or seasonal residents, docked at the bight. Courtesy of Michael X. Delli Carpini.

11

Shelter for the Labor Force?

DURING THE 1980S, and especially the 1990s, Key West became increasingly less affordable for public sector workers and those whose incomes depended primarily on the local tourism-based economy. Newcomers to Key West, often second-home buyers, could afford, and contributed to, the rising prices, while others were increasingly priced out of the market. One Key Wester described his neighborhood as transforming from one occupied by Conchs "who had a very strong feeling and respect for island life" to one occupied by the "likes of Calvin Klein, a Broadway producer, movie stars, and socialites from New York City."[1]

In 1981, Klein added the designer Angelo Donghia's house on Eaton Street to his roster of homes in Connecticut, Manhattan, and Fire Island, paying $975,000 for it, a purchase he described as "emotional." The escalation in the price of this Eaton Street residence was extraordinary, but real estate prices were increasing dramatically in most of Old Town, as well as, albeit to lesser degrees, in New Town and the neighborhood bordering Old Town, known as Midtown.[2]

Real estate appreciation was enhanced by the fact that the neighborhood designated as "Old Town," and recognized by the National Register of Historic Places as a historic district, roughly doubled in size in February 1983. In 1986, the city commission adopted an ordinance that reinforced its commitment to historic preservation, granting the Old Island Restoration Commission (OIRC) enhanced authority to review both new buildings and redevelopment in Old Town. Later in the year, the OIRC was renamed the Historic Architectural Review Commission (HARC). In 1998, out of concern that city commissioners sometimes undermined the OIRC's, and now HARC's, integrity, Key West voters solidified HARC's authority by passing a referendum that mandated that appeals from HARC would be heard by a local judge, rather than by the city commission.[3]

Not only were residential properties increasing in value, but commercial prices were also appreciating as the renovation of commercial buildings on Duval Street that had begun in the 1970s continued. For example, during the early 1980s, John Burgess and Jordon Meinster completed their renovation of four buildings in the 800 block of Duval that they had purchased in 1978. On the same block, Dennis Beaver gutted a building he had purchased in 1983, reinventing it as the Tropical Inn Guest House.[4]

New chain retail stores opened on Duval Street, with upscale chains replacing the local stores and chains that had traditionally served Key Westers. During the 1990s, a Bath & Body Works and a Coach store opened on the 400 and 500 blocks of Duval Street, respectively. A tourist chain attraction, Ripley's Believe It or Not, was also opened to visitors. Although chain stores did not dominate the business center of Duval Street, their presence increased toward the end of the century.

New art galleries opened on Duval Street, capitalizing on the growing number of tourists and affluent seasonal residents. By 1990, tourists could visit around twenty galleries, including long-standing ones such as the Gingerbread Square Gallery. Several more opened during the 1990s. Key West also attracted new artists who lived in the community either seasonally or year-round.[5]

Finding Housing: Class Matters

Some of these artists were fortunate enough to move to the community before housing prices escalated throughout most of the 1980s. Although prices dropped during the recession of 1982 and part of 1983, the average sales price of Key West residences increased about 29 percent between 1984 and 1986 and also rose significantly in 1987. Homeowners with mortgages shouldered significantly higher monthly payments than homeowners in the rest of the state did. Other buyers, however, flush with cash, had no need for a mortgage. Real estate brokers noticed a change in the type of buyer looking for real estate in Key West. One observed: "Where we once struggled with a working-class buyer qualifying for a $30,000 mortgage in order to buy a $40,000 house, it is now commonplace for a buyer to pay $300,000 cash." And some of these affluent buyers were converting homes that had been chopped up into apartments back to single-family homes.[6]

In addition, rents were rising fast. In 1979, the average rent in Key West was roughly equivalent to rents in the rest of the state, but by 1989 it had become considerably higher. In 1987, the president of the Key West Board of Realtors summarized the consequences of this increase: "When I first started out (about six years ago), finding a rental was easy, but jobs were scarce. Now it's just the other way around, plenty of jobs, but no place for a working person to live."[7]

A planning report issued in 1992 concluded, "The Key West housing market is characterized by high costs and low vacancy. It is a very tight market which undermines the island's economic well-being by limiting the labor supply, increasing business costs of operation and affecting the economic health of many Key West households." Due to the high cost of living, 20 to 25 percent of the workers in the city's hotels held second jobs. Still, the major hotels experienced a high turnover rate.[8]

Home prices continued to escalate in the 1990s. Although prices dropped between 1990 and 1991 during the national recession and again between 1993 and 1994, the overall trend was dramatically upward. By the mid-1990s, prices in Key West were among the highest in the United States. The average price of a single-family home rose to $265,800 in 2000, a figure that far exceeded the statewide average of $105,500. High solid waste and sewer fees added to citizens' bills. During most of the

1990s, Monroe County had the highest cost of living of all of Florida's 67 counties.[9]

Unlike those in Las Vegas, the service workers in Key West's tourism industry are not unionized. Further, the city commission has yet to adopt a "living wage" ordinance, although some have urged it to do so. Key West's unemployment rate remained less than 3 percent between 1995 and 2000, and reached a low of 2 percent in 2000. This did not, however, result in a significant increase in wages. The percentage of households paying more than 30 percent of their income on housing rose from 30.3 to 48.7 percent during the 1990s, rates significantly higher than the national average. Jobs in the tourism industry were filled increasingly by immigrants from Russia, the Czech Republic, and other eastern European countries and, to a lesser extent, from Latin America and the Caribbean.[10]

Several other factors besides the influx of wealthy people willing and able to pay high prices for a home to occupy either seasonally or year-round contributed to the shortage of affordable housing in Key West. Some were directly due to the growth in the tourism industry. The conversion of apartment buildings into guesthouses, for example, subtracted over one hundred apartments from the rental market in Key West between 1991 and 1994. Some investors converted apartments and single-family homes to short-term vacation rentals, making them unavailable for long-term rent. Even in Stock Island and elsewhere in the Lower Keys, where housing was more affordable, single-family units were being converted into short-term vacation rentals. Some former homes were converted to commercial uses, too, such as professional offices.[11]

From "Colored Town" to "Bahama Village": Tourism, Gentrification, and Key West's Black Community

In the historically black neighborhood west of Whitehead Street, housing prices lagged behind those of other Key West neighborhoods. The more limited gentrification here, however, ultimately resulted in the displacement of many black residents. In 1981, the city officially designated this neighborhood as "Bahama Village." The Key West Neighborhood Improvement Association, led by its director Roy Grant, initiated the name change in hopes of symbolizing the area's integration into Key West's growing tourism-based economy. Grant had charged in the mid-1970s that the city had slighted the neighborhood, contending, "No work has been done here in 50 years. The streets aren't swept, there's no drainage and it's very dirty."[12]

Now, the theory went, Bahama Village would benefit from the same economic trends that had impacted the rest of Key West. In Grant's words, "It's time for the black community to tie into the mainstream of the city's tourist economy." Mayor Sonny McCoy expressed similar hopes and suggested that a revitalized Bahama Village would enhance all of Key West: "New York has Greenwich Village. San Francisco has Chinatown. And Key West will have Bahama Village. The Bahamian ambience will only add to the charm of our island." In 1984, Mayor Richard Heyman noted, "Black residents of the community, in particular, have been left behind as Key West has moved from a Navy-oriented economy to a tourist-oriented economy. It's necessary to bring blacks into the mainstream of tourism."[13]

The inclusion of Bahama Village in the festivities preceding the Fantasy Fest night parade symbolized the effort to integrate the newly named neighborhood into Key West's tourism economy. In 1981, Bahama Village Night drew some tourists and locals to the neighborhood. Then, the Goombay Festival, a traditional Bahamian celebration, became an annual event held just prior to Fantasy Fest. The Tourist Development Council regularly provided the organizers with funds to help them publicize the events and pay their expenses.[14]

Not all of Key West's blacks viewed the city's designation of "Bahama Village" and its support for Goombay as a positive trend for the black community. From their perspective, the most alarming trend was gentrification, which had begun to change the texture of their neighborhood. As early as 1979, some pointed to early signs of gentrification that were the result of at least two factors. One was the expectation that Truman Annex, the abandoned Navy property adjacent to the neighborhood, would be redeveloped as an upscale residential community. Another was the significant increase in land values in most of Old Town resulted in a large gap between land values there and in what became known as Bahama Village, which made the neighborhood increasingly attractive to investors and new residents. In addition, Bahama Village lay within the expanded historic district, which only increased its appeal for investors.[15]

During the 1980s, Bahama Village was gentrifying and attracting more whites. Ervin Higgs, the Monroe County Property Appraiser, noted that, due primarily to higher taxes and utility costs, it was becoming financially difficult for the current residents of the neighborhood to remain there. Many homeowners in Bahama Village sold their homes and moved elsewhere, unable to resist the offers of between $80,000 and $100,000 for their properties. Higgs observed that a common practice was for non-Bahama Village residents to buy homes there, renovate them, and then sell them at a profit. By the mid-1990s, investors were often razing the houses they purchased in Bahama Village and replacing them with new homes.[16]

Other homes in Bahama Village were converted into commercial property, and additional commercial development was initiated in the area. By the end of the 1990s, however, few new black-owned businesses had opened. And those in Bahama Village who were concerned about the escalating gentrification of the neighborhood saw little they could do to slow the process.

The formation of the Bahama Conch Community Land Trust was the major response to gentrification. Organized in 1995, the trust's stated goal was to retain housing for longtime residents and to provide quality affordable housing in Bahama Village. As of April 1998, it had purchased no homes and had secured only limited financing. That month, however, the city commission transferred $269,000 from the Monroe County Land Authority to the Land Trust, allowing it to purchase three homes in Bahama Village and create nine units of affordable housing. Its success, however, remained limited, and by 2010 it had become moribund.[17]

The Exodus to Central Florida

Blacks were not the only ones moving out of Key West. During the 1980s and 1990s, many white Conchs also left the city. Most moved to communities in Central Florida, such as Ocala, Lakeland, and Sebring, as well as to the Tampa Bay area. Grace Fallon, who had moved to Ocala in 1978, began organizing reunions as more and more Conchs relocated to Central Florida. In 1983, only around twenty former Key Westers responded to her efforts to organize a reunion, but just a few years later several hundred attended the event. One of the T-shirts sold in Key West shops read, "Will the Last Conch Leaving Key West Please Bring the Flag," while another quipped, "KW Conchs, Endangered Species."[18]

The motives for the moves varied, as had been the case in the late 1970s, but the rising cost of living certainly contributed to the exodus. Until the passage of Florida's "Save Our Homes" constitutional amendment in 1992, the assessed value of owner-occupied residences in Florida could increase without limit. Therefore, as homeowners sold at inflated prices, their neighbors who chose to remain behind often saw dramatic increases in their property taxes. Beginning in 1995, when the amendment went into effect, annual increases in assessments were capped, so increased property taxes were unlikely to have been the cause of many homeowners' decisions to move elsewhere. Still, the cost of living in Key West drove some homeowners out even after the amendment was implemented.[19]

Some Conch renters relocated because they realized it would be difficult for them to afford a home in Key West. Richard Feger, a third-generation Conch, moved from Key West to Ocala in the 1980s. He had grown up in Key West, served in Vietnam, returned home, and got married. In 1978, Feger purchased a seafood business, and he proceeded to fish commercially part-time, buy a mobile home, and begin saving for a permanent one. Ultimately, however, he left Key West, partially because of the increasing cost of living, which derived primarily from the jump in electricity rates. In his first month in business in 1978, his electric bill was $98.40. Two years later, it was close to $500. At the same time, housing costs in Key West were increasing, and he felt he had a slim chance of being able to afford a home of his own. Not only was housing expensive but jobs offering career advancement were relatively scarce. One family emphasized that they left Key West because there "just wasn't enough opportunity."[20]

Noneconomic factors also contributed to some Conchs' decisions to relocate. One woman, for example, left Key West with her family in 2000 for Asheville, North Carolina, because, as she put it, "the island that I grew up on was gone." She recalled waking in the night to the noise from motorcycles and drunken tourists, and she often found empty beer cans on her front lawn: "Key West is where the rest of the world can come and let their hair down and do what they want at the expense of the local population. I guess they don't think about the fact that average families live here."[21]

Of course, some who had managed to purchase a home and still owned it a decade or more later seized the opportunity to sell at a significant profit. They could then live mortgage-free in a larger house elsewhere. Regardless of their reasons for moving, some later had a change of heart. Generally, however, rising housing prices made it impossible for them to move back to Key West. In the words of one relocated Conch, "When you sell out in Key West, there's no way you could ever afford to go back. It's a one-way road off The Rock."[22]

For longtime Conchs who stayed on "The Rock," Key West was no longer the community they had known. Ygnacio Carbonell, an eighty-one-year-old Conch, bemoaned, "Key West has changed. I don't like it. It's getting worse every year. The home feeling is completely gone. When you go to Pantry Pride or Publix, you don't see anybody to pass the day anymore." As one Conch put it, "I feel like a stranger in my own town," a feeling that many who left Key West probably shared.[23]

Development and Affordable Housing in a Tourism-based Economy: Politicians and Policy

By the mid-1980s, Key West's city officials were well aware that the city's tourism-based economy had created a mismatch between the tourism industry's need for employees and the ability of those employees, as well as other private service workers and public employees, to find affordable housing. During the first half of the decade, the number of residential housing units increased by only 10 percent, while the number of transient housing units (primarily hotels, motels, and guesthouses) increased by 55.5 percent. In 1986, tourist accommodations accounted for 25 percent of the non-military residential units in Key West, up from 19 percent in 1980.[24]

The Growth Management Ordinance (GMO) of 1986 was designed to curb the rapid development of hotels and expensive homes in Key West and to enhance the supply of affordable housing. The GMO represented a potentially significant change from the status quo. It limited the number of units that could be approved each year to 300 and restricted the city to approving only one transient unit for every four new residential units. Also, 50 percent of the residential units had to be affordable. Affordability applied to both rent levels and home prices, and both rentals and homes had to remain affordable for five years. The Key West City Planning Department forecast that the GMO would lead to a dramatic decrease in the growth of hotels, motels, and guesthouses, allowing the supply of residential housing, and especially of affordable units, to catch up with the demand.[25]

The city commission revised the GMO in December 1986, increasing the ratio of transient to residential units from 1 to 4 to 1 to 3 and thereby allowing more transient units to be constructed. The revision also reduced the proportion of housing that had to be affordable from 50 to 40 percent. Nevertheless, the revised ordinance still represented a change from the status quo in Key West and was an unprecedented public regulation of development.[26]

Many in Key West agreed with the sentiment of the local historian Sharon Wells, who insisted that the GMO was necessary if Key West's small-town atmosphere was to be retained, and with Captain Tony, who noted, "before [the GMO], it was like the rape of the island. There were no laws. No one wanted to stop these people. The law was necessary." Others, however, joined with the vice president of the Chamber of Commerce in calling the GMO too stringent and arguing that it would hurt the city's economy by slowing growth. Even those who criticized the GMO, however, including some employers in the tourism industry, recognized the need for affordable housing. The *Citizen*, in an editorial published on January 1, 1989, included on its wish list for the new year a moratorium on new motel and hotel development until plans for the 500 affordable housing units that the city dearly needed were complete.[27]

In spite of this widespread sentiment and the goal of the ordinance, however, the city commission sometimes rejected proposals for affordable housing. For example, in 1988, it rejected a proposal to build an affordable housing complex on North Roosevelt Boulevard. Mayor Heyman took the press to the site and urged the community to support the Bayview project, which was proposed by two local businessmen, Peter Rosasco and Gary Blum. The project would offer approximately 400 apartments with rents ranging from $350 to $640 a month, considerably lower than the threshold of what the GMO had deemed affordable. Although the GMO did not require it, the Bayview project would establish income limits for eligible tenants. Heyman emphasized that the site of the proposed development was close to places of employment and served by public transportation. It also had the advantage of being near enough to retail stores that many tenants could bike or walk to them.[28]

The proposal did not receive a warm welcome from the city commission. Commissioner Harry Powell, who had emphasized during his campaign that Key West needed to take steps to maintain the diversity of its population, expressed concerns about the project and suggested that with 400 low-rent units the development might become a "slum." Even Commissioner Jimmy Weekley, who had been the primary initiator of the GMO, voiced reservations about Bayview's density. The developers and their attorney appeared several times before the commission and responded to questions regarding the project's density and its impact on Key West's infrastructure, including its roads and sewage system. In response to the commission's concerns, the developers modified the project, decreasing it to 246 units, of which only 82 were designated as "affordable." In spite of these changes, in May 1988 the commission voted, 3 to 2, to reject the site plan. Heyman later complained that the experience of the Bayview developers would likely discourage others from proposing affordable housing projects. Indeed, the following month, developers of a proposed affordable housing project across from the Bayview site withdrew their application.[29]

In late 1991, city staff reported that they were uncertain of exactly how many new residential and transient units had been completed since the passage of the GMO. It was clear, however, that the GMO contributed to the supply of affordable housing to only a limited extent. Ocean Walk apartments and Las Salinas, both located in the SeaSide development on the east end of the island, added affordable rental units and condominiums, respectively. The GMO ordinance, however, only mandated that the units remain affordable for five years; as such, the long-term supply of affordable housing was not assured. Further, there was no stipulation that the purchased units be owner-occupied. For example, investors purchased many of the units in Las Salinas, rented them out to tenants, and then sold them for a significant profit five years later. The redevelopment of the Truman Annex naval base further showed the limitations of the GMO.[30]

Truman Annex

During the 1980s, the land that had once housed the Truman Annex Naval Station became the focus of a development struggle. Once a major component of Key West's naval facilities, the base was decommissioned in 1974 and was to be transformed to nonmilitary uses. Up for grabs, however, was who would develop and what type of development would take place on this prime land just a few blocks west of Duval Street.

From the mid-1970s until the land was sold in 1986, space in some of the buildings was rented inexpensively to writers, artists, craftspeople, and a variety of small businesses. In addition, liveaboards anchored their boats in the nearshore waters and in the former submarine basin at the Naval Station. In the words of the sculptor John Martini, who rented a studio at the Annex, "It was a wonderful moment when all that was Key West at that time was present. The boat people, the small craftsmen, and small business people . . . the artists and writers, bubbas and all just inside a gate across from the Green Parrot [a popular bar]." This community, however, proved short-lived, and the area soon transitioned from a military use to one more compatible with the island's shift toward wealthy seasonal residents and tourism.[31]

In the late 1970s, Denis Anderson, the director of the Key West and Lower Keys Development Corporation (Devcorp), an organization formed to oversee the transition of the land from federal control, predicted that multiple investors would compete to develop the property and that work would begin in late 1980 or early 1981. Anderson also anticipated that the redeveloped Annex would serve Key West's tourism-based economy and would likely feature a hotel and separate ports for yachts and cruise ships.[32]

After Devcorp lost its federal funding, the city commission organized the Key West Redevelopment Agency (RDA) and in mid-1979 appointed a five-member board to work with the General Services Administration, the federal agency responsible for arranging the sale of Truman Annex. It soon became apparent that the RDA's plans included no affordable housing. Rather, the area was to accommodate primarily expensive housing and hotels. Roy Grant, and others in the neighborhood soon to be designated as Bahama Village, voiced concern that the redevelopment would fuel gentrification and thus displace members of their community. Save Our Waterfront, a group led by the local architect Tom Pope, expressed his fear that Truman Annex would become a gated community that would limit the public's access. Ed Crusoe, a Key West Bar pilot, argued that the converted Truman Annex should include a shipyard to provide jobs for the workers who had lost their jobs when the naval shipyard closed.[33]

These concerns, however, generally fell on deaf ears at the RDA, which at its meeting in December 1979 considered its "final plan" for the Annex. According to the plan, low and moderate-income housing was incompatible with the optimal development of Truman Annex, which, instead, was to be developed with "the objective of maximizing employment opportunities, increasing the tax rolls and expanding the city's economic base." Optimal development included the construction of a resort hotel, a marina with a cruise port and yacht club, commercial space including offices and restaurants, and housing for residents and vacationers. The city commission, after hearing the protests of several groups, voted against the RDA's proposal. Still, the plan represented the general vision of the RDA over the next several years and of developers interested in the Truman Annex property.[34]

In 1983, the RDA was apparently in the process of solidifying an agreement with the Sarasota developer and attorney John Dent and his partners in the Key West Harbour Development Corporation. Dent offered to purchase the property for $12 million from the federal government, convey it to Key West, and then sign a ninety-nine-year lease and development agreement with the city. Dent's plan called for preserving and renovating some of the historic buildings in the Truman Annex and constructing about 160,000 square feet of office and retail commercial space, a 500-room resort hotel with a marina, and town houses and condominiums. Dent and his partners also envisioned building luxury housing on Tank Island, a small island located less than a mile off shore that the Navy had dredged in the 1960s and used to house two oil storage tanks. Unlike the RDA's plan, Dent's proposal also included some "moderate income" housing. Both the developer and the RDA denied "rumors" that the public would lose access to the waterfront property and that fences and gates would separate the development from the rest of the city. The RDA's director, Steve McDaniel, emphasized that the community would benefit from the additional tourists, businesses, and tax receipts the development would generate.[35]

An article published in 1984 set the scene for the redeveloped Navy property based upon McDaniel's and Dent's plans: "You live on Tank Island . . . today is Monday, a work day, so you choose to take the ferry into Key West and leave your boat docked at the Tank Island marina. As you head into the new marina at Truman Annex, you notice that one of the many cruise ships which use the new cruise ship port is docking.

. . . You also notice that the new 500-room hotel appears practically full. . . . There is little automobile traffic, as much of the development has been built with pedestrian walkways instead of streets. . . . You stroll by the renovated Truman White House, through the historic commercial district and into the quiet residential area."[36]

Dent and McDaniel interpreted this vision as a residential and tourist environment that was nothing more than an expansion of Key West's Old Town. Dent emphasized, "It's been our intent in our development to reflect Key West. We want to make sure that when it's finished it looks just like Old Key West." In reality, the development reflected a new vision of Key West, one frequented by cruise ship passengers and inhabited primarily by affluent residents, both year-round and seasonal. It was adjacent to Bahama Village, but could not be farther removed in terms of style and atmosphere; it was near the bars and entertainment on Duval and Front Streets in Old Town, but also a world of its own.[37]

The deal, however, fell apart in March and April 1986. A major factor working against it was the composition of the new city commission, which, after the city elections in 1985, included George Halloran and Jimmy Weekley, rather than Jose Balbontin and James Mira, who had both backed Dent's proposed development. Most of the new city commissioners sought lower density projects than what Dent and the old commission had agreed to; moreover, they agreed with the citizen groups that felt McDaniel had been representing Dent's interests rather than those of the wider community. The negotiations with Dent ended without an agreement.[38]

Many now wondered whether an arrangement could be reached with any private developer. Mel Fisher, the treasure hunter whose team had recently found the *Atocha* treasure, presented the RDA with an offer. Never at a loss for words or ideas, Fisher proposed a pirate theme park as the perfect reuse of the former Navy base. Fisher walked into RDA headquarters loaded with two chests of silver, along with certified checks and a letter of credit, and said, "The money's on the table." In spite of this dramatic offer, however, the deal did not go through.[39]

Instead, the land was sold at a GSA auction on September 10, 1986, twelve years after the base closed. The buyer was Pritam Singh, the purchase price just over $17 million. Singh was neither a Conch nor a long-time Key West business figure. He was born in Massachusetts in 1952, as Paul Arthur Labombard Jr. He first visited Key West in 1969, when he hitchhiked down to the southernmost city after graduating from high school in Maine. In Key West, he found a "mutual society of long-hairs." Labombard, as he was still known, slept on the porch of a local inn and also sometimes camped with other hippies on Christmas Tree (Wisteria) Island in the Gulf, an undeveloped island near the Key West Bight.[40]

After a few months in Key West, he moved on to Tallahassee and other Florida communities, working as a laborer on construction projects. Labombard eventually left Florida, was arrested at an anti-Vietnam May Day demonstration in Washington, D.C., and served five days in jail. He then moved to a commune near Amherst, Massachusetts, founded by the followers of a Sikh spiritual leader. Here, in 1971, at the age of nineteen, Labombard changed his name to Pritam Singh, meaning "God's beloved royal lion," and adopted the Sikh religion. Five years later, Singh found himself a devout believer in the Sikh faith but disillusioned with the founder of the community. He traveled to India in 1976 with his wife and daughter and became active in the Sikh drive for independence from India. For a couple of years, Singh traveled between India and the United States, speaking as an advocate for the Sikhs' cause.[41]

In 1979, Singh's life took a different turn. He moved back to Maine and entered the development business in Portland. Singh attracted wealthy backers and garnered significant profits in real estate development. Then, in 1986, he read in the *New York Times* about an auction in Key West for the former Navy land. Singh successfully outbid his competitors at the auction. Shortly after buying Truman Annex, Singh and his colleagues stayed at the Pier House, which, at $250 a night, was a far cry from Christmas Tree Island.[42]

The formal transfer of the property to Singh's newly formed Truman Annex Co. occurred on March 11, 1987, and Singh's master plan was made public at a town meeting in July. It included the renovation of the Little White House and other historic buildings. The Customs House was to be turned into a yacht club and restaurant. The development plan also envisioned a 150-unit luxury hotel overlooking a marina, adjacent to Mallory Square. In addition, it called for retail and office buildings, an artist's building with studio and living space, a recreational area, a 90-room hotel on Tank Island, and 125 units of what Singh called "rental housing," but the city called "affordable housing."[43]

Shortly after purchasing the property, however, Singh dramatically changed some of his stated plans. For example, he served artists who

had been renting space from the RDA with an eviction notice and provided them no option of moving to an "artist's building." John Martini
recollected:

> Singh made many promises: artists' space over commercial build-
> ings, a true community integrated in every way into the Old Town.
> . . . I should have guessed the true outcome when Pritam visited at
> my studio. He raved over the special feeling of the brick building
> with huge roof beams in which I worked. He told me that this space
> would be the spiritual center for the entire project. I was moved un-
> til a few days later I received my eviction notice, one of the first to
> be given to anyone. Well, I thought, he must be determined to start
> off with the space that would spiritually define his vision. Within a
> week after I moved out he moved in the lawnmowers for the annex.
> This would be as spiritual as the space ever became.[44]

Singh soon faced financial difficulties, and in 1990 he declared bank-
ruptcy. He did organize a new company called the Truman Annex Real
Estate Company that constructed homes on Truman Annex, but, due to
his financial problems, most of the nonresidential uses of Truman Annex
were ultimately completed by other parties. Ocean Properties, based in
South Florida, purchased Tank Island from Singh's creditors, renamed it
Sunset Key, and developed luxury housing on it. Ocean Properties also
developed the Hilton Key West Resort & Marina (later the Westin) adjacent to Mallory Square, which included several cottages on Sunset Key.
In addition, Ocean Properties developed Pier B as a cruise ship port that
was owned by the hotel.[45]

Most of the housing units served as homes for relatively wealthy,
and primarily seasonal, newcomers to the island. Key West had long attracted winter residents. Many of its prominent writers left during the
summer, as did many workers in tourism. Increasingly, however, wealthy
purchasers of second homes targeted Key West as a community where
they could spend part of each year and likely secure a profitable investment. During the 1990s and early twenty-first century, many of these
purchasers of second (and third and fourth) homes sought out Truman
Annex. By the early 2000s, during the summer months, one could wan-
der through most of Truman Annex and not see a soul.[46]

Ultimately, despite Singh's construction of housing deemed affordable under the GMO, the Truman Annex development did little to help

the cause of affordable housing on the island. Singh sold several of the homes that were priced at below market value to his colleagues. His employees and other insiders purchased 42 of the first 85 affordable homes before sales even opened to the public. For a majority of these purchasers, their Truman Annex properties served as second homes or as investments they could rent short-term to tourists or long-term to Key West residents. Many of the units that initially sold at affordable prices were rented at market rates after the five-year limit expired. A number of the "affordable" homes also sold around the five-year mark at market values, which were well above the affordable range. In 2004, the 600-square-foot, one-bedroom condominiums in the Shipyard, originally built as affordable housing, were selling for above $400,000.[47]

In July 1979, Robert Duffy, an attorney with Legal Services of the Florida Keys, published a letter in the *Citizen*. He wrote:

> For generations all manner of economic and social life-styles have co-existed in Key West—wealthy and poor together. But this co-existence is being gravely threatened by the proposed plan for the surplus military property on Truman Annex. Continuation of a colorful, affordable, integrated island paradise is being swapped by this plan for a pale sterile, merely-passable tourist trap and wealthy get-away. . . . Truman Annex should be made to meet the overall needs of the community, integrated into the rest of the city and made usable and available to all income levels.

Duffy argued that this was especially important because homes in Key West were "being bought up by speculators who raise the land values and rents." The ultimate development of Truman Annex realized Duffy's worst fears. A resident of Aspen, Colorado, in the 1990s reacted to the upscaling of the community with the following observation: "The eccentric's hideout was becoming affluent America's playground." Certainly, some Key Westers felt similarly about the changes to their city, changes that the redevelopment of Truman Annex only accelerated.[48]

ROGO

At the time Truman Annex was being developed, Key West was entering a new phase regarding growth policy and affordable housing. In 1993, the city commission adopted a "Building Permit Allocation and Vested

Rights Ordinance," commonly referred to as the "Rate of Growth Ordinance" (ROGO). ROGO made the number of transient and residential units that could be constructed in Key West dependent on the city's ability to evacuate in the event of a hurricane. Florida's Department of Community Affairs (DCA) had exerted substantial pressure on Monroe County to adopt a policy to slow and stabilize development, and, in response, Monroe County staff and consultants devised the county's ROGO. DCA then required Key West to adopt a similar ordinance. The city's ROGO also limited the growth of new transient units to no more than one for every three new residential units, as was stipulated in the GMO. And ROGO mandated that 30 percent of the new residential units be "affordable," down from the 40 percent in the GMO.[49]

Although ROGO was a new policy, its provisions and goals were, in fact, similar to those of the GMO. Both ordinances limited new construction and also sought to slow the growth of transient units and to provide more affordable housing. Like the GMO, however, the city did not implement ROGO in a way entirely compatible with its goals. By the first quarter of 1997, the city had already permitted almost enough new construction to exhaust its ROGO allotment. The proportion of these units that were transient also exceeded the 25-percent limit, in part due to the actions undertaken by the city commission just prior to ROGO's adoption, actions that nevertheless violated the city's GMO. Sitting as the Board of Adjustment (BOA), the city commission regularly granted variances in Old Town that allowed for higher densities and often granted "special exceptions" to owners wishing to transform their apartment buildings into guesthouses. Between February 1992 and January 1993, the BOA approved fifty-one additional transient units, as well as twenty-seven residential units, only six of which qualified as affordable housing. According to David Ethridge, the editor of *Solares Hill*, beginning in early 1992, the BOA made it clear that "dense is the name, transient is the game."[50]

Last Stand protested many of these guesthouse conversions, but the BOA routinely approved them, ignoring their escalating squeeze on affordable housing. At least one city commissioner had made it quite clear that affordable housing was not her priority. Virginia Panico, later hired as the executive vice president of the Key West Chamber of Commerce, recognized the problem, saying, "Sure, it's becoming harder for working class people to live here," but concluded, "So what? It's becoming harder for them to live anywhere." Despite several warnings from DCA, in a single evening in July 1993 alone, the BOA approved conversions that added 39 new transient units. Finally, toward the end of 1993, the DCA challenged over twenty of the variances and special exceptions BOA had granted, primarily those permitting transient units in residential neighborhoods. In May 1994, the DCA agreed to withdraw its challenges to these variances if the city would begin to enforce its own laws and no longer allow density variances or special exceptions. The DCA's intervention proved effective. In December 1995, Key West stopped issuing additional permits for new transient units. As was the case with the GMO, however, ROGO's impact on the city's supply of affordable housing was limited.[51]

Key West at the End of the Century

In the mayoral race of 1997, Dennis Wardlow, who had been elected mayor in 1981, 1991, 1993, and 1995, chose not to seek reelection. Several new candidates joined the race, and the runoff came down to a showdown between the old guard, represented by Charlie Ramos, and those critical of the direction in which Key West was moving, represented by Sheila Mullins. Ramos had been a major force in Key West's politics in the early 1960s, when he defeated longtime incumbent Bernard Papy in the Democratic primary for state representative in 1962, but he stepped down after serving just one term in office. According to many Key Westers, he became a borderline hermit, gaining hundreds of pounds and spending days in his pajamas. Mullins, on the other hand, was an activist and worked with Last Stand and other citizen groups. She first arrived in Key West in the early 1970s while on vacation. When her car broke down during her visit, she decided to stay.[52]

During the runoff, Ramos declared that the race was between a third-generation Conch and a newcomer, and he presented Mullins's campaign as a war waged by power-hungry newcomers on the people who had built the island and made it attractive. In fact, he called Jimmy Weekley, a city commissioner at the time, a "turncoat Conch" for supporting Mullins. In the end, Mullins defeated Ramos by a wide margin and became Key West's first woman mayor.[53]

Along with Mullins, several incumbents were reelected to the city commission, which, with the adoption of district elections in 1993, had been expanded from five to seven members (including the mayor). Jimmy Weekley and Sally Lewis, both generally supportive of growth management and affordable housing, were both reelected. Carmen Turner, an African American from an established Conch family who often sided with Weekley and Lewis, also retained her seat.

During Mullins's administration, the commission adopted a policy limiting the ability of homeowners to rent their homes and condominiums to tourists on a short-term basis, a policy Mullins argued was necessary if the supply of affordable rental housing was to be increased. Her administration also initiated improvements to the sewage system to protect the nearshore waters from additional pollution. The commission was frequently criticized, however, for its long meetings that seemed to lack leadership.

In the election of 1999, Weekley opposed Mullins and secured an easy victory, gaining 59.3 percent of the votes to Mullins's 30.2 percent and trouncing the three other candidates, including an artist who changed his legal name to Captain Outrageous prior to the campaign. Also elected to office were two gay men. Jeremy Anthony and Tom Oosterhoudt. Anthony, a twenty-year resident of Key West, took the seat of Sally Lewis, who did not seek reelection. Oosterhoudt, who moved to Key West in the early 1980s, based his campaign partially on his success in bringing a symphony to Key West.[54]

The commission that took office in 1999 included two gay men, two women (one white and one black), and two white male Conchs who represented primarily the more traditional Conch families. The mayor, Jimmy Weekley, was himself a Conch and won the race with support from the gay and environmental communities. Most saw him as a mayor who would unite the different segments of the community. The commission, to a significant extent, reflected the city's makeup. Although the political officeholders were diverse, many continued to debate whether Key West, more generally, was losing its character and its uniqueness.

By the early 1990s, even the Key West Hotel and Motel Association was raising this concern. Their proposed agenda for the Tourist Development Council in 1993 included sharing the findings of a survey they had conducted. They concluded, "visitors consider Key West a special, unique place, not a manufactured environment like Disney World or many other destinations ruined by overbuilding and a raft of common franchise operations. The large Historic District with its wooden houses, past and current literary and artistic characters and the Conch traditions are our main features."[55]

The association felt the TDC should market those aspects of Key West that the survey identified as being attractive to tourists. The city's "historic treasures," including the museums and homes in the historic district, were among these attractive qualities, as was the "laid back lifestyle." Tourists also valued the waters for fishing, diving, and snorkeling, and the ideal climate. The survey suggested that visitors to Key West also appreciated the island's "eccentric characters" and the nightlife on Duval Street. In the first decade of the twenty-first century, issues of class, character, and the "marketing" of Key West continued to divide the community. Could Key West retain its character in the face of ever more cruise ship passengers and wealthy tourists and residents? And, even if so, could the island also provide housing for its public-sector and tourism-industry workers?

12

Island Tensions in the Twenty-First Century

Mass Tourism and Rising Real Estate Values in a "Unique" Community

THE FIRST YEARS OF the twenty-first century brought two very different trends to Key West that accelerated those first noticeable in the 1980s. On the one hand, mass tourism engulfed the island to a greater extent than ever before, manifesting primarily in the increased number of cruise ship passengers. On the other hand, real estate prices skyrocketed as, among other things, wealthy seasonal residents purchased homes and investors engaged in speculation. This real estate appreciation impacted the housing market, the tourism industry, and the culture of the island. Many worried that these trends would threaten the island's character, uniqueness, and inclusiveness. However, as had always been the case, people's feelings about changes in the community were mixed.

The Key West Chamber of Commerce estimated that between 1996 and 2003 the number of tourists visiting Key West increased by more than a million, for a total of approximately 2.6 million visitors in 2003.

The numbers decreased in 2004 and 2005 but remained above those of the late 1990s. The greatest source for this increase in visitors was the growing cruise ship trade (see appendix). In 1996, 393,000 cruise ship passengers visited Key West, representing about 28 percent of the island's tourists; by 2003, the number of passengers disembarking in Key West topped 1,067,000 and constituted about 42 percent of Key West's tourist trade. Almost daily, passenger ships would arrive at Mallory Dock, which the city owned, Pier B, which the Hilton Hotel (now the Westin) owned, or at the Outer Mole, which the Navy still owned but leased to Key West to service cruise ships. Indeed, Key West's volume of cruise ship traffic increased to rank among the highest in the world, with one estimate placing Key West as the world's fourth busiest port in 2003. Clearly, the protests by Last Stand and Reef Relief had had very little impact on the policies of the city or the practices of the cruise ship lines.[1]

No single reason could account for the increase in the number of cruise ship passengers. Cruising, in general, was becoming more popular with Americans. The terrorist attacks on September 11, 2001, in New York and Washington, D.C., also played a role, with some cruise ship lines substituting European destinations with ports closer to home. Between 2001 and 2002, the number of passengers arriving in Key West rose more than 50 percent, from 679,000 to over 1,030,000. The decrease in 2004, to 934,000 cruise ship passengers, stemmed partially from the threat of hurricanes in the fall and partially from the closure of the Outer Mole Pier from May through October 2004 for dredging of the harbor. The number arriving in 2005 dropped approximately 1 percent from that of 2004. However, in 2004, a ferry company began service between Key West and Fort Myers, transporting passengers to and from a city-built terminal at the Key West Bight, and this service partially compensated for the decrease in the number of cruise ship passengers. Many of those arriving via ferry in Key West left the same day, making their economic impact on the island similar to that of the cruise ship passengers.[2]

Key West: Spoiled Community or Tourist Mecca—The Outsider View

Key West's increase in tourism, and especially in cruise ship traffic, made it an object of criticism in a widely publicized analysis of tourist destinations. In March 2004, an article published in the *National Geographic*

Traveler magazine characterized Key West as a tourist destination gone bad. The magazine's "destination scorecard" ranked 115 tourist destinations from around the world as "Good," "Not so Bad," or "Getting Ugly." Key West ranked third from the bottom in the "Getting Ugly" group. The article gave Key West a rating of "bad" for both its tourism management and its likely future outlook, and a "warning" for its aesthetics.[3]

However, as had often been the case since the 1930s, people's responses to the situation were mixed. The same week the article in the *Traveler* appeared, an article in the *New York Times* travel section praised Key West. The author, having visited with his wife and two children, had few negatives to report and praised the range of activities available to visitors: "A Key West vacation means different things to different people. For some, it's one long bar crawl. For others, Key West is all about the water: fishing, snorkeling, sailing, jet skiing, parasailing. . . . Then there's cultural Key West, with an extraordinary collection of Victorian houses and a rich literary history." In March 2004, the *Island* magazine website also praised Key West, including it among its "Top 10 Island Picks" in the world, along with such destinations as Fiji, Tahiti, Cancun, Kauai, and Martha's Vineyard.[4]

Evaluations in publications and websites targeting gay tourists also concluded that Key West was a desirable place to vacation. For example, a travel website of gay and lesbian newspapers proclaimed, "Key West still remains one of the nation's most popular gay getaways," and noted that only Provincetown, Palm Springs, and Fort Lauderdale "offer such an abundance of gay-oriented accommodations." In December 2003, *Out and About*, a prominent gay publication, named Key West as the most desirable winter vacation destination for gays and lesbians.[5]

Key West: Spoiled or Attractive Community—The Insider View

Key Westers themselves remained divided on their views of tourism and its impact. Several of Key West's literary figures wrote critically of the changes in the community. Joy Williams's *Travel Guide to Key West and the Florida Keys* was first published in 1987, and several updated editions were released. In the 2003 edition, Williams added an "Afterword," in which she declared that Key West had changed for the worse and that the island had achieved "the critical mass of a totally tourist-based economy." A "business-development oligarchy prevailed" on the island, she continued, regardless of the "promoted carefree image." Williams concluded, "rascally Key West has fallen hard for its own commodification." The oligarchy had successfully promoted Key West to tourists, but it was no longer the community she had treasured. Although she still owned a home in Key West, she now spent relatively little time there.[6]

Rosalind Brackenbury, another Key West author who often wrote articles in *Solares Hill*, generally shared Williams's perspective. She reminded readers that, in earlier decades, Key West had displayed the "charm of the unexpected, the irregular, the slightly decrepit, the sun-worn . . . chickens, eccentric people." Now, Key West's atmosphere had changed for a variety of reasons, including rapid development and mass tourism. Greed had led to more tourism, development, and overcrowding, "giving in to the lowest common denominator, ignoring any sense of scale, from cruise ships to the monstrous concrete developments out on South Roosevelt."[7]

By this time, Last Stand shared its membership with a new group, Committee for a Livable Old Town, and the two organizations criticized mass tourism and those who promoted it. The Committee for a Livable Old Town apparently drew inspiration from the "Conch Republic's" secession in 1982, as well as from Hemingway's indignation at the tourists who gazed at his house. The Committee threatened, presumably facetiously, to initiate the secession of Old Town from Key West in protest of the numerous Conch Trains and Old Town Trolleys that had taken over the streets and carried tourists who gawked at their homes. Over time, it evolved into a cohesive group with a sophisticated website that, according to one of its leaders, represented the voices of the residents of Key West who shared a different perspective from the Key West Chamber of Commerce. Its website displayed several advertisements bearing statements such as "DID YOU KNOW . . . ? CRUISE SHIPS DODGE TAXES," and "DID YOU KNOW . . . ? CONCH TRAINS CAUSE TRAFFIC JAMS."[8]

HTA's president, Ed Swift, was the obvious target of some of the website's advertisements and vehemently disagreed with his critics. In June 2004, he distributed a nine-page letter documenting his response to the article published in the *National Geographic Traveler* and, in effect, to those Key Westers who criticized the city's shift toward mass tourism. His bottom line was that Key West was a far better community than it had been after the Navy downsized in the 1970s. Swift noted that a survey conducted around that time showed that 80 percent of Americans did not know where Key West was located. Certainly, some who had managed to find it were quite pleased that most had never heard of the island. But Swift saw things differently, exclaiming, "We've come a long way baby."

True, Swift admitted, tourism had created inconveniences for residents, such as noise and traffic. (Swift lived in a residential suburb of Key West, a safe distance from the tourists.) He concluded, however, "It's how we make our living as a city and [without tourism] our favorite restaurants wouldn't be here, the playhouse would not survive, the art shows and house tours wouldn't happen, restoration would not have been viable and most importantly the majority of Key Westers could not pay their bills or be able to stay on the island. Most of us must share our island to survive." Swift was one of the organizers of Community for a Better Key West, which operated a website and sponsored advertisements in support of mass tourism. Although its stated purpose was to offer a "balanced" viewpoint, one could find little on the site that was critical of the growth of tourism. It claimed, for example, "Our (the tourism) industry is clean, non-polluting and self promoting (if we do a good job)." The site also included a picture of a young girl with the caption, "Tourism has made my school a better place." Nearly all of the testimonials bore the heading "Tourism Benefits Us All."[9]

A survey conducted in 2004 of Key West's population found that many fell somewhere in between Swift's positivity and Last Stand's and the Committee for a Livable Old Town's negativity regarding increased tourism. The Community Foundation of the Florida Keys, a nonprofit philanthropic organization founded in 1996, initiated a study of Key Westers' attitudes regarding tourism, conducted by the well-known pollster and Key West resident, Lou Harris, and his son. The results of their telephone survey indicated that the citizens of Key West generally accepted the tourism-based economy but also wanted to stem the growth of tourism and to see the government regulate the tourism industry.

The survey found that 76 percent of Key West's residents "felt favorable" about their city's reputation as a popular destination. While they were not as overwhelmingly supportive of Key West's economy's heavy dependence on tourism, a majority, 59 percent, viewed this positively. Most agreed, however, that Key West would not benefit from a further increase in tourism. Only 19 percent wanted to see an increase in the number of visitors, compared with 59 percent who wanted the numbers to remain stable and 21 percent who wanted the number of visitors to decrease.

The study also indicated that Key West's supposedly laissez-faire attitude, which had always characterized the island only partially, did not extend to its residents' attitudes regarding the right relationship between government and tourist businesses. While 58 percent opposed "micromanaging the tourist industry," 85 percent agreed with the statement, "However much our economy benefits from the tourist industry, it is simply overwhelming our city and our natural environment. Our city government has a responsibility to protect our quality of life and the character of our community." An overwhelming majority reported that the city commission's top priority should be to "give equal consideration to the concerns of residents and the tourist industry and strike a reasonable balance between the two when conflicts arise." Only 30 percent felt that Key West's government was already providing this balance. Rather, 40 percent believed the government "usually favored" the tourism industry and another 22 percent thought it "always favored" the tourism industry.

The Tourist Development Council

The public's perspective on the TDC was somewhat contradictory. Although 68 percent of respondents thought the TDC was doing a good and necessary job to bolster the economy of the city and the county, 46 percent believed the TDC no longer needed to spend money on advertising because Key West was sufficiently established as a tourist destination. Even the *Citizen* suggested that the TDC, which had been originally designed to provide economic benefits to the entire community, was now primarily benefiting a few. It was unlikely, the *Citizen* suggested, that the TDC would ever agree that Key West and the Keys had enough tourism, because a majority of its board members directly benefited from continued growth. The *Citizen* proposed that the public interest might be better served by reducing the "bed tax" and replacing it with a "community impact tax" to help finance public improvements in the community. Elected officials, however, did not seriously consider this proposal.[10]

The TDC tried to steer a middle course. In April 2004, its director, Harold Wheeler, released a "white paper" to the TDC board titled "Tourism

Impacts/Quality of Life Issues," in which he emphasized that the TDC's primary goal was to promote "quality tourism," not "mass tourism." Wheeler noted that the TDC strove to attract people between the ages of 35 and 54, with household incomes of at least $75,000. And he suggested that the TDC's annual sponsorship of several fishing tournaments, as well of plays and music at local venues such as the Red Barn Theatre and Tennessee Williams Fine Arts Center, helped to attract that type of tourist.[11]

According to Wheeler, the fact that spring breakers and cruise ship passengers constituted an increasing share of visitors contributed to the "danger of losing the unique character of Key West and the Keys" and the "image of being quaint." According to Wheeler, the consumers the TDC was targeting visited the Keys for their natural beauty, marine environment, and things that are "quaint, unique, charming, cultural." He stressed that locals' concerns were compatible with the "eco-tourism" market the TDC targeted. Wheeler concluded that the TDC should "promote the most upscale, responsible traveler from whom we can profit, but who also will respect and help protect our natural resources."[12]

Committee Reports and Policy Initiatives: Symbolism in Action

The TDC, however, had relatively little direct influence on the character of Duval Street, cruise ship policy, or most other policy issues of concern to residents or tourists. These remained the city's responsibility. In late 2003, before the article appeared in *National Geographic Traveler*, Mayor Jimmy Weekley appointed a task force to study tourism's impact on Key West. He also convened a Key West Resident/Visitor Planning Committee, whose members were appointed by the mayor and city commission. The Planning Committee issued its final report in November 2004, presenting the city commission with a series of recommendations. The committee made no suggestions regarding the controversial cruise ship issue, but it did conclude that the city commission needed to consider additional policies and regulations regarding code enforcement, noise pollution, cleanliness, and several other quality-of-life issues. Mayor Weekley agreed that Key West had to "change what people consider Key West" to be and had to find a middle ground, if both tourism and residents' quality of life were to be maintained. For example, while Duval

Street should retain some "funkiness," Old Town's residents should not be burdened with loud music late at night.[13]

The report had little, if any, impact on public policy. As Julio Avael, the city manager, later recalled, the report was shelved and nothing was accomplished. Still, around the time the task force and the committee were meeting, the city commission was wrestling with several issues related to the experiences of tourists in Key West and the character of Key West as a tourist and residential community. Two of these issues were code enforcement and "adult uses." In neither case were significant changes made, primarily out of concern that increased regulation would hurt existing businesses and undermine the "openness" of Duval Street, an openness that some criticized but that many tourists obviously welcomed.[14]

In 2004, the city commission directed Charles Stephenson, the city's director of code enforcement, to enforce existing code regulations on Duval Street. According to Stephenson, "We used to be unique. It's now getting trashy and vulgar." At a meeting that May, some commissioners voiced concerns about the noise emanating from clubs on Duval, as well as about revelers carrying "open containers" of alcohol on the streets, hawkers in front of bars, palm weavers, and street performers.[15]

Many suspected, however, that little would change. Even Weekley admitted that the city had a reputation for passing ordinances and then refusing to enforce them. Dennis Cooper, the publisher of the weekly paper, *Key West The Newspaper*, often remarked that in Key West laws were, at most, selectively enforced. Still, during a weekend in May, the city issued about thirty citations to businesses in violation of codes, including the illegal display of signage and flags and the illegal sale of merchandise on the sidewalks. Business owners were also warned that should they fail to comply with the codes, they would have to appear before a hearing master. Citations continued to be issued in June.[16]

The codes themselves also came under scrutiny. The *Citizen* contended that the city needed to decide which ordinances to keep or add, and then enforce these ordinances and rescind all others. In an editorial, the *Citizen* urged the city to find solutions to real problems "without changing the character of Key West or altering a small part of what makes this island unique by taking the existing rights from our local businesses." Cooper reminded readers, "The festive atmosphere on Duval Street is famous around the world. It is a major tourist attraction. While we agree that some clean-up is in order, we hope that the ultimate objective is not to close down the party altogether."[17]

On June 16, 2004, the city commission met to discuss its policy options for Duval Street, and Commissioner Ed Scales articulated a similar sentiment. "Let's make no mistake," he noted, "the HRCC-1 [the Duval Street zoning district] is the economic engine that this city runs on." He warned the commission to be careful not to adopt additional regulations that might deter tourists from visiting. Businesses' freedom from government regulation was part of what made Key West unique, and this uniqueness added to Key West's allure as a tourist destination. The *Citizen* found some merit in this approach but cautioned that a cost-benefit analysis to Key West's current "anything and everything goes" attitude might indicate that the economic engine needed some mending.[18]

Some in Key West suggested that the many adult businesses were a legitimate target for such mending. In Las Vegas, the primary reason male tourists leave the gambling resorts on The Strip is to visit nude or topless clubs located nearby. In Key West, however, several such businesses were conveniently located on and near Duval Street, and, of course, not all of the adult entertainment involved women dancing for male audiences. In fact, part of this concern about "adult uses" grew out of a conflict regarding a controversial proposal for a complex on upper Duval that would include a venue for "adult" shows catering to gay tourists and residents. Faced with significant opposition from residents living nearby and difficulties attracting adequate financing, its developers backed out of the venture. City commissioner Carmen Turner then initiated a discussion about the need for an "adult use" ordinance.[19]

Advertisements in Key West's newspapers enticed customers to adult establishments. For example, one could have a "Naked Lunch" at a "clothing optional Bar & Restaurant" just a "step from Duval" in Key West's historic district. After lunch, one could visit the clothing-optional Garden of Eden on Duval, an open-air bar on the third floor of a three-bar complex. One could also visit "Christy Sweets' Totally Private Personal Dances," where visitors could "Get Naked Too!" just "5 doors from Duval Street." Customers were reassured that Christy's establishment was free of smoke and alcohol. On upper Duval, one could visit the Key West Scrub Club, which featured "Live, Nude, Adult Entertainment in

Private Rooms," with "Escorts available 24/7." Nude entertainment was also available at Teaser's on both Truman Avenue and lower Duval. In addition, a new adult superstore had just opened off of lower Duval, and additional establishments near upper Duval catered primarily to a gay and lesbian audience. Ultimately, the city determined that there were fourteen adult businesses operating in Key West. This number, however, did not include the clothing-optional bars, the drag clubs, and the Topless Fishing Charters of America, which offered charter fishing ventures in boats staffed by topless women and whose owner declared "This is for everyone to have a fine, fun time and come back with great pictures of the fish and your friends, too."[20]

City commissioners disagreed about the necessity of an ordinance that would restrict the number of adult venues. Tom Oosterhoudt, who represented much of Old Town, opposed such restrictions and contended that the main supporters of such a strict ordinance were the wealthy residents new to Key West: "It's getting to be this retirement city with this gentrification, which I hate." Key West, he lamented, was losing its identity as the "laid-back, wild, wild West Town" it used to be. The Pistol and Enema website, the self-proclaimed "gay information source of Key West," protested, "Good God, this is turning into a Republican town." Christy Sweet, who had been involved in disputes with the city over the legality of her business, agreed with Oosterhoudt's analysis. According to Sweet, the wealthy people who were paying outrageous prices for second homes in Key West were "a different group of people" and "not as open to adult entertainment." Commissioner Carmen Turner, however, supported a strict ordinance and stressed that the nudity on display during Fantasy Fest should not be taken to represent "who we are as a community."[21]

In early July, the commission passed an ordinance, 6 to 1, regarding adult venues. The ordinance, however, could hardly be considered a clamp down on adult clubs, and indeed Turner, who favored stricter controls, was the only dissenting vote. The law granted adult-business standing to nine establishments. Six other adult businesses were allowed to continue as "nonconforming" uses but would lose their status if their businesses were sold. The ordinance also included another category that was primarily designed to protect the adult cabaret at La Te Da. In addition, in response to reports that a gay porn star had masturbated on the stage of a bar during PrideFest, three of the commissioners urged that the proposed law include language prohibiting sexual acts at the clubs. This prohibition, however, was not added.[22]

Ultimately, the ordinance actually benefited the gay-oriented establishments on upper Duval Street because it recognized them as legitimate adult-entertainment venues. The gay businesses and Key West Business Guild had lobbied the city commission to ensure that these clubs would not be hurt by the ordinance, and the commissioners had responded positively. Oosterhoudt, the primary spokesperson for their concerns, emphasized, "We do want to keep our uniqueness and funkiness," and felt that the ordinance reflected "the more freewheeling, free-spirited legacy of Key West's history . . . of live and let live."[23]

Generica

Although Key West's ratio of the number of "adult use" clubs to the number of citizens was considerably higher than the national norm, if not the highest, many argued that Key West had drifted toward "generica." A frequently cited example of this trend was the rising number of chain stores on Duval Street. Among the critics of this trend were some advocates of tourism, who argued that Key West's "uniqueness" was important for drawing tourists. Other critics, however, blamed the tourists who generated the demand for chain stores and condemned the growth of mass tourism. Lower Duval Street had several newer franchise stores. A Walgreens drug store had opened, as well as several franchise retail stores and restaurants, including Coach, Chico's, Express, the Hard Rock Café, and Wendy's. A Hooters and a Planet Hollywood had opened for a short time before closing.

In September 2003, the Key West Planning Board unanimously recommended a ban on chain stores in the Key West Bight (a.k.a., the Historic Seaport) area, on the section of upper Duval near the Atlantic Ocean, which had a different zoning designation than lower Duval and was considered an arts district, and the Bahama Village business district along Petronia Street. Key West's head city planner emphasized that this ordinance was necessary if the historical character of Key West and its "small town feel" were to be protected. The small Keys community of Islamorada had already instituted a citywide ban on chain stores, a measure that the Key West Planning Board had noted. Still, the city commission failed to adopt this ordinance. Most of the commissioners worried about being faced with a lawsuit, and they also recognized that chains had already established such a strong presence on Duval that the ordinance would essentially amount to too little, too late. Therefore, Coach and Christy Sweets' could continue to coexist just a few doors from each other.[24]

Chickens, Uniqueness, and Tourism Promotion

Few communities have resident gangs of chickens roaming around. This was a unique feature of Key West. The question was whether it was desirable. Historically, many families in Key West had raised chickens for food, and gambling on cockfights was also a way of life for many Conchs. By the 1980s, few fights, if any, were held in Key West, although they remained common in other areas of the Keys. In 1989, Monroe County deputies raided property on Rockland Key owned by "Woodsie" Niles, a county code enforcement inspector, on a tip that it was being used as a cockfighting pit. The sheriff temporarily placed several hundred cocks in custody but ultimately returned them to their owner for lack of a feasible plan for what to do with them.[25]

In the early 1990s, the Key West writer and performer Ben Harrison wrote *A Poultry Operetta*, based loosely on the raid on Niles's property. The lyrics empathized with the fighting cocks, noting, "I would not want to be a chick raised to fry/In a Styrofoam package on a grocery store aisle/Well, I'd rather fight even though I might die/I'd rather fight to my death than lay eggs or fry." Others in Key West, however, were concerned less about the chickens' quality of life, or death, than about their own well-being. Periodically, Key Westers complained that the chickens were too noisy. For example, Joseph "Cactus Joe" Zorskey, owner of the Cactus Terrace Motel on Truman Avenue, complained to the city commission in 1960 that the noisy roosters annoyed his guests and kept them awake at night.

As Key West gentrified, many newcomers saw the chickens as more of a nuisance than a "quaint" reminder of old Key West. And after Hurricane Georges in 1998 upended many of the trees the chickens liked to roost in, the city government began receiving more complaints about chickens roaming in citizens' yards. In 2004, an estimated 2,000 chickens were enjoying their island life when the city paid a local barber, Armando Parra

Sr., $20 a chicken to round them up. The chickens were to be shipped to a farm, where presumably they could live happily. Later that year, the chicken wars took an ugly turn. In October, 45 chickens were found dead in Old Town, apparently the victims of poisoning.[26]

Many supported the war against the chickens. Some environmentalists, for example, complained that the chicken droppings contributed to the pollution of nearshore waters. Others tired of chickens in their yards. One resident called the sleep deprivation she suffered due to the noisy roosters a "form of torture."

Others, however, fought on the side of the chickens. Most prominent among these was Katha Sheehan, "the Chicken Lady," who opened a Chicken Store on Duval Street that sold chicken-related items. Sheehan viewed the chickens as an important component of Key West's historic heritage. Others agreed. One letter addressed to the *Citizen* noted: "I grew up in Key West and . . . [have a] suggestion: if you don't like the chickens, then you should leave. They are a part of Key West." Another responded to the environmentalists' concerns: "So the Key West chickens have to go because somehow their poop gets into the water? What about osprey, doves, pelicans, fish, eagles, sea gulls, cormorants and those migrating turkey buzzards? Are they all some non-pooping species?" Two tourists on a return visit to Key West were disappointed to hear about the chicken-catcher's quest to round up the fowl, declaring, "that's what people come here for! Something different!"[27]

Although it was uncertain which side would prevail, it was clear that the chicken war was attracting attention to Key West. A board member of the Tourist Development Association (TDA) proposed to the TDA and to Market Share Company, the firm that contracted with the TDA to produce Fantasy Fest each year, that they stage a new festival, ChickenFest. The idea caught on, and the TDA and Market Share announced in January 2004 that the inaugural ChickenFest Key West would be held that June. The organizer of the event for Market Share emphasized, "The visitors who come to Key West love to see the quirkiness of the island, and the chickens exemplify some of that eccentricity." Whether or not the chickens continued to thrive, Key West's tourism promoters would find a way to use Key West's "historic heritage" to draw more tourists to the island. ChickenFest only made it two years, a shorter life span than that enjoyed by many of Key West's chickens. It failed to attract many tourists to Key West, and it lost many of its sponsors and most of its TDC funding.[28]

The Cultural Amenities of Home

Chickens roamed the streets of Key West long after ChickenFest and the city's chicken-catching campaign were things of the past, but the question of what constituted the city's uniqueness continued to be raised. It soon became clear that many new residents of and seasonal visitors to Key West were less interested in the trappings of uniqueness, as described by Kirkwood, Buffett, Captain Tony, and many others, than in having access to the cultural amenities of the communities where many of them lived for the rest of the year. Key West might still be the "anti-Hamptons" in the sense of lacking pretension, and the city's prominent gay community also distinguished it from other places and certainly from other small towns. Uniqueness, however, could not replace access to amenities and convenience. In fact, the TDC's dual emphasis on "quality tourism" and "uniqueness" was uneasy at best. The TDC's desire to attract wealthier tourists was, however, compatible with that of many of the community's more affluent residents, year-round or seasonal alike, who wanted to expand the island's cultural offerings.

The gentrification of Old Town, along with the influx of wealthier, winter residents, reinforced the community's inclination, and its ability, to sustain the arts. The Waterfront Playhouse near Mallory Square and the Red Barn Theatre on Duval Street, both long-standing venues, offered professional plays featuring local as well as out-of-town actors. In addition, the Founders Society, an organization comprising Key West citizens, both year-round and seasonal, raised significant sums of money to support the Tennessee Williams Fine Arts Center, which had opened in 1979 on the Stock Island campus of the Florida Keys Community College.

Newer cultural organizations also formed. The Key West Film Society was founded in 1998. After initially screening films at several locations, the society raised $1.5 million to lease and renovate a building on Eaton Street, just a half block from Duval Street. Jean Carper, the successful author of health and nutrition books and now a Key West resident, contributed $200,000 to the drive, and many others also donated. The Tropic Cinema opened for business in 2004 and showed films daily. Its executive director noted, "There's a fair measure of New Englanders, New Yorkers, a lot of people from St. Louis, Chicago and points in between. They all navigated to Key West because of its . . . allure and found it wanting for intellectual stimulation."[29]

In 1997, Sebrina Maria Alfonso, a several generation Conch, took the lead in organizing the Key West Symphony Orchestra, becoming its music director and conductor. Other Conchs and newcomers provided support, and the Key West Symphony Orchestra held its first performance in 1998 at the Tennessee Williams Fine Arts Center. Another musical group, the Key West Pops Orchestra, came together in 1999. Then, on New Year's Eve, 2001, the Island Opera Theatre staged its first production. Several new art galleries also opened. In July 2004, the "Gallery Guide" issued by the Florida Keys Council of the Arts listed forty-seven different galleries.

Key West was now recognized as an attractive tourist destination for those with artistic proclivities. In December 2001, an article published in *USA Today* titled "10 great places with arts-filled spaces" included Key West among its top ten smaller communities. In June 2004, *American Style* magazine, a national arts publication, reported that Key West ranked 25th in its readers' poll of which cities to visit on a "cultural road trip." The next year, the same magazine ranked Key West 20th in its "Top 25 Arts Destinations" poll of cities with populations under 100,000.[30]

Many of the galleries catered to tourists and locals interested in relatively inexpensive art. Others, however, appealed to a wealthier clientele. In May 2005, Eric Charest-Weinberg opened a gallery on Duval with the primary goal of moving the galleries in Key West "to a higher level." Before moving to Key West from his home in Montreal, Charest-Weinberg considered opening a gallery in Palm Beach or Miami but concluded that Key West, with its wealthy visitors and seasonal residents, was the ideal site for his gallery.[31]

In 2005, the local artist and art commentator Judi Bradford summarized the changes in Key West, as represented by Charest-Weinberg and other new galleries. She observed, "one change that is taking place in galleries is the shift from local artists to 'collectible artists.'" Although galleries that emphasized local artists, such as Lucky Street Gallery and Gallery on Greene, remained, Bradford noted that more galleries were "opening up who carry the contemporary masters whose value to collectors is established." She expressed concern that the tide would turn away from local and emerging artists. She also feared that the common perception of Key West as the "anti-Hamptons" was under fire by those who wanted to "Hamptonize" Key West's art scene.[32]

Not only was the changing art market working against emerging artists, so, too, was the changing real estate market. Dean Walters, the Island Opera Theatre's director and cofounder, moved to Key West in the mid-1980s. Walters later compared Key West's attraction to actors, singers, painters, and writers to that of Greenwich Village in the past. "There's just a certain atmosphere that draws that talent down here—a laid-back, pretty-much-anything-goes atmosphere—which allows artistic minds to really create because they're not held in a box so much."[33]

Key West, however, like Greenwich Village, had become unaffordable to most aspiring writers and artists. In New York, these artists often moved to less expensive neighborhoods. In Key West, some moved to Stock Island, which still had some older affordable housing, but even there, housing prices were on the rise.

The Rodel Foundation, organized in Key West in 1999 by William and Peyton Budinger, who had moved to Key West earlier in the decade, addressed this difficulty and tried to provide an environment where young artists could foster their talents. Peyton Budinger took the lead in Rodel's financing of a new nonprofit, The Studios of Key West, which was incorporated in 2006 and leased the newly renovated historic Armory building on White Street. The Studios provided studio space for young artists and sponsored talks by writers and artists. Decades earlier, young writers and artists had rented space in the abandoned Navy property that later became Truman Annex. Now, The Studios tried to recreate this opportunity for young artists by providing them with low-rent studio space, with the aim of eventually providing affordable housing. Still, in Key West's expensive housing market, this effort could have only a limited impact. The mission of The Studios became increasingly difficult to accomplish after it lost its funding from the Rodel Foundation in 2009, although other businesses and individuals in the community stepped up to provide support.[34]

Property Trumps Tourism?

Rising property values not only made the housing market unaffordable for aspiring artist and writers but also changed the nature of tourism on the island. In fact, the first years of the twenty-first century saw skyrocketing real estate prices that rivaled tourism as the dominant economic engine in Key West, contributed to the upscaling of tourist accommodations on the island, and, in some respects, diminished the city's uniqueness. In 2004, Michael L. Kilgore, the editor of *Celebrate*, Key West's gay newspaper at the time, highlighted the impact of rising real estate prices. He wrote, "It's just economics, after all. The old Conchs figured it out long ago, cashed out and moved to Ocala. And now all the homes and guesthouses gays fixed up are commanding prices as high as San Francisco or Boston. The issue isn't about tourism—long-term, day-trippers, gay, straight, or otherwise. It's about a new real estate–based economy that's making tourism—and us—irrelevant." He concluded, quoting Pogo, "We have met the enemy and he is us."[35]

Greg Needham, the publisher of *Celebrate*, echoed Kilgore's sentiment, contending that Key West was "seeing the end of tourism as we have known it." He further argued, "You can talk all you want about tourism being the 'economic engine,' but the real estate economy has trumped the oft-talked about tourist economy. Priorities have shifted, city government has signed on and new residents are setting the agenda. The battle may be over before we could even figure out how, or who, to fight." Needham predicted that Key West would increasingly attract one of two types of tourists, the wealthy seasonal resident and the day-tripper (primarily cruise ship passengers), with fewer total tourists. This trend, along with the fact that a high percentage of condominiums and homes were sold as second homes, would lead to a reduced demand for tourism-related services and a loss of jobs, trends that many recent and future property purchasers might welcome. Key West would become the next Hamptons or Vail, Colorado, albeit with cruise ships.[36]

The head of the Innkeepers Association noted that with the rising property values, banks were often unwilling to grant mortgages to purchasers of guesthouses who wanted to retain the properties as tourist quarters. As such, some tourist accommodations were sold and converted to condominiums or to single-family residences, which seasonal residents were more likely to purchase. The difficulty these accommodations faced in hiring labor due to the lack of affordable housing contributed to this trend.[37]

Another development related to Key West's rising property values and its appeal to seasonal residents and investors was the conversion of hotels and motels to condo hotels, a trend also evident in other tourist areas such as Miami, Orlando, and Las Vegas. Hotel or motel owners who successfully converted their properties to condo hotels—that is, to condominiums whose transient licenses allowed their owners to rent out their units on a short-term basis—could garner huge profits.

The impact of these conversions, however, was unclear. If purchasers lived in their units for several months, island businesses that relied on a steady turnover of tourists would likely be hurt. Although advocates of "quality" tourism might applaud the downturn in total visitors to the island, others in the community would suffer. Recognizing the potential consequences of such conversions, the Key West City Commission in December 2004 imposed a 180-day moratorium on them and then extended this moratorium into August. It also directed the Key West Planning Department to analyze the issue, and the TDC initiated its own study.[38]

Regardless of the impact, it was clear that real estate appreciation was driving the conversions, and investors, both Key Westers and out-of-towners, were likely to purchase the units. The TDC report concluded, "The demand for condominium units created as part of lodging property conversions is really part of a larger drive for real estate as an investment which has seen substantial increases over the past three years. Weary of the stock market, and seeking to capitalize on historically low interest rates, individuals have been turning to real estate as an investment source and/or to purchase a second home." Many who purchased the converted units did so not to secure long-term rental income or a vacation home, but to "flip" the property, hopefully at a sizable profit. Although many left the stock market to play at real estate instead, they treated the units as "stock." Their goal was to buy low and sell high, ideally before the converted units were even completed.[39]

Atlantic Shores was one of the establishments scheduled to convert from a motel to a condo hotel. Atlantic Shores Resort, Ltd. had purchased Atlantic Shores in the mid-1990s. The company's partners renovated the property, which catered primarily to gays and lesbians and included a clothing-optional pool whose sign read, "We don't discriminate against heterosexuals." In 2004, Meisel Capital Partners negotiated a merger with Atlantic Shores Resort, Ltd. Meisel had already purchased the Santa Maria Motel located next to Atlantic Shores, razed it, and was building a condo hotel on the site. The new partnership formulated plans to demolish Atlantic Shores and replace it with a brand-new 58-unit condo hotel.

It submitted its proposal to the city before the city commission adopted its moratorium, and in June 2005 the city commission approved the redevelopment of Atlantic Shores.[40]

Michael Browning, one of the partners in Atlantic Shores Resort, Ltd., had formerly co-owned the Sea Shell Motel and International Youth Hostel, which in 1993 charged guests $13 a night for a bunk. When that same year the city commission considered a committee's recommendation that Key West strive to attract more wealthy travelers, Browning complained that Key West's visitors should reflect the diversity of its permanent residents. Now, more than a decade later, Browning's perspective had changed significantly. He justified the redevelopment of Atlantic Shores by noting that he and his partners were merely responding to the market. Key West was now attracting wealthier visitors who wanted luxury facilities, not a small 1950s-style motel room. However, one of Browning's partners, Rich Ferrell, offered a different perspective. Ferrell was critical of the waning of Key West's unique atmosphere due to rising property values and those who sought to profit from them. He preferred the earlier vision of owning "a hotel to serve the gay community and to keep affordable rooms on the waterfront." Soon after, he sold his share of Atlantic Shores Resort, Ltd.[41]

Many of the Atlantic Shores' guests greeted the news of the sale and renovation with consternation. One noted, "It is a Key West institution. . . . You can go there and get a drink and talk with some real nice people. It's a locals' hangout . . . it's the type of place where no matter if you are rich or poor, gay or straight, everyone is treated the same. . . . I'm going to miss it. Where are we going to go?" The owner of the concession booth at the Shores' pool added, "What was cool about the Shores was that you would get a couple staying at the Casa Marina sitting around having a drink with some kid from the Youth Hostel naked." A drag queen who had performed at Atlantic Shores concluded, "It's the end of an era."[42]

Atlantic Shores closed it doors in May 2007. As it turned out, the Shores' new owners decided not to proceed with the planned conversion but instead sold the property to Southernmost Hotels & Resorts, which owned a nearby hotel and guesthouses. Southernmost Hotels razed Atlantic Shores and constructed new upscale rooms on its site. The tea dances and fundraisers for those down on their luck became a thing of the past, as did the clothing-optional pool and deck area. As one of the sellers of Atlantic Shores asserted, "This island is going upscale."[43]

During the same period, the Spottswood Companies, Inc., owned by the daughter and three sons of the former State Senator John Spottswood, redeveloped the Holiday Inn Beachside, which had opened in the early 1960s on North Roosevelt Blvd. in Key West, just over the bridge from Stock Island, as the Beachside Resort & Conference Center. The Spottswood Companies had earlier built several time-share developments in Key West and was a major developer elsewhere in the Keys. This condo hotel opened in the fall of 2007, came under Marriott management in December 2008, and charged rates far in excess of what the former Holiday Inn had charged. The Spottswood Companies also submitted plans to the city to raze several other moderately priced motels near the new Beachside Resort and build a major convention center and hotel. The entrance to Key West would be transformed such that one entering over the bridge would see new luxurious buildings rather than modest motels. In addition, Pritam Singh, the developer of Truman Annex, converted the Hampton Inn on North Roosevelt to the Parrot Key Hotel and Resort, another condo hotel. Even some of the already expensive hotels were going more upscale. In 2005, LXR Luxury Resorts & Hotels, an affiliate of the Blackstone Group private investment firm, assumed ownership of the Casa Marina and the Reach and initiated major renovations of both properties. Then, in 2008, both came under the management of Hilton's luxury brand, the Waldorf Astoria Hotels and Resorts.

Average room rates in Key West, which were already high, increased further in 2007, in part because of the limited number of rooms available to tourists due to the upgrading of facilities. The Reach was closed for renovation, and the Casa Marina had only limited rooms available.[44] In addition, the more moderately priced facilities, such as the Holiday Inn Beachside, had become things of the past. In mid-2007, the Florida Keys ranked third in the United States, behind only New York and San Francisco, in the average price of hotel rooms. Smith Travel Reports found that of fifteen major global tourism markets, only Paris, London, Dubai, and New York were more expensive than the Florida Keys. The business editor for the *Citizen* wrote, "whenever somebody I know is looking to take a trip or honeymoon, instead of saying, 'you should come to Key

West,' my response usually is, 'It's too bad Key West is so expensive. You'd love it here.'"[45]

By the mid-2000s, Key West had more to offer to both its affluent residents and its wealthier tourists. To many, Key West was now a more desirable community to visit and call home than ever before. It offered significant cultural amenities and upscale accommodations. The question remained, however, of how much was left of the Key West that had once lured so many creative individuals, owing, at least in part, to the community's perceived uniqueness. And how much remained of the town so many Conchs had once called home? And, even if some aspects of its uniqueness remained, who could afford to enjoy and live in this new Key West? These and related questions, which addressed issues of both culture and class, were salient in a town whose newly adopted motto was "One Human Family."

13

One Human Family?

IN OCTOBER 2000, the Key West City Commission endorsed "One Human Family" as the city's official philosophy. The proclamation began, "Key West is an enlightened island community that is passionate about all living together as caring, sharing neighbors; and that each of us are dedicated to making our home as close to 'paradise' as we can." It further declared, "We want to proclaim that the truth, as we see it, is that there is no 'them,' there is just 'us,' *all* of us, together as ONE HUMAN FAMILY, now and forever." In endorsing this motto, the commission proclaimed its acceptance of equality between gays and straights and suggested that Key West was, more generally, a unique, open, and egalitarian community.

The Key West artist J. T. Thompson originated the "One Human Family" theme, which was already a popular bumper sticker by the time the city commission adopted it as Key West's motto. In 2001, the Monroe County Commission followed Key West's lead and adopted the phrase as the philosophy of the Florida Keys. To some Key Westers, the motto rang true—their island was, in fact, "One Human Family." Others, however, viewed this motto with more skepticism. Both positions had some validity. Some aspects of Key West were compatible with the official motto. In other respects, however, the community fell short.[1]

Gay Rights and Organizations

The Key West City Commission continued to support policy advocated by gay rights activists, policy that was compatible with the "One Human Family" motto. In July 2001, the city commission proclaimed that Key West welcomed same-sex binational couples and asked the Immigration and Naturalization Service to afford these couples the same rights and treatment granted to married couples. Later in the year, openly gay City Commissioners Tom Oosterhoudt and Jeremy Anthony were both reelected, and Oosterhoudt introduced an amendment to the city's Human Rights Ordinance adding protections for transgendered individuals. In January 2003, before Anthony's death from AIDS, the city commission unanimously voted to ban discrimination based on "gender identity or expression," thereby becoming the first city in Florida to pass such a protection for transgendered individuals.[2]

After the election in 2003, Oosterhoudt was the only openly gay city commissioner. Still, in March 2004, shortly after President Bush advocated a constitutional amendment forbidding gay marriages, the commission passed a resolution supporting same-sex marriages and urging cities and counties in Florida to recognize gay marriages performed outside the state. Although the resolution was merely symbolic—Florida's law recognized only marriages between a man and a woman and forbade communities from recognizing same-sex marriages performed elsewhere—the hundreds gathered in city hall applauded the vote.[3]

The Gay and Lesbian Community Center and other organizers of PrideFest 2003 garnered national attention when participants unfurled a "Sea-to-Sea" gay pride flag that stretched the length of Duval Street from the Atlantic to the Gulf in commemoration of the twenty-fifth anniversary of the creation of the rainbow flag in San Francisco. In Key West, PrideFest organizers intended the flag to symbolize that Key West was "One Human Family." The Key West City Commission and Monroe County Commission affirmed their commitment to the motto when they both declared August 12–14, 2005, as "Hillsborough Pride in Exile Days," in response to the refusal by the Board of County Commissioners of Hillsborough County, Florida, to support or recognize gay pride events.[4]

Key West's gay community and its relationships with the wider community were different in the early 2000s than they were in the 1970s and 1980s. In several ways, the distinctions between gay and straight had broken down. For example, Key West's gay population was no longer concentrated in Old Town. Many gay renovators of Old Town homes had long since sold them to straight purchasers, many of them seasonal residents. Gays and lesbians were as likely to live in Midtown or New Town as in Old Town. They chose these neighborhoods for the same reasons others might, and they faced no obstacles in doing so.

The tourism sector had shifted in a similar direction. While gay visitors sometimes still chose to stay at gay guesthouses, many stayed elsewhere, be it in a guesthouse or a chain hotel. Key West's most popular lesbian guesthouse, Pearl's Rainbow, adopted an "all welcome" policy in 2010, in part because fewer lesbian tourists were opting to stay in lesbian-only accommodations.

In the city commission elections of 2007, Teri Johnston, a lesbian, was elected city commissioner from Midtown, and she was reelected without opposition in 2011. And in 2008, another lesbian, Heather Carruthers, the owner of Pearl's Rainbow, was elected to the county commission in a countywide election. Sexual orientation was largely irrelevant in these elections. Both had been active in the successful effort to persuade the state to lower the windstorm insurance rates in Key West and the rest of Monroe County, and they based their campaigns to a significant extent on this effort.

Not all of these phenomena represented dramatic shifts from those of the 1980s. For example, Richard Heyman garnered strong support from wide segments of the Key West community in his mayoral election in 1987. Nor were these trends unique to Key West. That more gays and lesbians preferred to stay in accommodations not restricted by sexual orientation reflected society's more widespread support of gay rights. Still, Key West by the end of the century was a town that was nonjudgmental with regard to sexual orientation. While some in the gay community bemoaned the loss of the gay enclave in Old Town, as well as other changes that united the once separate worlds of gays and straights, most felt the changes made the city more reflective of its motto "One Human Family."

Christmas Tree Island

The "One Human Family" philosophy can also be interpreted as a call for policy based on community discussion and debate rather than on the private needs of political insiders and growth and development interests whose decisions were made behind closed doors. Key West had experienced both of these decision-making styles in previous decades. In 2007, the city's "family" was divided by a proposal to annex an uninhabited island to the city so developers could transform it into a sister community of Sunset Key, the nearby island of multimillion-dollar homes. The proposed developers of the island were Ocean Properties Limited, who had developed Sunset Key and the Westin Hotel adjacent to Mallory Square, and the Bernstein family, the owner of Wisteria Island, popularly known as Christmas Tree Island. A grassroots effort organized to try to block the developers' initiative.

Wisteria Island was formed from the dredging in Key West Harbor that began in the 1890s and continued on and off for decades. In the 1930s, State Representative Bernard Papy purchased the island, selling it at a considerable profit in the mid-1950s to the newly organized Wisteria Corporation, which announced plans to build homes and a yacht club there. Instead, in 1967 it sold the still undeveloped island to a company controlled by Benjamin Bernstein, a major landowner on Stock Island. In 1972, Bernstein's company bought 150 acres of bay bottom around the island. The Bernstein family retained possession of the island and bay bottom after Benjamin died in 1974, and at the time of the proposed annexation, Roger Bernstein, a lawyer in the Miami area, was the primary family member to participate.[5]

In the 1960s and 1970s, Christmas Tree Island served as a campground for hippies. Later, homeless people inhabited the island, and a large number of liveaboards docked in the waters nearby. Now, Bernstein and the Walsh family, which controlled Ocean Properties, envisioned a very different island, one inhabited, for at least part of the year, by multimillionaires living in multimillion-dollar homes.

The developers had much to gain from the annexation. Under county land-use and zoning regulations, only two homes could be built on the 21-acre island. If Key West annexed it, as many as over 150 units could be allowed. The newspaper publisher Dennis Cooper concluded, "It's about helping a small group of already-rich developers make a few more million dollars." Many agreed with his analysis.[6]

Initially, it appeared that the annexation would proceed exactly as the island's owner and prospective developer wished. In May 2007, the city commission approved the annexation, 5 to 2. Under the city commission's rules, a majority would have to support the annexation again in a final vote. Prior to this vote, however, Cooper's newspaper generated significant publicity about the issue, and citizens mobilized against the annexation.[7]

Advocates of the annexation emphasized that Key West would garner tax revenues from the expensive homes built on the island. City Commissioner Harry Bethel concluded that supporting the annexation was "simple economics": "You can leave a bunch of homeless people camping out there now, or you can develop and gain revenue from it." The *Citizen* agreed. True, boaters who anchored near the island would likely lose this privilege, and the island's squatters would certainly be a thing of the past, but, the newspaper suggested, the island could "serve as a model for environmentally friendly development." In its May editorial, the *Citizen* concluded that while the changes might be sad to some, "change has always been part of Key West's character and history."[8]

Others recognized that many of these changes did not merely reflect the "character" of Key West or the inexorable forces of history but rather the impact of public policy. The question was, who would influence that policy? The adoption of the tourist tax, the limit on building heights, and the designation and expansion of the historic district were among those governmental policies that had dramatically impacted Key West's character and, ultimately, its history.

City Commissioners Bill Verge and Mark Rossi had voted against the annexation and remained opposed to it. By the end of June 2007, over 1,000 citizens had signed a petition against the annexation. Many of them felt that developing the island would move Key West even further toward becoming a community of expensive and largely seasonal homes that was unaffordable for the average worker. In fact, an explicit connection to the lack of affordable housing was the consequence of development on the liveaboards who anchored nearby. According to one organizer of the petition, "That's the last bastion of affordable housing in Key West. People just think it's ridiculous to build condos out there just so people from somewhere else can live in them a few weeks or months out of the year."[9]

It also came to light in Cooper's *Key West The Newspaper* that three city commissioners, as well as the police chief, had been treated to an expensive dinner on May 10 at Latitudes Beach Café on Sunset Key. While the name "Latitudes" was likely meant to remind diners at the restaurant of images in Jimmy Buffett's popular song, "Changes in Latitudes, Changes in Attitudes," the $39 lobster dinner was probably not exactly what Buffett had in mind when he wrote the song. The Key West political insider Bob Dean had invited the commissioners and the police chief to the restaurant and picked up the tab. Dean, the owner of Dean-Lopez Funeral Home, was a longtime presence on the Key West political and business scene. Michael Walsh, one of the sons of the Walsh family that owned Ocean Properties, also happened to be at the dinner. Although the accusations had not yet been made public, federal prosecutors were investigating Ocean Properties for allegedly providing favors to Palm Beach County commissioners to court their support for a downtown convention center hotel in West Palm Beach.[10]

The three commissioners later reported that they did not discuss the annexation that night and that the event was a retirement party for Harry Bethel, whose term on the city commission was to expire in about five months. At the time of the dinner, the final vote on the annexation was to take place on May 15. The commission, however, postponed the vote because Mayor Morgan McPherson and Commissioner Rossi were absent.[11]

Likely due to the citizens' petition and the newspaper coverage of the dinner on Sunset Key, by the end of June a majority of the city commissioners were in support of a referendum on whether the city should annex the island. Recognizing the vote was unlikely to go their way, the developers withdrew their proposal. The citizen-organized Wisteria Island Committee, however, realizing the developers could reapply at a future date, circulated a petition calling for a referendum to amend the city charter such that any annexation would require citizen approval. Bruce Ritson, a former accountant who had moved from New Jersey to Key West in the 1970s, headed the committee, which was required to secure signatures from 10 percent of Key West's registered voters in order to get the issue on the ballot. The committee was successful in securing the necessary signatures, and voters overwhelmingly approved the amendment. At least for the time being, Christmas Tree Island would remain undeveloped. Its owners, however, decided that they also wanted it unoccupied and posted large "No Trespassing" signs in plain sight.[12]

Rising Housing Prices

While gays had won entry into the social, economic and political systems of Key West, and citizens had sometimes defeated development interests, many Key Westers, both straight and gay, struggled to find affordable housing. In the mid-1980s and early 1990s, the city commission had adopted policy designed to alleviate this problem, but the situation intensified during the 1990s and in the early years of the twenty-first century as prices escalated even more. In terms of the availability of housing for Key West's workforce, the community was far from "One Human Family."

Between 2000 and 2005, the median sales price of a single-family home in Key West rose 191 percent, from $275,000 to $800,000. An analysis of the sales prices of single-family homes in Old Town, completed in April 2005 by a Key West realty company, found that the average price had risen 294 percent between the first quarter of 2000 and the first quarter of 2005. In January 2005, the lowest priced single-family home for sale in Key West was a one-bedroom, 623-square-foot home; the asking price was $599,000. That month, 142 houses were listed for more than $1 million, with only ten single-family homes on offer for under $700,000. Although condominiums were less expensive than single-family homes, their average sales price also increased dramatically, from a median of $152,900 in 2000 to $545,000 in 2005. In January 2005, the least expensive condominium on the market, a 331-square-feet unit, was listed for $399,000.[13]

These increasing prices were primarily a function of the demand created by those who did not live in Key West year-round. Purchasing a house was out of reach for most who relied on Key West's labor market for their incomes. In 1999, the median household income of the island's year-round residents was only about 10 percent higher than that of the state, but by 2005, Key West's average housing price was approximately triple that of the state (see appendix). Few buyers of single-family homes and condominiums homesteaded their properties, a tax benefit reserved for primary residences. Even in the mid- and late 1990s, only around 50 percent of single-family homes were homesteaded, but this figure dropped significantly between 2003 and 2005, reaching a low of 27 percent in 2004. Condominiums were even less likely to be homesteaded. In the late 1990s, about 25 percent of condominiums were homesteaded, but by 2004, that proportion had dropped to 17 percent and by 2005 to 11 percent. In addition, these official figures likely understated the percentage of homes and condos not used as primary residences, because some owners fraudulently homesteaded their properties in order to pay lower property taxes. Increasingly, those purchasing homes and condominiums in Key West were using them as vacation or seasonal homes or as investment properties.[14]

The conversion of apartments to condominiums reinforced this trend of investor ownership and more expensive housing. In 2004 alone, the owners of 229 apartments, representing approximately 5 percent of the long-term rentals in the city, initiated the conversion process. Most of these condominium conversions were purchased by investors. In 2004 and early 2005, only 32 of the 229 condominium conversions were owner occupied. The rents charged on the remaining condominiums generally exceeded those charged before the conversion, thereby making Key West's rental market less affordable.[15]

The market in Key West condominiums, both conversions and existing units, was increasingly based on speculation and enabled by the lending practices of financial institutions that, as it turned out, were by no means unique to Key West. A vice president with a Key West bank noted in 2005 that his institution's accepted debt-to-income ratios for condominium purchases had risen considerably. He pointed out, prophetically, that should prices stop escalating, many would likely default on their mortgages.

Transient Rentals

The significant number of Key West homes and condominiums owned by those who lived in the community part-time or not at all intensified the debate over transient rentals. This conflict addressed how, in their quest for profit, investors in Key West real estate affected the availability of affordable housing for Key West's workforce, as well as how short-term vacation rentals impacted established neighborhoods. The issue was whether these investors should have the right to secure income from short-term tourists, who were defined as those renting a condominium or house for less than thirty days. Some owners had procured transient licenses that allowed them to rent their property for any length of time, but in the mid-1990s the city stopped issuing any additional transient licenses.

Nevertheless, owners who had not secured such licenses still sought to rent their properties to short-term tourists. In their view, their property rights should grant them the latitude to profit from the tourists' desire to vacation in paradise. Those who wanted to limit transient rentals argued that property owners would be more likely to enter long-term leases with Key Westers if they could not rent to short-term tourists, which in turn would increase, or at least stop the decrease in, the supply of housing for Key West's workforce. In addition, they contended that residents of Key West's neighborhoods that included relatively few tourist accommodations should not have to subject themselves to a continual influx of tourists, who might, in fact, act like noisy vacationers enjoying themselves away from home.

In 1996, the city commission adopted an ordinance that capped the number of short-term rental licenses and stopped the issuance of new licenses. In 1998, the commission adopted another ordinance that imposed fines on those who rented out unlicensed homes to tourists for less than thirty days. Several property owners challenged the 1998 ordinance. The most successful of these lawsuits was initiated by Opie and Kathy Rollison, owners of property in Truman Annex. In April 2004, the appeals court decided that the Rollisons could rent their condo on a transient basis, because they had been doing so for less than half the year since before 1998 when the ordinance was adopted. The court ruled that before Key West passed the ordinance, the city exercised an informal policy that allowed owners to profit from short-term rentals for less than six months of the year.[16]

Some Key Westers vehemently opposed the *Rollison* decision, and John Mertz, a former chair of the Key West Planning Board, organized a political action committee to express support for the enforcement of the transient rental ordinance. They secured a victory in August 2004 when Florida's Third District Court of Appeal rejected an appeal of the *Abbe* case of 2003, in which an administrative judge had ruled that the city's ordinance was valid and enforceable.[17]

Therefore, the city's ordinance applied to all owners of unlicensed transients units who had not rented their units for less than six months a year prior to the passage of the law. By this time, however, this ordinance likely had only a limited impact on the supply of affordable housing for Key West's workforce. The dramatic increase in property values, along with the sale of many condos and homes between 2001 and 2004, produced a market affordable only to those who never intended to cover their mortgages through renting their property, either long-term to Key Westers or short-term to tourists. Many chose to simply let their property sit empty when they were not in Key West or else rent them to tourists for the legal minimum of thirty days. And if they did lease them on an ongoing basis, most public sector and tourism industry workers were unlikely to be able to afford the rent. The ordinance may have helped to accomplish one of its goals, which was to protect neighborhood residents from a succession of short-term tourists. By the mid-2000s, however, the relationship between transient rentals and the lack of affordable housing in Key West was indirect at best.

Affordable Housing

The shortage of affordable housing continued to drive the rapid turnover of workers in the tourism industry. The Key West Chamber of Commerce estimated that Key West lost approximately 750 workers in 2002, primarily because of the high cost of living, and especially of housing. A study conducted by the TDC found that employers in tourism in Key West had a significantly higher turnover rate than that of the county and of the tourism industry nationwide.[18]

As was the case in the 1990s, many employers relied heavily on immigrant workers. Under the federal Immigration and Nationality Act, when there was an inadequate supply of local workers, employers were allowed to recruit international workers for seasonal jobs. The TDC's survey of employers found that 27 percent of tourism-related businesses, primarily lodging establishments, bars, and restaurants, employed temporary foreign workers, although many suggested that the true percentage was much higher. Most of these workers came from Eastern European countries, with the remainder coming primarily from Canada, Mexico, Central America, and the Caribbean.[19]

Many immigrants arrived in Key West on their own, documented or undocumented. Some came to the island as volunteers with nonprofit organizations and were provided with housing in exchange for work. After completing their volunteer duty, some of these immigrants stayed in Key West. Several of Key West's tourism businesses arranged for a contracting company to supply them with foreign workers. Other foreign workers were brought in by independent "contractors," who arranged for their housing, often squeezing six or more people into a small apartment, and took a share of the immigrants' paychecks. Periodically, the federal government raided establishments that hired undocumented workers. These raids, however, were rare.

To attract and retain a workforce, some employers in the private sector assisted their employees with housing. The Chamber of Commerce's "Salary and Survey Report" in 2005 found that 17 percent of private-sector employers provided their employees with some kind of housing benefit. Affordable housing projects initiated by governmental agencies increased the number of apartments available to workers, although these apartments were rented more commonly to workers in the public sector than to those in the tourism industry. One of these projects, Roosevelt Gardens, provided workers with new apartments on North Roosevelt Boulevard. The Key West Housing Authority owned and managed the ninety-six apartments that opened for occupancy in late 2004. In February 2004, the Housing Authority purchased the Poinciana apartments from the Navy and made them available to civilian workers. In addition, the real estate affiliate of Historic Tours of America completed workforce housing projects on Stock Island and in Key West, and Habitat for Humanity built housing in the Lower Keys and renovated apartments in Key West.[20]

These additions, although welcome, were by no means adequate, and even additional developments were unlikely to contribute enough affordable housing units to redress the problem. Although the city's ROGO ordinance of 1993 required that at least 30 percent of the housing units in new developments be "affordable," by the 2000s this requirement had become less relevant to the issue of affordable housing. Market-rate units were generally no longer available to builders. In addition, projects deemed to be "redevelopments" were not required to make 30 percent of their units affordable. As redevelopments, neither condo hotel projects nor condominium conversions in Key West were subject to the city's affordable housing requirement.[21]

One controversial recommendation to potentially increase the supply of affordable housing was to "revisit" the building height limit that had been adopted in the 1970s. True, developers were sometimes able to skirt the four-story legal limit with creative measuring, but the ordinance clearly prevented high-rise development in the city. Last Stand and its allies, fearful that the city commission might revise the ordinance, had persuaded voters in 1998 to approve a referendum that added the four-story height limitation to the city charter. The amendment also mandated that any developer who wanted to exceed the limits had to secure approval from the voters in a referendum election. Given the difficulty of getting approval for taller buildings, no developers had requested a height variance since the charter amendment.[22]

The proposal to link the issue of affordable housing with that of building height landed on the political agenda in December 2004, when Mayor Jimmy Weekley asked the planning board to support a policy that allowed developers of affordable housing in New Town to exceed the four-story limit. City Commissioner Ed Scales and the *Citizen* both supported this proposal. Among its opponents were City Commissioner Harry Bethel, who represented New Town; HARC's chair, George Born; and Last Stand. In February 2005, the Key West Planning Board effectively killed this idea when it recommended against either changing the city's existing height limits or eliminating the necessity of a referendum to grant exceptions to these limits.[23]

Two studies completed in 2007 documented the continuing dearth of affordable housing in Key West. One of the studies found that 37 percent of respondents worked more than one job. Respondents also cited the cost of housing as the number one reason to leave Key West. The other study documented the significant discrepancy between housing prices and rents and income levels. This affordability gap contributed to a 6-percent decrease in the county's population between 2000 and 2007 and a 14-percent decrease in the number of residents between the ages of 20 and 54. From 2000 to 2009, Key West's population declined from 25,478 to 22,463 (see appendix).[24]

The Homeless

Key West's homeless population existed on the margins, or altogether outside, of Key West's "One Human Family." The city estimated that in April 2002 approximately 860 homeless people lived in Key West, and by December that number had increased to almost 1,000. In the 1920s, Key West's businesspeople and governing officials had clearly indicated their intolerance for "hoboes" from the North interfering with their efforts to attract tourists, and the reaction in the late 1990s and early 2000s was similar. Authorities generally saw homelessness in terms of violations of the law, rather than as reflecting the general issue of affordable housing or the mental and physical health problems some of the homeless suffered.[25] The city's primary policy was to arrest the homeless and charge them with violating "open container," "aggressive panhandling," and other ordinances. The Monroe County Court would often sentence the homeless to 29 days in jail, whereas in Miami the same violations would earn a sentence of a single day.[26]

In late 2002, Key West initiated another policy to reduce the number of homeless—buy them a one-way bus ticket to Miami and pay Miami-Dade County officials to provide for them in their shelters. Mayor Weekley explained the need for the proposal this way: "Here we are advertising as a relaxed, laid-back scene, a place where you can leave your troubles and stress behind. [Instead,] you get here and there are all these people on the street, and it puts your stress level up again." As the executive director of the National Coalition for the Homeless noted, "Homeless people are viewed as anti-tourist." An article in the *New York Times* headlined "Key West Trying to Put New Locks on Paradise," on the city's policies toward the homeless, suggested that some were not welcome in Key West's "family." In the end, Miami graciously rejected this overture.[27]

Instead, the Key West Commission took several steps to make the city less hospitable to the homeless: It closed a public beach where many of the homeless congregated. It expanded the city's no-panhandling ordinance to cover almost the entire historic district of Key West. And it forbade camping in the wetlands. The final adoption and implementation of this third measure was delayed until after a "summit" on the homeless was held in January 2003. After the summit, the city agreed to establish either a temporary or permanent emergency shelter, although it took no steps to do so in 2003. In January 2004, the Florida Department of Environmental Protection declared the section of the Salt Pond wetlands near Smathers Beach, where many homeless camped, environmentally sensitive, opening the door for the city to evict the homeless. In February, the city placed "No Trespassing" signs in the area. The city police and code enforcement officers then raided the beach before dawn, issued trespassing warnings, and ordered the homeless and other campers to vacate within twenty-four hours.[28]

Before the police returned, most of the homeless had moved to the nearby Bridle Path, owned by the Monroe County Land Authority, and to Higgs Beach, a nearby county-owned facility, where they were promised they would not face arrest. This promise was due less to the good will of city officials than to the *Pottinger* case in Miami, where the court suggested that cities could not evict the homeless from public property unless they had established alternative places for them to go. Even before the raid, the city and county had considered providing the homeless with a facility on Stock Island near the sheriff's detention center, complete with showers, bathrooms, and Quonset huts. At its meeting on March 16, 2004, the Key West City Commission voted to jointly fund, with Monroe County, a facility on Stock Island as a "safe zone." Once it was complete, officials, assuming they had complied with the mandate of the *Pottinger* decision, would set about removing the homeless from the Bridle Path and Higgs Beach. They would be given the option of leaving the Lower Keys, going to jail, or moving to the safe zone.[29]

The safe zone opened in July 2004 and shortly thereafter reached its eighty-person capacity. In early October, the homeless people who made regular use of the safe zone were informed that the facility was being transformed into an "overnight temporary shelter." The homeless were given a few days notice that the new procedures required them to leave every morning at 7:30 with all their personal belongings. If they wished to return at night to sleep, they had to check in at 7 p.m. John Jones, the city's assistant city manager, agreed with the new policy of the Florida Keys Outreach Coalition (FKOC), which managed the facility, remarking, "We don't want to have a Club Med for homeless here. We need to move them out, and help them." Many who lived in the shelter argued that the new policy meant they would have to return to the street and the beaches during the day, where they would face the possibility of arrest, especially those who worked at night and now had no place to sleep during the day. One resident summarized his fate as follows: "I'm getting used to moving, and I'm getting used to losing."[30]

In January 2005, the Southern Homeless Assistance League, a coalition of nonprofit organizations serving the homeless, estimated that the number of homeless living in shelters in Key West had increased during the previous three years. Reverend Stephen Braddock, the chair of the league, presented a generally optimistic review of the situation, concluding, "something is working," including more of the homeless moving into transitional housing. The national advocacy organization, the National Coalition for the Homeless, agreed that Key West's policy regarding the homeless had improved with the opening of the Stock Island facilities and the adoption of other related initiatives. In its report in 2004, the coalition had listed Key West as one of the twenty "meanest cities" in the nation in terms of its homeless policy. In its 2005 report, the coalition removed Key West from the list.[31]

One Human Family?

The community's "One Human Family" motto certainly rang true to many Key West residents during the first years of the new century. Any new owner of residential property in Key West, be they year-round or seasonal, were welcome to participate in the community's cultural and philanthropic institutions. There was no "exclusive" club that admitted only those citizens who had lived in the Keys for generations. Gay organizations and individuals were welcome participants in, and often the primary organizers of, many community activities. Several women served on boards and in executive positions in community organizations, and the Woman's Club was one of the more respected groups in the city.

Long-standing civic organizations such as Rotary International funded community projects, and Key Westers often organized fundraisers for friends' health care and other needs. In 2005, J. T. Thompson was among those who organized the Sister Season Fund to raise money for workers in tourism-related industries who needed temporary help to make ends meet due to illness or other problems. Several island residents organized the Community Foundation of the Florida Keys in 1996, expanding its efforts in 2004 after hiring a full-time president. The foundation's fundraising efforts dramatically enhanced the island's philanthropic work in a way that was compatible with the "One Human Family" motto.

In terms of the economic circumstances of its different members, however, the Key West family was probably never more unequal. The community attracted wealthy, primarily seasonal, newcomers in the 1990s and first years of the new century, and these newcomers bid up the prices of the few available pieces of real estate. In the process, the city became less affordable to those members of its workforce who had not had the good fortune to arrive years earlier and purchase a home or condominium. And even those who had purchased homes faced high property insurance costs, a burden to those with modest incomes. Some of Key West's residents, both Conchs and those who had moved to the island in earlier decades, chose to profit from selling their homes after they increased in value, but many were involuntarily displaced as apartments were converted to condominiums and as costs increased. Key West was now a community where relatively few had long-term roots.[32]

Jimmy Weekley, the former mayor, bemoaned in 2005, "I hate to see people doing that (leaving), because we are losing our history." Key West's City Planner, Ty Symroski, voiced a similar sentiment. "A lot of these people are regular local people engaged in regular, local jobs and when they sell, they are not selling their housing to . . . people like them, they are selling to people who will not be regular local people." He concluded, "We are a community that is not replacing itself."[33]

The writer Rosalind Brackenbury felt similarly. She wrote that her block in Old Town now included six empty houses. One had been purchased by a couple for cash about a year earlier, and they had not visited the house since. Rumor had it that they were in Rome. Another home was in the process of being gutted and rebuilt at twice the size. A local developer had purchased two others and was replacing them with one much larger home. Brackenbury wrote, "the houses where there used to be neighborhoods are being bought up, the trees cut down, swimming pools inserted, houses 'mansionized' . . . and they are locked up and left."[34]

Key West's family was by no means stable. The island had always been subject to change, and the question of what type of community it would become remained. It seemed unlikely that Key West would attract many young, creative people interested in the arts or business, or that it would entice younger families who might participate in the Little League and other civic organizations. Living costs were high and economic opportunities were few, and these circumstances limited the type of family Key West could become.

Conclusion

IN 1983, the writer Bill Manville, who had moved to Key West with his wife, author Nancy Friday, in the late 1970s, praised Key West's uniqueness: "What appeals to us is the island's cosmopolitan atmosphere, the way different levels of society interconnect. You go to a party here, and you're liable to meet anyone from the Mayor to a drug smuggler to Tennessee Williams. There is no country club, really . . . and the Stock Island golf course is going bankrupt for lack of paying customers. . . . I mean it's America, yet at the same time it's not America. It's Key West." A magazine article published on Key West in 1984 suggested that even though its physical structures were being renovated, Key West remained "different": "Today, boutiques and art galleries are the rage in this Florida outpost. But despite such encroachments, it remains a haven for authentic characters and 'perverse minds.'"[1]

Not everyone agreed, however, that Key West had maintained its cosmopolitan uniqueness, or, at least, that it was likely to do so for long. In an article published in 1983, John Stavro, based upon interviews with several Key Westers, raised a concern many shared: "The ultimate worry for Key West is not one of buildings or open spaces, but something less tangible. It is how to keep the eclectic, Bohemian mix of people who have made up the character of Key West for decades. If the island becomes a rich-man's paradise . . . that spirit will be gone." Stavro cited another article, published in *Holiday* by Budd Schulberg in 1949, that warned, "In time, unfortunately, if too many professional boosters have their way, the Keys may change. . . . The Keys seem to be in for a boom that would transform them into exactly the kind of place most of the permanent settlers and the tourists have come there to avoid."[2]

Stavro's and Schulberg's articles assumed that Key West had long been a unique place and was now threatened by a newfound popularity. In fact, the island has always been both similar to and different from other places. Key West's uniqueness has been tempered, in part, by more general cultural and economic trends: the countercultural movement of the 1960s and 1970s, the widespread drug use during those and later decades, the increased openness of the gay population after the Stonewall riots of June 1969, the real estate boom of the early twenty-first century, periodic economic downtowns, and the growth of leisure time and discretionary income that contributed to the expansion of global tourism.

Key West's hospitable island climate and small size, along with other of its qualities, however, often magnified more general trends. Key West's gay population, which grew significantly in the 1970s and 1980s, soon constituted a higher percentage of the population in Key West than in virtually any other U.S. city. Soaring real estate prices dramatically affected not just one neighborhood, section, or group of people in Key West but almost all of the island's geography and population. Nor was there a "tourist bubble" where tourists congregated to the exclusion of the rest of the island, although Old Town was the focus of most who visited.

One heralded aspect of Key West's uniqueness is its "live-and-let-live" ethos, which has made the island hospitable to diverse populations. The prevalence of this ethos, and as such its relevance to Key West's uniqueness, however, has been overstated. Tensions between labor and management within the cigar industry and on the federal New Deal projects were common. Later, conflicts arose over issues related to development and tourism, as often occurred in other communities. The bitter rhetoric that characterized Key West's elections in the 1980s and 1990s often pitted Conchs against newcomers, who were accused of trying to seize power from the locals in order to reinvent the community. Still, this "live-and-let-live" ethos is not just a construct of the Key West Chamber of Commerce or Tourist Development Council to encourage visitors to "Come as You Are" to the island paradise. The community has indeed been home to diverse groups of people who have gotten along reasonably well on a small island.

The legendary Captain Tony Tarracino died in November 2008. Until just a few months before his death, Captain Tony could sometimes still be found at Captain Tony's Saloon, sharing his stories with locals and tourists drinking there, especially if they were female. It mattered none that Captain Tony no longer owned the bar; for many, it was his tavern and his island. True, Hemingway and Buffett were better known than Tony, and their association with the town likely brought more tourists to Key West than his did. And Ed Swift and his business partners, as well as others, had a bigger impact on Key West's tourism and real estate industries than Tony ever did. But Key West is known for its spirit and character, and Captain Tony embodied this spirit from the time he moved to the community in the late 1940s.

Tony likely would have felt at home on the island during Key West's earlier eras. His love for the sea makes it easy to imagine him as the captain of a wrecker racing to be the first to reach a ship that had run aground on the reef. And his working-class background would have led him to fit in comfortably with the workforce in the cigar industry. Of course, during the New Deal era, Tony would have frequented Sloppy Joe's, conversing with Hemingway and the myriad characters who visited the bar.[3]

Captain Tony's lifestyle jibed with a "live-and-let-live" culture, but he also embodied the spirit of those concerned about the community's future. He realized that a "live-and-let-live" attitude might also lead to a laissez-faire system where developers could build wherever and whenever they chose and, in the process, destroy the character of the island he loved. His several unsuccessful runs for mayor, and his one victory, grew out of his desire to slow changes on the island even as he embraced tourism. Captain Tony's journey in Key West, from shrimp-boat worker to charter-boat captain to proprietor of a popular bar, highlights the transitions and complexities of the island community.

As a charter-boat captain and bar owner, he benefited from the increased tourist trade in Key West, although his bar attracted all segments of Key West's population. The media often sought his opinion, and as mayor he bragged about his ability to attract more tourists to the island. However, before and during his term in office, he fought developers who wanted to build large hotels to serve those tourists. Tony and others, including citizen activists and elected officials, sought to balance the development of residential housing and tourist accommodations with the needs of the municipal and tourist-industry workforce for affordable housing. In this endeavor, they had only limited success, and Key West moved toward an economy based on high-end tourism and real estate.

As the end of the first decade of the twenty-first century approached, some echoed the doubts that have been raised for decades about the quality of Key West as a tourist destination. Fodor's *Florida 2009* edition, while praising Key West for its weather, architecture, and "laid-back lifestyle," made sure to point out that "much has been lost to those eager for a buck." It described Duval Street resembling "a miniature Las Vegas lined with garish signs for T-shirt shops and tour company offices. Cruise ships dwarf the town's skyline and fill the streets with day-trippers." Still, as had long been the case, many voiced a different, more favorable opinion. For example, readers voting in *Florida Magazine*'s 2009 opinion poll ranked Duval Street as the state's best main street for the third consecutive year. The magazine characterized Duval as having a "rhythm all its own," including "souvenir shops, famous art galleries, bars, boutique shops, seafood restaurants and theaters."[4]

An article published in a travel magazine earlier in the decade provides some insight into the persistence of contrasting views of the island. In discussing the variety of places to stay in Key West, it noted that choosing a place "mirrors, in a way, the town's own existential dilemma. Guesthouses represent the past—eccentric, architecturally distinctive. Resorts signify Key West's evolution into a mainstream destination. At one extreme are inns, campy enough to make Liberace look like Charlton Heston; at the other, property much like those anywhere in America. Between the two poles, however, are places of character and comfort."[5]

In other words, Key West remained a popular tourist destination in part because it offered a variety of places to stay—from the unique to the generic. Similarly, while several chain restaurants did business on

Duval, so did numerous locally owned restaurants, either on the avenue or within walking distance. Neither all of the accommodations nor all of the restaurants offer Key West's visitors unique experiences, but, then again, Key West has always been both unique and mainstream. What it has not always been, but has surely become, is a community affordable primarily for the wealthy.

Key West's rising real estate values during most of the 1990s and the first half of the next decade greatly exceeded the national average. The real estate market, however, mirrored that of many other communities: investors bought and flipped houses; people who prospered during the stock market and high-tech booms of the 1990s bought vacation homes; developers converted apartments to condominiums and motels to condo hotels. Housing was increasingly priced beyond the reach of middle-class families and workers in the tourism industry and public sector. New cultural institutions formed that were supported by the increasingly wealthy population that lived, at least seasonally, on the island. Few communities the size of Key West boasted both an opera company and a symphony.

The serious recession that began in late 2007 and the global financial crisis of 2008 caused Key West to lose some of the trappings of the wealthy community it had become. The Island Opera Theatre closed its doors. Then, in 2010, the Key West Symphony Orchestra, facing financial problems, changed its name to the South Florida Symphony and tried to expand to include Fort Lauderdale and West Palm Beach. Despite these efforts, the symphony cancelled its 2011 season, and its future remains uncertain.

The recession and financial crisis dramatically impacted the real estate market. In 2009, the Spottswood Companies placed their plan to redevelop the entrance to Key West on Roosevelt Boulevard by replacing inexpensive motels with a convention center and upscale hotel on indefinite hold. The condo hotel developers faced challenges selling their units in the weaker market.

Even before the recession, however, the severe flooding in October 2005 brought on by Hurricane Wilma contributed to a slow down in the real estate market. Sales of residential properties declined significantly between 2005 and 2006, and the inventory of unsold homes and condos increased. Although the number of residential property transactions rose slightly in 2007, the average sales price of residences in Key West decreased 10 percent from 2006, and property sat longer on the market before selling, if it sold at all.[6]

Prices dropped further at the end of the decade, and, as in other markets, the number of short sales and foreclosures increased. The median selling price of a single-family home decreased 36 percent, from $645,390 in 2007 to $410,000 in 2010. Condominium and townhouse prices decreased even more dramatically, from $520,000 in 2007 to $290,000 in 2010 or 44 percent. Rents also decreased. Some who had once been priced out of the market could now afford to buy a home. Still, Key West was a relatively expensive housing market, and workers in tourism and other service sectors continued to struggle economically.[7]

The tourism industry, however, did not experience the decline that the real estate industry suffered. The number of tourists staying in Key West overnight increased slightly each year between 2005 and 2009 (see appendix). While room rates dropped toward the end of the decade, in 2009, the average room rates, as well as the occupancy rates, in the Keys were the highest in the state, and Key West's average daily room rate exceeded that of the rest of the Keys. The rising real estate prices in the first years of the new century challenged tourism's place as the most important component of Key West's economy, but as sales in real estate slowed, the emphasis on drawing in tourists to the island increased. In mid-2009, the state legislature authorized a penny increase in the tourist tax, as requested by the TDC and other tourism interests. Now the TDC would have more to spend on events and advertising aimed at drawing tourists to a place now branded as "Close To Perfect—Far From Normal."[8]

Although the phrase "far from normal" was open to various interpretations, many officials in the tourism industry have long celebrated Key West as "America's Caribbean Island" and its difference from other U.S. destinations. Many now wondered about the potential impact on Key West should travel restrictions to and from Cuba—that Caribbean nation located just ninety miles from Key West and the home country of many who had arrived in Key West during the late 1800s and afterward—be lifted. Some felt it would mean fewer visitors to Key West, while others saw it as an opportunity to entice even more tourists to Key West. The Tourist Development Council and city officials prepared to advocate that Key West be declared a port of entry for Cuba and then strive to attract tourists to visit both destinations under the motto "Two nations. One vacation." An editorial in the *Citizen* suggested that the city's heritage fit well with this goal: "Key West's historic Cuban ties and the people and cultures that so influenced the character of the community . . . gives the Southernmost City a strong foundation for renewed ties. In a sense, the city's future may reside in its past."[9]

Public relations firms may indeed succeed in making this pitch. In reality, however, the Key West of today is far from the Key West that was once heavily influenced by the island's Cuban and Bahamian population. Key West has been reinvented, to some extent by Conchs, but to a more significant extent by others. In 2007, Marcella Morgan, herself a third-generation Conch, produced the film *When Paradise Was Ours*, which features interviews with several Conchs, most of them in their 70s and 80s, talking about the Key West of their youth and of their parents' generation. Many of the families they knew have since moved from the island, either recently or long ago. They report feeling that the island has changed in many ways and is no longer "their" town.

The reinvention of Key West will continue, shaped by national and global factors as well as local policies. No matter where that leads in the long run, Key West will remain a tourist town with much to offer visitors. While many in the town have embraced change, Key Westers have also fought, with some success, against the tourist culture's homogenizing effects. The citizens of Key West will continue to value their community for a variety of reasons. Still, we may well wonder whether the sons and daughters of average-income Conchs, aspiring writers and artists, public sector employees, tourism industry workers, and others will be able to afford to live and participate in the community. What quality of life will be available to them? With effort, and luck, the Conch Republic may yet be able to become "One Human Family."

ACKNOWLEDGMENTS

Many people generously contributed to this manuscript. Dennis Judd, Scott Keeter, and Todd Swanstrom read different versions of large segments of the manuscripts over the years and always offered constructive suggestions. Rosemary Jann read and made detailed comments on much of the manuscript. Her talents as a writer and English professor greatly contributed to the final product. Jack Fernandez and Jim Handly edited the manuscript. Several others also critiqued sections of my work. These include Bob Beauregard, John Capouya, Allison DeFoor, Bob Ingalls, Robin Jones, Judy Kass, Roy Kass, Adam Labonte, James Lopez, Ted Muller, Linda Musante, Terry Parssinen, Rich Piper, and William Wright.

Several students at the University of Tampa assisted me by writing papers on different aspects of Key West and by commenting on my work. I would like to thank Cassie Greatens, Sheri Huelster, Jason Kahn, Adam Labonte, Elizabeth Rozman, and Ashley Wazowicz.

A number of people in Key West always were willing to help me out. The late Ed Little read sections of the manuscript and often provided insights into Key West's maritime history. I, and many other students of Key West history, will greatly miss him. Ty Symroski, the island's former city planner, read several chapters and often enlightened me about development issues in the community. Peter Ilchuk provided enlightening commentary on the political campaigns and administrations of Richard Heyman. Laurie McChesney offered insights into the real-estate market in Key West and provided me with relevant documents; Rita Brown, Bob Muens, Bobby Nesbitt, and Lenore Troia informed me about the cultural scene in Key West during the last few decades. Robert Pardon read some of my work and gave me helpful suggestions from the perspective of a Conch who had played major roles in the city's public utility and tourism industries. George Born helped me understand the importance of historic preservation in Key West. Amy Kimball-Murley provided me with helpful information about the cruise ship industry in Key West, and Jessica Bennett, the director of market research for the Monroe County Tourist Development Council, often gave me data on tourism trends in the city. Ray Blazevic, who I often encountered at the Key West library, always had interesting things to tell me about Key West. Dennis Cooper, the publisher of *Key West The Newspaper*, allowed me to examine his archives and to copy relevant articles.

I often stayed at Eden House during my visits to Key West. Mike and Colleen Eden were always a pleasure to see. Mike educated me about the Key West he first experienced in the 1970s. Bob, Gary, Morgan, Pasha, and others who worked at Eden House made me feel at home. Bob's "get your ass out of bed" wakeup calls reminded me that I wasn't staying at the Hilton. During the last few years of my research, I often stayed at the house on Elizabeth Street owned by my friends, John and Karen O'Leary. They could not have been more generous.

The two reviewers for the University Press of Florida, Lee Irby and Brewster Chamberlin, were both outstanding. Mr. Chamberlin saved me from making several factual mistakes. I was fortunate that the press chose Penelope Cray to copyedit the manuscript. She was a pleasure to work with. Gary Mormino, the coeditor of this book series, often sent me newspaper articles and archival material from his extensive files. Michael X. Delli Carpini, Tony Gregory, Scott Keeter, and Stuart Newman Associates allowed me to use their images, and Peter Kraaft prepared the Key West map for the book. Jim Beckman and Maria Beckman helped me select which images to include.

Marlyn Pethe, the director of the University of Tampa Macdonald-Kelce Library, helped me with census material. Several of the reference librarians there, including Art Bagley, Elizabeth Barron, Melisandre Hilliker, Jeanne Vince, and Mickey Wells, always were willing to assist me. Sue Felter, Louise Hane, and Lisa Valentine graciously took care of my many interlibrary loan and other requests. Diane Keffer, the staff assistant at the University's College of Social Sciences, Mathematics and Education, helped prepare this manuscript. The Faculty Development Committee at the University of Tampa provided me with several grants that enabled me to visit Key West. I think they often doubted that I was actually working during my trips to the island, so it is fortunate that I finally wrote something.

Tom Hambright, the head of the history section at the Key West Public Library and the Monroe County Historian, was indispensable during the decade I spent on this project. He provided me with access to the library's archives, read and made comments on the entire manuscript, and always was willing to answer my sometimes bizarre questions.

Robin Jones, my wife, talked me into beginning this project after we visited Key West in 2000. Her ulterior motive clearly was to spend more time in Key West, which was fine with me. This book is dedicated to Robin.

APPENDIX

Table 1. Population Trends in Key West, by Decade, 1830–2009

Year	Total
1830	517
1840	688
1850	2,645
1860	2,913
1870	5,016
1880	9,890
1890	18,080
1900	17,114
1910	19,945
1920	18,749
1930	12,831
1940	13,323
1950	26,433
1960	33,956
1970	29,312
1980	24,292
1990	24,832
2000	25,478
2009	22,463

Sources: Browne, *Key West: The Old and the New*, 173; Planning Department, City of Key West, "Statistical Abstract City of Key West," March 2004, 2; U.S. Census Bureau, American FactFinder, http://factfinder.census.gov (retrieved February 26, 2011).

Table 2. Tourism Indicators in Key West, 1984–1999

	Total			Percentage Change		
Year	Bed Tax Revenues	Deplanements	Cruise ship Passengers	Bed Tax Revenues	Deplanements	Cruise Passeng
1984	556,614	104,232	-	-	-	-
1985	825,936	95,032	-	-	-1.2	-
1986	1,038,350	135,008	46,000	25.7	42.1	-
1987	1,946,606	160,703	-	8.75	19	-
1988	2,306,210	159,553	-	18.5	-93	-
1989	2,605,604	149,805	-	13	-3.9	-
1990	2,978,499	192,777	132,840	14.3	28.7	-
1991	3,282,886	185,438	112,810	10.2	-3.8	-15.1
1992	3,391,592	198,562	139,680	3.3	7.1	23.8
1993	3,828,627	216,372	255,570	12.9	9	83
1994	4,059,544	243,404	452,300	6	12.5	77
1995	4,297,481	242,147	398,370	5.9	-0.5	-11.9
1996	4,795,515	271,714	393,340	11.6	12.2	-1.3
1997	5,237,446	267,732	561,550	9.2	-1.5	42.8
1998	5,408,216	257,574	586,390	3.3	-3.8	4.4
1999	5,696,390	268,940	609,860	5.3	4.4	4

Sources: Key West International Airport; City of Key West Finance Department; Thomas J. Murray & Associates, "The Impacts," 16, 18.
Note: The bed tax in Key West was increased from 2 to 3 percent in November 1986.

Table 3. Tourism Indicators in Key West, 2000–2010

	Total			Percentage Change		
Year	Bed Tax Revenues	Deplanements	Cruise ship Passengers	Bed Tax Revenues	Deplanements	Cruise s Passeng
2000	6,228,176	275,386	664,487			
2001	6,425,114	255,850	678,988	3.2	-7.10%	2.2%
2002	6,419,684	259,314	1,030,504	-0.1	1.40%	51.80%
2003	6,850,321	286,833	1,067,222	6.7	10.60%	3.60%
2004	7,271,371	291,501	934,070	6.1	1.60%	-12.50%
2005	7,220,187	313,869	924,233	-0.7	7.70%	-1.1%
2006	7,421,576	276,154	888,193	2.8	-12.00%	-3.9%
2007	7,893,266	263,788	816,919	6.4	-4.50%	-8.00%
2008	8,165,768	222,198	740,932	3.5	-15.80%	-9.30%
2009	9,372,137	229,313	859,409	14.8	3.20%	16.00%
2010	11,461,977	277,966	850,270	22.30%	21.2%	—1.1%

Source: Key West Chamber of Commerce, "Statistics on Tourism," http://www.keywestchamber.org/PI trends.
Note: The bed tax was increased from 3 to 4 percent in June 2009.

Table 4. Key West/Florida Median Owner-occupied Home Values from 1960 to 2009 and Key West/Florida Median Household Incomes in 1999

Year	Key West Home Values	State of Florida
1960	$10,700	$11,800
1970	$14,419	$15,084
1979	$58,600	$45,300
1990	$147,400	$77,100
2000	$265,800	$105,500
2005–9	$640,000	$211,300
1999 Median Household Income	$43,021	$38,819

Source: U.S. Bureau of the Census, County and City Data Book, 1962: 5, 499; County and City Data Book, 1973: 21, 671; County and City Data Book, 1983: 7, 828; County and City Data Book, 1994: 8; http://factfinder.census.gov, FactFinder, 1990, HO23B Median Value; "Key West (city), Florida," http://quickfacts.census.gov; U.S. Census Bureau, "Key West city, Florida," 2005–2009 American Community Survey 5-Year Estimates; U.S. Census Bureau, "Florida Selected Housing Characteristics: 2005–2009."

Table 5. Tourism Trends, 2003–2009

Year	Overnight Visitors	Day Trippers	Cruise ship Passengers	Total Visitors
2003	1,309,559	242,268	1,067,222	2,619,049
2004	1,303,633	241,172	934,070	2,478,875
2005	1,046,111	237,460	925,795	2,209,366
2006	1,063,752	196,794	888,183	2,148,729
2007	1,094,647	202,510	816,919	2,114,076
2008	1,112,978	205,901	739,218	2,058,097
2009	1,165,327	206,263	859,409	2,230,999

Source: Key West Chamber of Commerce, "Key West and Monroe County Demographics," http://www.keywestchamber.org (retrieved February 26, 2011).

NOTES

Introduction

1. King, *The Conch that Roared*.

2. Matt Schudel, "Capt. Tony Tarracino—Saloonkeeper, Mayor, Eccentric of Key West," *Washington Post*, November 16, 2008.

3. Judd and Fainstein, eds., *The Tourist City*, 12–13; Traub, *The Devil's Playground*, xiv; Shaw and Williams, *Critical Issues*, 225.

4. Souther, *New Orleans On Parade*, 14. Also see Gotham, *Authentic New Orleans*, 7–13.

5. Hoffman, Fainstein, and Judd, eds., *Cities and Visitors*. Also see Meethan, *Tourism in Global Society*, and Wasserstrom, *China's Brave New World*, especially chapter 15. A significant literature debates whether tourists do in fact value a "unique" destination and seek "authenticity." See MacCannell, *The Tourist*; Rojek and Urry, "Transformations of Travel and Theory"; Ritzer and Liska, "'McDisneyization' and 'Post-Tourism'"; and Craik, "The Culture of Tourism." A good review of the literature on typologies of tourists' motivations and the characteristics of destinations they find desirable is provided in Shaw and Williams, *Critical Issues in Tourism*, 78–85. For a review of some of the literature related to this issue, see Prentice, "Tourist Motivation and Typologies."

6. See Gotham, *Authentic New Orleans*, and Gotham, "Tourism Gentrification"; Fainstein, Hoffman and Judd, "Introduction," *Cities and Visitors*, 2. Also see Williams, "Toward a Political Economy of Tourism," 70–71.

7. A "live-and-let-live" philosophy was among the cultural characteristics attributed to the "unconventional cities" studied in Sharp, *Morality Politics in American Cities*, 26, 28. Elazar, *American Federalism*, focuses on cultural differences among states and regions. Key West has typically displayed Elazar's "individualistic," rather than moralistic or traditionalistic, political culture.

See Raymer, *Key West Collection*, for articles by the Key West newspaper columnist who emphasized the prevalence of a "laissez-faire" culture in Key West.

8. Also see Gottdiener, *The Theming of America*, 6–8.

9. Harrison, *Undying Love*.

10. Gotham, *Authentic New Orleans*, 19. Also see Meethan, *Tourism in Global Society*; Butler, ed., *The Tourism Area Life Cycle*, Vols. 1 and 2, and Shaw and Williams, *Critical Issues in Tourism*.

11. Brown, *Inventing New England*; see Britton, "Tourism, Capital and Place." Studies of the growth of tourism in some cities conclude, however, that its increase is not due primarily to conscious efforts to attract tourists. See Ehrlich and Dreier, "The New Boston Discovers the Old Tourism and the Struggle for a Livable City," and Terhorst, van de Ven, and Deben, "Amsterdam."

12. "Theater; 'West Side Story': The Beginnings Of Something Great," *New York Times* (hereafter, *NYT*), October 21, 1990.

13. See, for example, Zukin, *The Culture of Cities*.

14. Kennedy, *Grits and Grunts*.

15. Cox, *A Key West Companion*, 194.

16. See Andy Newman interview, December 18, 2008; Rojek, *Leisure Theory*; Getz, *Festivals, Special Events, and Tourism*.

17. Phil Caputo, "Phil Caputo on Key West," *Florida Keys Magazine*, May 1987: 20–27; Rothman, *Devil's Bargains*.

18. Beauregard, *When America Became Suburban*, 77, emphasizes this point regarding the movement into central cities in the 1990s. I have added, "and comfortable." See Gotham, "Tourism Gentrification." Also see Zukin, "Gentrification" and *Naked City*. KPMG, "Key West Base Reuse Plan," 28; City of Key West Planning Department, "2002 Statistical Abstract," 106.

19. Davis, "Another Caribbean Conquest," 175; *MH*, April 8, 1989.

20. Beauregard, "City of Superlatives" and "Radical Uniqueness and the Flight from Urban Theory"; Julius Stone, "Key West Is to be Restored," *NYT*, August 12, 1934; Davis, "New World Symphony With A Few Sour Notes."

Chapter 1. Key West's First Hundred Years: Wrecking, the Military, Cigar Making, and a Few Tourists

1. Sears, *Sacred Places*; Aron, *Working at Play*; Stronge, *The Sunshine Economy*, 76–77.

2. An Invalid, *A Winter in the West Indies and Florida*, viii, 128.

3. An Invalid, *A Winter in the West Indies and Florida*, 132, 138.

4. "Key West," *NYT*, December 26, 1857; "Key West Enjoyments," *New York Daily Times*, March 30, 1855.

5. Viele, *The Florida Keys*, 37; Browne, *Key West*, 13–14; Diddle, "Adjudication of Ship-wrecking Claims at Key West in 1831"; Stebbins, *City of Intrigue, Nest of Revolution*, 11.

6. Cox, *A Key West Companion*; Tom Hambright, interview, January 28, 2011.

7. Milanich, *Florida Indians and the Invasion from Europe*; Tom Hambright, interview, March 7, 2005; Hahn, *Missions to the Calusa*; Browne, *Key West*; Viele, *The Florida Keys*.

8. Gannon, *Florida*; Browne, *Key West*; Stebbins, *City of Intrigue, Nest of Revolution*; Viele, *The Florida Keys*; Marvin, *A Treatise on the Law of Wreck and Salvage*.

9. Marvin, *A Treatise on the Law of Wreck and Salvage*, 2; Viele, *The Florida Keys*, 48–49.

10. Browne, *Key West*; Viele, *The Florida Keys*; Barnett, "Inventing the Conch Republic"; Schroeder, "Fisheries of Key West and the Clam Industry of Southern Florida"; Witzell, "The Origin of the Florida Sponge Fishery."

11. Viele, "Lt. Perry and the US Schooner Shark in Pirate Waters"; Jameson, "Porter and the Pirates"; Browne, *Key West*, 73; Hambright, "Military History of the Florida Keys"; Roth, "150 Years of Defense Activity in Key West, 1820–1970."

12. Jameson, *East Martello Tower*; Stebbins, *City of Intrigue, Nest of Revolution*; Camp, "Captain Brannan's Dilemma"; Lester, "Key West During the Civil War," iii. After President Lincoln called for the blockade of the southern port, the Navy in Key West was designated in April 1861 as the headquarters of the Gulf Blocking Squadron, and many of the blockade running ships that Union forces captured were brought to Key West (Roth, "150 Years of Defense Activity in Key West, 1820–1970"; see Meinig, *The Shaping of America*, 480–81, 510–11).

13. Westfall, *Key West*; Browne, *Key West*, 67; Wells, *Forgotten Legacy*, 18; Smith, "Engineering Slavery." In January 1818, Key West was incorporated as the City of Key West. In November 1828, a new charter changed its designation to that of a town, and then in 1832 it was again incorporated as a city (Browne, *Key West*, 50–51).

14. Hambright and Hambright, *Key West Historic Memorial Sculpture Garden*; MH, June 18, 1999; Corey Malcom, interview, May 20, 2010.

15. Browne, *Key West*; Proby, *Audubon in Florida*; Audubon, "Three Floridian Episodes," 56–57; Hammond, "Wreckers and Wrecking on the Florida Reef, 1829–1832," 240.

16. Hammond, "Sketches of the Florida Keys, 1829–1833," 74–75; Hammond, "Wreckers," 248.

17. Patrick, ed., "William Adee Whiteheads," 64, 71.

18. Black, "Richard Fitzpatrick's," 56 (for quote on Pardon Greene); Browne, *Key West*, 67.

19. Browne, *Key West*, 38, 39.

20. "Commercial Cities and Towns," 54, 56; *NYT*, July 7, 1854; Denham and Huneycutt, eds., *Echoes from a Distant Frontier*, 245.

21. "Heritage Online." http://persi.heritagequestonline.com (last accessed August 20, 2009).

22. Paine, "Over the Florida Keys by Rail," 405; Brown Jr., "The Civil War, 1861–1865"; Black, "Richard Fitzpatricks' South Florida, 1822–1840," 47.

23. Viele, *The Florida Keys*, 49, 171; Westfall, *Key West*. In 1889, the state legislature expanded Key West's city limits to include the entire island, but this increased the population of Key West by only a few people (Browne, *Key West*, 55).

24. Roth, "150 Years of Defense Activity in Key West, 1820–1970"; Roth, "The

Military Utilization of Key West and the Dry Tortugas from 1822–1900"; Langley and Langley, *Key West and The Spanish-American War*; Pais, "The Battleship *Maine*"; "Naval Air Station."

25. Schroeder, "Fisheries of Key West and the Clam Industry of Southern Florida," 2, 59; Stebbins, *City of Intrigue, Nest of Revolution*, 66. For some, the term *conch* had negative connotations. As late as 1949, *Webster's New International Dictionary of the English Language* included as one definition of *conch*, "One of an inferior class of whites in Florida and vicinity" (553). An earlier dictionary, *The Shorter Oxford*, defined *conch* as "A nickname for the lower class of inhabitants of the Bahamas, the Florida Keys, etc., from their use of conchs as food" (361). A reporter from New York visiting Key West in 1884 noted: "The natives of the Florida Keys, as well as of most of the Bahama Islands, are known all over the Southern country as Conchs, just as we speak of Florida crackers. It is a name usually applied in derision, but the Conchs themselves do not seem at all ashamed of it" ("Visit to Key West," 4).

26. Browne, *Key West*; Munroe, "Sponge and Spongers of the Florida Reef"; Witzell, "The Origin of the Florida Sponge Fishery." Sponging continued for decades in Key West, but its contribution to Key West's economy had become insignificant even before the 1939 sponge blight that devastated sponging throughout Florida (Schroeder, "Fisheries of Key West and the Clam Industry of Southern Florida," 55).

27. Witzell, "The Origin, Evolution, and Demise of the U.S. Sea Turtle Fisheries"; Knight, "Norberg Thompson."

28. Stebbins, "1885 Schedule"; Westfall, *Key West*.

29. Johnson, *The Bahamas from Slavery to Servitude, 1783–1933*; Foster, *Conchtown USA*.

30. Stebbins, "1885 Schedule." In 1885, 4,871 inhabitants, or 36 percent of the city's population, were either born in Key West or elsewhere in Florida, 4,410 (33%) were born in Cuba, and 3,260 (24%) were born in the Bahamas. In addition to those born in Cuba, another 575 were the sons or daughters of Cuban immigrants.

31. Westfall, *Key West*; Poyo, "Cuban Revolutionaries and Monroe County Reconstruction Politics, 1868–1876"; Skidmore, "Cubans by Choice"; Hambright and Hambright, *Key West Historic Memorial Sculpture Garden*; Born, *Historic Florida Keys*; "Florida's State Board of Health."

32. Poyo, "Cuban Patriots in Key West, 1878–1886"; Stebbins, "The Insurgents of Key West"; Poyo, "Key West and the Cuban Ten Years War"; Langley and Langley, *Key West and the Spanish-American War*, 16–17; Ronning, *José Martí and the Émigré Colony in Key West*.

33. Browne, *Key West*; Zahav, "The Key West Jewish Community." Some of Key West's Jewish leaders joined with the city's Cubans to provide financial support for Cuban independence (Browne, *Key West*, 170; Fuller, "History of St. Mary's, Star of the Sea, Key West, Florida"; Langley and Langley, *Key West and the Spanish-American War*, 17).

34. Wells, *Forgotten Legacy*; Sawyer and Wells-Bowie, *Key West*.

35. Brown Jr., *Florida's Black Public Officials*, 47; Terry Schmida, "Black History Month," *The Key West Citizen* (hereafter, *Citizen*), February 4, 2001.

36. Poyo, "Cuban Revolutionaries and Monroe County Reconstruction Politics, 1868–1876"; Brown Jr., *Florida's Black Public Officials*, 63–68, 173; Browne, *Key West*, 55; Rivers and Brown, "African Americans in South Florida."

37. Nolan, Shriver, and Nidy, "Cultural Resource Survey"; URS, "Key West Historic Resources Survey"; Born, *Preserving Paradise*.

38. Viele, *The Florida Keys*, 55; George Born, "Curry Family's Lasting Legacy," *Citizen*, March 13, 2005.

39. Chamberlin, "A History of Key West," 34; Tom Hambright, interview, January 8, 2008. In 1892, a new city hall building was constructed on Greene Street to replace the structure that had burned in the fire of 1886. Another city hall was constructed in 1962. The Greene Street building was then referred to as Old City Hall (Cox, *A Key West Companion*, 99–100).

40. Browne, *Key West*, 81; "Along the Florida Reef," 285. Mueller, *Steamships of the Two Henrys*, 23–37. On tourism in Florida during this era, see Stronge, *The Sunshine Economy*.

41. Browne, *Key West*, 82; Mueller, *Steamships of the Two Henrys*, 61–72.

42. Brinton, *A Guide-Book of Florida and the South for Tourists, Invalids and Emigrants*, 97; Ronning, *José Martí and the Émigré Colony in Key West*, 48, 62; Rhodes and Dumont, *A Guide to Florida for Tourists, Sportsmen and Settlers*, 406.

43. "Mark Twain in Key West," 15.

44. "Visit to Key West in 1884": 5–6.

45. Dodge, "Subtropical Florida," 14–15.

46. Rhodes and Dumont, *A Guide to Florida for Tourists, Sportsmen and Settlers*, 204.

47. Ibid., 204–6.

48. Barbour, *Florida for Tourists, Invalids, and Settlers*, 152. Winslow Homer visited Key West in 1886 and 1903 and completed several paintings during his visits (Griffin, *Winslow Homer*).

49. Henshall, *Camping and Cruising in Florida*, 120–21.

50. Cited in Gallagher, "The Dynamic Cuban Émigré Society of Key West," 2; Cited in Langley and Langley, *Key West*, 7.

51. Paine, "Over the Florida Keys by Rail"; Milo Smith + Associates, Inc., "Research and Analysis"; Browne, *Key West*, preface, vii; Corliss, "Building the Overseas Railway to Key West"; Hopkins, "The Development of The Overseas Highway," 49.

52. *Announcement*; Standiford, *Last Train to Paradise*; Allen, "Looking Forward."

53. Harris, "The Florida East Coast Railway and What It Means to Key West"; Beehler, "Key West From a Strategic Point of View"; Browne, *Key West*, 212–13.

54. Standiford, *Last Train to Paradise*, 215.

55. Mueller, *Steamships of the Two Henrys*, 204–5. The car ferries carried northward sugar, fruits, and vegetables grown in Cuba.

56. Little, "The Origins of a Sports Fishing Mecca"; Hambright and Hambright, *Key West Historic Memorial Sculpture Garden*, 23; Born, *Historic Florida Keys*; Willis, *The New and Greater Key West Florida Told in Picture and Story*.

57. Ogle, *Key West*, 117; *Tampa Morning Tribune* (hereafter, *TMT*), December 14, 1909, December 26, 1909, November 22, 1909.

Chapter 2. The Not-So-Roaring Twenties

1. Frazer and Guthrie, *The Florida Land Boom*; Grunwald, *The Swamp*; City of Key West Planning Department, "Statistical Abstract," 2004; *Citizen*, July 30, 1926, January 21, 2006; Mayo, *The Sixth Census of the State of Florida 1935*, 1935; Mayo, *The Fifth Census*

of the State of Florida Taken in the Year 1925; McRae, *The Fourth Census of the State of Florida Taken in the Year 1915*; Mayo, *The Sixth Census of the State of Florida 1935*. The county's black population dropped from 26 percent of the population in 1915 to 18 percent in 1925 (Mayo, *The Fifth Census*, 57–59). The boundaries of Monroe County were changed in 1928 and the city limits of Key West were extended in 1928 to include the golf course that was built on Stock Island (Mayo, *The Sixth Census of the State of Florida 1935*, 149). The city's new territory was mostly unpopulated (Tom Hambright, interview, February 20, 2006). It is likely that many of the blacks who left Key West moved to the Miami area. In 1920, Miami was second only to New York City in its number of black immigrants, primarily from the Bahamas (Dunn, *Black Miami in the Twentieth Century*, 98).

2. *MH*, June 18, 1920.

3. Kennedy, *Grits and Grunts*, 86–89; Stuart McIver, "Key West's Bloodiest Christmas," *Sunshine*, December 11, 1994; Peter Rosasco, "Key West Tale of a Christmas Past: The Lynching of Manuel Cabeza," *Solares Hill* (hereafter, *SH*), December 16, 1993; Schmida, *True Crime Stories of Key West and the Florida Keys*, Vol. 2, 72–79. A letter from the Klan of the Keys No. 42, Knights of the Ku Klux Klan to Mrs. Claude Sawyer, June 30, 1924, refers to Mr. Chas. H. Ketchum, a Key West resident, as the Grand Dragon of the Ku Klux Klan of Florida (letter in possession of Tom Hambright, Key West Library).

4. Harris, "Key West," 58; Mueller, *Steamships*, 206; Hopkins, "The Development of The Overseas Highway," 50.

5. Long, "Workers on Relief, 1934–1938, in Key West"; Reilly, *Tropical Surge*; Westfall, *Key West*; Harris, "Key West"; Tom Hambright, interview, January 11, 2008; Roth, "150 Years of Defense Activity in Key West, 1820–1970," 47. The Naval Air Station's personnel were transferred out of Key West and many of its buildings were either abandoned or moved elsewhere.

6. Harris, "Key West"; *MH*, July 20, 1921; Between 1919 and 1928, the number of rooms in lodging accommodations in Florida quintupled. In 1928, Dade County, which included Miami, had far more rooms than any other county (Stronge, *The Sunshine Economy*, 90–91).

7. Braden, *The Architecture of Leisure*; Cole, *The Casa Marina*; *MH*, December 31, 1920; Ogle, *Key West*.

8. *MH*, July 11, 1921, July 15, 1921. On tourism initiatives in other communities, see Starnes, "Introduction," *Southern Journeys* and Berkowitz, "A 'New Deal' for Leisure."

9. Ephemera Collection, Ke 776–800, #788, University of Florida Special Collections, P. K. Yonge Library of Florida History. The brochure does not include a publication date, but it appears to have been written in 1923. Although it does not designate an author or sponsor specifically, it does note that those wanting more information about Monroe County and Key West should contact the Chamber of Commerce in Key West.

10. *Citizen*, December 19, 1923, December 13, 1923, November 15, 1923.

11. *Citizen*, February 13, 1924. The *Citizen* emphasized that Key West's major attraction was its climate, another being its outstanding fishing.

12. *Citizen*, December 13, 1923, January 11, 1924.

13. *Citizen*, February 25, 1926; Little, "The Origins of a Sports Fishing Mecca."

14. Johnson, *The Bahamas from Slavery to Servitude, 1783–1933*, 111; Julia Moore, "Will Gomez," *SH*, June 1981; Willoughby, *Rum War at Sea*; White, *By-Line*, 138.

15. Dean, Love. "Rum Runners Days in Keys are Recalled," *Florida Keys Magazine*,

First quarter 1979: 11–15, 35; White and Smiley, *History of Key West*, 72–73; Willoughby, *Rum War at Sea*; *Citizen*, February 26, 1926; Earl R. Adams, "Dry Era Busy One on Keys," *Miami Herald* (hereafter, *MH*), May 10, 1946.

16. Burt Garnett, "Rum-running in the Economy of the Keys," *Citizen*, February 5, 1967.

17. England, "America's Island of Felicity," 44.

18. Elmer Davis, "The Hounds of Spring," *The New Yorker*, Vol. 2. (March 13, 1926): 20; Davis, "Another Caribbean Conquest," 172.

19. Dos Passos, *The Fourteenth Chronicle*, 337, 357, 385, 391; See Shaughnessy, *Sloppy Joe's*, 14–19.

20. Elmer Davis, "The Hounds of Spring." *The New Yorker*, Vol. 2. (March 13, 1926): 20.

21. With the exception of Lena Johnson, who in 1927 was the first woman to be elected to the commission, during this era the city commission was composed of white men (*Citizen*, November 14, 1927, November 16, 1927, November 17, 1927). *Citizen*, April 16, 1926. On the increase in automobile travel during the 1920s, see Jakle, *The Tourist*. On small towns lobbying for highway connection and improvements during the decade, see Jakle, *The American Small Town*. For a discussion of municipal autocamps and of private autocamp grounds that charged for admission during the 1920s, see Belasco, *Americans on the Road*.

22. Hopkins, "The Development of The Overseas Highway." The freeholders approved the $300,000 bond issue in an election on October 16, 1923 (*Citizen*, January 11, 1924). Bethel, *First Overseas Highway to Key West, Florida*. A series of bond issues financed projects related to the highway (Snead, "Florida Overseas Highway"); *Citizen*, January 2, 1924, March 9, 1926.

23. *Citizen*, July 12, 1926, August 11, 1926, March 19, 1926; *Citizen*, August 13, 1926, August 16, 1926.

24. Hopkins, "The Development of The Overseas Highway"; Bethel, *First Overseas Highway to Key West, Florida*; Lovering, *Reporter in Paradise*; Ogle, *Key West*, 140.

25. *Citizen*, July 14, 1926.

26. *Citizen*, January 9, 1924.

27. *Citizen*, August 16, 1926; The Florida Keys Land Trust, "Ecology of the Salt Ponds"; *Citizen*, March 9, 1926; Frazer and Guthrie, *The Florida Land Boom*.

28. "Official Souvenir Key West Extension of the Florida East Coast Railway," issued by Oversea Railroad Extension Celebration Committee of Key West, written by George M. Chapin. Printed by The Record Co., St. Augustine, Florida. Ephemera Collection, railroads 2666 to 2715, #2711, University of Florida Special Collections, P. K. Yonge Library of Florida History. Porter was one of the sons of Dr. Joseph Yates Porter and Louise Curry, the daughter of William Curry (Chapin, *Florida*, 315–16); "The Beginnings of Key West," *SH*, September 1984; *Citizen*, March 9, 1926; *Coral Tribune*, December 14, 1956; Browne, *Key West*, 56, 63, 102; *Citizen*, March 19, 1926.

29. Ogle, *Key West*, 132; *Citizen*, March 26, 1926.

30. *MH*, April 12, 1987; *Citizen*, January 18, 1987, April 4, 1999. Another hotel built during the decade was the Gibson Hotel on Fleming Street.

31. *Citizen*, 4, 15 March, February 22, 1926. Citizens from other communities were purchasing property in Key West during this period, with the OverSea company serving

as the broker in many of these transactions. Many properties were brought for speculative purposes and quickly resold.

32. Ephemera Collection, Ja-Ke 741–75, #773, University of Florida Special Collections, P. K. Yonge Library of Florida History. No specific date is provided for this publication, but using various references one can discern that it was 1925. Although the publication does not include the name of its sponsor or author, it notes that those interested in additional information should contact the Key West Chamber of Commerce.

33. Ephemera Collection, Ja-Ke 741–75, #773, University of Florida Special Collections, P. K. Yonge Library of Florida History.

34. For a discussion of the expansion of speculation in Florida's real estate market in 1924 and 1925 and the beginning of the collapse in 1926, see Stronge, *The Sunshine Economy*. Among the factors that contributed to the real estate collapse was the hurricane that hit the state in September 1926 (Barnes, *Florida's Hurricane History*, 111–26). "The Beginnings of Key West," *SH*, September 1984.

35. The passenger plane left Key West at 8:00 a.m. and reached Havana at 9:15 a.m., with the return flight leaving Havana at 3:45 p.m.(Simons and Withington, *The History of Flight*, 89); "The Beginnings of Key West," *SH*, September 1984.

36. Bethel, *First Overseas Highway to Key West, Florida*; Hopkins, "The Development of The Overseas Highway"; Knowles, *Category 5*; Tom Hambright, interview, June 9, 2009.

Chapter 3. The Depression and War Years: Tourism Dreams Give Way to Military Realities

1. Mayo, *The Sixth Census of the State of Florida 1935*, 80; City of Key West Planning Department, "Statistical Abstract, 2004"; Long, "Key West and the New Deal"; Key West Administration, *Key West in Transition*, 59–61. The state legislature passed an act that formally recognized the city council's abdication of its authority to the Governor of the State of Florida. The legislature passed another act granting the governor the authority to remove from office any elected or appointed officers of the City of Key West until December 31, 1936 (Chapter 17573 [No. 802], Senate Bill No. 833; Chapter 17572 [No. 801], Senate Bill No. 900, filed in Office Secretary of State June 10, 1935).

2. President Roosevelt signed the Federal Emergency Relief Act in May 1933 and appointed Harry Hopkins as its head. Initially, funds dispersed to states and cities were to provide cash and necessities to the indigent, but the focus soon shifted to include projects to provide work for the unemployed. In November 1933, Roosevelt signed an executive order that created the Civil Works Administration (CWA), which focused on funding public projects to create jobs. Many of those hired by the CWA had been on the FERA rolls. The CWA operated until the end of March 1934, leaving the FERA as the primary federal agency responsible for work relief programs. Some who the CWA had hired switched to work on FERA projects, while others went on the relief rolls (Taylor, *American-Made*, 100–142). For a good overview of federal programs in Florida during this era, see Stuart and Stack, eds., *The New Deal in South Florida*. Key West Administration, *Key West in Transition*, "Foreword." Stetson Kennedy (*Palmetto Country*, 253) reported that Conchs told him, "Besides conchs, grits and grunts is our favorite eats." They also noted, "We can't afford much else, but even if we could, I guess they would still be our favorites."

3. Key West Administration, *Key West in Transition*, "Foreword." Long, "Workers on Relief, 1934–1938, in Key West"; *TMT*, July 6, 1934. For a discussion of tourism during the Depression and the role of communities and the federal government in promoting tourism, see Berkowitz, "A 'New Deal' For Leisure." On the increase in spending on travel between 1934 and 1938, and then again during the 1940–41 season, see Belasco, *Americans on the Road*, 154–65. On vacationing during the Depression, see Aron, *Working at Play*, 237–57. For a discussion of tourism in Florida during the Great Depression, see Stronge, *The Sunshine Economy*, 141–42.

4. *Palm Beach Times*, August 25, 1935. In August 1935, the county commission authorized Mayor Malone to apply for funds from the federal government to finance a water pipeline that would extend from the mainland to Key West (Heinlein, "Key West Search for Fresh Water, Part Three"). Davis, "New World Symphony With A Few Sour Notes"; *TMT*, July 10, 1934; Key West Administration, *Key West Guide Book*; Key West Administration, *Key West in Transition*; *Palm Beach Times*, July 4, 1935; *Citizen*, January 3, 1936.

5. Key West Administration, *Key West in Transition*; *Tampa Times*, September 11, 1934; Long, "Key West and the New Deal, 1934–1936"; Writers' Program, *A Guide to Key West*, 1949: 52–53; Ephemera Ke 776–800, #776, "The Key West Art Gallery Caroline Lowe House," 1935.

6. Ephemera, Ke 801–25, #819, "Key West," n.d.

7. Ephemera, Ke 801–25, #819, "Key West," n.d. This emphasis on Key West's difference from other towns in the United States paralleled New Orleans's efforts to distinguish itself. In Souther's words, "Tourist guides in the 1940s and 1950s emphasized that one could in effect visit a foreign land just by traveling to the Crescent City" ("Making 'America's Most Interesting City,'" 115). Also see Desmond, *Staging Tourism*, 39, which examines advertising in Hawaii in the 1920s and efforts to attract tourists to the state by suggesting they would encounter "life now much as it was a century ago."

8. *MH*, July 26, 1936.

9. Taylor, *American-Made*; Key West Administration, *Key West in Transition*, 9–20.

10. Boulard, "State of Emergency," 175; *Palatka Daily News*, April 9, 1935; Green, *Looking for the New Deal*, 85.

11. Boulard, "State of Emergency," 177; Davis, "New World Symphony With A Few Sour Notes," 651.

12. Davis, "New World Symphony With A Few Sour Notes," 651.

13. Davis, "New World Symphony With A Few Sour Notes," 651–52; See Scandura, *Down in the Dumps*, 96, 98.

14. Marvin H. Walker, "Key West Has Its Kingfish," *Florida Grower* (March 1935): 7; *Florida Times-Union*, April 24, 1935.

15. *Pasco Co. Free Press*, April 26, 1935. Work on the Key West pool on Roosevelt Boulevard began in May 1935 (*MH*, May 27, 1935). In June, Gilfond announced that local laborers on work relief had been working on improving Pan American (Meacham) Field (*Citizen*, June 22, 1935). *The Key Sun*, August 30, 1935.

16. The WPA and Veterans Administration also were involved with the program (Knowles, *Category 5*, 43, 289–90). Also see Standiford, *Last Train to Paradise*; Scott, *Hemingway's Hurricane*; Taylor, *American-Made*; Mueller, *Steamships of the Two Henrys*.

17. Manucy and Hale, "Three Key West Winter Seasons, 1934–1936"; *Ocala Star*, November 1, 1935. The total number of guests staying in Key West's hotels during the

December-March 1935–36 tourist season fell to 7,697, down from 8,844 the year before. During the 1933–34 season, 4,295 tourists had stayed in Key West's hotels. The Casa Marina was closed during the 1933–34 season and open from December through March for the next two years. The Oversea Hotel was also closed during the 1933–34 season and reopened only in February 1935, after being rehabilitated by the FERA workers (Manucy and Hale, "Three Key West Winter Seasons, 1934–1936").

18. The KWA reported that the number of Key Westers on the relief rolls dropped from 2,000 in 1934 to 1,600 in February 1935, but had increased again to 1,700 by the end of March, the end of the tourist season (*Florida Times-Union*, April 28, 1935, October 17, 1935; KWA, *Key West Guide Book*, 13–14); *Citizen*, July 12, 1935. An analysis conducted for WPA by Manucy and Falk, however, reported significantly higher numbers of relief recipients during this period ("A Survey"). President Roosevelt signed an executive order to create the Works Progress Administration (WPA) in May 1935. Henry Hopkins headed the WPA and transferred several FERA administrators to the new administration (Taylor, *American-Made*, 170–80).

19. *Citizen*, August 19, 1935, August 21, 1935, February 24, 1936; *Florida Times-Union*, December 13, 1935; *MH*, October 25, 1935. Projects included the improving of Atlantic Boulevard, the dredging of Garrison Bight to accommodate small craft, and the construction of a reservoir annex in the aquarium. The WPA also employed some people involved in the Writers' Project.

20. *MH*, February 25, 1936; *Citizen*, February 24, 1936; "La Semana Alegre."

21. *Citizen*, May 29, 1935.

22. *Pensacola News*, December 3, 1935; *Bradenton Herald*, December 4, 1935; St. Petersburg Times (hereafter *SPT*), December 5, 1935; *TMT*, December 5, 1935, December 6, 1935; *MH*, December 8, 1935; *Florida Keys Sun*, December 13, 1935; *Citizen*, December 20, 1935.

23. *Citizen*, August 4, 1936; *Miami Tribune*, August 11, 1936.

24. Haines Colbert, "King of the Keys," *The Miami News*, May 31, 1959; Bud Jacobson, "Beers, Banks, and Burials," *SH*, December 1976.

25. Hopkins, "The Development of The Overseas Highway"; Drye, "Tempting the Fate"; Heinlein, "Key West Search for Fresh Water, Part Three"; *Citizen*, June 2, 1936, July 13, 1936; *MH*, July 19, 1936.

26. *TMT*, March 30, 1938; Hopkins, "The Development of The Overseas Highway"; Heinlein, "Key West Search for Fresh Water, Part Three"; *MH*, August 23, 1936; Mack Dryden, "Bridge Building Moves Ahead," *Florida Keys Magazine*, Fourth quarter 1978: 8, 10–11.

27. Tennessee Williams, "Homage to Key West," *Harper's Bazaar*, January 1973: 50–51.

28. Federal Writers' Project, "Key West Guide," circa 1936, 48. See also Writers' Program of the Work Projects Administration, *A Guide to Key West*, 1949.

29. *St. Augustine Record*, September 21, 1937; *Citizen*, September 15, 1937.

30. Ephemera, Ke 776–800, No. 791, 1939, "In The 'Good Old Summer Time' The Key West Chamber of Commerce Welcomes To Our City." This was the third edition of the booklet.

31. Ernie Pyle, "Philosophy of Key West: What India's Mahatma Gandhi Needs," *TMT*, January 29, 1939.

32. Letter from Lieutenant Colonel G. D. Hatfield, U.S. Marine Corps (Retd.), to Governor Spessard Holland, August 2, 1941, in Florida State Archives, Department of State, Series 406, Monroe Co., letter on the station head of the United States Marine Corps, Office of the Commanding Officer, Marine Barracks, Naval Station, Key West, Florida.

33. Raymer, "The Bad Old Days." Some Key Westers referred to the area around Mom's in Key West's black neighborhood west of Whitehead Street as "jungle town." Others used the term *jungle town* more generally to refer to this neighborhood (Scandura, *Down in the Dumps*; Sister Theresa Cecilia Lowe, interview, June 22, 2009).

34. The Key West Administration published another guidebook in September 1935, *Key West Guide Book: An Aid to the Visitor—Fall and Winter 1935–1936*. It still listed Hemingway's house as one of its "points of interest," but included a note that it was a "private residence, not open to the public" (43). See also, Federal Writers' Project, Work Projects Administration, *Florida*, which enumerates a number of Key West's attractions. Ephemera, Ke 801–25, #819, "Key West," n.d. On literary tourism, see Rojek, *Ways of Escape*, 152–60.

35. Meyers, *Hemingway*, 207; Plath and Simons, *Remembering Ernest Hemingway*, 87–101.

36. Reynolds, *Hemingway: The American Homecoming*; Born, *Historic Florida Keys*, 60; Reynolds, *Hemingway: the 1930s*; Moorehead, ed., *The Letters of Martha Gellhorn*; Kaufelt, *Key West Writers and Their Houses*, 11. Hemingway worked on many of his books in several different locations. For example, in 1948, he wrote that *A Farewell to Arms* was written in "Paris, France, Key West, Florida, Piggott, Arkansas, Kansas City, Missouri, Sheridan, Wyoming, and the first draft of it was finished near Big Horn in Wyoming. . . . It was rewritten in the fall and winter of 1928 in Key West and the final rewriting was finished in Paris in the spring of 1929" (Bruccoli, *Hemingway*, 96).

37. Richardson, *Wallace Stevens*, 124–25. Hemingway describes this fight in a letter he wrote to Sara Murphy in February 1936 (Miller, ed., *Letters from the Lost Generation*, 157–58).

38. Shaughnessy, *Sloppy Joe's*; According to T.J. English in *Havana Nocturne*, Sloppy Joe's was the best-known bar in Havana and was frequented by U.S. tourists. Kennedy, *Grits and Grunts*; Nancy Klingener, "A Living Legend of the Left," *SH*, July 27, 2007; Stetson Kennedy, interview, July 16, 2007.

39. Moorehead, ed., *The Letters of Martha Gellhorn*.

40. Wolfe, "The Poor Are Different from You and Me," 161; Ernest Hemingway, "Who Murdered the Vets? A First Hand Report on the Florida Hurricane," *New Masses*, September 1935: 9–10.

41. Reynolds, *Hemingway: The 1930s*, 303.

42. Reynolds, *Hemingway: The 1930s*, 196–97.

43. Stevens, ed., *Letters of Wallace Stevens*, 274, 355, 386, 806.

44. *Citizen*, December 13, 1934, November 28, 1979; Thompson, ed., *Selected Letters of Robert Frost*, 414–15; Grade, ed., *Family Letters of Robert and Elinor Frost*, 181.

45. *Citizen*, February 7, 1940, November 23, 1983, February 14, 1952, May 31, 1970.

46. Nina Wilcox Putnam, "South from Miami," *Collier's*, December 18, 1937: 18, 38–39; Moorehead, ed., *The Letters of Martha Gellhorn*, 44.

47. Hayman, *Tennessee Williams*; Tennessee Williams, "Homage to Key West," *Harper's Bazaar*, January 1973: 50–51. In a letter written in Key West in 1941, Williams noted

that he associated with Elizabeth Bishop, John Dewey, James Farrell, and others. He also noted that in the evening he consorted with "B-girls, transients and sailors at Sloppy Joe's or the Starlight Gambling Casino" (Devlin and Tischler, eds., *Selected Letters of Tennessee Williams*, Vol. 1, 305). Devlin and Tischler, eds., *Selected Letters of Tennessee Williams*, Vol. 1, 304.

48. Bishop, *Edgar Allan Poe and The Juke-Box*; Ellis, *Art and Memory in the Work of Elizabeth Bishop*; Millier, *Elizabeth Bishop*.

49. Bishop, *Edgar Allan Poe and The Juke-Box*; Millier, *Elizabeth Bishop*; Ellis, *Art and Memory in the Work of Elizabeth Bishop*, 45. Also see Martin, *The Education of John Dewey*, and Arthur Phillips, "Elizabeth Bishop: Poet of the Way Things Are," *SH*, January 1989.

50. Giroux, ed., *One Art*, 75–76.

51. Ellis, *Art and Memory in the Work of Elizabeth Bishop*, 138.

52. Millier, *Elizabeth Bishop*, 159. Bishop's letter was addressed to Charlotte Russell, April 2, 1942, from Bishop's home on Margaret Street (Giroux, ed., *One Art*, 106.)

53. Heinlein, "Key West's Naval Hospital"; Roth, "150 Years of Defense Activity in Key West, 1820–1970"; Sigrid Arne, "Wartime Boom Days Pull Key West Out of Doldrums as Navy Moves In," *The San Diego Union*, April 4, 1943; *Citizen*, September 9, 1944.

54. Roth, "150 Years of Defense Activity in Key West, 1820–1970;" Tom Hambright, interview, July 11, 2007; Mickler, "Key West in World War II."

55. Mickler, "Key West in World War II"; Hambright, "German U-Boats Assault Florida Keys," 1.

56. Sigrid Arne, "Wartime Boom Days Pull Key West Out of Doldrums as Navy Moves In," *The San Diego Union*, April 4, 1943.

57. Hopkins, "The Development of The Overseas Highway"; Heinlein, "Key West Search for Fresh Water, Part Three."

58. Sigrid Arne, "Wartime Boom Days Pull Key West Out of Doldrums as Navy Moves In," *The San Diego Union*, April 4, 1943; Edie Hall Smith, "The Casa: A Grand Hotel Lives on in Style," *Times-Union and Journal*, Jacksonville, March 7, 1982; Mickler, "Key West in World War II." The Housing Authority completed Porter Homes in 1942, making them available to war workers and service families. The Housing Authority also completed Poinciana Housing Project that year and expanded it several times over the next two years. It housed some military personnel, but most of its tenants were civilians employed by the military.

59. Cohen and Leon, "Bahama Village Redevelopment Plan, City of Key West, Florida." Four city blocks were condemned and purchased in 1942 to acquire land for expanding the base ("The United States Navy and the City of Key West, Florida," Information Pamphlet, Ephemera, Ke 801–25, No. 806, circa 1952). Benedict Thielen, "The Cities of America: Key West," *Saturday Evening Post* 221 (January 22, 1949): 20, 84–89.

60. Rev. Arthur B. Dimmick to Franklin D. Roosevelt, October 19, 1935, FDR Papers.

61. Meyer Berger, "Old Key West Awakes," *NYT*, March 21, 1937.

Chapter 4. Key West 1945–1970: Not a Clean Well-Lighted Place

1. Raymer, *Key West Collection*.

2. City of Key West Planning Department, "Statistical Abstract," 2004. The 1970 Census tables list Key West's population as 27,563, but the corrected population, which was not listed in the tables, was 29,312 (U.S. Bureau of the Census, Vol. 1, "Characteristics

of the Population," part 11, Florida section 1, "1970 Census of Population," 11–16). The 1960 Census estimated that of the total population in Key West, 2,554 lived in a newly annexed area of the city and 31,402 lived in the area that constituted Key West in 1950 (U.S. Bureau of the Census, *Census of Population, 1960* Vol. 1, "Characteristics of the Population," Part 11, Florida, Table 9., 11–17).

3. In 1959, 8.5 percent of Key West's families earned $10,000 or more, compared to 11.1 percent of the entire state. Of the 22 cities in Florida with a population of 25,000 and over, Key West had the lowest percentage of families earning more than $10,000. Key West's median income in 1959 was $4,736, placing it 12th among cities in Florida, which had a statewide median income of $4,722 (U.S. Bureau of the Census, *County and City Data Book* 1962, 497). Key West's median family income in 1969 was $6,918, which was lower than that of all but two of the state's 28 comparable cities. The statewide median family income that year was $8,261 (U.S. Bureau of the Census, *County and City Data Book* 1962; U.S. Bureau of the Census, *County and City Data Book* 1972). In 1973, Monroe County was the only county in the southern half of the peninsula with a per capita income below the national average (Stronge, *The Sunshine Economy*).

4. Williams, *Key West Conch Talk*.

5. Sawyer and Wells-Bowie, *Key West*.

6. The prominent Conchs included Norberg Thompson, before he died in 1951, Maitland Adams, Clarence Higgs, John Spottswood, and Joe Pinder. Conchs dominated the boards of the major banks. In 1960, Monroe County had only four banking institutions (Bud Jacobson, "Banking with the Conchs: 1st Federal Savings & Loan Success Story," *SH*, February 1984).

7. In 1970, 21 percent of Key West's population was of "foreign stock" (U.S. Bureau of the Census, *City and County Data Book 1972*, 667): 1,815 persons were foreign born and another 3,930 were of foreign or mixed parentage. Of these, 2,399 (42 percent) were from Cuba and only 142 from "other America." The 1970 census recorded that Key West included 6,685 residents of "Spanish language" and 3,293 of Spanish origin or descent (U.S. Bureau of the Census, *1970 Census of Population*, Vol. 1, "Characteristics of the Population," part 11, Florida section 1, Table 102).

8. *NYT*, December 11, 1960; *Citizen*, January 17, 1961.

9. City Commissioner Carmen Turner, interview, July 22, 2004. The other public housing complex the Navy wanted transferred was the Poinciana extension. Fort Village included 74 dwelling units, and the Poinciana included about 550 (*MH*, August 7, 1953, August 8, 1953).

10. McDonald, "The Lincoln Theater"; *MH*, April 4, 1965, April 21, 1968; *Citizen*, January 25, 1987. The Monroe Theater admitted blacks to the balcony as early as the 1930s (Sister T. C. Lowe, personal correspondence, September 29, 2009).

11. *Citizen*, March 6, 1969. Major was probably the most politically active and influential African American in Key West during the 1960s. Roosevelt Sands, Sr. was another significant black community leader.

12. *Citizen*, March 15, 1947; Richard H. Rovere, "Our Far-Flung Correspondents: 'End of the Line,'" *The New Yorker*, December 15, 1951; Hambright, "German U-Boats Assault Florida Keys"; Milo Smith + Associates, Inc., "Research and Analysis"; White and Smiley, *History of Key West*; Gibb, "An Economic and Social Analysis of the Impact of the Military Role in Key West, Florida"; *MH*, October 26, 1962; *Citizen*, October 28, 1962;

Key West Salt Ponds Committee, "The Key West Salt Ponds and Development"; *Citizen*, October 23, 1962, November 23, 1962.

13. Dobbs, *One Minute to Midnight*, 100.

14. Milo Smith + Associates, Inc., "Research and Analysis," 28E; See Gibb, "An Economic and Social Analysis of the Impact of the Military Role in Key West, Florida," 7.

15. Little, "An Overview of the Evolution of the Historic Seaport at Key West Bight"; "Key West/Marathon: The Twin Capitals of Florida Keys Fishing," *The Fish Boat*, March 1984; *Tampa Sunday Tribune*, February 12, 1950. In the 1950s, the primary locations for the shrimp fleets in Florida were Key West, Fort Myers, and Fort Myers Beach (Stronge, *The Sunshine Economy*, 178).

16. *Citizen*, February 6, 1951; Milo Smith + Associates, Inc., "Research and Analysis"; Knight, "Norberg Thompson."

17. *Citizen*, May 22, 1947.

18. Corcoran, *Key West in Black and White*, 168; Phil Caputo, "Phil Caputo on Key West," *Florida Keys Magazine*, May 1987: 20–27; Little, "An Overview of the Evolution of the Historic Seaport at Key West Bight."

19. A dancer at the club was also arrested and charged with indecent exposure, and Judge Archer fined two women for wearing shorts that were "too short" (*MH*, August 5, 1945).

20. *Citizen*, April 29, 1948, August 8, 1960. The robbery charges against Cagnina were dropped. Shortly afterward, he resigned from the police force. Later, Cagnina was charged several times with various crimes and was convicted in 1981 of several federal charges, including cocaine trafficking and racketeering, for which he was sentenced to thirty years in jail. Cagnina was associated with the Trafficante criminal organization based in Tampa (Schmida, *True Crime Stories of Key West and the Florida Keys*). During at least some of this era, the Trafficante organization apparently played a role in the bolita gambling in Key West (Deitche, *The Silent Don*). George Warren interview, January 7, 2008.

21. *Citizen*, May 24, 1947; Benedict Thielen, "The Cities of America: Key West," *Saturday Evening Post* 221 (January 22, 1949): 20, 84–89.

22. *Citizen*, April 16, 1948, May 19, 1948.

23. *Citizen*, May 19, 1948.

24. *Citizen*, May 19, 1948.

25. *Citizen*, May 19, 1948.

26. John Bonner, "Lid Put on Key West Gambling as Warren Arrives," *MH*, October 30, 1951; Stephen Trumbull, "Gambling Wide-Open in Key West: Downtown Bars Have Roulette, Blackjack, Dice; Many Sailors Among Customers," *MH*, February 6, 1950.

27. John Bonner, "What Gambling? 'Surprised' Key West Asks after Exposure," *MH*, October 31, 1951.

28. John Bonner, "What Gambling? 'Surprised' Key West Asks after Exposure," *MH*, October 31, 1951.

29. *MH*, February 16, 1967; *SPT*, February 1, 1955.

30. Helen Worden, "Key West Has Character: America's Southernmost City, Four Hours and Twenty-Nine Bridges from Miami, has a Pirate Past and Tourist Present," *Holiday*, October 1946; Gwen Harrison, "Stomach Weak? Shun Cockfights in Key West,"

MH, February 11, 1956; Ralph Morrow, "When the White Rooster was the Cock of the Walk," *Citizen*, October 23, 2001.

31. John Bonner, "Lid Put on Key West Gambling as Warren Arrives," *MH*, October 30, 1951; Sawyer, *Only in Key West*, 18.

32. *Citizen*, July 10, 1960; Bud Jacobson, "JP's and Constables," *SH*, June 1981; *Citizen*, December 3, 1961, December 5, 1961, February 13, 1966; *MH*, December 10, 1961, August 7, 1966.

33. Bud Jacobson, "JP's and Constables," *SH*, June 1981; Bud Jacobson, "Bolita is More Fun Than Dope," *SH*, December 1982.

34. Langley, "City Electric System"; *Citizen*, October 22, 1969; Bob Padron, interview, July 14, 2004. In the years that Papy dominated the board, when a vacancy occurred in any of its four positions, other than the mayor's, the board would appoint a replacement by majority vote (*MH*, September 28, 1968).

35. *Citizen*, October 12, 1989; *MH*, October 21, 1989.

36. *MH*, February 28, 1968.

37. *Citizen*, October 22, 1969; Bob Padron, interview, July 14, 2004.

38. *Citizen*, October 22, 1969; *MH*, September 28, 1968; Langley, "City Electric System."

39. *Citizen*, October 22, 1969, July 15, 1969; Langley, "City Electric System."

40. Adam, *The Rise of a Gay and Lesbian Movement*, 63.

41. Hayman, *Tennessee Williams*; *MH*, June 28, 1987; Williams, *Memoirs*.

42. Devlin and Tischler, eds., *Selected Letters of Tennessee Williams*, Vol. 2; Williams, *Memoirs*; *Citizen*, December 7, 1995; Ogle, *Key West*, 188.

43. Dodé, *Gay Key West*, 39; *Citizen*, January 12, 1986; Altobello and Pierce, *Literary Sands*; Tennessee Williams, "Homage to Key West," *Harper's Bazaar*, January 1973: 50–51.

44. *MH*, September 10, 1987; Hale, "The Gnädiges Fräulein"; *Citizen*, January 12, 1986, May 4, 1976, April 17, 1977; *MH*, May 23, 1976; Hayman, *Tennessee Williams*.

45. *Citizen*, March 29, 1970.

46. *Citizen*, January 11, 1959; Tennessee Williams, "Homage to Key West," *Harper's Bazaar*, January 1973.

47. Kaufelt, *Key West Writers and Their Houses*, 69–77.

48. Raymer, "Conch Chowder," *Citizen*, June 29, 1969.

49. Morris, *Coast to Coast*, 99; Ebensten, *Home and Abroad*, 251. The description Ebensten quotes from *Coast to Coast* is actually a combination of different statements that Morris included in his chapter on Key West, rather than a direct quote from the chapter.

50. Eileen Moore Quinn, "Henry Faulkner," *SH*, June–July 1980; House, *The Outrageous Life of Henry Faulkner*.

51. Dodé, *Memories of Key West*; Eileen Moore Quinn, "Henry Faulkner," *SH*, June–July 1980.

52. *MH*, June 14, 1968; *Citizen*, June 14, 1968, April 9, 1978, January 1, 1984.

53. The Army Air Corps took over the site of the Meacham Field airport during the Second World War and then turned it over to the Navy. After the war, the county leased the airport from Key West Realty ("The Beginnings of Key West"); Hambright and Hambright, *Key West Historic Memorial Sculpture Garden*.

54. *Citizen*, May 1, 1952; July 3, 1957.

55. *Citizen*, December 25, 1960.

56. Key West Salt Ponds Committee, "The Key West Salt Ponds and Development"; Ed Knight, interview, July 2004; Bud Jacobson, "Charlie Toppino and His Sons Dominating the County's Growth Since 1934," *SH*, May 1988.

57. Milo Smith + Associates, Inc., "Research and Analysis," 14B.

58. Al Burt, "Ellis in Wonderland," *MH Tropic Magazine*, May 16, 1982.

59. *Citizen*, April 24, 1960.

60. Hambright and Hambright, *Key West Historic Memorial Sculpture Garden*; *Citizen*, June 7, 1953; Richard H. Rovere, "Our Far-Flung Correspondents: 'End of the Line,'" *The New Yorker*, December 15, 1951; *MH*, December 5, 1969; *Citizen*, January 16, 1983.

Chapter 5. Postwar Tourism

1. Benedict Thielen, "The Cities of America: Key West," *Saturday Evening Post* 221 (January 22, 1949): 89.

2. Mormino, *Land of Sunshine, State of Dreams*.

3. *Citizen*, September 9, 1944.

4. Ephemera, Ke 801–25, #814. The Key West Chamber of Commerce published the leaflet. No date is given, but it refers to plans to open ferry service between Key West and Havana for cars in 1947, suggesting that it probably was published soon after the war ended. The brochure emphasized that visitors would find no "tourist bubble" in Key West (see Judd, "Constructing the Tourist Bubble").

5. Wolz and Hayo, *The Legacy of the Harry S. Truman Little White House, Key West*, 139.

6. Wolz and Hayo, *The Legacy of the Harry S. Truman Little White House, Key West*, 44.

7. Wolz and Hayo, *The Legacy of the Harry S. Truman Little White House, Key West*, 50.

8. Langello, "Log of the President's Vacation Trip to Key West," November 17–23, 1946; Rigdon, "Log of President Truman's Trip to Puerto Rico"; Rigdon, "Log of President Truman's Fifth Trip to Key West." Rigdon, "Log of President Truman's 9th Visit to Key West"; Wolz and Hayo, *The Legacy of the Harry S. Truman Little White House, Key West*.

9. *Citizen*, November 16, 1948; Wolz and Hayo, *The Legacy of the Harry S. Truman Little White House, Key West*.

10. *Citizen*, January 10, 1960.

11. *MH*, November 16, 1962, November 27, 1962; *NYT*, October 28, 1962; *Citizen*, September 9, 1960.

12. Ephemera, Ke 776–800, No. 793, n.d. Although this brochure was not dated, it apparently was published in the early 1960s. An advertisement from 1959 reminded tourists that they could drive their own car down the "unique" Overseas Highway or travel from Miami via Greyhound Bus ("Key West Tourist News," Winter-Summer 1959).

13. *Citizen*, September 4, 1960. Rand was a well-known "fan dancer."

14. In 1947, the city purchased from the State of Florida much of the submerged land in the Garrison Bight. In January 1949, the city leased to the Key West Charter Boatman's Association some of the bight area, including the seawall along North Roosevelt Boulevard that tourists driving into downtown Key West were sure to notice. Many of the charter boats then moved from the Craig Docks and other locations to the Garrison

Bight (Little, "The Origins of a Sports Fishing Mecca"). Marcia W. Fitch, "Art and the Tourist Trade," *Citizen*, November 21, 1960.

15. Tom Hambright, personal correspondence, April 5, 2007. For example, a newsletter of the Florida News Bureau of the Florida Development Commission released on June 22, 1967 noted the Hemingway House as one of the "points not to be missed" (Hampton Dunn Collection, Monroe County, Key West, pt. 2, University of South Florida Special Collections).

16. John Dorschner, "The Great Conch Train War," *MH Tropic Magazine*, September 9, 1973; *Citizen*, January 27, 1972.

17. *Citizen*, February 19, 2005; Dodé, *Gay Key West*, 157.

18. *Citizen*, February 4, 1960, November 6, 1963, January 27, 1972; John Dorschner, "The Great Conch Train War," *MH Tropic Magazine*, September 9, 1973.

19. George Born, "The First Stirrings of History," *Citizen*, March 12, 2006; Sherrill and Aiello, *Key West*, 37; Martha Thompson and David Johnson, "History Preserved," *Florida Keys Magazine*, Third quarter 1979: 34–37. There is an extensive literature on historic preservation in cities and its relationship to tourism. See Jakle, *The Tourist*; Souther, *New Orleans on Parade*, and Hamer, *History in Urban Places*.

20. *Citizen*, March 13, 1960, March 17, 1960.

21. *Citizen*, January 26, 1960, March 22, 1960.

22. *Citizen*, May 31, 1960.

23. *Citizen*, April 22, 1960.

24. Sherrill and Aiello, *Key West*; *Citizen*, April 14, 1960; *Citizen*, October 17, 1960, October 9, 1960. The Old Island Restoration Foundation (OIRF) organized a publicity committee that would focus on advertising Key West to potential tourists. At the 1965 annual meeting of the OIRF, the publicity committee reported that the OIRF had distributed articles on Old Island Days to 300 different newspapers ("Annual Meeting, Old Island Restoration Foundation, Inc., April 14, 1965," available in the Florida History room in the Key West Public Library).

25. *Citizen*, June 5, 1960.

26. Resolution No. 25–60; *Citizen*, August 12, 1960, September 4, 1960, November 20, 1960, February 24, 1966; "History of Design Guidelines," May 2002.

27. Cox, *A Key West Companion*, 82. Those who violated the statute were subject to a fine of less than $100 or sent to prison for a period of not more than 90 days, or both (Chapter 69-1187).

28. White, *Louise White Shows You Key West*; *Citizen*, June 12, 1960, December 7, 1976.

29. *MH*, September 1, 1963; *Citizen*, May 19, 1960, January 6, 1960, January 21, 1960.

30. *Citizen*, January 27, 1960, January 31, 1960, February 7, 1960, February 14, 1960.

31. *MH*, February 17, 1962; CE Maguire, Inc., "Community and Neighborhood Impact Study," 57; Hazel Lowe, "Florida's Keys Catch on Fire," *The Saturday Gazette*, Montreal, January 17, 1981; OIRF and City of Key West, "Dedication," February 1, 1963; Milo Smith + Associates, Inc., "Research and Analysis," 82E. The dedication of what was then called both the convention hall and the community center took place in February 1962. The "Dedication of Old Mallory Square and the Unveiling of The Porter Anti-Pirate Marker" occurred on February 1, 1963.

32. *Citizen*, March 4, 1960, December 21, 1960, December 22, 1960, February 1, 1968; *MH*, June 14, 1968.

33. *Citizen*, November 5, 1961; Christine Arnold Dolen, "See Key West: There's More to Conch Culture than Sun and Sloppy Joe's," *MH*, January 7, 1990.

34. *Citizen*, June 10, 1960; Bud Jacobson, "Key West Hand-Prints: 30 Years Young This Year," *SH*, December 1981.

35. Apparently, blacks were not always met with open arms in some of Key West's favorite tourist destinations. An article published in 1969 describes what unfolded when two young African American men entered Sloppy Joe's and ordered a drink. The waitress went to the jukebox and played Al Jolson's version of "Look away, Dixieland." The men left the bar, and the waitress reported, "That usually takes care of that" (Charles Patrick, "Key West," *SPT*, August 31, 1969).

36. Kermit Lewin, interview, July 13, 2004; *MH*, April 7, 1959; *Citizen*, October 31, 1963, November 6, 1963. In 1967, voters rejected an urban renewal plan that specifically targeted the Poinciana area, including about 500 low-rent apartments, about half of which were vacant. In 1969, voters rejected another urban renewal referendum by a margin of 2 to 1 (*MH*, October 28, 1963, November 1, 1963, November 9, 1963; *MH*, November 5, 1969).

37. *MH*, June 10, 1971.

38. David Wolkowsky, interview, January 18, 2008; William Wright, "David Wolkowsky: The Prince of Key West," *SH*, May 1990; *MH*, June 10, 1971; *Citizen*, September 18, 1977; White, *Louise White Shows You Key West*.

39. Bud Jacobson, "Morgan Bird and The Oldest Bar," *SH*, May 1982; *MH*, March 12, 1969; Bellavance-Johnson, *Tennessee Williams in Key West and Miami*, 11. It also briefly housed the Duval Club, after Sloppy Joe's moved (*Citizen*, April 14, 1963).

40. Bud Jacobson, "'A' Is For Artists," *SH*, March 1986.

41. Bud Jacobson, "'A' Is For Artists," *SH*, March 1986; Bud Jacobson, "Morgan Bird and The Oldest Bar," *SH*, May 1982.

42. *MH*, December 30, 1977; David Wolkowsky, interview, January 10, 2008; Rob Jordan, "Tropical Splendor: How David Wolkowsky Helped Shape Modern Florida," *Home Miami*, February 2008: 48–55; William Wright, interview, January 17, 2008. In the early 1970s, the writers Nancy Friday and Bill Manville learned about the Pier House from Tennessee Williams while they were visiting Palm Beach. They drove to Key West, stayed at the Pier House, and met Wolkowsky. They then purchased a house in Key West in 1978 (*Citizen*, March 19, 1978; Susan Nadler, "Nobody Owns a Mercedes," *Florida Keys Magazine*, March 1986: 44–53).

43. *Newsweek*, March 9, 1953; Office of Economic Adjustment, "Report of Community Visit," 12; *MH*, September 25, 1970.

44. *Newsweek*, March 9, 1953; Office of Economic Adjustment, "Report of Community Visit," 12; *NYT*, August 7, 1966; *MH*, September 25, 1970.

45. Milo Smith + Associates, Inc., "Research and Analysis"; *Citizen*, August 4, 1960. For a discussion of the development of motor courts, hotels, and motels in the United States between the 1930s and the 1950s, see Belasco, *Americans on the Road*, 150–73. Also see Jakle, Sculle, and Rogers, *The Motel in America*.

46. *Citizen*, February 28, 1959, March 18, 1960, April 8, 1960, May 8, 1961, April 28, 1967; *MH*, October 7, 1961; *MH*, June 30, 1964.

47. *NYT*, August 18, 1964; *MH*, February 16, 1967; *Citizen*, September 29, 1975; Edie

Hall Smith, "The Casa: A Grand Hotel Lives on in Style," *Times-Union and Journal*, Jacksonville, March 7, 1982.

48. *Citizen*, October 23, 1962, November 23, 1962, September 29, 1975.

49. Cited in Sherill and Aiello, *Key West*, 46.

50. Arlo Haskell, "Where Charles Olson Turned Against the Tide," *SH*, January 11, 2008; Jose Yglesias, "Key West: Of Sailors, Shrimps and the Way It Was," *Venture*, February 1969: 67–76. For a discussion of the often contested interpretations of what era and characteristics in a community's history should be considered "authentic," see Dolgon, *The End of the Hamptons*, 68–75. For observations on how recent visitors to Nice, France, like those more than a century ago, bemoaned the "fact" that, compared to just a few decades earlier, the area had been ruined, see Kanigel, *High Season in Nice*, 7–8.

51. Bud Jacobson, "The Gang that Started the Sunset Celebration," *Key West The Newspaper* (hereafter, *KWTN*), February 4, 1994.

52. Bud Jacobson, "The Gang that Started the Sunset Celebration," *KWTN*, February 4, 1994; *Citizen*, February 19, 2005.

53. On November 3, 1964, voters in Monroe County rejected a referendum to create a toll road through the Keys.

Chapter 6. Island of Intrigue: Key West in the 1970s

1. Bluestone and Harrison, *The Deindustrialization of America*; Zukin, *Loft Living*; City of Key West Planning Department, "Statistical Abstract," 2004.

2. Milo Smith + Associates, Inc., "Reuse Plan"; CE Maguire, Inc., "Community and Neighborhood Impact Study"; Office of Economic Adjustment, "Report of Community Visit to Key West, Florida."

3. Jon Nordheimer, "Key West Anxious Over Navy Cutback," *The Tampa Tribune-Times*, November 1, 1970; Tom Hambright, interview, July 15, 2006; Milo Smith + Associates, Inc., "Reuse Plan"; Gibb, "An Economic and Social Analysis of the Impact of the Military Role in Key West, Florida"; Office of Economic Adjustment, "Report of Community Visit to Key West, Florida," 11.

4. Hill, "The Political Economy of Military Base Redevelopment," 120–23; Milo Smith + Associates, Inc., "Reuse Plan," 53. Figures on military and related personnel are available in the Florida History room at the Key West Public Library in the reports of "Military Personnel, Their Dependents and Civilian DOD Personnel in the Key West Area." Also see, "Key West Vanishing Detail?," *Ladycom*, June 1978: 13–20 and Key West City Planning Department, "City Action Plan Supplementary," April 1985, 31.

5. Office of Economic Adjustment, "Report of Community Visit to Key West, Florida"; Milo Smith + Associates, Inc., "Reuse Plan"; Little, "An Overview of the Evolution of the Historic Seaport at Key West Bight"; Schittone, "Tourism vs. Commercial Fishers."

6. *U.S. News and World Report*, April 9, 1984; Al Burt, "In Florida," *MH Tropic Magazine*, April 13, 1980; *The Montreal Gazette*, May 15, 1980; Harrison, *Off to the Side*, 242.

7. *Citizen*, January 6, 1976; Susan Sachs, "Busted: Drug Arrests Reach into Establishment," *MH*, March 16, 1980; *MH*, May 31, 1985.

8. *Keynoter*, September 11, 1975.

9. *Citizen*, September 9, 1975; *MH*, September 10, 1975; Eric Deggans, "A State Stranger Than Fiction," *SPT*, February 29, 2004.

10. *Citizen*, February 24, 1976, March 11, 1976, May 31, 1985; *MH*, May 31, 1985, February 25, 1976; Carl Hiaasen, "Big Bubba: As Pot Probe Widens, Manny James Vanishes," *MH*, March 20, 1980; *Citizen*, December 16, 2001.

11. *Newsweek*, January 19, 1976; *MH*, March 14, 1976, March 24, 1976; *Citizen*, April 4, 1976, April 13, 1976; Schmida, *True Crime Stories of Key West and the Florida Keys*, 114–25.

12. Patty Shillington, "Ex-Commissioner Convicted in Drug Case," *MH*, June 22, 1985.

13. The "Smuggler's Island" series ran March 16-21, 1980; For example, see Carl Hiaasen, "Big Bubba: As Pot Probe Widens, Manny James Vanishes," *MH*, March 20, 1980.

14. *Citizen*, October 9, 1980; *Keynoter*, November 20, 1980, March 5, 1981.

15. *MH*, September 11, 1985; Jaggers, *Billy Freeman, Florida Keys Sheriff*. For a more general discussion of drug smuggling in Florida, see William S. Ellis, "Florida: A Time for Reckoning," *National Geographic*, August 1982.

16. Schmida, *True Crime Stories of Key West and the Florida Keys*, Vol. 2, 98–108; *SH*, May 1985; *MH*, May 31, 1985; *Citizen*, August 7, 1985; Allison DeFoor, interview, January 7, 2001; Tom Hambright, interview, July 15, 2006. The Key West Police Department was characterized as a Racketeer Influenced and Corrupt Organization (RICO) in this case. Those involved in the enterprise included narcotics traffickers, an attorney, and Key West Police Officers. See 837 F.2d 1509 24 Fed. R. Evid. Serv. 1001 United States of American, Plaintiff-Appellee, v. Raymond Casamayor, Defendant-Appellant, et. Al, No. 85–5602, 85–5628. United States Court of Appeals, Eleventh Circuit, February 23, 1988.

17. *MH*, May 31, 1985; Bud Jacobson, "Federal Dope Trial Topples Cops and Politicians," *SH*, December 1989.

18. *Newsweek*, January 19, 1976.

19. Frederick Burger, "Jimmy Buffett," *MH Tropic Magazine*, January 20, 1980. See Ryan, *The Parrot Head Companion*.

20. Pearsall, "New Key West"; Buffett, *A Pirate Looks at Fifty*, 123–25.

21. Dodé, *Memories of Key West*, "Introduction."

22. Humphrey, with Lewine, *The Jimmy Buffett Scrapbook*, 100; Corcoran, *Jimmy Buffett*, 33. Another popular hangout was the West Indies Lounge, in the Queen's Table restaurant at the Santa Maria Motel ("The Santa Maria," *Citizen*, November 16, 1997; Mark Howell, "Extreme Makeover at the Santa Maria," *SH*, December 31, 2004).

23. Lyon, *The Search for the Atocha*.

24. John Dorschner, "Melvin and the Pirates," *MH Tropic Magazine*, July 20, 1980; Pearsall, "New Key West"; *Citizen*, August 2, 2008. The diver Rick Gage also died in that incident.

25. Lyon, *The Search for the Atocha*, 87.

26. Kathleen J. Hargreaves, "The Reel Capt. Tony," *MH Tropic Magazine*, August 31, 1980; *MH*, October 22, 1989.

27. John Martini, interview, July 4, 2005.

28. Ed Little, interview, July 14, 2005; *SH*, May 26, 2006; *Citizen*, March 3, 1985; Lori Capullo, "Key West Perspectives: Island Life Inspires Masterpieces," *Florida Home and Garden*, March 1989: 86–92.

29. Congdon and Bucuvalas, *Just Above the Water*; Frank, *Mario Sanchez*.

30. *Citizen*, April 23, 1976; *MH*, January 28, 1979; Rita Brown, interview, July 28,

2005; Gary McDonald, interview, July 6, 2006; Margaret Walker, "Revival in Key West: Tennessee Williams and the Cast of Characters," *Gold Coast Pictorial* (June 1976): 30–37.

31. Gary McDonald, interview, July 6, 2006.

32. Edmund V. White, e-mail correspondence, February 3, 2008.

33. *Citizen*, January 12, 1995; Arthur Phillips, "A Morning with Richard Wilbur," *SH*, May 1989; Andrea Chambers, "Up Front," *People Magazine*, February 1981: 24–28; *MH*, March 11, 1984.

34. *Publishers Weekly*, May 10, 1985; *SH*, May 1986; *Citizen*, March 31, 1986; Nancy Klingener, "Last Words," *MH*, January 24, 1994.

35. *Citizen*, January 8, 1995; Brinnin, *Truman Capote*, 144.

36. Brinnin remained a winter resident until he died in 1998 (*NYT*, June 30, 1998). His biography, *Truman Capote: Dear Heart, Old Buddy*, includes many references to Key West.

37. *SH*, May 1986; *Citizen*, January 25, 1985, February 5, 1978; *Keynoter*, February 26, 1981; *MH*, January 30, 1995; Bill Anderson, "Philip H. Burton: The Quiet Man of Angela Street," *SH*, December 1987: 3–9. Burton lived in Key West until he suffered a stroke in 1993.

38. Rampersad, *Ralph Ellison*, 504–5, 559–60.

39. Kaufelt, *Key West Writers and Their Houses*, 128; "A Key West Canticle," *After Dark*, January 1978: 40–61; *Citizen*, January 19, 1964, April 23, 1989; Albin Krebs, "Key West: Anyone's Place in the Sun," *NYT Magazine*, December 31, 1978.

40. *Citizen*, December 17, 2000; John Dorschner, "Portrait of the Author As a Young Director," *MH Tropic Magazine*, October 13, 1974; Kaufelt, *Key West Writers and Their Houses*, 90.

41. Ryan, *The Parrot Head Companion*, 34; Kaufelt, *Key West Writers and Their Houses*, 89; *Citizen*, January 22, 1984.

42. Harrison, *Off to the Side*, 231; Susan Nadler, "Nobody Owns a Mercedes," *Florida Keys Magazine*, March 1986: 44–53.

43. Humphrey, with Lewine, *The Jimmy Buffett Scrapbook*, 100; Harrison, *Off to the Side*, 242, 273.

44. Wenner and Seymour, *Gonzo*, 226.

45. Rogak, *A Boy Named Shel*.

46. Lurie, *Familiar Spirits*, 130, 123.

Chapter 7. Key West in Transition

1. One preservationist estimated that about seventy percent of the restoration of "Conch" homes in Old Town was undertaken by the gay community (Cox, *A Key West Companion*, 183). On the important role gays played in gentrifying neighborhoods in several cities, see Abraham, *Metropolitan Lovers*.

2. Milo Smith + Associates, Inc., "Research and Analysis."

3. Martha Thompson and David Johnson, "History Preserved," *Florida Keys Magazine*, Third quarter 1979: 34–37.

4. George Born, interview, July 16, 2007; CE Maguire, Inc., "Community and Neighborhood Impact Study"; URS, "Key West Historic"; Martha Thompson and David Johnson, "History Preserved," *Florida Keys Magazine*, Third quarter 1979: 34–37.

5. Tucker and Langley, "Florida's Keys"; Patricia G. Gruber, "How Ohio Key

Disappeared," *MH Tropic Magazine*, June 18, 1972; *Citizen*, January 3, 1973. In April 1976, the Florida Keys Aqueduct Authority board imposed a "no exception moratorium" on new water connections. Previously, the FKAA had granted numerous exceptions to the moratorium (*Citizen*, April 8, 1976).

6. George Born, "Design Attributes of Old Places," *Citizen*, September 26, 2004.

7. Georgia Tasker, "Inside a Designer's Key West Sanctuary," *MH Tropic Magazine*, May 28, 1978; *Citizen*, August 11, 2002.

8. Albin Krebs, "Key West: Anyone's Place in the Sun," *NYT Magazine*, December 31, 1978; *MH*, May 28, 1978; *Tampa Tribune-Times*, December 21, 1980. See Branchik, "Out in the Market"; Gotham, "Tourism Gentrification."

9. The *Citizen* reported in 1969 that on the three major business blocks of Duval Street (probably the 400, 500, and 600 blocks), there were sixteen vacant stores. It also noted that some restoration and improvement had been completed, such as Marion Stevens' restoration of her building as an art gallery and David Wolkowsky's restoration of a corner (October 5, 1969); Sonny McCoy, interview, July 13, 2007.

10. *Citizen*, February 15, 1978.

11. Laurie Karnatz, "Love of Past Drives HTA," *Citizen*, August 8, 2004; Timothy O'Hara, "Belland Works Behind the Scenes," *Citizen*, August 8, 2004; Ed Swift, interview, March 5, 2001. A study conducted in 1978 of property owners on Duval Street found that Old Town Key West Development Corporation was a major property owner. Old Town owned 23 of the 33 parcels of land on the 600 block as well as some of the 700 block. David Wolkowsky also owned part of the 700 block. The Spottswood family owned the La Concha Hotel, the parking lot across from it on Duval Street, and two buildings on the 500 block of Duval. Hilario Ramos owned the property on the 200 block that the Lopez Distributors occupied as well as the house at the end of Duval that was referred to as the southernmost house. In all, more than fifty different owners owned the property and buildings on Duval Street (*Citizen*, July 30, 1978). Swift emphasized that their "restoration" work was not intended to return Key West's downtown to what it had once been. He noted, "If you reconstructed Key West as it actually was you'd have dirt streets, no sidewalks, dilapidated and unpainted buildings and garbage in the alleys. It'd be impossible to reproduce even if you wanted to. Instead, we're creating what people want to think of as Key West, with a mixture of New England, Conch and Bahamian architecture" (News release from the Communications Group, "Casa Marina Joins Boom in Key West Restoration," June 21, 1978; Hampton Dunn Collection, Monroe County, Key West, pt. 3, University of South Florida Special Collections).

12. *SPT*, September 12, 1978; Milo Smith + Associates, Inc., "Reuse Plan"; Stronge, *The Sunshine Economy*; CE Maguire, Inc., "Community and Neighborhood Impact Study."

13. CE Maguire, Inc., "Community and Neighborhood Impact Study"; Key West City Planning Department, "City Action Plan," September 1986: 23. The figures given in these two sources vary slightly.

14. Tom Corcoran, e-mail to author, December 24, 2006; *Citizen*, April 15, 1977, January 15, 1978; *Keynoter*, June 23, 1993; Barry Stavro, "Key West: Putting Itself Back Together—Again," *Florida Trend* (February 1983): 58–63.

15. *MH*, December 30, 1977; *Citizen*, December 30, 1977.

16. Pearsall, "New Key West."

17. Alice K. Turner, "Why Key West?," *New York* magazine, March 20, 1978.

18. Alice K. Turner, "Why Key West?," *New York* magazine, March 20, 1978.

19. Albin Krebs, "Key West: Anyone's Place in the Sun," *NYT Magazine*, December 31, 1978.

20. Corcoran, *Jimmy Buffett*, 13.

21. Jack Lange, "The Other Side of Key West," *MH Tropic Magazine*, November 26, 1978.

22. Al Burt, "The Trouble with Key West," *MH Tropic Magazine*, September 17, 1978; Philip Morgan, "The Sun Sets on Key West," *The Tampa Tribune–The Tampa Times*, May 14, 1978.

23. Joan Kufrin, "Why Are All These People Squinting at the Sun?," *MH Tropic Magazine*, April 10, 1977; Philip Morgan, "The Sun Sets on Key West," *The Tampa Tribune–The Tampa Times*, May 14, 1978. In the late 1960s, the Key West Police Department made it known that hippies were unwelcome in Key West. In February 1968, Police Chief Armando Perez Jr. said he had ordered his officers to "pick up" anyone on the streets without "visible means of support." He noted the increase in hippies in Key West and observed that their long hair made them easy to pick out. Perez said that those convicted of being vagrants could choose to leave town, instead of "permanently working" for the city in jail (*Citizen*, February 1, 1968).

24. *Citizen*, February 1, 1973, January 10, 1973, January 15, 1973, January 16, 1973; *Citizen*, January 2, 1975.

25. *MH*, March 15, 1966; Tom Hambright, interview, July 15, 2006; *Citizen*, August 24, 1975.

26. Little, "An Overview of the Evolution of the Historic Seaport at Key West Bight"; Ed Little, e-mail to author, June 27, 2005; Malcom, "Turtle Industry in Key West."

27. Tony Falcone, interview, September 10, 2009; Margo McCollum, "Lookout New Orleans, Here Comes . . . Key West Fantasy Fest," *Florida Keys Magazine*, First quarter 1980: 38–41.

28. *Citizen*, October 28, 1979, October 29, 1979, October 30, 1979, October 30, 1980.

29. Judi Bradford, "Fantasy Fest Evolves from Local Event to National Prominence," *Fantasy Fest 2000* (Official Magazine); *Citizen*, October 26, 1999, October 29, 1999; Margo McCollum, "Lookout New Orleans, Here Comes . . . Key West Fantasy Fest," *Florida Keys Magazine*, First quarter 1980: 38–41. The protest against Air Florida group was focused on the loud noise the planes created, but it also captured the broader opposition to increased tourism and development in Key West. The attorney Henry Lee Morgenstern initiated a lawsuit (Henry Lee Morgenstern, interview, January 3, 2008).

30. DiNovo, "Analysis"; *Citizen*, August 31, 1977, June 22, 1977; Sandra Higgs, interview, June 29, 2008.

31. *Citizen*, July 19, 1978, July 20, 1978, August 2, 1978.

32. *Citizen*, December 24, 1978.

33. *Citizen*, August 15, 1979, September 19, 1979, December 23, 1979; Mack Dryden, "A Hot Issue: Bed Tax Debate Heats Up Throughout County," *Florida Keys Magazine*, Fourth quarter 1979: 10–11. Don Nettleton, the president of the Greater Key West Chamber, reported that riders on the Conch Tour Train had decreased thirty percent from the previous year, and he noted that the county commission had not increased the $139,000 appropriation for advertising the Keys for six years (*Citizen*, August 3, 1979).

34. *Citizen*, January 30, 1980, March 10, 1980, December 4, 1980.

35. *Citizen*, January 30, 1980.

36. *Citizen*, March 12, 1980, October 12, 1980, November 1, 1981. Around the time of the referendum election, a breakdown at the desalinization plant on Stock Island left residents and tourists with limited or no water, especially those on upper stories (*Fort Lauderdale News*, March 10, 1980). The city's sewage facilities were also deemed inadequate. In August 1979, the Florida Department of Environmental Regulation alleged that since 1975 the city had discharged effluent including untreated human waste into the Ninth Street and Riviera Canal systems (*Sentinel Star*, August 14, 1979).

37. Windhorn and Langley, *Yesterday's Key West*, 26–27.

38. *Citizen*, June 5, 1973, July 1, 1973, July 3, 1973. On the increasing popularity of condominiums in Florida from the 1960s onward, see Stronge, *The Sunshine Economy*, 193–94. Also see Mormino, *Land of Sunshine, State of Dreams*, 67.

39. *Citizen*, July 3, 1973; Mack Dryden, "Bill Westray," *SH*, September 1979; Bill Westray, "Rest Beach," *SH*, April 1977.

40. *Citizen*, July 3, 1974; *Fort Lauderdale News and Sun-Sentinel*, August 26, 1973; Denver *Post*, January 9, 1974.

41. *MH*, May 3, 1974; *Citizen*, November 5, 1974.

42. Mark Howell, "Founder of *SH* Dies at 74," *SH*, February 13, 2011; David L. Langford, "Key West Pirates Lair to Crash Pad," *Orlando Sentinel*, November 22, 1970.

43. Barry Stavro, "Key West: Putting Itself Back Together—Again," *Florida Trend* (February 1983): 58–63.

44. "Travel: The Restoration of Key West," *Fiesta*, March 1978: 16–18.

45. Albin Krebs, "Key West: Anyone's Place in the Sun," *NYT Magazine*, December 31, 1978.

46. Philip Morgan, "The Sun Sets on Key West," *The Tampa Tribune–The Tampa Times*, May 14, 1978.

47. Tom Corcoran, email to author; Mormino, *Land of Sunshine, State of Dreams*.

48. CE Maguire, Inc., "Community and Neighborhood Impact Study," 97–99.

49. The Monroe County Property Appraiser's Office reported that property values in Key West increased 48.7 percent between 1977 and 1978 ("Property Appraisal is Shocker," *Florida Keys Magazine*, Fourth quarter 1978: 9).

50. *Citizen*, January 6, 1980; Tennessee Williams, "Homage to Key West," *Harper's Bazaar*, January 1973: 50–51.

Chapter 8. The Gay Community and the Transformation of Key West

1. City of Key West Planning Department, "Statistical Abstract," 2004; Key West City Planning Department, "City Action Plan Supplementary Report No. 2"; *Citizen*, May 2, 1994; KPMG, "Key West Base Reuse Plan," July 7, 1987.

2. Key West City Planning Department, City Action Plan, April 1985; City of Key West Planning Department, "Statistical Abstract," 2004. The Puerto Rican segment of Key West's population remained relatively stable during the 1990s, decreasing from 287 to 284 (constituting 1.1 percent of Key West's population in 2000). The Mexican population increased from 238 to 371 (constituting 1.5 percent of Key West's population in 2000). (City of Key West Planning Department, "Statistical Abstract," 2004).

3. Plantec Corporation, "Affordable Housing Study"; Jim Brooks, NAS Information

Officer, interview, July 24, 2007; Hammer, et al., "Fiscal Impact of Growth Management, Key West, Florida." According to the Hammer, et al. analysis, retirees generated approximately 17 percent of the jobs in Key West in 1990. For example, retirees accounted for about one-third of the demand for health care services, equivalent to about 250 jobs.

4. *FL Keys Mag.*, July 1983, 41; Gates and Ost, *The Gay and Lesbian Atlas*, 24–30. Key West was not ranked among the top communities for lesbians. According to one estimate, around 500 lesbians, compared with 4,200 gay men, lived in Key West in 1990 (Anne Carlisle, "The Invisible Revolution: Lesbians in Business," *SH*, December 1990). Castells, *The City and the Grassroots*, 143.

5. Beatrice MacGuire, "Key West," *enRoute*, December 1982, 64. See Kip Blevin, "Pride and Prejudice," *SH*, August 1990; Dodé, *Gay Key West*. For a discussion of Provincetown's gay community, see Krahulik, *Provincetown*.

6. *Citizen*, April 6, 1992, March 23, 1986; *MH*, October 26, 1986.

7. Tucker, "Key West, Florida," 292.

8. Corcoran, *Jimmy Buffett*; Gordon Ross, interview, July 18, 2003. See Abraham, *Metropolitan Lovers*, on the importance of the gay and lesbian population in the street life of many cities during this era.

9. Barry Stavro, "Key West: Putting Itself Back Together—Again," *Florida Trend* (February 1983): 58–63; Kreloff, "Key West." The Hog's Breath Bar later occupied this site.

10. *Citizen*, October 24, 1976; Kreloff, "Key West," 4. The site later became Rumrunners.

11. "A Key West Canticle," *After Dark*, January 1978: 40–61; Dodé, *Gay Key West*, 98; Anne Carlisle, "The Invisible Revolution: Lesbians in Business," *SH*, December 1990.

12. The Copa was a popular club in Fort Lauderdale, and the owners of that club were involved in opening the Key West Copa (Dodé, *Gay Key West*, 139); Scott Fusaro, "Blaze Claimed Copa, Doused before Destroying More," *Citizen*, August 8, 2005; Williams, *The Florida Keys*, 182.

13. Jim Gilleran, interview, August 14, 2008. See Rupp and Taylor, *Drag Queens at the 801 Cabaret*.

14. White, *States of Desire*, 216; Patricia Bellew, "Gays in Key West Seeking to Create a Tourist Mecca," *MH*, May 16, 1982; Anne Carlisle, "The Invisible Revolution: Lesbians in Business," *SH*, December 1990. Rainbow House was a popular guesthouse for lesbian tourists.

15. Jon Allen, interview, March 12, 2005; *SH*, May 30, 1996; *MH*, November 2, 1980; Rupp and Taylor, *Drag Queens at the 801 Cabaret*, 52. Formica died in 1993 (Nathan Gay, "La Te Da: Keeping the Tea Dance tradition alive," *Citizen*, July 15, 2007).

16. *MH*, November 2, 1980; U.P.I., February 22, 1982; www.digi-watch.com (last accessed October 22, 2006).

17. *Citizen*, August 10, 2002.

18. *Citizen*, August 19, 2002; "A Key West Canticle," *After Dark*, January 1978: 40–61; *MH*, March 18, 1979.

19. Tony Falcone, interview, July 17, 2004.

20. *SPT*, February 4, 1979; Patricia Bellew, "Gays in Key West Seeking to Create a Tourist Mecca," *MH*, May 16, 1982; Eileen Moore Quinn, "The Key West Business Guild,"

SH, November 1980; Dennis Beaver, interview, July 20, 2006; Forsyth, "Sexuality and Space."

21. Paul Cherry, "Metropolitan Community Church, Key West," *SH*, April 1987. The Metropolitan Community Church was organized in Los Angeles in the late 1960s and officially became the MCC in 1970. It was the first self-identified gay congregation in the United States (Kaiser, *The Gay Metropolis, 1940–1996*; Adam, *The Rise of a Gay and Lesbian Movement*). Washingtonblade.com, May 26, 2003; *MH*, May 24, 2003.

22. *SPT*, October 9, 1989; *SH*, September 23, 2003; Gordon Ross, interview, July 18, 2003; *SH*, March 3, 1994; *Island News*, March 16, 2001; *SH*, May 8, 1997; Jim Gilleran, interview, August 14, 2008.

23. Steve Smith, interview, January 8, 2006.

24. Gordon Ross, "Gordon Ross Remembers . . . ," *Conch Color*, November 28–December 4, 2008.

25. *Citizen*, December 2, 1997; *SH*, November 30, 2001; www.cyberconch.com/aidskw.

26. *SH*, June 6, 2003; Constance Gilbert, "Gay and Lesbian Community Center Enters its 10th Year," *Citizen*, March 11, 2007.

27. *Citizen*, September 4, 2005. McLernan lived in Key West until 2004, when he moved to Miami Beach. He died in 2005.

28. *NYT*, September 17, 1994. For an analysis of the role of gays in urban politics, see Bailey, *Gay Politics, Urban Politics*. Also see Button, Rienzo, and Wald, *Private Lives, Public Conflicts*.

29. Peter Ilchuk, e-mail, February 2, 2007.

30. Peter Ilchuk, interview, July 14, 2000. Just two years before Heyman's election to the city commission, Miami voters had passed a referendum that rescinded the city's gay rights ordinance (Adam, *The Rise of a Gay and Lesbian Movement*).

31. *Citizen*, April 6, 1982.

32. Kermit Lewin was mayor from 1963 to 1969. Delio Cobo, who had previously served as mayor from 1957 to 1961, served again from 1969 to 1971. Charles "Sonny" McCoy was mayor from 1971 to 1981.

33. Mayor Sonny McCoy decided not to seek reelection in 1981, after serving five terms in office. For a balanced perspective on McCoy's terms in office, see *Citizen*, November 8, 1981. *MH*, November 2, 1983; Al Burt, "Conch Stew," *MH Tropic Magazine*, May 9, 1982.

34. Patricia Bellew, "Gays in Key West Seeking to Create a Tourist Mecca," *MH*, May 16, 1982.

35. Al Burt, "The King is Dead; Long Live the King," *MH Tropic Magazine*, June 6, 1982.

36. *Citizen*, March 7, 1983; *MH*, November 2, 1982.

37. *Citizen*, July 8, 1983; *MH*, October 23, 1983; Peter Ilchuk, e-mail, February 2, 2007.

38. Peter Ilchuk and June Keith, interviewed on Walsh tapes, located in the Gay and Lesbian Community Center; *Citizen*, June 29, 1982.

39. Gary Boulard, "The Building of Key West: Paradise Lost?" *SH*, June 1983; *Citizen*, October 25, 1983.

40. *Citizen*, June 2, 1983, July 29, 1983. The other African American elected to office during this decade was Dr. Otha Cox (*Citizen*, October 7, 2004). Cox was elected to the Utility Board of Key West in 1978, which governed the City Electric System (CES), and

he continued to serve in that capacity until his death in 2004. At the time of his death, he was the vice chairman of the utility, by then called Keys Energy Service. Cox also served on the Monroe County Tourist Development Council.

41. Peter Ilchuk, interview, July 14, 2000; *Citizen*, June 26, 1983, November 16, 1983.

42. Tucker, "Key West, Florida," 296; Peter Ilchuk and June Keith, interviewed on Walsh tapes, located in the Gay and Lesbian Community Center; Peter Ilchuk, interview, July 14, 2000.

43. *Citizen*, November 4, 1987; *NYT*, September 17, 1994.

44. *SH*, November 30, 1995; *NYT*, December 2, 1995; White, *States of Desire*, 216.

45. *NYT*, December 2, 1995; *KWTN*, December 1, 1995, December 8, 1995; Sheila Mullins, interview, June 9, 2001.

46. Bob Pardon, interview, July 27, 2007; Tom Hambright, interview, July 16, 2005. Women were not allowed to join the Yacht Club until 1990.

47. Peter Ilchuk, e-mail, February 2, 1997; *Citizen*, September 5, 1991.

48. *SH*, January 18, 1996, January 15, 1998. For a discussion of the factors that contributed to the passage of gay rights legislation nationwide, see Button, Rienzo, and Wald, *Private Lives, Public Conflicts*.

Chapter 9. Key West in the 1980s and 1990s: Bringing in the Tourists

1. Stronge, *The Sunshine Economy*; Becky Iannotta, "Welcome to the U.S.," *Citizen*, April 17, 2005.

2. *Citizen*, November 1, 1981, November 5, 1981. The Latin American Chamber of Commerce of the Lower Keys was involved in a variety of activities. In 1979, it sponsored the Canavales de Cayo Hueso parade and other festivities during a week of activities (*Citizen*, May 14, 1979). The tax would be applied to stays of six months or less at hotels, apartments, motels, apartment motels, rooming houses, tourist or trailer camps, and condominiums.

3. *Citizen*, November 5, 1981, February 13, 1983; *Keynoter*, February 9, 1984. The BOCC also created five taxing districts within the county, one of which encompassed Key West, and required that the TDC include at least one member from each of these districts. The advertising initially focused on South Florida (*Citizen*, April 29, 1982).

4. *MH Tropic Magazine*, April 18, 1982; Hopkins, "The Development of The Overseas Highway," 56; David Ethridge, "Grid-Lock: Latest Warning," *Florida Keys Magazine*, March 1987.

5. Tom Hambright, interview, July 12, 2007; *Citizen*, August 17, 1979, December 28, 1980; Key West Salt Ponds Committee, "The Key West Salt Ponds and Development"; Langley, "City Electric System."

6. *Citizen*, March 16, 1980, March 17, 1980; Heinlein, "Key West Search for Fresh Water, Part Three"; Ellen Sugarman, "Development: A Dissenting Opinion," *SH*, November 1987; Key West City Planning Department, "City Action Plan Phase One." In a referendum held on February 6, 1979, voters approved a $53 million loan from the federal government for a new pipeline and related improvements, such as water treatment facilities (*Citizen*, November 3, 1981).

7. Sandra Higgs, interview, June 26, 2008; Andy Newman, interview, December 18, 2008. Newman and Associates were responsible for both advertising and media rela-

tions for the Keys until 1986, when Tinsley Advertising of Miami received the contract for advertising.

8. *Citizen*, April 22, 1982, April 23, 1982; King, *The Conch that Roared*.

9. King, *The Conch that Roared*.

10. Roach, "Promoting Paradise."

11. Dennis Wardlow, interview, July 19, 2007.

12. David Paul Horan, interview, June 25, 2010; King, *The Conch that Roared*.

13. These included John Magliola, a radio commentator, and Townsend Kieffer, a news reporter. Ed Swift offers a slightly different view of the secession. According to Swift, he, Magliola, Kieffer, and Bitner conceived of the idea, and then Swift called Wardlow, who immediately agreed (Ed Swift, interview, August 12, 2008).

14. *Citizen*, April 22, 1982.

15. Britton, "Tourism, Capital, and Place," 465; Craik, "The Culture of Tourism," 125. Richard Starnes suggests that southern tourism fits into three general categories (*Southern Journeys*, 2). Environmental tourism includes scenic beauty, beaches, hiking, and fishing, and destination tourism includes attractions created to draw tourists, such as gambling casinos. The third category, cultural and heritage tourism, includes Civil War battlefields and historic districts. By the end of the 1980s, Key West's tourism industry clearly included aspects of all three categories, and more. Ted Ownby ("Nobody Knows the Troubles I've Seen," 247–48) found that many southern communities and states emphasize "variety" in their effort to attract tourists, a characteristic that also applies to Key West.

16. *Citizen*, November 2, 1980, October 30, 1980.

17. "Fantasy Fest 2000 Official Magazine"; *Citizen*, November 2, 1981; *Citizen*, April 1, 1986, October 31, 1986, October 15, 1989; *Citizen*, October 21, 1996.

18. *Citizen*, October 29, 1999; *Citizen*, October 27, 1995; *Citizen*, October 30, 1998.

19. *MH*, October 23, 1990; *Citizen*, October 23, 1990, October 24, 1990, October 25, 1993, October 24, 1999.

20. *Citizen*, October 29, 1980.

21. *MH*, October 25, 1985; *MH*, October 23, 1990.

22. *MH*, November 10, 1992; *Citizen*, November 2, 1992.

23. *Citizen*, October 24, 1993, November 1, 1993; *Citizen*, August 17, 1994, October 28, 1994.

24. *Citizen*, August 17, 1994, October 28, 1994, October 30, 1994; *Citizen*, October 29, 1995.

25. *MH*, April 18, 1996.

26. See Cocks, "The Chamber of Commerce's Carnival."

27. Patricia Bellew, "Gays in Key West Seeking to Create a Tourist Mecca," *MH*, May 16, 1982; Keynoter, September 11, 1991; Steve Smith, interview, January 8, 2007.

28. *SH*, May 2, 2003; Dodé, *Gay Key West*; Rupp and Taylor, *Drag Queens at the 801 Cabaret*.

29. *Celebrate*, August 22–September 4, 2002; *Citizen*, August 8, 1994; Vicki Weeks, interview, Summer 2006; Pam Doto, "Key West Hosts Week-Long Lady's Night," *SH*, September 5, 1996; *SH*, August 28, 1997; *Citizen*, September 3, 1997; *SH*, September 7–13, 1998. By the late 1980s, Atlantic Shores had become a primary sponsor of the events.

30. Diane Beruldsen, interview, October 17, 2006.

31. http://www.tripsmarter.com/keywest/archives/events/women-flag-football. htm (last accessed October 16, 2006); Diane Beruldsen, interview, October 17, 2006. McGillis moved to Key West with her husband in 1993 and lived there for several years (*Tampa Tribune*, March 21, 1993).

32. Miller, *In Search of Gay America*, 277.

33. Dennis Beaver, interview, July 20, 2006; *Citizen*, July 14, 1994; Constance Gilbert, "Light the Skies!," *Celebrate*, June 10–23, 2004; Rupp and Taylor, *Drag Queens at the 801 Cabaret*.

34. "Hemingway Slept Here, So the Town Cashes In," *NYT*, July 25, 1994.

35. McIver, *Hemingway's Key West*.

36. Mireya Navarro, "In Key West, A Farewell to Arm-Wrestling?," *NYT*, May 11, 1997; *SH*, April 10, 1997; Mireya Navarro, "Squabbling Over How to Honor 'Papa,'" *NYT*, July 7, 1997; Carol Shaughnessy, interview, December 19, 2008.

37. "Hemingway Slept Here, So the Town Cashes In," *NYT*, July 25, 1994.

38. David Kaufelt, interview, March 9, 2005.

39. Christine Arnold Dolen, "See Key West: There's More to Conch Culture than Sun and Sloppy Joe's," *MH*, January 7, 1990; David Kaufelt, interview, March 9, 2005.

40. *SH*, March 26, 1998.

41. Humphrey, with Lewine, *The Jimmy Buffett Scrapbook*, 141–42.

42. *SH*, May 14, 1998. On the relationship between music and tourism, see Gibson and Connell, *Music and Tourism*.

43. *SH*, April 14, 2006, May 12, 2006.

44. Sarah Nicholls, Christine Vogt, and Soo Hyun Jun, "Heeding The Call For Heritage Tourism," *Parks and Recreation*, September 2004: 38–47. Also see Prentice, "Revisiting 'Heritage'"; Bender and Delaune, "Historic Structure Report."

45. http:///melfisher.org (last accessed October 16, 2006). The Mel Fisher Maritime Heritage Society was the not-for-profit organization that ran the facility, which was one of the most popular of Key West's heritage sites, attracting about 228,000 visitors in 2003 and 219,000 in 2005. The Ernest Hemingway House Museum does not provide exact figures on attendance, but reports that they average between 400 and 600 visitors a day, for a total of approximately 182,500 a year (based on 500 visitors a day). In 2005, other sites attracted the following number of visitors: Fort Zackary Taylor State Historical Site—300,000; Key West Lighthouse Museum—87,563; Ripley's Believe It or Not—86,000; the Harry S. Truman Little White House—65,000; the Key West Museum of Art and History—53,247; the Botanical Gardens—25,000; East Martello Museum—11,677; the Oldest House Museum—11,677 (American Association of Museums, *The Official Museum Directory*, 2004, 2006).

46. *Citizen*, March 3, 2003; www://funandsun.com (last accessed October 15, 2006).

47. *SH*, February 26, 1999; *SH*, September 9, 2005.

48. Wolz and Hayo, *The Legacy of the Harry S. Truman Little White House, Key West*; Bob Wolz, interview, July 17, 2004.

49. Laurie Karnatz, "Tracking HTA," *Citizen*, August 5, 2004; Laurie Karnatz, "Love of Past Drives HTA Front Man," *Citizen*, August 8, 2004; Piper Smith, e-mail, April 26, 2006.

50. *Citizen*, September 8, 2006, October 8, 2008; "Duck Tour Case Holds a Few Lessons for City," *Citizen*, March 28, 2009; "Inside the Ducks Case," *KWTN*, October 17,

2008; Laurie Karnatz, "Tracking HTA's Impact on Cities,," *Citizen*, August 8, 2004; *SH*, December 11, 1998.

51. Bob Wolz, interview, July 17, 2004.

52. *Citizen*, January 20, 1993; *MH*, August 10, 1969. Albert Kee died in 2003.

53. Keith, *Postcards from Paradise*; *MH*, September 10, 1989; *Citizen*, October 20, 1989.

54. Sally Lewis, interview, April 3, 2000; *Citizen*, October 12, 1997; *MH*, September 13, 1997.

55. See Shaw and Williams, *Critical Issues in Tourism*, 211–43, and Costa and Martinotti, "Sociological Theories." Some of the points that Costa and Martinotti make regarding Venice also apply to Key West. Like Venice, the majority of those who visit Key West do so more for its "atmosphere" than to take advantage of culture and art (i.e., museums, galleries, etc.). Of course, the city's atmosphere during Fantasy Fest, for example, differs from that of most weekends. It is also likely that the "tourist gaze" in Key West, as in Venice, combines both the "romantic" and "collective" gazes discussed by Urry (*The Tourist Gaze*, 43–45). Many tourists in Key West appreciate the architecture and foliage in Old Town, which constitute examples of the romantic gaze. Certainly, however, the sunset scene at Mallory Square and the crowded sidewalks and bars on Duval Street in the evenings constitute examples of the collective gaze, where other visitors, as well as locals, are the primary attractions of the tourist experience.

56. "Florida Keys Magazine: Real Estate, 1987: 24."

57. KPMG, et al., "Key West Base Reuse Plan"; Thomas J. Murray and Associates, "The Impacts of the Cruise Ship Industry on the Quality of Life in Key West," 67; Smith, "Among Touram"; *Citizen*, March 28, 1997. On the importance of public expenditures to enhance tourism and for a more general discussion of the economics of tourism, see Urry, *The Tourist Gaze*, Chapter 3 and 105–9. Also see Judd, ed., *The Infrastructure of Play*.

58. Hammer, et al., "Fiscal Impact of Growth Management, Key West, Florida," 15; KPMG, "Key West Base," 41; Thomas J. Murray and Associates, "The Impacts of the Cruise Ship Industry on the Quality of Life in Key West," 18.

59. The bed tax receipts in constant dollars were $4,193,143 in 1990 and $6,524,789 in 2000 (Thomas J. Murray and Associates, "The Impacts of the Cruise Ship Industry on the Quality of Life in Key West," 17).

60. Johnnie White, "Tourism: The Key's Economic Engine," *Florida Keys Magazine*, September 1987: 17–23; Hammer, et al., "Fiscal Impact of Growth Management, Key West, Florida," 9; KPMG, "Key West Base," 20. In the retail sector, jobs in accommodations and food services dominated, with retail sales being next most important (U.S. Bureau of the Census, "American Fact Finder").

61. Bermello, et al., "Key West Base Reuse Plan"; *Citizen*, February 24, 1987; Hammer, et al., "Fiscal Impact of Growth Management, Key West, Florida"; KPMG, "Key West Base"; Thomas J. Murray and Associates, City of Key West Annual Budget FY 2001–2, 55–56.

62. *Citizen*, January 20, 1986.

63. *Citizen*, January 20, 1986.

64. *Citizen*, May 6, 1986. The improvements underway in 1984 were primarily financed by a state grant (*Citizen*, January 20, 1986).

65. Key West Cultural Preservation Society, "Spirit of Sunset"; *Citizen*, January 16, 1997.

66. Kuralt, *Charles Kuralt's America*, 33.

67. Dodé, *Memories of Key West*, 17.

Chapter 10. The Politics of Tourism and Development

1. For example, Amsterdam is known for both its libertarian atmosphere with regard to social mores and its traditionally activist government (Terhorst, van de Ven and Deben, "Amsterdam"). Also see DeLeon's work on San Francisco, *Left Coast City*. For general discussions of tourism and political conflict, see Hall, *Tourism and Politics*, and Hall and Jenkins, *Tourism and Public Policy*.

2. *Reporter*, April 21, 1988, June 30, 1988; *Citizen*, April 12, 1989. The Florida Keys Federation of Chambers of Commerce represented the Monroe County Tourist Development Council's Cultural Events Umbrella and recommended the funding allocation. As such, the Chambers played a major role in the allocation of countywide funding, rather than just allocations within District 1 (*Citizen*, September 4, 1994).

3. *MH*, May 24, 1989, July 16, 1989; *Citizen*, February 10, 1993.

4. The BOCC appointed the nine members of the Tourist Development Council, who each served four-year terms. Three of the nine TDC members were required to be operators or owners of tourist accommodations in Monroe County, with one of these three associated with the accommodations industry in Key West. Three other TDC members were required to be associated with the tourist industry but could not be owners or operators of hotels (*KWTN*, March 15, 1996).

5. The proposal was controversial, partially because those who opposed regulations had resisted a meaningful state-mandated land-use plan that would restrict development, and they argued that the state of Florida, not the tourists, should pay for the lost revenues that would result from the land-use plan (*Citizen*, March 1, 1988).

6. *Citizen*, September 5, 1999; *SH*, March 12, 1998, June 18, 1999, September 3, 1999; *Citizen*, August 5, 2001; Marion Robinson, interview, March 1, 2008; *MH*, September 12, 1999.

7. *USA Today*, September 1, 1999; *MH*, August 26, 1999; *Newsweek*, July 27, 1998; *Fodor's99 Florida*, 230.

8. *Citizen*, August 15, 1999; *SH*, November 12, 1999, February 11, 2000; Bill Wickers, interview, February 15, 2008. After the terrorist attacks on September 11, 2001, this percentage shrank to 25 percent out of the perceived necessity of spending more on advertising to mitigate the expected downturn in tourism.

9. Wendy Tucker, "Local Boatyard Demolition Begins for Motel Complex Construction," *Citizen*, July 21, 1977. Figures for 1980 and 1985 are from Key West City Planning Dept., "City Action Plan," September 1986, 12; figures for 1990 are from "Future Land Use Element Data Inventory and Analysis," City of Key West Comprehensive Plan, July 1993, 1–24; figures for 1999 are from Key West Chamber of Commerce, "Relocation Information." In 1997, the TDC estimated that a count of transient units in the city, including the "phantoms," would raise the total number of rooms to around 6,400. Michael Ingram, the chair of the TDC, estimated that the actual figure might have been as high as 8,000 rooms (Mark Howell, "Any Room For More Rooms?," *SH*, April 3, 1997).

10. In 2000, La Concha was renovated once again and became a Crowne Plaza Hotel Resort (*Citizen*, November 26, 2000).

11. The first of its two buildings opened in late 1983. In November 1984, Reflections was sold to Ocean Key House Associates and the project was transformed from time-shares to the first "luxury suite hotel" in Key West (*Citizen*, January 23, 1983; Stacy Willits, "SeaSide brings Sea of Change," *Citizen*, November 21, 2004; Gary Boulard, "The Building of Key West: Paradise Lost?," *SH*, June 1983; *Citizen*, February 1, 1984; Henry Lee Morgenstern, interview, January 3, 2008).

12. *SH*, September 1983. Key West had been designated as an Area of Critical State Concern in 1975, but was removed from this in 1981 after the state approved the city's land-use plan.

13. *Citizen*, August 15, 1984, September 14, 1984, September 23, 1984, July 15, 1985. There were a long series of votes on different aspects of the project. On many, but not all, votes, Heyman and Halloran opposed the developer, while Emma Cates, Joe Balbontin, and Mira voted in the developer's favor (for example, see *Citizen*, April 20, 1984, April 23, 1984). See Henry Lee Morgenstern, "Why Development is Above the Law in Key West," *SH*, October 1985.

14. *Citizen*, November 18, 1985.

15. White, "The Selling of the Small-Town Commission," 70, 72; *Citizen*, December 4, 1985.

16. *Citizen*, June 30, 1987.

17. White, "The Selling of the Small-Town Commission," 62.

18. Emmy Nicklin, "O, Captain! My Captain!," *Key West Magazine*, February/March 2008: 14; *Citizen*, May 3, 1990; White, "The Selling of the Small-Town Commission."

19. Alexander Cockburn, "Summit Can't Hold a Candle to Key West Politics," *Wall Street Journal*, November 14, 1985; White, "The Selling of the Small-Town Commission," 62.

20. *Citizen*, November 7, 1989; *MH*, October 22, 1989; *SPT*, February 7, 1990.

21. *Citizen*, November 10, 1989; *Citizen*, "Tradewinds," May 3, 1990.

22. *SH*, May 1990, 6–7; October 31–November 13, 1991.

23. "The Beginnings of Key West," *SH*, September 1984.

24. Key West Salt Ponds Committee, "The Key West Salt Ponds and Development," 5.

25. Key West Salt Ponds Committee, "The Key West Salt Ponds and Development"; Joan Borel, interview, July 1, 2006.

26. James Hendrick, interview, July 3, 2006.

27. Tucker and Langley, "Florida's Keys"; Bill Westray, "Editorial on Critical State Concern," *SH*, March 1983.

28. Larry Marks, interview, July 6, 2006; *MH*, March 4, 1987.

29. In September 1985, Circuit Judge M. Ignatius Lester ruled that the previous approvals issued for 1,120 units were "valid and in full force and effect." Nevertheless, the developer did not immediately proceed with the project.

30. *Citizen*, October 29, 1986.

31. *Citizen*, February 10, 1988; *MH*, November 24, 1987, October 2, 1988; Stacy Willits, "SeaSide brings Sea of Change," *Citizen*, November 21, 2004.

32. The first was Ocean Walk apartments. The others included Las Salinas Condominiums, the Salt Pond Condominiums, Sunrise Suites (a condo hotel), and Seaside

Residences townhouses (Stacy Willits, "SeaSide brings Sea of Change," *Citizen*, November 21, 2004).

33. Marion C. Robinson, "Salt Pond Update: An Interview with Joan Borel," *SH*, March 1989.

34. *Keynoter*, February 10, 1988, March 12, 1988; *Citizen*, March 2, 1987, August 2, 1987; John Cole, "Building on the Beach: Developers, Environmentalists and Government Struggle over the Future of Smathers-Salt Pond area," *SH*, March 15–31, 1991.

35. Braun, "A Strategic Plan for the Key West Salt Ponds," 18; *Citizen*, July 7, 2005.

36. Key West City Planning Department, "City Action Plan," April 1985; Marsha Gordon, "Commercial Fishing," *Florida Keys Magazine*, January 1984: 18–19; Schittone, "Tourism vs. Commercial Fishers"; Hammer, et al., "Fiscal Impact of Growth Management, Key West, Florida," 8.

37. Little, "An Overview of the Evolution of the Historic Seaport at Key West Bight"; Schittone, "Tourism vs. Commercial Fishers."

38. *Citizen*, June 5, 1985; Ellen Sugarman, "The Fight to Save Commercial Fishing," *SH*, June 1985.

39. "Key West Bight Preserved"; Keysnews.com, May 24, 2004.

40. Ed Little, e-mail to author, January 9, 2007.

41. *Citizen*, April 2, 1984, May 26, 1992; Julio Avael, interview, July 11, 2007.

42. Emily Roach, "Is Key West Economy in Ship Shape?," *Citizen*, January 17, 1999; *Citizen*, April 22, 1998.

43. Emily Roach, "Is Key West Economy in Ship Shape?," *Citizen*, January 17, 1999.

44. www.reefrelief.org (last accessed October 28, 2009); *Citizen*, May 22, 1992. For a discussion of the benefits and costs of cruise ships in the Caribbean, see Pattullo, "Sailing into the Sunset."

45. *Citizen*, October 19, 1995; Emily Roach, "Is Key West Economy in Ship Shape?," *Citizen*, January 17, 1999.

46. See "Executive Summary" of the Thomas J. Murray and Associates study, "Impacts of the Cruise Ship Industry" Amy Kimball-Murley, e-mail to author, August 10, 2011.

47. Tom Hambright, interview, August 7, 2008; John Cole, "The Only Home We've Ever Had," *SH*, January 1991; Matt Dukes Jordan, "What a Wonderful World It Could Be: Peary Court Ten Years after The Fall," *SH*, April 13, 2001; Elizabeth M. Smith, "Peary Court: It Ain't Over 'Till it's Over," *SH*, April 1990.

48. Elizabeth M. Smith, "Peary Court: It Ain't Over 'Till it's Over," *SH*, April 1990; J. D. Dooley, "Can Peary Court Be Saved?," *SH*, June 1991.

49. Matt Dukes Jordan, "What a Wonderful World It Could Be: Peary Court Ten Years after The Fall," *SH*, April 13, 2001; Schmida, *True Crime Stories of Key West and the Florida Keys*, Vol. 2.

50. *SH*, July 1991, April 18–May 1, 1991; J. D. Dooley, "Can Peary Court Be Saved?," *SH*, June 1991.

51. *SH*, February 13–26, 1992, February 27–March 18, 1992, March 19–April 1, 1992, April 2–15, 1992, December 17–30, 1992.

52. Laura Griffin, "D-day for the Mad Bomber," *SPT*, April 3, 1994; *Citizen*, July 17, 1994; *KWTN*, September 9, 1994.

53. Emily Roach, "The Final Chapter: Houseboat Row had a Storybook Beginning and a Mournful Ending," *Citizen*, June 17, 2001.

54. *MH*, April 3, 1974; June Keith, "Houseboat Row: Should It Stay or Should It Go?," *SH*, August 1990; Emily Roach, "The Final Chapter: Houseboat Row had a Storybook Beginning and a Mournful Ending," *Citizen*, June 17, 2001.

55. John Leslie, "Houseboat Row," *SH*, April 1982; June Keith, "Houseboat Row: Should It Stay or Should It Go?," *SH*, August 1990. The two agencies were the Department of Natural Resources (DNR) and the Department of Environmental Regulation (DER).

56. Katha Sheehan, "Proposed Houseboat Pact Presented to PATA Board," *Citizen*, October 12, 1988; June Keith, "Houseboat Row: Should It Stay or Should It Go?," *SH*, August 1990.

57. *Citizen*, May 7, 1995; Emily Roach, "The Final Chapter: Houseboat Row had a Storybook Beginning and a Mournful Ending," *Citizen*, June 17, 2001.

58. *SH*, February 12, 1998; *SH*, March 26, 1998; *Citizen*, April 9, 1998.

59. Cabinet Meeting Agendas, May 25, 1999; Emily Roach, "The Final Chapter: Houseboat Row had a Storybook Beginning and a Mournful Ending," *Citizen*, June 17, 2001; Jim Carrier, "In Devastated Keys, a Call to Improve," *NYT*, October 26, 1998.

60. Christina Cheakalos, "Bye, Bye Bubba, Bye, Bye Darlin'," *MH*, November 6, 1988.

Chapter 11. Shelter for the Labor Force?

1. Tim Barrus, "Islands in the Stream: A Second Opinion," *SH*, November 1985: 56–59.

2. Barry Stavro, "Key West: Putting Itself Back Together—Again," *Florida Trend* (February 1983): 58–63.

3. Marsha Gordon, "The Real Estate Story of Monroe County," *Florida Keys Magazine*, July 1983; "History of Design Guidelines," May 14, 2002; *Citizen*, January 8, 1986, October 8, 1986. The original area designated as the Historic District of Key West in 1965 was in 1972 included in the National Register of Historic Places. The local district was then expanded, and in 1983 the Department of the Interior included it in the National Register of Historic Places (*Citizen*, March 15, 1983).

4. *MH*, August 4, 1985.

5. Christine Arnold Dolen, "See Key West: There's More to Conch Culture than Sun and Sloppy Joe's," *MH*, January 7, 1990; Marko Fields, "Art as Business," *SH*, October 1989.

6. *Florida Keys Magazine*, July 1983: 41; Marsha Gordon, "The Real Estate Story of Monroe County," *Florida Keys Magazine*, July 1983; *Florida Keys Magazine*: Real Estate, 1987. Pamela Mason, "To Live, Work and Hope to Buy a Home in Key West," *SH*, May 1990; *Citizen*, May 6, 1994; Johnnie White, "Florida Keys Real Estate," *Florida Keys Magazine*, March 1988: 34–39.

7. *Citizen*, May 6, 1994; *Florida Keys Magazine: Real Estate*, 1987, 33. In 1979, the average rent in Key West was $255 a month; by 1989 it had risen to $608, compared to $481 for the entire state.

8. Hammer, et al., "Fiscal Impact of Growth Management Key West, Florida," 41.

9. KPMG, "Key West Base," 28, 19; City of Key West Planning Department, "Evalu-

ation and Appraisal Report," 16; City of Key West Planning Department, "Statistical Abstract, 2002."

10. Rothman, *Neon Metropolis*; Key West Chamber of Commerce, "Economic Trends"; Thomas J. Murray and Associates, "The Impacts of the Cruise Ship," 5. For a discussion of labor markets in the tourism industry, see Shaw and Williams, *Critical Issues*, Chapter 7 and Gladstone and Fainstein, "Regulating Hospitality."

11. City of Key West Planning Department, "Evaluation and Appraisal Report," 18; Christina Cheakalos, "Bye, Bye Bubba, Bye, Bye Darlin'," *MH*, November 6, 1988.

12. Cohen and Leon, "Bahama Village Redevelopment Plan, City of Key West, Florida"; *MH*, September 19, 1976.

13. *Citizen*, September 13, 1981; *MH*, October 22, 1981; Alden Solovy, "Some Interesting Projects Around Key West," *SH*, April 1984.

14. *Citizen*, October 29, 1981; *Island Life*, October 20, 1988; Mark Howell, "Concerned Citizens Rush to Raise Cash to Save Goombay," *SH*, October 3, 1996.

15. *MH*, April 8, 1979; Cohen and Leon, "Bahama Village Redevelopment Plan, City of Key West, Florida," 20.

16. Ann Boese, "Racial Unrest in Key West," *SH*, November 1990; KPMG, "Key West Reuse Plan"; Cohen and Leon, "Bahama Village Redevelopment Plan, City of Key West, Florida," App C; Also see Dan Keating, "Gentrification Enriches Keys, but Blacks Don't Share Wealth," *MH*, March 3, 1992.

17. *Citizen*, April 8, 1998. Drug trafficking occurred in Bahama Village, although it is difficult to know to what extent. For example, thirty-three persons were arrested in September 1996 for soliciting to buy crack. Drug dealers from Miami were involved with some of the drug activity (*Citizen*, September 9, 1996).

18. Sarah Hollander, "Where the 'Old Conchs' Go!," *Citizen*, December 31, 1995; Grace Fallon, interview, July 12, 2005; Phoebe Redner Coan, "Conch Exodus: Justa and DeWitt Roberts," *SH*, June 1982.

19. *Citizen*, December 31, 1995.

20. Al Burt, "Leaving the Rock," *MH Tropic Magazine*, October 18, 1981; *Citizen*, September 19, 2000.

21. *Citizen*, September 19, 2000.

22. Al Burt, "Leaving the Rock," *MH Tropic Magazine*, October 18, 1981.

23. *Citizen*, December 31, 1995; *MH*, February 28, 1995; Andrew Saunders, interview, June 17, 2004.

24. Key West City Planning Department, "City Action Plan Supplementary Report No. 3."

25. *Citizen*, June 16, 1987; *MH*, October 4, 1987; City of Key West Growth Management Ordinance, Ordinance No. 86–20, adopted August 1986; Geddy Svelkauskas, "Affordable Housing at the Annex: Some People Are more Equal than Others," *SH*, January 1990; Hammer, et al., "Fiscal Impact of Growth Management, Key West, Florida." The 300-unit limit constituted seven percent of the number of units remaining to "build out," or the maximum number of units allowed under the existing zoning code.

26. City of Key West Growth Management Ordinance (amended), Ordinance No. 86–40.

27. *MH*, October 4, 1987; *Citizen*, January 1, 1989.

28. *Citizen*, January 10, 1988.

29. *Citizen*, May 17, 1988; *MH*, June 23, 1988.

30. Richard Hatch, "Buildout!," *SH*, November 14–26, 1991; Hammer, et al., "Fiscal Impact of Growth Management, Key West, Florida," 45. Purchasers of the condos had to agree to sell for a minimal profit for the first five years. After that, there was no limit on the sales price.

31. John Martini, "The Surreal World: Truman Annex Before the Auction," *SH*, September 8, 2006.

32. "Navy Pullout May Not be all Bad," *Florida Keys Magazine*, Third quarter 1978: 9–11; Mack Dryden, "Naval Station Could be Major Key West Attraction," *Florida Keys Magazine*, First quarter 1978: 10–12, 14; Mack Dryden, "Key West Navy Base May Go Public Soon," *Florida Keys Magazine*, Third quarter 1979: 38–39.

33. Mack Dryden, "What Next On The Base," *SH*, May 1979; Richard Marsh, "Summer of Discontent: The Navy Base Controversy," *SH*, August 1979; *Citizen*, January 8, 1980.

34. *Citizen*, December 13, 1979; In January 1980, the city commission unanimously voted down the RDA's plan for Truman Annex (*Citizen*, January 8, 1980).

35. Becky Iannotta, "Paradise Lost," *Citizen*, September 10, 2006; Alden Solovy, "Truman Annex: The $387,500.00 Development," *Florida Keys Magazine*, May 1984: 22–25.

36. Alden Solovy, "Truman Annex: The $387,500.00 Development," *Florida Keys Magazine*, May 1984: 22–25.

37. Alden Solovy, "Truman Annex: The $387,500.00 Development," *Florida Keys Magazine*, May 1984: 22–25.

38. *Citizen*, March 3, 1986, March 9, 1986, March 12, 1986; *Citizen*, March 16, 1987; John Dent, interview, September 25, 2006.

39. *MH*, August 31, 1986; Becky Iannotta, "Paradise Lost," *Citizen*, September 10, 2006; George Murphy, "A Reporter's Notes: Eight Months of RDA-Watching," *SH*, June/July 1985.

40. *Citizen*, April 1, 1986, September 14, 1986; Curtis Gillespie, "Singh's Last Song," *Key West Magazine*, February/March 2008: 24–35.

41. Kip Blevin, "Truman Annex On Shaky Grounds," *SH*, December 1990; Curtis Gillespie, "Singh's Last Song," *Key West Magazine*, February/March 2008: 24–35.

42. Curtis Gillespie, "Singh's Last Song," *Key West Magazine*, February/March 2008: 24–35; *Citizen*, April 1, 1986, September 14, 1986.

43. Ellen Sugarman, "The Best Revenge: Pritam Singh and The Truman Annex," *Florida Keys Magazine Real Estate* (1987): 36–39.

44. John Martini, "The Surreal World: Truman Annex Before the Auction," *SH*, September 8, 2006.

45. Hill, "Measuring Success in the Redevelopment of Former Military Bases"; Lee Irby, "510 Greene Street," *SH*, November 2–18, 1992; *KWTN*, June 2, 1995.

46. On vacation homes in tourist communities, see Hettinger, *Living And Working In Paradise*.

47. Hill, "Measuring Success in the Redevelopment of Former Military Bases"; Geddy Svelkauskas, "Affordable Housing at the Annex: Some People Are more Equal than Others," *SH*, January 1990; Hammer, et al., "Fiscal Impact of Growth Management, Key West, Florida," 47; Laurie McChelsey, interview, June 6, 2004. Completed, the develop-

ment at Truman Annex boasted 304 homes and 281 condos (Becky Iannotta, "Paradise Lost," *Citizen*, September 10, 2006).

48. *Citizen*, July 8, 1979; Rothman, *Devil's Bargains*, 250.

49. City of Key West Building Permit Allocation and Vested Rights Ordinance, Ordinance No.93–37; Ty Symroski, memo, March 1, 2005; City of Key West Building Permit Allocation and Vested Rights Ordinance, Ordinance No.93–37, provision 5.05, 9; Ty Symroski, email to author, July 18, 2011.

50. KPMG Peat, "Key West Base," 33; *SH*, August 28, 1997, April 22, 1993, July 29, 1993.

51. Dr. Jake Rutherford, interview, March 8, 2005; Bill Belleville, "Key West: Wasting Away in Condoville," *The Orlando Sentinel*, April 15, 1990; *SH*, September 9, 1993, July 29, 1993, June 23, 1994, February 24, 1994; Key West Planning Department, "The Impact."

52. *Citizen*, October 26, 1997; Sheila Mullins, interview, June 9, 2001.

53. *Citizen*, October 5, 1997, October 9, 1997, November 5, 1997.

54. *Citizen*, October 6, 1999.

55. The statement was dated September 22, 1993 (provided to author by Matt Babich).

Chapter 12. Island Tensions in the Twenty-First Century: Mass Tourism and Rising Real Estate Values in a "Unique" Community

1. http://www.keywestchamber.org (last accessed August 3, 2008). Key West Vision 2020 Five Year Progress Review Draft 1 May 2004, F:/Jessica/vision 2020/2003 update/revision i.doc, 1; *Celebrate*, January 23–February 5, 2003.

2. *Keynoter*, February 19, 2003; *Citizen*, April 9, 2004; information provided by Key West Bight Board.

3. "Destination Scorecard," *National Geographic Traveler*, March 2004: 60–67.

4. Seth Margolis, "South Florida on a Whim and a Budget," *NYT*, February 22, 2004; *Islands*, March 24, 2004, www.islands.com.

5. February 21, 2003 (among the sponsors of the website were the *Washington Blade* and the *New York Blade*); *Celebrate*, January 8–21, 2004.

6. Williams, *The Florida Keys*, 272–75.

7. Rosalind Brackenbury, "The Ugly Issue," *SH*, February 27, 2004.

8. Keysnews.com, April 26, 2004.

9. http://www.communityforabetterkeywest.com, May 16, 2004, March 21, 2005.

10. *Citizen*, May 21, 2004.

11. Keysnews.com, April 13, 2004.

12. Wayne Markham, "Perhaps We're Finally Seeing Common Ground on Tourism," *Keynoter.com*. April 16, 2004.

13. Keysnews.com, April 3, 2004; Key West Res/Vis Planning Plan, November 29, 2004; *Keynoter*, April 12, 2004; *Keynoter*, January 29, 2005.

14. Julio Avael, interview, July 19, 2007.

15. Keynoter.com, May 21, 2004; Keysnews.com, May 26, 2004, June 21, 2004.

16. Mark Howell, "What Happens When You Mess with Duval," *SH*, June 4, 2004; Keysnews.com, "Today in History," June 7, 2004; Keynoter.com, May 21, 2004; *Keynoter*, June 20, 2004.

17. Keysnews.com, May 30, 2004; Dennis Reeves Cooper, "The City Commission's Mandate to the KWPD: Clean Up Duval Street," *KWTN*, May 21, 2004.

18. Keysnews.com, June 17, 2004, June 21, 2004.

19. Jon Allen, interview, March 7, 2005; Fox, *In The Desert of Desire*, 120.

20. Keysnews.com, May 5, 2004; Keynoter.com, April 7, 2004.

21. *MH*, April 25, 2004.

22. *Citizen*, July 6, 2004, July 8, 2004; *Keynoter*, July 7, 2004.

23. Jon Allen, interview, March 7, 2005; Nick Madigan, "Key West, Suddenly Shy, Puts Pasties on its Party," *NYT*, October 20, 2004.

24. *Citizen*, September 19, 2003; Tom Oosterhoudt, interview, October 22, 2009. Not all would agree that the chain stores detracted from the appeal of Key West. See Ritzer, *Enchanting a Disenchanted World*, 120–21, who argued that the average tourist's primary goal is increasingly the "consumption of goods." Presumably, for many, purchasing these goods at chain stores would be as desirable as buying them at locally owned stores.

25. *SPT*, February 13, 2004; *KWTN*, January 9, 2004.

26. Gerry Wood, "Cock-A-Doodle-Don," *MH Tropic Magazine*, January 19, 1992; Ben Harrison, interview, June 30, 2008; *Citizen*, April 7, 1960; *The Orlando Sentinel*, January 15, 2004; Kewsnews.com, January 21, 2004; Scott Fusaro, "Foul Play Suspected in Deaths of 45 Fowl," *Citizen*, October 12, 2004.

27. *Orlando Sentinel*, January 15, 2004; Keysnews.com, October 10, 2003; Keysnews.com, January 8, 2004; Rosalind Brackenbury, "Talking to Tourists," *Keysnews.com*, March 26, 2004.

28. Linda O'Brien, interview, July 1, 2008; Keysnews.com, January 15, 2004; *Citizen*, July 2, 2005.

29. V. K. Gibson, "Let's Make A Deal," *SH*, June–July 1986; Christine Arnold Dolen, "See Key West: There's More to Conch Culture than Sun and Sloppy Joe's," *MH*, January 7, 1990; *SH*, August 19, 2005; Stacy Willits, "Big Money," *Citizen*, November 7, 2004; Mike Shields, interview, January 14, 2008; MiamiHerald.com, May 30, 2004. See Zukin ("Gentrification") for a discussion of the relationship between gentrifiers and cultural institutions.

30. *USA Today*, December 14, 2001; Keysnews.com, June 17, 2004; *Citizen*, May 8, 2005.

31. Eric Charest-Weinberg, interview, July 19, 2005.

32. Judi Bradford, "Gallery Business is Changing," *L'Attitudes*, August 27, 2005; Judie Bradford, interview, July 5, 2005.

33. Wisniewski, "Dean Walters Pioneering Keys' Opera."

34. Bob Muen, interview, August 13, 2008; Bobby Nesbitt, interview, July 15, 2003; Mark Howell, "When the Walls of the City Shake," *SH*, July 16, 2004.

35. *Celebrate*, May 27–June 9, 2004.

36. *Celebrate*, June 24–July 7, 2004.

37. Randy Osipow, interview, July 26, 2004.

38. Bennett, "Study of the Impact of Condominium Conversions to The Florida Keys and Key West."

39. Bennett, "Study of the Impact of Condominium Conversions to The Florida Keys and Key West," 7.

40. Nathan Gay, "New Shores? Old Shores?," *Celebrate*, December 23, 2004–January 5, 2005; *Citizen*, June 2, 2005.

41. *MH*, April 5, 1993; Nathan Gay, "New Shores? Old Shores?," *Celebrate*, December 23, 2004–January 5, 2005.

42. *Citizen*, March 25, 2007.

43. *Citizen*, March 25, 2007, July 28, 2007.

44. *Keysnews.com*, November 2, 2008; Bennett, "Study of the Impact of Condominium Conversions to The Florida Keys and Key West," 32–35.

45. *Citizen*, June 20, 2007; Ann-Margaret Sobota, "Paint by Numbers," *Citizen*, July 15, 2007.

Chapter 13. One Human Family?

1. *SH*, June 1, 2001. Thompson initially printed about 25,000 bumper stickers on his own. He then received financial support from fundraisers and various contributors (J. T. Thompson, interview, July 16, 2008); Key West Travel e-News, July 2005.

2. *Citizen*, July 4, 2001; *Celebrate*, January 9–22, 2003, May 1–14, 2003; *Keynoter*, March 19, 2003.

3. *MH*, March 17, 2004; Keysnews.com, March 17, 2004.

4. Tampa is the county seat of Hillsborough County, but Tampa's city officials did not support, and Mayor Pam Iorio criticized, the county's action.

5. *Citizen*, April 29, 2007; *Citizen*, May 3, 2007; Tamara Lush, "Key West Wrangle: Sides Square Off over Christmas Tree Island," *Miami New Times*, November 1, 2007.

6. *Citizen*, April 29, 2007; Tamara Lush, "Key West Wrangle: Sides Square Off over Christmas Tree Island," *Miami New Times*, November 1, 2007.

7. *Citizen*, May 3, 2007.

8. Miamiherald.com, May 6, 2007; Tamara Lush, "Key West Wrangle: Sides Square Off over Christmas Tree Island," *Miami New Times*, November 1, 2007; *Citizen*, May 8, 2007.

9. *Citizen*, April 29, 2007; Tamara Lush, "Key West Wrangle: Sides Square Off over Christmas Tree Island," *Miami New Times*, November 1, 2007.

10. Dennis Reeves Cooper, "Wisteria Island: The Power Dinner on Sunset Key," *KWTN*, June 22, 2007; Tom Duboco, "Feds Ask If Hotel Deal Tied to Gifts," *PalmBeachPost.com*, June 22, 2008.

11. *Citizen*, June 21, 2007.

12. *Citizen*, June 27, 2007, August 17, 2007, October 4, 2007; Tamara Lush, "Key West Wrangle: Sides Square Off over Christmas Tree Island," *Miami New Times*, November 1, 2007.

13. Key West Chamber of Commerce, "Community Information," www.keywestchamber.org (last accessed December 7, 2007). Keith Flatt, interview, July 13, 2005; *Tampa Tribune*, January 17, 2005; *Tampa Tribune*, January 17, 2005; www.coldwellbanker.com (Home Price Index); *SPT*, October 2, 2004; *Keynoter*, September 28, 2005.

14. Key West Chamber of Commerce, "Community Information." www.keywestchamber.org (last accessed December 7, 2007); On second homes, see Muller, "Mobility, Tourism, and Second Homes."

15. *Citizen*, February 27, 2005, February 28, 2005.

16. *Citizen*, April 23, 2004, July 8, 2004.

17. *Citizen*, December 5, 2004, August 17, 2004.

18. Ginny Haller, "Working in America," *Citizen*, May 25, 2003; Bennett, "Study of the Monroe County Tourism Workforce." Another contributing factor to the turnover was that only about 60 percent of private employers, compared with virtually all of the public sector employers, provided health insurance plans (not all of which were employer financed).

19. Ginny Haller, "Working in America," *Citizen*, May 25, 2003.

20. *Keynoter*, January 17, 2004, May 28, 2005; Bennett, "Study of the Monroe County"; *Citizen*, December 15, 2004, August 8, 2008. Key West also had some mobile homes that provided affordable housing (Mark Howell, "Downtown Key West Trailer Court to Close," *SH*, July 29, 2005). One factor that contributed to making "housing" less affordable was that after the city established, in 1998, an 81-buoy mooring field in the harbor north of N. Roosevelt, it evicted liveaboards who refused to tie up to the buoys (*Keynoter*, July 10, 2004; Mark Howell, "'Send the Squatters Packing.'" *SH*, July 9, 2004).

21. Key West Planning Department, "The Impact of Hotels Redeveloping and Converting to Residential Uses in Key West," 39; Bennett, "Study of the Impact of Condominium Conversions to The Florida Keys and Key West," 29.

22. *Citizen*, December 18, 2004.

23. *Citizen*, December 18, 2004, December 26, 2004; *Citizen*, January 24, 2005, February 4, 2005.

24. Bennett, "Study of the Impact of Condominium Conversions to The Florida Keys and Key West"; Larson, "City of Key West Worker Satisfaction Survey Final Report"; Metropolitan Center of Florida International University, "Monroe County, Florida, Affordable Housing Needs Assessment."

25. *Citizen*, January 6, 2003; *MH*, December 24, 2002.

26. Sam Kaufman, interview, July 2, 2008.

27. Tamara Lush, "Key West Wrangle: Sides Square Off over Christmas Tree Island," *Miami New Times*, November 1, 2007; *Tampa Tribune*, May 8, 2004; *Citizen*, December 30, 2002; Dana Canedy, "Key West Trying to Put New Locks on Paradise," *NYT*, January 14, 2003.

28. *Citizen*, March 17, 2003, March 10, 2004, March 11, 2004, March 12, 2004; *Tampa Tribune*, March 8, 2004.

29. *Citizen*, March 12, 2004, March 16, 2004, March 17, 2004; Mark Howell, "The Safe Zone Screw Up: How It Happened," *SH*, June 18, 2004.

30. *Citizen*, July 1, 2004, October 4, 2004, October 6, 2004.

31. *Citizen*, January 29, 2005; National Coalition for the Homeless, "Illegal to be Homeless 2004 Report"; Brady Dennis, "Tough on the Homeless, City Deemed Heartless," *Tampabay.com*, January 30, 2006.

32. For a discussion of neo-natives in resort communities, see Rothman, *Devil's Bargains*.

33. *Tampa Tribune*, January 17, 2005; *MH*, January 10, 2005.

34. Rosalind Brackenbury, "Is Anybody Out There?," *SH*, June 10, 2005.

Conclusion

1. Warner, "Key West Writers," 6; *U.S. News and World Report*, April 9, 1984.

2. Barry Stavro, "Key West: Putting Itself Back Together—Again," *Florida Trend* (February 1983): 63.

3. See Tarracino and Manard, *Life Lessons of a Legend*.

4. *Fodor's Florida* 2009, 490–91; *Florida Monthly*, September 2009, 18.

5. Peter Frank, "Best of the Florida Keys," *Travel+Leisure*, March 2003, http://www.travelandleisure.com.

6. Key West Chamber of Commerce, "Chamber Chowder," May 2007; "Tropical Breeze," Summer 2006; *Citizen*, April 1, 2007.

7. Key West Association of Realtors, "December 2010 Key West Statistical Analysis," www.keywestrealtors.org (last accessed February 26, 2011)

8. MCTDC, Smith Travel Research, for September 2008, available on Monroe County website, last accessed November 27, 2008; *Citizen*, April 12, 2009; Key West Chamber of Commerce website, "Key West Bed Tax—Third Penny Collection of Bed Tax Year-to-Date Percentage Change from Prior Years," last accessed August 2, 2011.

9. Douglas Hanks, "Cuba to Compete with Florida Tourism," *Chicagotribune.com*, May 4, 2009; *Citizen*, February 17, 2009.

BIBLIOGRAPHY

Abraham, Julie. *Metropolitan Lovers: The Homosexuality of Cities*. Minneapolis: University of Minnesota Press, 2009.

Adam, Barry D. *The Rise of a Gay and Lesbian Movement*. Rev. ed. New York: Twayne Publishers, 1995.

Allen, Geo. W. "Looking Forward." In *The New and Greater Key West, Florida: Told in Picture and Story*, Comp. J. A. Willis. Key West: J. A. Willis, under the auspices of the Key West Board of Trade, 1914. Reprint, N.p., 1990.

"Along the Florida Reef." In *Tales of Old Florida*, edited by Frank Oppel and Tony Meisel, 265–309. Secaucus, N.J.: Castle, 1987.

Altobello, Patricia, and Deirdre Pierce. *Literary Sands of Key West*. Washington, D.C.: Starrhill Press, 1996.

American Association of Museums. *The Official Museum Directory, 2004*. 34th ed. N.C.: National Register Publishing, 2003.

———. *The Official Museum Directory, 2006*. 36th ed. N.C: National Register Publishing, 2005.

An Invalid. *A Winter in the West Indies and Florida*. New York: Wily and Putnam, 1839.

Announcement: Key West Extension of the Florida East Coach Railway opened January 22, 1912. Reprint by The Conch Tour Train, 1987.

Aron, Cindy S. *Working at Play: A History of Vacations in the United States*. New York: Oxford University Press, 1999.

Audubon, John James. "Three Floridian Episodes." *Tequesta* 5 (1945): 52–68.

Bailey, Robert W. *Gay Politics, Urban Politics: Identity and Economics in the Urban Setting*. New York: Columbia University Press, 1999.

Barbour, George M. *Florida for Tourists, Invalids, and Settlers*. New York: D. Appleton and Company, 1882.

Barnes, Jay. *Florida's Hurricane History*. 2nd ed. Chapel Hill: The University of North Carolina Press, 2007.

Barnett, William C. "Inventing the Conch Republic: The Creation of Key West as an Escape from Modern America." *The Florida Historical Quarterly* 88 (Fall 2009): 139–72.

Barrus, Tim. "Islands in the Stream: A Second Opinion." *Solares Hill*, November 1985: 56–59.

Beauregard, Robert A. "City of Superlatives." *City and Community* 2, no. 3 (September 2003): 183–99.

———. *When America Became Suburban*. Minneapolis: University of Minnesota Press, 2006.

———. "Radical Uniqueness and the Flight from Urban Theory." In *The City Revisited: Urban Theory From Chicago, Los Angeles, New York*, edited by Dennis R. Judd and Dick Simpson, 186–202. Minneapolis: University of Minnesota Press, 2011.

Beehler, Commodore W. H. "Key West from a Strategic Point of View." In *The New and Greater Key West Florida Told in Picture and Story*, Comp. J. A. Willis. Key West: J. A. Willis, under the auspices of the Key West Board of Trade, 1914. Reprint, N.p., 1990.

Belasco, Warren James. *Americans on the Road: From Autocamp to Motel, 1910–1945*. Cambridge: The MIT Press, 1979.

Bellavance-Johnson, Marsha. *Tennessee Williams in Key West and Miami*. Ketchum, Idaho: The Computer Lab, 1989.

Bender and Delaune Architects, P.A. "Historic Structure Report: The Old Custom House and Post Office, Key West, Florida." September 30, 1992.

Bennett, Jessica. "Study of the Impact of Condominium Conversions to The Florida Keys and Key West." Prepared for the Monroe County Tourist Development Council Board of Directors, August 2005.

———. "Study of the Monroe County Tourism Workforce." Key West: The Florida Keys and Key West Monroe County Tourism Development Council, August 2006.

Berkowitz, Michael. "A 'New Deal' for Leisure: Making Mass Tourism during the Great Depression." In *Being Elsewhere: Tourism, Consumer Culture, and Identity in Modern Europe and North America*, edited by Shelley Baranowski and Ellen Furlough, 185–212. Ann Arbor: The University of Michigan Press, 2001.

Bermello Ajamil and Partners, Inc., Florida Conflict Resolution Consortium, Sullins Stuart, The Market Share Company, and Tindall Oliver and Associates, Inc. "Key West Base Reuse Plan Data Collection and Resource Evaluation Report." Draft for review, June 9, 1997.

Bethel, Rod. *First Overseas Highway to Key West, Florida*. N.p.: Printed by author, 1989.

Bishop, Elizabeth. *Edgar Allan Poe and The Juke-Box: Uncollected Poems, Drafts, and Fragments*. Edited by Alice Quinn. New York: FSG, 2006.

Black, Hugo L., III. "Richard Fitzpatrick's South Florida, 1822–1840; Part 1: Key West Phase." Introduction by Charlton W. Tebeau. *Tequesta* 40 (1980): 47–77.

Bluestone, Barry, and Bennett Harrison. *The Deindustrialization of America: Plant Closing, Community Abandonment, and the Dismantling of Basic Industry.* New York: Basic Books, 1982.

Born, George Walter. *Historic Florida Keys: An Illustrated History of Key West and The Keys.* Published for the Historic Florida Keys Foundation, Inc. San Antonio, Tex.: Historical Publishing Network, a division of Lammert Incorporated, 2003.

Born, George. *Preserving Paradise: The Architectural Heritage and History of the Florida Keys.* Charleston, S.C.: The History Press, 2006.

Boulard, Gary. "'State of Emergency': Key West in the Great Depression." *Florida Historical Quarterly* 67, no. 2 (October 1988): 166–83.

Braden, Susan R. *The Architecture of Leisure: The Florida Resort Hotels of Henry Flagler and Henry Plant.* Gainesville: University Press of Florida, 2002.

Branchik, Blaine J. "Out in the Market: A History of the Gay Market Segment in the United States." *Journal of Macromarketing* 22, no. 1 (June 2002): 86–97.

Braun, D. Greg. "A Strategic Plan for the Key West Salt Ponds." Draft, July 2000.

Brinnin, John Malcolm. *Truman Capote: Dear Heart, Old Buddy.* New York: Delacorte Press, 1986.

Brinton, Daniel G. *A Guide-Book of Florida and the South for Tourists, Invalids and Emigrants, with a map of the St. John River.* Jacksonville: Columbus Drew, 1869. A Facsimile reproduction. Gainesville: The University Presses of Florida, 1978.

Britton, S. G. "Tourism, Capital, and Place: Towards a Critical Geography of Tourism." *Environment and Planning D: Society and Space* 9: 451–78.

Brown, Canter Jr. "The Civil War, 1861–1865." In *The New History of Florida*, edited by Michael Gannon, 231–48. Gainesville: University Press of Florida, 1996.

———. *Florida's Black Public Officials, 1867–1924.* Tuscaloosa: University of Alabama Press, 1998.

Brown, Dona. *Inventing New England: Regional Tourism in the Nineteenth Century.* Washington, D.C.: Smithsonian Institution Press, 1995.

Browne, Jefferson B. *Key West: The Old and The New.* St. Augustine: The Record Company Printers and Publishers, 1912. Facsimile Reproduction of the 1912 Edition. Gainesville: University of Florida Press, 1973.

Bruccoli, Matthew J., ed., with Judith S. Baughman. *Hemingway and the Mechanism of Fame Statements, Public Letters, Introductions, Forewords, Prefaces, Blurbs, Reviews, and Endorsements.* Columbia: University of South Carolina Press, 2006.

Buffett, Jimmy. *A Pirate Looks at Fifty.* New York: Fawcett Crest, 1998.

Butler, Richard W., ed. *The Tourism Area Life Cycle.* Vol. 1, *Applications and Modifications.* Clevedon, UK: Channel View Publications, 2006.

———., ed. *The Tourism Area Life Cycle.* Vol. 2, *Conceptual and Theoretical Issues.* Clevedon, UK: Channel View Publications, 2006.

Button, James W., Barbara A. Rienzo, and Kenneth D. Wald. *Private Lives, Public Conflicts: Battles over Gay Rights in American Communities.* Washington, D.C.: CQ Press, 1997.

Cabinet Meeting Agendas, May 25, 1999, Board of Trustees of the Internal Improvement Trust Fund, State of Florida.

Camp, Vaughan, Jr. "Captain Brannan's Dilemma: Key West 1861." *Tequesta* 20 (1960): 31–44.

Capullo, Lori. "Key West Perspectives Island Life Inspires Masterpieces." *Florida Home and Garden*, March 1989: 86–92.

Carrier, Jim. "In Devastated Keys, a Call to Improve." *New York Times*, October 26, 1998.

Castells, Manuel. *The City and the Grassroots*. Berkeley: University of California Press, 1983.

CE Maguire, Inc. "Community and Neighborhood Impact Study." Truman Annex Redevelopment, August 1981.

Chamberlin, Brewster. "A History of Key West: A Chronology." Mimeo, August 21, 2007. Draft provided by the author.

Chapin, George M. *Florida, 1513–1913: Past, Present and Future*. Chicago: The S. J. Clarke Publishing Company, 1914.

City of Key West Building Permit Allocation and Vested Rights Ordinance, Ordinance No.93–37, adopted, August 1993.

City of Key West Comprehensive Plan, July 1993, Solin and Associates, Inc. Planning Consultants.

City of Key West Growth Management Ordinance, Ordinance No. 86–20, adopted August 1986.

City of Key West Growth Management Ordinance (amended), Ordinance No. 86–40, adopted December 1986.

City of Key West, Florida. "Annual Budget for the Fiscal Year October 1, 2001 to September 30, 2002."

City of Key West Planning Department. "Evaluation and Appraisal Report of the Key West Comprehensive Plan." May 13, 2002.

———. "2002 Statistical Abstract."

———. "Statistical Abstract City of Key West." March 2004.

Cocks, Catherine. "The Chamber of Commerce's Carnival: City Festivals and Urban Tourism in the United States, 1890–1915." In *Being Elsewhere: Tourism, Consumer Culture, and Identity in Modern Europe and North America*, edited by Shelley Baranowski and Ellen Furlough, 89–107. Ann Arbor: The University of Michigan Press, 2001.

Cohen, Thaddeus, and Sienna Leon. "Bahama Village Redevelopment Plan, City of Key West, Florida." July 1995. Available in the Florida History room of the Key West Public Library.

Cole, John. *The Casa Marina: Historic House by the Sea*. Key West: Scarma Bay Publishing Company, 1992.

"Commercial Cities and Towns of the United States." *Hunt's Merchants' Magazine and Commercial Review* 26, (January–June 1852): 52–60.

Congdon, Kristin G., and Tina Bucuvalas. *Just Above the Water: Florida Folk Art*. Jackson: University Press of Mississippi, 2006.

Corcoran, Tom. *Jimmy Buffett: The Key West Years*. Marathon, Fla.: The Ketch and Yawl Press, 2006.

———. *Key West in Black And White*. Marathon, Fla.: The Ketch and Yawl Press, 2007.

Corliss, Carlton J. "Building the Overseas Railway to Key West." *Tequesta* 13 (1953): 3–21.

Costa, Nicolo, and Guido Martinotti. "Sociological Theories of Tourism and Regulation Theory." In *Cities and Visitors Regulating People, Markets, and City Space*, edited by Lily Hoffman, Susan F. Fainstein, and Dennis R. Judd, 53–71. Malden, Mass.: Blackwell, 2003.

Cox, Christopher. *A Key West Companion*. New York: St. Martin's Press, 1983.

Craik, Jennifer. "The Culture of Tourism." In *Touring Cultures Transformations of Travel and Theory*, edited by C. Rojek and J. Urry, 113–36. New York: Routledge, 1997.

Davis, Elmer. "The Hounds of Spring." *The New Yorker* 2 (March 13, 1926): 19–20.

———. "Another Caribbean Conquest." *Harper's Magazine* 158 (January 1929): 168–76.

———. "New World Symphony With A Few Sour Notes." *Harper's Magazine* 170 (May 1935): 641–52.

"A Decade of Giving! How a Dream Became Reality." *Community Foundation of the Florida Keys*, Spring 2006: 1, 4–5.

Deitche, Scott M. *The Silent Don: The Criminal Underworld of Santo Trafficante Jr*. Fort Lee, N.J.: Barricade Books Inc., 2009.

DeLeon, Richard Edward. *Left Coast City: Progressive Politics in San Francisco, 1975–1991*. Lawrence: University Press of Kansas, 1992.

Denham, James M., and Keith L. Huneycutt, eds. *Echoes from a Distant Frontier: The Brown Sisters' Correspondence from Antebellum Florida*. Columbia: University of South Carolina Press, 2004.

Desmond, Jane. *Staging Tourism: Bodies on Display from Waikiki to Sea World*. Chicago: University of Chicago Press, 1999.

Devlin, Albert, and Nancy M. Tischler, eds. *Selected Letters of Tennessee Williams*. Vol. 1, *1920–1945*. Sewanee, Tenn.: University of the South, 2000.

———. *Selected Letters of Tennessee Williams*. Vol. ll, *1945–1957*. Sewanee, Tenn.: University of the South, 2004.

Diddle, Albert W. "Adjudication of Shipwrecking Claims at Key West in 1831." *Tequesta* 6 (1946): 44–49.

DiNovo, Joseph. "Analysis of the Potential Use of the Local Option Tourist Development Tax to Preserve Green Space in Monroe County, Florida." Unpublished report to Board of Trustees, Last Stand, June 16, 1999. Manuscript in possession of author.

Dobbs, Michael. *One Minute to Midnight: Kennedy, Khrushchev, and Castro on the Brink of Nuclear War*. New York: Alfred A. Knopf, 2008.

Dodé, Lee. *Gay Key West: Cruisin' Duval*. Key West: Arete Publishing, 1998.

———. *Memories of Key West: The Sixties, Seventies, Eighties, and into the Nineties*. N.p.: n.d.

Dodge, Charles Richards. "Subtropical Florida." In *Tales of Old Florida*, edited by Frank Oppel and Tony Meisel, 9–26. Secaucus, N.J.: Castle, 1987.

Dolgon, Corey. *The End of the Hamptons: Scenes from the Class Struggle in America's Paradise*. New York: New York University Press, 2005.

Dos Passos, John. *The Fourteenth Chronicle: Letters and Diaries of John Dos Passos*. Edited by Townsend Ludington. Boston: Gambit Incorporated, 1973.

Drye, Willie. "Tempting the Fate: Bonus Veterans, the Florida Keys, and the Storm of the Century." *Tequesta* 65 (2005): 5–36.

Dunn, Marvin. *Black Miami in the Twentieth Century*. Gainesville: University Press of Florida, 1997.

Ebensten, Hanns. *Home and Abroad*. Chapel Hill, N.C.: Professional Press, 2004.

Ehrlich, Bruce, and Peter Dreir. "The New Boston Discovers the Old Tourism and the Struggle for a Livable City." In *The Tourist City*, ed. Dennis R. Judd and Susan S. Fainstein, 155–78. New Haven, Conn.: Yale University Press, 1999.

Elazar, Daniel J. *American Federalism: A View from the States*. 2nd ed. New York: Thomas Y. Crowell Company, 1972.

Ellis, Jonathan. *Art and Memory in the Work of Elizabeth Bishop*. Burlington, Vt.: Ashgate, 2006.

England, George Allan. "America's Island of Felicity." *Travel Magazine* 50, no. 3 (January 1928): 13–17, 43–44.

English, T. J. *Havana Nocturne*. New York: William Morrow, 2007.

Fainstein, Susan S., Lily M. Hoffman, and Dennis R. Judd. "Introduction." In *Cities and Visitors Regulating People, Markets, and City Space*, ed. Susan S. Fainstein, Lily Hoffman and Dennis R. Judd, 1–18. Malden, Mass.: Blackwell, 2003.

Federal Writers' Project, Work Projects Administration for the State of Florida. *Florida: A Guide to the Southernmost State*. New York: Oxford University Press, 1939.

Federal Writers' Project, WPA. "Key West Guide." Typescript, Circa 1936. Available in University of Florida Special Collections, P. K. Yonge Library of Florida History.

Florida Keys Land Trust, Inc. "Ecology of the Salt Ponds: The Salt Ponds of Key West," n.d. Available in the Florida History room of the Key West Public Library.

"Florida's State Board of Health." *Florida Keys Sea Heritage Journal* 18, no. 1 (Fall 2007): 3–7.

Fodor's Florida 2009. New York: Fodor's Travel, 2009.

Fodor's 99 Florida. New York: Fodor's Travel Publications, 1998.

Forsyth, Ann. "Sexuality and Space: Nonconformist Populations and Planning Practice." *Journal of Planning Literature*, February 2001: 339–58.

Foster, Charles C. *Conchtown USA: Bahamian Fisherfolk in Riviera Beach, Florida*. Boca Raton: Florida Atlantic University Press, 1991.

Fox, William I. *In The Desert of Desire: Las Vegas and the Culture of Spectacle*. Las Vegas: University of Nevada Press, 2005.

Frank, Nance. *Mario Sanchez: Before and After*. Key West, Fla.: Key West Press, 1977.

Frazer, William, and John J. Guthrie Jr. *The Florida Land Boom: Speculation, Money, and the Banks*. Westport, Conn.: Quorum Books, 1995.

Fuller, Florence. "History of St. Mary's, Star of the Sea, Key West, Florida." n.d. Available in Catholic Church file, Florida History room, Key West Public Library.

Gallagher, Nicole Elizabeth. "The Dynamic Cuban Émigré Society of Key West: A Community Study from 1868 to 1895." Honors thesis, University of North Carolina, Chapel Hill, 2004.

Gannon, Michael. *Florida: A Short History*. Gainesville: University Press of Florida, 1993.

Gates, Gary J., and Jason Ost. *The Gay and Lesbian Atlas*. Washington, D.C.: The Urban Institute Press, 2004.

Getz, Donald. *Festivals, Special Events, and Tourism*. New York: Van Nostrand Reinhold, 1990.

Gibb, William L. "An Economic and Social Analysis of the Impact of the Military Role in Key West, Florida." May 11, 1970. Available in University of Florida Special Collections, P. K. Yonge Library of Florida History.

Gibson, Chris, and John Connell. *Music and Tourism: On the Road Again*. Clevedon, UK: Channel View Publications, 2005.

Giroux, Robert, ed. *One Art: Letters of Elizabeth Bishop*. New York: The Noonday Press, 1994.

Gladstone, David L., and Susan S. Fainstein. "Regulating Hospitality: Tourism Workers in New York and Los Angeles." In *Cities and Visitors: Regulating People, Markets, and City Space*, ed. Lily M. Hoffman, Susan S. Fainstein, and Dennis R. Judd, 145–66. Malden, Mass.: Blackwell, 2003.

Gotham, Kevin Fox. "Tourism Gentrification: The Case of New Orleans' Vieux Carre (French Quarter)." *Urban Studies* 42, no. 7, (June 2005): 1099–1121.

———. *Authentic New Orleans: Tourism, Culture, and Race In The Big Easy*. New York: New York University Press, 2007.

Gottdiener, Mark. *The Theming of America: American Dreams, Media Fantasies, and Themed Environments*. 2nd ed. Boulder, Colo.: Westview Press, 2001.

Grade, Arnold, ed. *Family Letters of Robert and Elinor Frost*. Albany: State University of New York Press, 1972.

Green, Elma C., ed. *Looking For The New Deal: Florida Women's Letters during the Great Depression*. Colombia: The University of South Carolina Press, 2007.

Griffin, Randall C. *Winslow Homer: An American Vision*. New York: Phaidon, 2006.

Grunwald, Michael. *The Swamp: The Everglades, Florida, and the Politics of Paradise*. New York: Simon and Schuster, 2006.

Hahn, John A., ed. and trans. *Missions to the Calusa*. Gainesville: University Presses of Florida, 1991.

Hale, Allean. "The Gnädiges Fräulein: Tennessee Williams's Clown Show." In *The Undiscovered Country: The Later Plays of Tennessee Williams*, ed. Philip C. Kolin, 40–53. New York: Peter Lang, 2002.

Hall, Colin Michael. *Tourism and Politics: Policy, Power and Place*. New York: John Wiley and Sons, 1994.

Hall, Colin Michael, and John M. Jenkins. *Tourism and Public Policy*. New York: Routledge, 1995.

Hambright, Thomas L. "Military History of the Florida Keys." In *The Florida Keys Environmental Story: A Panorama of the Environment Culture and History of Monroe County, Florida*, ed. Dan Gallagher, 117–20. N.p.: Seacamp Association, Inc., 1997.

Hambright, Tom. "German U-Boats Assault Florida Keys." *Florida Keys Sea Heritage Journal* 2, no. 4 (Summer 1992): 1, 4–6, 10–11.

Hambright, Tom, and Lynda Hambright. *Key West Historic Memorial Sculpture Garden: Key West's 36 Most Influential People and Their Times*. Key West: Friends of Mallory Square, Inc., 1997.

Hamer, David. *History in Urban Places: The Historic Districts of the United States*. Columbus: Ohio State University Press, 1998.

Hammer, Siler, George Associates. "Fiscal Impact of Growth Management, Key West, Florida." Silver Spring, Md.: Printed by author, January 1992.

Hammond, E. A. "Wreckers and Wrecking on the Florida Reef, 1829–1832." *Florida Historical Quarterly* 41, no. 3 (1963): 239–74.

———. "Sketches of the Florida Keys, 1829–1833." *Tequesta* 29 (1969): 73–94.

Harris, Sam. "Key West: The Gibraltar of America." *Suniland: A Magazine of Florida* 1, no. 1 (October 1924): 57–58, 96.

Harris, W. Hunt. "The Florida East Coast Railway and What It Means to Key West." In *The New and Greater Key West Florida Told in Picture and Story*, comp. J. A. Willis. Key West: J. A. Willis, under the auspices of the Key West Board of Trade, 1914. Reprint, N.p., 1990.

Harrison, Ben. *Undying Love*. Far Hill, N.J.: New Horizon Press, 2008.

Harrison, Jim. *Off to the Side*. New York: Grove Press, 2002.

Hayman, Ronald. *Tennessee Williams: Everyone Else Is an Audience*. New Haven: Yale University Press, 1993.

Heinlein, Carston R. "Key West's Naval Hospital." *Florida Keys Sea Heritage Journal* 3, no. 1 (Fall 1992): 8–13.

———. "Key West Search for Fresh Water, Part Three." *Florida Keys Sea Heritage Journal* 16, no. 3 (Spring 2006): 1, 3–15.

Henshall, James A. *Camping and Cruising in Florida*. Cincinnati: Robert Clarke and Co., 1884.

Hettinger, William S. *Living And Working In Paradise: Why Housing Is Too Expensive and What Communities Can Do About It*. Windham, Conn.: Thames River Publishing, 2005.

Hill, Catherine Alison. "The Political Economy of Military Base Redevelopment: An Evaluation of Four Converted Naval Bases." PhD diss., Rutgers, The State University of New Jersey, 1998.

Hill, Catherine. "Measuring Success in the Redevelopment of Former Military Bases: Evidence from a Case Study of the Truman Annex in Key West, Florida." *Economic Development Quarterly*, August 2000: 265–75.

"History of Design Guidelines in Key West." May 14, 2002, mimeo provided to the author by George Born.

Hoffman, Lily M., Susan S. Fainstein, and Dennis Judd, eds. *Cities and Visitors: Regulating People, Markets, and City Space*. Malden, Mass.: Blackwell, 2003.

Hopkins, Alice. "The Development of The Overseas Highway." *Tequesta* 46 (1986): 48–58.

House, Charles. *The Outrageous Life of Henry Faulkner: Portrait of an Appalachian Artist*. Knoxville: The University of Tennessee Press, 1988.

Humphrey, Mark, with Harris Lewine. *The Jimmy Buffett Scrapbook*. 3rd ed. New York: Citadel Press Kensington Publishing Corporation, 2000.

Jaggers, Annie Laura. *Billy Freeman, Florida Keys Sheriff*. Key West: Cayo Publishing, 2000.

Jakle, John A. *The American Small Town*. Hamden, Conn.: Archon Books, 1982.

———. *The Tourist: Travel in Twentieth-Century North America*. Lincoln: University of Nebraska Press, 1985.

Jakle, John A., Keith A. Sculle, and Jefferson S. Rogers. *The Motel in America*. Baltimore: The Johns Hopkins University Press, 1996.

Jameson, Colin G. *East Martello Tower*. Key West: The Key West Art and Historical Society, Inc., 1992.

———. "Porter and the Pirates: The Navy's First Two Years in Key West, 1823–1825." *Florida Keys Sea Heritage Journal* 4, no. 4 (Summer 1994): 1, 4–7, 10–15.

Johnson, Howard. *The Bahamas from Slavery to Servitude, 1783–1933*. Gainesville: University Press of Florida, 1996.

Judd, Dennis R. "Constructing the Tourist Bubble." In *The Tourist City*, edited by Dennis R. Judd and Susan S. Fainstein, 35–53. New Haven: Yale University Press, 1999.

———, ed. *The Infrastructure of Play: Building the Tourist City*. Armonk, N.Y.: M. E. Sharpe, 2003.

Judd, Dennis R., and Susan S. Fainstein, eds. *The Tourist City*. New Haven: Yale University Press, 1999.

Kaiser, Charles. *The Gay Metropolis, 1940–1996*. New York: Houghton Mifflin Company, 1997.

Kanigel, Robert. *High Season in Nice: How One French Riviera Town Has Seduced Travelers for Two Thousand Years*. London: Abacus, 2002.

Kaufelt, Lynn Mitsuko. *Key West Writers and Their Houses*. Sarasota, Fla.: Pineapple Press, Inc., 1986.

Keith, June. *Postcards from Paradise: Romancing Key West*. Key West, Fla.: Palm Island Press, 1995.

Kennedy, Stetson. *Palmetto Country*. New York: Duell, Sloan and Pearce, 1942.

———. *Grits and Grunts: Folkloric Key West*. Sarasota, Fla.: Pineapple Press, Inc., 2008.

Key West Administration. *Key West in Transition: A Guide Book for Visitors*. N.C.: Key West Administration, December 1934.

Key West Administration. *Key West Guide Book: An Aid To The Visitor—Fall and Winter 1935–36*. N.C.: Key West Administration, September 1935.

"Key West Bight Preserved." *Florida Keys Sea Heritage Journal* 1, no. 4 (Summer 1991): 7.

Key West Chamber of Commerce. "Economic Trends." Circa 2001.

———. "Relocation Information." 2002.

———. "Chamber Chowder." May 2007.

Key West City Planning Department. "City Action Plan, Phase 1 Report, Database Development Growth Projections, Infrastructure Analysis." August 1984.

———. "City Action Plan Supplementary Report No. 2, Demographics." April 1985.

———. "City Action Plan Supplementary Report No. 3, Housing and Land Use." September 1986.

Key West Cultural Preservation Society, Inc. "Spirit of Sunset: Welcome to Key West Mallory Square Program, Summer Souvenir Edition." May 20, 1986.

Key West Planning Department. "The Impact of Hotels Redeveloping and Converting to Residential Uses in Key West." Presented to the City Commission, August 2, 2005.

Key West Salt Ponds Committee (KWSPC). "The Key West Salt Ponds and Development." November 1, 1983.

King, Gregory. *The Conch That Roared*. Lexington, Ky.: Weston and Wright Publishing Company, 1997.

Knight, Edward B. "Norberg Thompson." *Florida Keys Sea Heritage Journal* 8, no. 1 (Fall 1997): 1, 10–13.

Knowles, Thomas Neil. *Category 5: The 1935 Labor Day Hurricane*. Gainesville: University Press of Florida, 2009.

KPMG Peat Marwick LLP Real Estate, Mortgage and Hospitality Consulting, Bermello, Ajamil, Partners, Inc. "Key West Base Reuse Plan: Economic and Market Analysis of Selected Opportunities and Uses." July 7, 1997. Draft for review.

Krahulik, Karen Christel. *Provincetown: From Pilgrim Landing to Gay Resort*. New York: New York University Press, 2005.

Kreloff, Martin. "Key West–The Last Resort." *Alive*, July 1977: 4, 6–7.

Kuralt, Charles. *Charles Kuralt's America*. New York: G. P. Putnam's Sons, 1995.

"La Semana Alegre." February 23–29, 1936. Available in WPA/FERA files, Florida History room, Key West Public Library.

Langello, Charles J. U.S.N., "Log of the President's Vacation Trip to Key West, Florida, 17–23 November 1946." Available in the Florida History room of the Key West Public Library.

Langley, Wright. "City Electric System: Bringing Power to the People for 50 years, 1943–1993." N.p, n.d., report commissioned by the utility from Wright Langley.

Langley, Wright, and Joan Langley. *Key West: Images of the Past*. Key West: Christopher C. Belland and Edwin O. Swift, III, 1982.

———. *Key West and The Spanish-American War*. Key West: Langley Press, Inc., 1998.

Larson, Karen A. "City of Key West Worker Satisfaction Survey Final Report." Submitted to Mayor Morgan McPherson and City Commission, et al., December 17, 2007.

Lester, Donald Gordon. "Key West During the Civil War." Master's thesis, University of Miami, 1949.

Lew, Alan A., C. Michael Hall, and Alan M. Williams, eds. *A Companion to Tourism*. Malden, Mass.: Blackwell, 2004.

Little, Edward J. Jr. "The Origins of a Sports Fishing Mecca: Key West's Legendary Charterboat Row." *Florida Keys Sea Heritage Journal* 8, no. 4 (Summer 1998): 4–5.

———. "An Overview of the Evolution of the Historic Seaport at Key West Bight." *Florida Keys Sea Heritage Journal* 10, no. 3 (Spring 2000): 3–7, 15.

Long, Durward. "Key West and the New Deal, 1934–1936." *Florida Historical Quarterly* 46 (January 1968): 209–18.

———. "Workers on Relief, 1934–1938, in Key West." *Tequesta* 28 (1968): 53–61.

Lovering, Frank W. *Reporter in Paradise*. Key West: Key West Sunprint, Inc., 1934.

Lurie, Alison. *Familiar Spirits: A Memoir of James Merrill and David Jackson*. New York: Penguin Books, 2001.

Lyon, Eugene. *The Search for the Atocha*. New York: Harper and Row, 1979.

MacCannell, Dean. *The Tourist: A New Theory of the Leisure Class*. Berkeley: University of California Press, 1999.

Malcom, Corey. "Turtle Industry in Key West." *Florida Keys Sea Heritage Journal* 19, no. 3 (Spring 2009): 1, 3–15.

Manucy, Albert C., and Mary K. Falk. "A Survey Showing the Economic Status of Key West, Florida from August 1933 through August 1935." WPA Proj. 194, Fla., December 1935, Key West, Florida. Available in WPA/FERA file in Florida History room, Key West Public Library.

Manucy, Albert C., and Joe Hale. "Three Key West Winter Seasons, 1934–1936." Tourist and Traffic Statistics from Files of Florida Works Progress Administration, District Five, Project 194. Key West: April 1936. Available in University of Florida Special Collections, P. K. Yonge Library of Florida History.

"Mark Twain in Key West." *Florida Keys Sea Heritage Journal* 13, no. 2 (Winter 2002–03): 1, 12–15.

Marvin, William. *A Treatise on the Law of Wreck and Salvage*. Boston: Little, Brown and Company, 1858.

Martin, Jay. *The Education of John Dewey: A Biography*. New York: Columbia University Press, 2002.

Mayo, Nathan. *The Fifth Census of the State of Florida Taken in the Year 1925*. Tallahassee, Fla.: Appleyard, 1925.

———. *The Sixth Census of the State of Florida 1935*. N.p., 1935.

McDonald, Bridget. "The Lincoln Theater: Gone and Nearly Forgotten." In *Meet Me at the Tropic*. Key West Film Society, N.d.

McIver, Stuart B. *Hemingway's Key West*. Sarasota, Fla.: Pineapple Press, 1993.

McRae, W. A. *The Fourth Census of the State of Florida Taken in the Year 1915*. Tallahassee, Fla.: T. J. Appleyard, State Printer, 1925.

Meethan, Kevin. *Tourism in Global Society: Place, Culture, Consumption*. New York: Palgrave, 2001.

Meinig, D. W. *The Shaping of America: A Geographical Perspective on 500 Years of History*. Vol. 2, *Continental America 1800–1867*. New Haven: Yale University Press, 1993.

Metropolitan Center of Florida International University. "Monroe County, Florida, Affordable Housing Needs Assessment." Prepared for The Partnership for Community Housing and The Rodel Foundation of Key West, 2007.

Meyers, Jeffrey. *Hemingway: A Biography*. New York: Harper and Row, 1985.

Mickler, J. R. "Key West in World War II: A History of the Naval Station and Naval Operating Base." N.p., 1945. Available in the Florida History room of the Key West Public Library.

Milanich, Jerald T. *Florida Indians and the Invasion from Europe*. Gainesville: University Press of Florida, 1995.

Miller, Neil. *In Search of Gay America: Women and Men in a Time of Change*. New York: The Atlantic Monthly Press, 1989.

Millier, Brett C. *Elizabeth Bishop: Life and the Memory of It*. Berkeley: University of California Press, 1993.

Miller, Linda Patterson, ed. *Letters from the Lost Generation: Gerald and Sara Murphy and Friends*. New Brunswick: Rutgers University Press, 1991.

Milo Smith + Associates, Inc. "Research and Analysis." Part 1 of a comprehensive planning report for the City of Key West, Florida, for the Florida Development Commission, Tallahassee, Florida, April 20, 1967.

———. "Reuse Plan Surplus Naval Properties." Key West Florida, June 1975.

Moorehead, Caroline. *Gellhorn: A Twentieth-Century Life*. New York: Henry Holt and Company, 2003.

———, ed. *The Letters of Martha Gellhorn*. London: Chatto and Windus, 2006.

Mormino, Gary. *Land of Sunshine, State of Dreams: A Social History of Modern Florida*. Gainesville: University Press of Florida, 2005.

Morris, Jan. *Coast to Coast: A Journey across 1950s America*. San Francisco: Travelers' Tales, 2002.

Mueller, Edward A. *Steamships of the Two Henrys: Being An Account of the Maritime Activities of Henry Morrison Flagler and Henry Bradley Plant*. DeLeon Springs, Fla.: E. O. Painter Printing Co., 1996.

Muller, Dieter, K. "Mobility, Tourism, and Second Homes." In *A Companion to Tourism*, edited by Alan A. Lew, C. Michael Hall, and Allan M. Williams, 387–98. Malden, Mass.: Blackwell, 2004.

Munroe, Kirk. "Sponge and Spongers of the Florida Reef." In *Tales of Old Florida*, edited by Frank Oppel and Tony Meisel, 29–39. Secaucus, N.J.: Castle, 1987.

National Coalition for the Homeless, "Illegal to Be Homeless 2004 Report." http://www.nationalhomeless.org. Last accessed August 3, 2008.

"Naval Air Station, Key West in World War One." *Florida Keys Sea Heritage Journal* 9, no. 4 (Summer 1999): 1, 13–15.

Nolan, Terence H., William Carl Shiver, and L. Scott Nidy. "Cultural Resource Survey of Key West." Miscellaneous Project Report Series No. 48. N.p.: Bureau of Historic Sites and Properties Division of Archives, History and Records Management, Department of State of the State of Florida, May 1979. Available in the Florida History room of the Key West Public Library.

Office of Economic Adjustment (OEA), Office of the Assistant Secretary of Defense. "Report of Community Visit to Key West, Florida." The Pentagon: Washington D.C., November 1972. Available in the Florida History room of the Key West Public Library.

Ogle, Maureen. *Key West: History of An Island of Dreams*. Gainesville: University Press of Florida, 2003.

Old Island Restoration Foundation and The City of Key West, Fla. (OIRF). Dedication of Old Mallory Square and the Unveiling of The Porter Anti-Pirate Marker, February 1, 1963, Old Mallory Square, 4 p.m. Available in the Florida History room of the Key West Public Library.

Ownby, Ted. "Nobody Knows the Troubles I've Seen, but Does Anybody Want to Hear about Them When They're on Vacation." In *Southern Journeys: Tourism, History, and Culture in the Modern South*, edited by Richard D. Starnes, 240–49. Tuscaloosa: University of Alabama Press, 2003.

Paine, Ralph D. "Over the Florida Keys by Rail." In *Tales of Old Florida*, edited by Frank Oppel and Tony Meisel, 405–14. Secaucus, N.J.: Castle, 1987.

Pais, Joseph G. "The Battleship *Maine*: A Key West Legacy." *Florida Keys Sea Heritage Journal* 8, no. 2 (Winter 1997/98): 1, 10–14.

Patrick, Rember W, ed. "William Adee Whitehead's Description of Key West." *Tequesta* 12 (1952): 61–73.

Pattullo, Polly. "Sailing into the Sunset." In *Tourists and Tourism: A Reader*, edited by Sharon Bohn Gmelch, 339–58. Long Grove, Ill.: Waveland Press, Inc., 2004.

Pearsall, Bill. "New Key West: A Transition from Bustling Navy Town to Thriving Cruising Center Is in the Works." *Yachting* (November 1974): 67, 122–124.

Plantec Corporation. "Affordable Housing Study." Prepared for Affordable Housing Study Committee, Key West. Jacksonville, Florida, October 1987.

Plath, James, and Frank Simons. *Remembering Ernest Hemingway*. Key West: The Ketch and Yawl Press, 1999.

Poyo, Gerald E. "Cuban Revolutionaries and Monroe County Reconstruction Politics, 1868–1876." *Florida Historical Quarterly* 55, no. 4 (April 1977): 407–22.

———. "Key West and the Cuban Ten Years War." *Florida Historical Quarterly* 57, no. 3 (January 1979): 289–307.

———. "Cuban Patriots in Key West, 1878–1886: Guardians at the Separatist Ideal." *Florida Historical Quarterly* 61, no. 1 (July 1982): 20–36.

Prentice, Richard. "Revisiting 'Heritage': A Key Sector of the (then) "New" Tourism'– Out with the 'New' and Out With 'Heritage'?" In *Classic Reviews in Tourism*, edited by Chris Cooper, 164–91. Buffalo: Channel View Publications, 2003.

———. "Tourist Motivation and Typologies." In *A Companion to Tourism*, edited by Alan A. Lew, C. Michael Hall, and Allan M. Williams, 261–79. Malden, Mass.: Blackwell, 2004.

Proby, Kathryn Hall. *Audubon in Florida*. Coral Cables: University of Miami Press, 1974.

Rampersad, Arnold. *Ralph Ellison*. New York: Alfred A. Knopf, 2007.

Raymer, Dorothy. *Key West Collection*. Key West: The Ketch and Yawl Press, 1999.

———. "The Bad Old Days." In *Key West Collection*, by Dorothy Raymer, 3–8. Key West: The Ketch and Yawl Press, 1999.

Reilly, Benjamin. *Tropical Surge: A History of Ambition and Disaster on the Florida Shore*. Sarasota, Fla.: Pineapple Press, Inc., 2005.

Reynolds, Michael. *Hemingway: The American Homecoming*. Malden, Mass.: Blackwell, 1992.

———. *Hemingway: The 1930s*. New York: W. W. Norton and Company, 1997.

Rhodes, Harrison, and Mary Wolfe Dumont. *A Guide to Florida for Tourists, Sportsmen and Settlers*. New York: Dodd, Mead and Company, 1912.

Richardson, Joan. *Wallace Stevens: The Later Years, 1923–1955*. New York: William Morrow, 1988.

Rigdon, William M., Lieut-Comdr., U.S.N., comp. "Log of President Truman's Trip to Puerto Rico, The Virgin Islands, Guantanamo Bay, Cuba, and Key West, Florida, 20 February 1948 to 5 March 1948." Available in the Florida History room of the Key West Public Library.

———. "Log of President Truman's Fifth Trip to Key West, Florida, November 7–21, 1948."

———. "Log of President Truman's 9th Visit to Key West, Florida, and Ft. Jefferson National Monument, 2–22 March 1951." Available in the Florida History room of the Key West Public Library.

Ritzer, George. *Enchanting a Disenchanted World*. 2nd ed. Thousand Oaks, Calif.: Pine Forge Press, 2005.

Ritzer, George, and Allan Liska. "'McDisneyization' and 'Post-Tourism': Complementary Perspectives on Contemporary Tourism." In *Touring Cultures: Transformations of Travel and Theory*, edited by C. Rojek and J. Urry, 96–109. New York: Routledge, 1997.

Rivers, Larry E., and Cantor Brown Jr. "African Americans in South Florida: A Home and a Haven for Reconstruction-era Leaders." *Tequesta* 56 (1996): 5–23.

Roach, Katharine. "Promoting Paradise: 25 Years of Keeping Key West in the News." *Key Wester* 3, no. 11 (September 2005): 24–27.

Rogak, Lisa. *A Boy Named Shel: The Life and Times of Shel Silverstein*. New York: Thomas Dunne Books, St. Martin's Press, 2007.

Rojek, Chris. *Ways of Escape: Modern Transformations in Leisure and Travel*. London: The MacMillan Press Ltd., 1993.

———. *Leisure Theory: Principles and Practice*. New York: Palgrave Macmillan, 2005.

Rojek, Chris, and John Urry, eds. *Touring Cultures: Transformations of Travel and Theory.* New York: Routledge, 1997.

Rojek, Chris, and John Urry. "Transformations of Travel and Theory." In *Touring Cultures: Transformations of Travel and Theory*, edited by Chris Rojek and John Urry, 1–19. New York: Routledge, 1997.

Ronning, C. Neale. *José Martí and the Émigré Colony in Key West: Leadership and State Formation.* New York: Praeger, 1990.

Roth, Clayton Dale Jr. "150 Years of Defense Activity in Key West, 1820–1970." *Tequesta* 30 (1970): 33–51.

———. "The Military Utilization of Key West and the Dry Tortugas from 1822–1900." Master's thesis, University of Miami, 1970.

Rothman, Hal K. *Devil's Bargains: Tourism in the Twentieth-Century American West.* Lawrence: University Press of Kansas, 1998.

———. *Neon Metropolis: How Las Vegas Started the Twenty-First Century.* New York: Routledge, 2002.

Rupp, Leila J., and Verta Taylor. *Drag Queens at the 801 Cabaret.* Chicago: University of Chicago Press, 2003.

Ryan, Thomas. *The Parrot Head Companion: An Insider's Guide to Jimmy Buffett.* Secaucus, N.J.: Carol Publishing Group, 1998.

Sawyer, Harry, Sr. *Only In Key West: A Humorous Reference Guide to Monroe County Politics.* Key West: Productions by Janet Griffith, 1997.

Sawyer, Norma Jean, and LaVerne Wells-Bowie. *Key West.* Charleston, S.C.: Arcadia Publishing, 2002.

Scandura, Jani. *Down in the Dumps: Place, Modernity, American Depression.* Durham: Duke University Press, 2008.

Schittone, Joseph. "Tourism vs. Commercial Fishers: Development and Changing Use of Key West and Stock Island, Florida." *Ocean and Coastal Management* 44 (2001): 15–37.

Schmida, Terry. *True Crime Stories of Key West and the Florida Keys.* N.p, 2006.

———. *True Crime Stories of Key West and the Florida Keys*, Vol. 2. Key West: Key West Crook Books, 2008.

Schroeder, William C. "Fisheries of Key West and the Clam Industry of Southern Florida." Bureau of Fisheries Document No. 962, Washington, D.C.: Government Printing Office, 1924.

Scott, Phil. *Hemingway's Hurricane: The Great Florida Keys Storm of 1935.* New York: McGraw Hill, 2006.

Sears, John F. *Sacred Places: American Tourist Attractions in the Nineteenth Century.* New York: Oxford University Press, 1989.

Sharp, Elaine B. *Morality Politics in American Cities.* Lawrence: University Press of Kansas, 2005.

Shaughnessy, Carol. *Sloppy Joe's: The Tradition Continues.* Key West: The Market Share Company, n.d.

Shaw, Gareth, and Allan W. Williams. *Critical Issues in Tourism: A Geographical Perspective.* 2nd ed. Malden, Mass.: Blackwell, 2002.

Sherrill, Chris, and Roger Aiello. *Key West: The Last Resort.* Key West: Key West Book and Card Company, 1981.

The Shorter Oxford English Dictionary on Historical Principles. Prepared by William Little. Volume 1 A–Me. London: George Newnes Limited, 1933.

Simons, David, and Thomas Withington. *The History of Flight: From Aviator Pioneers to Space Exploration.* New York: Barnes and Noble Books, 2004.

Skidmore, Thomas E. "Cubans by Choice: Carlos Manuel de Céspedes and José Martí." In *Imagining a Free Cuba: Carlos Manuel De Céspedes and José Martí,* edited by Jose Armor Y. Vazquez, 1–12, Occasional Paper #24. Providence, R.I.: The Thomas J. Watson Jr., Institute for International Studies, Brown University, 1996.

Smith, Dewitt C. III. "Among Touram: Community Study of Key West, Florida, a Small City at the Marginal Heart of American Culture." PhD diss., University of Chicago, 1998.

Smith, Mark A. "Engineering Slavery: The U.S. Army Corps of Engineers and Slavery at Key West." *The Florida Historical Quarterly* 86, no. 4 (Spring 2008): 498–526.

Snead, Chas. D. "Florida Overseas Highway: No Name Key To Lower Matecumbe, Monroe County, Florida." N.d., circa December 1929. Available in the Florida History room of the Key West Public Library.

Souther, J. Mark. "Making 'America's Most Interesting City': Tourism and the Construction of Cultural Image in New Orleans, 1940–1984." In *Southern Journeys: Tourism, History, and Culture in the Modern South,* edited by Richard D. Starnes, 114–37. Tuscaloosa: University of Alabama Press, 2003.

———. *New Orleans on Parade.* Baton Rouge: Louisiana State University Press, 2006.

Standiford, Les. *Last Train to Paradise: Henry Flagler and the Spectacular Rise and Fall of the Railroad that Crossed an Ocean.* New York: Three Rivers Press, 2002.

Starnes, Richard D., ed. *Southern Journeys: Tourism, History, and Culture in the Modern South.* Tuscaloosa: University of Alabama Press, 2003.

Stebbins, Consuelo E. "1885 Schedule of the Florida State Census for Key West, Fla., Monroe County." October 29, 2002. Available in the Florida History room of the Key West Public Library.

———. *City of Intrigue, Nest of Revolution: A Documentary History of Key West in the Nineteenth Century.* Gainesville: University Press of Florida, 2007.

———. "The Insurgents of Key West and the Expedition of 1895." *Florida Keys Sea Heritage Journal* 15, no. 1 (Fall 2004): 1, 10–15.

Stevens, Holly, ed. *Letters of Wallace Stevens.* New York: Alfred A. Knopf, 1966.

Stronge, William B. *The Sunshine Economy: An Economic History of Florida since the Civil War.* Gainesville: University Press of Florida, 2008.

Stuart, John A., and John F. Stack Jr., eds. *The New Deal in South Florida: Design, Policy, and Community Building.* Gainesville: University Press of Florida, 2008.

Tarracino, Captain Tony, and Brad Manard. *Life Lessons of a Legend.* N.p., 2008.

Taylor, Nick. *American-Made: The Enduring Legacy of the WPA; When FDR Put the Nation to Work.* New York: Bantam Books, 2008.

Terhorst, Peter, Jacques van de Ven, and Leon Deben. "Amsterdam: It's All in the Mix." In *Cities and Visitors,* ed. Lily M. Hoffman, Susan S. Fainstein, and Dennis R. Judd, 75–90. Malden, Mass.: Blackwell, 2001.

Thomas J. Murray and Associates, Inc. "The Impacts of the Cruise Ship Industry on the Quality of Life in Key West." Gloucester Point, Va.: Printed by author, April 8, 2005.

Thompson, Lawrance, ed. *Selected Letters of Robert Frost*. New York: Lawrance Thompson and Holt, Rinehart and Winston, Inc., 1964.

Traub, James. *The Devil's Playground: A Century of Pleasure and Profit in Times Square*. New York: Random House, 2004.

Tucker, Jeffrey, and Wright Langley. "Florida's Keys: Anguish in Paradise." *Florida Trend* 19, no. 1 (May 1976): 28–38.

Tucker, Scott. "Key West, Florida." In *Hometowns: Gay Men Write About Where They Belong*, edited by John Preston, 289–301. New York: Penguin Books, 1991.

Urry, John. *The Tourist Gaze*. 2nd ed. Thousand Oaks: Sage Publications, 2002.

URS. "Key West Historic Resources Survey Monroe County, Florida." Gaithersburg, Maryland: URS Corporation, Inc., September 30, 2004.

U.S. Bureau of the Census. American FactFinder. Geography Quick Report, Key West, Fla., data based on 1997 Economic Census.

———. *Census of Population: 1960*. Vol. 1, "Characteristics of the Population." Washington, D.C.: U.S. Government Printing Office, 1961.

———. *County and City Data Book 1962*. Washington, D.C.: U.S. Government Printing Office, 1962.

———. *1970 Census of Population*. Vol. 1., "Characteristics of the Population." Washington, D.C.: U.S. Government Printing Office, 1973.

———. *County and City Data Book 1972*. Washington, D.C.: U.S. Government Printing Office, 1973.

Viele, John. *The Florida Keys*. Vol. 3, *The Wreckers*. Sarasota, Fla.: Pineapple Press, Inc., 2001.

———. "Lt. Perry and the US Schooner Shark in Pirate Waters." *Florida Keys Sea Heritage Journal* 17, no. 3 (Spring 2007): 1, 12–15.

"Visit to Key West in 1884." *Florida Keys Sea Heritage Journal* 11, no. 4 (Summer 2001): 4–11, 15.

Warner, David. "Key West Writers." *Cimarron Review* (October 1982): 5–11.

Wasserstrom, Jeffrey N. *China's Brave New World—And Other Tales for Global Times*. Bloomington: Indiana University Press, 2007.

Webster's New International Dictionary of the English Language. 2nd ed. Springfield, Mass.: G. and C. Merriam Company Publishers, 1949.

Wells, Sharon. *Forgotten Legacy: Blacks in Nineteenth Century Key West*. Key West: Historic Key West Preservation Board, 1982.

Wenner, Jann S., and Corey Seymour. *Gonzo: The Life of Hunter S. Thompson; An Oral Biography*. New York: Little, Brown and Company, 2007.

Westfall, Loy Glenn. *Key West: Cigar City, USA*. N.p.: Printed by author, 1997.

White, Brooks. "The Selling of the Small-Town Commission: An Analysis of the Key West, Fla. City Elections, An Elections Yearbook for 1985." Key West: Printed by author, 1985. Available in the Florida History room of the Key West Public Library.

White, Edmund. *States of Desire: Travels in Gay America*. London: Picador, 1980.

White, Louise. *Louise White Shows You Key West: Guide to an Enchanting City*. St. Petersburg, Fla.: Great Outdoors Publishing Co., 1965.

White, Louise V., and Nora K. Smiley. *History of Key West: Today and Yesterday*. St. Petersburg, Fla.: Great Outdoors Publishing Co., 1959.

White, William, ed. *By-Line: Ernest Hemingway; Selected Articles and Dispatches of Four Decades*. New York: Charles Scribner's Sons, 1967.

Williams, Alan M. "Toward a Political Economy of Tourism." In *A Companion to Tourism*, edited by Alan A. Lew, C. Michael Hall, and Alan M. Williams, 61–73. Malden, Mass.: Blackwell, 2004.

Williams, Donnie. *Key West Conch Talk and Nicknames*. N.p.: Don Williams "Capture The Moments Video and Books," 2006.

Williams, Joy. *The Florida Keys: A History and Guide*. 10th ed. New York: Random House, 2003.

Williams, Tennessee. *Memoirs*. Sewanee, Tenn.: The University of the South, 1972.

Willis, J. A., comp. *The New and Greater Key West Florida Told in Picture and Story*. Key West: J. A. Willis, 1914. Reprint, N.p., 1990.

Willoughby, Malcolm. *Rum War at Sea*. Washington, D.C.: Government Printing Office, 1964.

Windhorn, Stan, and Wright Langley. *Yesterday's Key West*. Miami: E. A. Seemann Publishing, Inc., 1973.

Wisniewski, Anna. "Dean Walters Pioneering Keys' Opera." *Key Wester* 4, no. 1 (November 2005): 20–23.

Witzell, W. N. "The Origin, Evolution, and Demise of the U.S. Sea Turtle Fisheries." *Florida Keys Sea Heritage Journal* 7, no. 3 (Spring 1997): 1, 4–7, 10–15.

———. "The Origin of the Florida Sponge Fishery." *Florida Keys Sea Heritage Journal* 9, no. 3 (Spring 1999): 1, 10–13.

Wolfe, Susan J. "The Poor Are Different from You and Me." In *Key West Hemingway: A Reassessment*, ed. Kirk Curnutt and Gail D. Sinclair, 158–71. Gainesville: University Press of Florida, 2009.

Wolz, Robert, and Barbara Hayo. *The Legacy of the Harry S. Truman Little White House, Key West*. Key West: Historic Tours of America, Inc., 2004.

Writers' Program of the Work Projects Administration in the State of Florida. *A Guide to Key West*. Revised Second Edition. New York: Hastings House, 1949.

Zahav, Jonathan. "The Key West Jewish Community: One Hundred Years." Key West: Printed by author, 1987. Available in the Florida History room of the Key West Public Library.

Zukin, Sharon. *Loft Living*. Baltimore: The John Hopkins University Press, 1982.

———. "Gentrification: Culture and Capital in the Urban Core." *Annual Review of Sociology* 13(1987): 129–47.

———. *The Culture of Cities*. Cambridge, Mass.: Blackwell, 1995.

———. *Naked City: The Death and Life of Authentic Urban Places*. New York: Oxford University Press, 2010.

INDEX

Abbe court case, 276

Adams, Maitland, 82, 84

Adult uses, 254–57; Christy Sweets', 255–56, 258; Garden of Eden, 255; Key West Scrub Club, 255–56; nudity, 148, 265–66; Teaser's, 256

Affordable housing, 230, 245, 262, 263; in Bahama Village, 232; and Bayview Project, 235–36; and Growth Management Ordinance (GMO), 234–36; and liveaboards, 272; in New Town, 93; and Monroe County Land Authority, 200; and One Human Family, 274–79; provided by military, 82; and ROGO, 242–44; in Truman Annex, 241–42; in twentieth-first century, need for, 277–78. *See also* Key West Housing Authority

African Americans, 61; in Bahama Village, 230–32; in "colored town," 55; displacement by Navy, 61, 63; and elected office, 24, 170; employment discrimination against, 80–81; integration of, 80; and politics, 61, 70; in public housing, 80; and segregation,

23, 80; share of Key West's population, 17, 23, 32, 80; and slavery, 17; and Sloppy Joe's, 318n35; and tourism, 231; and urban renewal, 107. *See also* African Cemetery Memorial; Goombay Festival

African Cemetery Memorial, 17

Aguero, Charles, 152

AIDS, 164–65, 171, 186, 269; AIDS Help, 164–65, 180, 183; AIDS Memorial, 165

Albury, Willard, 51, 54

Alfonso, Sebrina Maria, 261

Allen, Joe, 178

Amsterdam, Bruce, 182

Anderson, Denis, 237

Annual Key West Songwriters' Festival, 187–88

Anthony, Jeremy, 245, 269

Anti-Hampton ethos, 4, 10, 260, 262

Antoniadis, Yiannis, 109

Aqua nightclub, 4, 162; Inga, 162

Architectural heritage, 24–25, 103. *See also* Historic District

Area of Critical State Concern (ACSC), 202–3, 207, 332n12

Argonaut Development Group, 208

Art galleries, 9, 123, 148, 228, 261; Artists Unlimited, 92, 123; Caroline Lowe House, 45–46; dePoo's Island Gallery, 92; East Martello Gallery, 112, 123, 148, 329n45; in East Martello Tower and West Martello Tower, 92; Gallery on Greene, 261; Gingerbread Square Gallery, 123, 228, 166; Key West Art Center, 105–6, 123; Lucky Street Gallery, 261

Ashley, Elizabeth, 126

Atocha. See Nuestra Señora de Atocha

Audubon, John James, 17, 18, 102; Audubon House, 102

Avael, Julio, 212, 254

Avila, Louis, 51

Bahama Conch Community Land Trust, 232

Bahama Village, 230, 231–32, 257

Bahamians, 6, 16, 19, 21, 22, 23, 24, 25, 77

Balbontin, Joe, 169, 203, 204, 239

Ball, Ed, 111

Banks, 313n6. *See also* First National Bank

Barbour, George, 28

Barnes, Michael, 217

Baron, Elliot, 212

Baron, Jack, 92

Barron, Clarence W., 39

Bars and restaurants: The Affair, 161; Anabek's Bar, 161; Bourbon Street Pub, 162, 184; Bull & Whistle, 188; Café 416, 161; Captain Tony's Saloon, 122, 160, 204, 287; Chart Room Bar, 121, 126, 143, 155; Claire's, 161; Delmonico's, 46, 87, 161, 170–71; El Cacique, 120–21; Full Moon Saloon, 121, 126; Garden of Eden, 255; Green Parrot, 188, 237; Hog's Breath Saloon, 188; Howie's Lounge, 160; John Brown's Bar, 123; La Te Da, 162, 163, 256; Logan's Lobster House, 90; Louie's Backyard, 121; Margaritaville restaurant, 188; Mascot Lounge, 83; Midget bar, 83; Monster bar, 144, 160, 161, 188; Old Anchor Inn, 121, 187; The Oldest Bar, 108, 122; One Saloon, 162; Pena's Garden of Roses, 47, 48; Queen's Table restaurant, 320n22; Ramonin's, 46; Red Doors Inn, 83; Sands Restaurant & Cocktail Lounge, 202; Sloppy Joe's, 36, 57–60, 108, 122, 185, 287; Twigg Bar, 161; West Key Bar, 83; West Indies Lounge, 320n22

Bauer, Charlie, 187, 188

Bayview housing project, 235–36. *See also* Affordable housing

Bayview Park, 184

Beattie, Ann, 186

Beaver, Dennis, 187, 228

Belland, Christopher, 142, 189, 190. *See also* Historic Tours of America (HTA); Old Town Key West Development

Belushi, John, 127

Berg, Donald, 151–52

Berger, Meyers, 64

Bernstein, Benjamin, 271

Bernstein, Leonard, 6, 160

Bernstein, Roger, 271

Beruldsen, Diane, 183, 184

Bethel, Harry, 215, 272, 273, 279

Big Pine Key, 52, 87, 119

Bird, Morgan, 108, 112

Bishop, Elizabeth, 6, 7, 60–61, 92

Bitch Sisters, 163

Bitner, Dennis, 166, 178, 328n13

Blackstone Group, 3, 266

Blum, Gary, 235

Blume, Judy, 186

Board of Adjustment (BOA), 243

Board of County Commissioners (BOCC), 41, 167, 168, 269, 309n4; abdication of governing authority, 44; and domestic-partner ordinance, 173; and Key West Administration, 45; One Human Family motto, 268; and Overseas Highway, 39, 41; and tourism advertising, 54; and Tourist Development Council (TDC), 149–51, 175, 198, 201, 327n3, 331n4

Boca Chica Field, 62, 81, 98, 115

Boca Chica Naval Air Station. *See* Boca Chica Field

Boese, Ann, 171

Bohemian lifestyle, 10, 59, 90, 218, 286

Bolita, 36, 53, 54, 84–87, 117. *See also* Gambling

Bone Island Press, 171

Bootlegging, 12, 36

Borel, Joan, 208–9

Born, George, 140–41, 279

Botanical Gardens, 50, 329n45

Brackenbury, Rosalind, 250, 283

Braddock, Stephen, 282

Bradford, Judi, 261

Bridle Path, 49, 281

Brinnin, John Malcolm, 125
Brinton, David G., 26
Brixey, Del, 159–60, 163
Brothels, 30, 55, 112
Brown, Bobby, 116–17
Brown, Canter, Jr., 24
Brown, Roderick, 123
Browne, Jefferson, 19
Browning, Michael, 265
Brumgart, Rex, 101, 108, 112, 145, 196
Bryant, Anita: anti-gay campaign, 7
Bubba system, 79, 105, 167, 168
Buckner, Rita, 123
Budinger, Peyton, 262
Budinger, William, 262
Buffett, Jimmy, 6, 11, 144, 286; arrival in Key
   West, 120; and Captain Tony, 122, 204; and
   Key West lifestyle, 121; local performances
   by, 160, 208; A Pirate Looks at Fifty, 121;
   songs by, 120, 122, 187, 273; support for
   Salt Ponds, 208; and Hunter Thompson,
   127; and tourism in Key West, 187. See also
   Meeting of the Minds
Buffett, Laurie, 126
Burbank Realty Company, 42
Burgess, John, 228
Burton, Philip, 125
Butler, Bob, 208
Butler, Coffee, 78, 160

Cabeza, Manuel, 33
Cagnina, Sam, 83, 314n20
Camp, Jim, 162
Campbell, Betty, 164
Canary Islands, 19, 22, 33
Capote, Truman, 90, 125, 155
Captain Outrageous, 245
Caputo, Philip, 9
Carbonell, John, 84
Carbonell, Louis, 84
Carbonell, Ygnacio, 234
Caro, Tom, 87
Caroline Lowe House, 45–46, 102
Caroline Street, 8, 45–46, 60, 83, 90, 102. See
   also Key West Bight; Historic Seaport
Carper, Jean, 260
Carruthers, Heather, 270
Casamayor Raymond ("Tito"), 119
Castells, Manuel, 159
Cates, Emma, 170, 203, 204
Cates, Janet Hill, 119–20
Cates, Michael, 119–20

Cayo Hueso, 14; Cayo Hueso, Ltd., 143
Celebrate (newspaper), 263
Center for Marine Conservation, 213
Céspedes, Carlos Manuel de, 23
Chain stores, 3, 95, 228, 257–58, 288,
   338n24
Chambers, Esther, 111
Charest-Weinberg, Eric, 261
Charley Toppino & Sons, 94
Chavez, Buddy, 78
Chickens, 4, 258–60; ChickenFest, 259, 260
Christmas Tree Island, 240, 271–74
Ciardi, John, 124, 125
Ciardi, Judith, 124
Cigar industry, 6, 16, 22, 23, 25, 27–28, 31, 33.
   See also Cuban population
Cisterns, 27, 63, 108, 149
City Electric Company, 87–88
City Electric System (CES), 80, 115, 176
City of Key West, 303n13, 303n23, 312–13n2
CityView Trolley Tours of Key West, 190
Civil War, 15–16, 303n12; Civil War Heritage
   Days Festival, 189
Civil Works Administration (CWA), 47, 308n2
Clark, Phil, 120
Club Bath, 166
Club Mandible, 127
Club Miramar, 47
Cock fighting, 30, 36, 57, 86, 258
Cocks, Catherine, 182
Code enforcement, 203, 253, 254–55
Colored town, 55, 107, 230. See also Bahama
   Village; Jungle town; Urban renewal
Commercial Club, 40
Commercial fishing, 8, 21, 62, 82, 115–16,
   209–11. See also Shrimp industry; Sponge
   industry; Turtle industry
Committee for a Livable Old Town, 250, 251
Community for a Better Key West, 251
Community Foundation of the Florida Keys,
   251, 282–83
Comparsas, 7, 78
ConAgra, 211
Conch Grove Compound, 126
Conch Republic, 1, 176–79
Conchs, 2, 6, 8, 10, 201; Elizabeth Bishop's
   view of, 61; and "bubba" system, 79, 167;
   and civic organizations, 79; and "Conch
   Town," 107; departure from Key West,
   10–11, 114, 154–55, 199, 232–33, 263,
   283–84; different meanings of, 304n25;
   employment for, 79; and gambling, 51, 55,

58; and gentrification, 154–55, 168; music and dance, importance of, 78; as name for Key Wester, 21; as name for shellfish, 21; and New Town development, 93–94; nicknames of, 78

Conch Tour Train, 101, 102, 112, 127, 148, 190, 194, 212, 250, 323n33

Condominiums, 9, 10, 204; condo hotels, 10, 263–66, 279, 289; conflicts over high rises, 152–53; conversions to, 263, 275, 279, 283, 289; homesteads, 275; La Brisa, 207; popularity in Florida, 324n38; prices of, 274, 290; in SeaSide, 208

Conkle, Bill, 148, 163

Conley, Vincent, 93

Convention center, 266, 289

Convent of Mary Immaculate, 104

Cooper, Dennis, 254, 271–72, 273. See also *Key West The Newspaper*

Copa, The, 161, 162, 164, 169

Corcoran, Tom, 83, 155

Corruption, 77, 84, 87–89, 94, 119. *See also* Drug smuggling

Cost of living, 10, 78, 154–55, 156, 229, 230, 232–33, 277–79, 283–84

County commission. *See* Board of County Commissioners (BOCC)

Covington, Jerome, 165

Cox, Otha, 326n40

Crane, Louise, 60

Crespo, Artemio, 87, 117

Cruise ships, 109, 192–93, 211–13, 248, 298, 299. *See also* Mallory Square; Outer Mole dock; Pier B

Crusoe, Ed, 237

Cuba, 30, 41, 42, 49, 79, 174–75, 290–91. *See also* Cuban Missile Crisis; Cuban population

Cuban Club, 23, 51, 78, 86

Cuban Missile Crisis, 81, 99, 110, 111

Cuban population, 6; and cigar industry, 6, 22–23; civic organizations of, 23; and Cuban independence, 22–23, 50–51, 162; cultural influence of, 120–21; depicted in tourism advertising, 46; and El Grito de Baire, 50–51; and Gatoville, 123; and Hotel Monroe, 26; and Mariel boatlift, 174–75, 180; migration to Key West, 22–23; and national lottery, 54; neighborhoods of, 23, 123; and Noche Alegre, 103; and politics, 24; restaurants and coffee houses of, 120–21, 54; and strikes on WPA, 51; and tourism promotion, 35–36, 100; and travel to Cuba,

79. *See also* Cuban Club; Mariel boatlift; San Carlos Institute; Sanchez, Mario

Cudjoe Key, 88

Curry, Leslie, 34, 39

Curry, Roland, 33, 37

Curry, William, 25

Curry family, 25

Customs House, 25, 188, 240. *See also* Key West Museum of Art and History in the Custom House

Daniel, Bernice Dickson, 100

Dean, Bob, 273; Dean-Lopez Funeral Home, 273

DeFoor, J. Allison, II, 119

de Marsan, Marie, 108

Dennis, Margaret, 216

Dennis, Morgan, 216

Dent, John, 238–39

dePoo, Suzie, 92

Dewey, John, 60, 92, 100, 108, 312n47

Dillard, Annie, 186

Dimmick, Arthur B., 64

Dion, Fred J., 84

Disney. *See* Walt Disney World

Division Street: renamed Truman Avenue, 98

Dodez, Lee, 101, 121, 123, 166, 196

Dodge, Charles Richards, 27, 28

Domestic-partner ordinance, 172–73

Donghia, Angelo, 141, 144, 227

Dos Passos, John, 38, 58, 100

Dos Passos, Katy, 58

Douglass High School, 80

Dredge and fill, 21, 40, 94–95, 140, 207

Dredger's Key, 62. *See also* Sigsbee Park

Drug smuggling, 9, 116–20, 121, 153, 177, 335n17

Drury, Jay, 123

Dry Tortugas, 16, 210

Duck Tours Safari, 190

Duffy, Robert, 242

Dupepe, Clancy, 143

Duval Street, 3, 4, 7, 8–9; ambience in 1950s, 91; adult-use establishments on, 255–57; art galleries on, 92, 105, 123, 228, 261; chain stores on, 228, 257–58; code enforcement, 253–55; criticisms of, 200–201; cruise-ship traffic on, 212; Cuban restaurants on, 120–21; decline in business activity, 95; divergent evaluations of, 288; gambling establishments on, 84; Jewish-owned retail stores on, 23; movie theaters on, 80;

Duval Street—*continued*
planning issues about, 169; renovation of, 139, 141–42; transition of, 9. *See also* Aqua nightclub; Bars and restaurants; Caroline Lowe House; Comparsas; Copa, The; Cuban Club; Fast Buck Freddie's; Havana Madrid nightclub; Historic District; Key West Woman's Club; Oldest House; Old Town; Russell House; San Carlos Institute; Southernmost House; Trade Winds
Eagleton, Thomas, 163
East Martello Tower, 16, 92, 112, 148, 188
Eaton Street, 30, 141, 227
Ebensten, Hanns, 91
801 Cabaret, 184; 801 Girls, 162, 184; Destray, 162; Margo, 162; Sushi, 162
El Grito de Baire, 50–51
Ellis, Terry, 94
Ellison, Ralph, 125
England, George Allen, 37
Epoch, The, 161
Ethridge, David, 243

Falcone, Tony, 148, 163, 182
Fallon, Grace, 232
Fantasy Fest, 7, 8, 148–49, 163, 164, 169, 180–84, 187, 191, 231
Farto, Joseph ("Bum"), 116, 118
Fast Buck Freddie's, 148, 181
Faulkner, Henry, 92
Fausto's, 203
Federal Emergency Relief Administration (FERA), 44, 47, 49, 50, 51, 59, 308n2, 309–10n17, 310n18. *See also* Key West Administration (KWA); Stone, Julius, Jr.
Feger, Richard, 233
Feiner, Sam, 199
Fernandez, Louis ("Blackie"), 86
Ferrell, Rich, 265
Ferris, John, 88
Ferry service: between Key West and Fort Myers, 248
Feuer, Anne Hemingway, 185–86
Finkelstein, Marty, 160; Marty Finkelstein Center, 165
Fire Island, 167, 227
Fires, 22, 24, 102, 161
First National Bank, 40–41
Fisher, Mel, 121–22, 188–89, 239. See also *Nuestra Señora de Atocha*
Fitch, Marcia, 100
Flagler, Henry, 26, 29, 30, 33, 34, 39, 40

Flagler Station Train Historeum, 211
Fleeming, John W. C. (later Fleming), 15
Fleming Street, 30, 45, 79, 83, 160, 162, 163
Florida-Caribbean Cruise Association, 212
Florida Department of Community Affairs (DCA), 202–3, 243–44. *See also* Area of Critical State Concern (ACSC)
Florida Department of Environmental Protection, 218, 281, 324n36
Florida Department of Natural Resources, 202
Florida East Coast Car Ferry Company, 30
Florida East Coast Railway, 29, 33, 39, 49, 211
Florida East Coast Railway Steamship Company, 26
Florida Keys Aqueduct Authority, 152, 176, 321n5
Florida Keys Aqueduct Commission (FKAC), 63, 115
Florida Keys Community College, 123, 166, 260
Florida Keys Council of the Arts, 261
Florida Keys Land Trust, 209
Florida Keys Outreach Coalition, 281
Florida Magazine, 288
Florida Pollution Control Board, 140, 207
Florida State Road Department, 62
Fonda, Peter, 126, 155
Fontis, Frank, 109
Formica, Lawrence, 162
Fort Jefferson, 16, 17
Fort Village Apartments, 63, 80
Fort Zachary Taylor, 16–17, 27, 47, 54, 178, 189, 329n45. *See also* Civil War: Civil War Heritage Days Festival; Sculpture Key West
Founders Society, 165–66, 260
Frank, Bill, 210
Freeman, Billy, 118–19
Freeman, Shirley, 172
Friday, Nancy, 285, 318n42
Friends of Florida Trust Fund, 208
Front Street, 25, 57, 105–6, 108–9, 111, 123, 160, 163, 188, 239
Frost, Elinor, 59, 186
Frost, Robert, 59, 100, 186–87
Fuhriman, Scott, 163

Gabriel, Robert, 24
Galey, Harry, 45, 51
Gambling, 30, 36–37, 53–54, 55, 77, 82–87, 111, 117, 122, 258. *See also* Bolita; Cock fighting
Garrison Bight, 100, 144, 217, 310n19, 316n14
Gato, Eduardo, 22

Gato dormitory, 63
Gatoville, 123
Gautier, Jefferson Davis, 118
Gay and Lesbian Community Center, 165, 187, 269
Gay population, 7, 89, 160–65, 166–72, 183–84, 256–57, 269–70. *See also* Fantasy Fest; Gay and Lesbian Community Center; Heyman, Richard; Key West Business Guild; Lesbian population; Metropolitan Community Church (MCC)
Gay Pride Week, 184. *See also* PrideFest
Geiger, Captain John, 102
Gellhorn, Martha, 57–58, 59–60
Generica, 257–58. *See also* Chain stores
Gentrification, 10, 139–40, 154–55, 159, 230–32, 256, 260. *See also* Housing prices; Truman Annex
Gilfond, M. E., 49
Gilleran, Jim, 161–62
Globalization, 2, 3
Goehring, Wilhelmina. *See* Harvey, Wilhelmina
Golan, Abraham, 93, 95
Golan, Margo, 95, 149, 150, 175
Golan, Sam, 95
Golden, Jack, 49
Goombay Festival, 231
Gordon Ross and Friends, 164
Graham, Bob, 118, 178
Graham, Mary Lee, 145, 146, 167
Grant, Roy, 230, 231, 237
Green, Pat, 180
Greene, Pardon C., 15, 18–19
Greene Street, 57, 92, 102, 112, 122, 108
Greene Street Theatre, 123–24
Greenwich Village, 48, 58, 59, 114, 231, 262
Growth Management Ordinance (GMO) of 1986, 234–35, 236, 241–42, 243, 244. *See also* Affordable housing
Gucinski, Adolph, 123
Guesthouses, 3, 7, 139, 148, 159, 162, 163, 193, 201, 230, 243, 263, 270, 288, 325n14; Alexander's, 163; Island House, 162, 170; La Te Da, 162, 163, 256; Lighbourn Inn, 163; New Orleans House, 161; Pearl's Rainbow, 270; Rainbow House, 325n14; Tropical Inn Guest House, 228. *See also* Key West Business Guild
Guild Hall, 123
Gulf Oil Company, 36, 109

Habitat for Humanity, 278
Hall, Peter, 90
Halloran, George, 170, 203, 210, 239, 332n13
Hambright, Tom, 62
Hammond, E. A., 18
HARC. *See* Historic Architectural Review Commission (HARC)
Harden, Hunter, 84
Harris, Lou, 251
Harrison, Ben, 258
Harrison, Jim, 116, 127
Harry S. Truman Little White House, 189, 329n45
Harvey, C. B., 99, 167
Harvey, Wilhelmina, 164, 167, 177
Havana, 14, 18, 26, 33–34, 36, 37, 41, 42, 43, 56, 57, 79
Havana Madrid nightclub, 47, 83
Helberg, Charles, 93, 95
Hemingway, Ernest, 4, 6, 9, 11, 56, 57, 58, 60, 100, 184–86; Hemingway Days, 184–86; Hemingway House, 4, 57, 58, 100–101, 112, 311n34, 329n45. *See also* Gellhorn, Martha; Pfeiffer, Pauline
Hendrick, James, 207
Henry, Peter, 148
Henshall, James, 28
Heritage House Museum, 186–87
Herlihy, James Leo, 90–91, 92, 126
Herman, Jerry, 160
Hernandez, Johnny, 118
Hersey, Barbara, 124
Hersey, John, 124, 144, 186
Heyman, Richard, 123, 166–71, 204, 210, 235–36, 270
Hiaasen, Carl, 117, 200
Higgs, Ervin, 231–32
Higgs, Sandra, 198
Hillsborough Pride in Exile Days, 269–70
Hippies, 146–47, 194, 195, 240, 271, 323n23
Historic Architectural Review Commission (HARC), 228, 279
Historic District, 104, 140–41, 169, 228, 240, 245–46. *See also* Historic Architectural Review Commission (HARC); Historic preservation; Old Island Restoration Commission (OIRC); Old Island Restoration Foundation (OIRF)
Historic preservation, 102–3, 104, 140, 147, 228
Historic Seaport, 8, 211, 257. *See also* Key West Bight

Historic Tours of America (HTA), 119–20, 189–91, 194, 212, 278. *See also* Old Town Key West Development; Swift, Edwin, III
Homeless, 36, 271–72, 280–82
Homer, Winslow, 305n48
Homesteaded property, 274–75
Hopper, Dennis, 126
Horan, David Paul, 149, 150, 178
Hotels, motels, and resorts: Atlantic Shores Motel, 163, 264–66; Beachside Resort & Conference Center, 266; Cactus Terrace Motel, 258; Casa Marina, 3, 34–35, 37, 45, 59, 63, 81, 99, 110, 143, 202, 266; Duval House (Hotel Duval), 26; Grand Key Resort Hotel, 208; Hampton Inn, 266; Hilton Hotel/Resort and Marina, 193, 195, 213, 214, 241, 248; Holiday Inn, 95, 202, 266; Hotel Monroe, 26; Island City House Hotel, 30; Key Ambassador Motel, 95, 109; Key Wester Hotel, 95, 109; La Concha, 41, 45, 49, 81, 89, 99, 110, 111, 125, 202; LXR Luxury Resorts & Hotels, 266; Oversea Hotel, 30, 35, 45; Panama Hotel, 30; Parrot Key Hotel and Resort, 266; Reach Hotel, 203, 204, 266; Santa Maria Motel, 264, 320n22; Sea Shell Motel and International Youth Hostel, 265; Southernmost Hotels & Resorts, 265; Southernmost Motel, 152; Town House Motor Inn, 81, 111; Waldorf Astoria Hotels and Resorts, 3, 266; Westin Hotel/Key West Resort & Marina, 3, 195, 241, 248, 271; Wyndham Hotels, 203. *See also* Condominiums: condo hotels; Golan, Margo; Tourism
Houseboat Row, 206, 216–18
Housing prices, 78, 156, 227–32, 274–75, 289–90
Huckel, William, 153
Human Rights Ordinance, 172, 269
Hurricanes, 2, 16, 22, 24, 30, 49, 50, 52, 58, 125, 206, 218, 243, 248, 258, 289
Hyman, Sam, 110, 111

Ignatius, Lester M., 153
Iguana man, 145
Ilchuk, Peter, 166, 172
Immigration, 19, 23, 230, 269, 277–78. *See also* Bahamians; Cuban population; Jewish population; Mariel boatlift; Spaniards
Innkeepers Association, 263
Invalids: visiting Key West, 12, 13
Isaac Allerton (ship), 191

Island in the Sun, 207–8, 209
Island Opera Theatre, 261, 262, 289

Jacobson, Bud, 112
James, Manuel, 117, 153
Jameson, Colin, 111
Jewish population, 23
Johns Committee, 89
Johnson, Avery, 45
Johnson, Bill, 106
Johnson, Earle S., 112
Johnston, Teri, 270
Jones, John, 281
Jungle town, 55. *See also* Bahama Village; Colored town; Urban renewal

Kaufelt, David, 186
Kaufelt, Lynn, 186
Kee, Rose, 170
Kee Seashell Corner, 191
Kennedy, John F., 99
Kerr, Richard, 168, 169, 170
Key Largo, 39
Key West Administration (KWA), 45, 47, 49, 51, 53, 56, 58, 64. *See also* Federal Emergency Relief Administration (FERA); Stone, Julius, Jr.
Key West Aloe, 148, 163, 212
Key West and Lower Keys Development Corporation (Devcorp), 237
Key West Aquarium, 47, 101, 104, 105, 144, 189–90
Key West Art & Historical Society, 92, 101, 166, 187, 203
Key West Arts Project, 45
Key West Bight, 8, 21, 36, 108, 116, 122, 147–48, 209–11, 248, 257. *See also* Caroline Street; Historic Seaport
Key West Board of Trade, 29
Key West Business Guild, 164, 166, 172, 173, 175, 178, 181–82, 183, 214, 257
Key West Chamber of Commerce, 40, 61, 62, 79, 99; advertising booklets during 1930s, 54; advertising after World War II, 97; and African American employment, 80–81; booster of tourism during 1920s, 34–35, 41–42; and commercial fishing district, 210; and cruise ships, 211; and Fantasy Fest, 181–82; and Growth Management Ordinance (GMO), 235; "Salary and Survey Report," 278; and secession, 178; split within, 150, 175; and Sunset Celebration,

146; and Tourist Development Council (TDC), 198

Key West Citizen, 35, 40, 100; and affordable housing, 235, 279; and bolita, 86–87; and Christmas Tree Island, 272; and city codes, 254; and cruise ships, 109; and Fantasy Fest, 182; and future relations with Cuba, 291; and historic preservation, 103, 104–5; and hoboes, 36; and Meacham's project, 41; and Overseas Highway, 39; and Sunset Celebration, 146, 194–95; and Tourist Development Council (TDC), 252; and tourist development tax, 150, 175; and Truman's visits, 98–99; and urban renewal, 107; and World Powerboat races, 180; during World War II, 62

Key West City Commission, 230, 245, 252, 253, 279; and adult uses, 255–57; and Bahama Village, 232; and black representation, 170; and Christmas Tree Island, 270–73; and code enforcement, 254–55; and commercial fishing district, 210–11; and Conch Train, 101; and condo hotels, 264–65; and cruise ships, 213; and elections of 1985, 239; and Fantasy Fest, 181–82; and gambling, 85; and Growth Management Ordinance (GMO), 235–36; and Richard Heyman, 166–70; and high-rise development, 152–53; and Hillsborough Pride in Exile Days, 269–70; and Historic Architectural Review Commission (HARC), 228; and historic district, 140; and homelessness, 280–81; and Houseboat Row, 217; and Human Rights Ordinance, 172–73; and Key West Art Center, 106, and Key West Bight, 210–11; and Meacham Field, 93; and Old Island Restoration Commission (OIRC), 104; and One Human Family, 268–69; and Peary Court, 214–15; and public housing, 80; and the Reach, 203; and Rate of Growth Ordinance (ROGO), 242–43; and Salt Ponds development, 207–9; and Southernmost Point, 192; and street hawking, 110; and Truman Annex, 237–39; and urban renewal, 107; and zoning, 94

Key West City Council: abdication of governing authority, 44

Key West Cultural Preservation Society (CPS), 194–95

Key West Film Society, 260–61

Key West Foundation Company, 41

Key West Fragrance and Cosmetics Factory. *See* Key West Aloe

Key West Hand Print Fabrics, 106, 112, 123, 148

Key West Harbor, 271

Key West Harbour Development Corporation, 238

Key West High School, 78; integration of, 80

Key West Historic Memorial Sculpture Garden, 172

Key West Hotel and Motel Association, 175, 178, 181–82, 191, 193, 205, 212, 214, 215–16

Key West Housing Authority, 63, 80, 278

Key West Improvement Company, 93, 95

Key West International Airport, 93, 192, 206, 298. *See also* Meacham Field

Key West Lesbian and Gay Pride Alliance, 184

Key West Lighthouse & Keepers Quarters Museum, 188. *See also* Lighthouse museum

Key West Literary Seminar, 186

Key West Maritime Historical Society, 210, 211

Key West Museum of Art and History in the Custom House, 25, 188, 329n45

Key West Naval Station, 16, 20–21, 30, 33, 55, 60–61, 81, 97–98, 115, 122, 141, 151, 191, 237. *See also* Boca Chica Field; Naval Air Station at Trumbo Point; Naval Operating Base; Truman Annex

Key West Neighborhood Improvement Association, 230

Key West Planning and Restoration Commission, 152, 207

Key West Planning Board, 257, 276, 279

Key West Planning Department, 203, 206, 234, 264

Key West Players, 106, 123, 124

Key West Police Department, 55, 61, 83–86, 90, 116, 117, 119, 164, 166, 170–71, 273, 281, 314n20, 320n16, 323n23

Key West Pops Orchestra, 261

Key West Port and Transit Authority (PATA), 194, 195

Key West Realty Board, 39

Key West Realty Company, 40, 42, 93

Key West Redevelopment Agency (RDA), 237–39, 241

Key West Resident/Visitor Planning Committee, 253, 254

Key West Rotary Club, 79, 107, 282

Key West Salt Ponds Committee, 206

Key West Symphony Orchestra, 10, 245, 261, 289

Key West The Newspaper, 254, 273. *See also* Cooper, Dennis

Key West Tourist Development Council, 175. *See also* Tourist Development Council (TDC)

Key West Utility Board, 87, 88, 168

Key West Volunteer Corps, 45

Key West Woman's Club, 25, 79, 106, 124, 146, 164, 282

Key West Wreckers Club, 164–65

Key West Writers Workshop, 185, 186

Key West Yacht Club, 105, 172, 327n46

Kidder, Margot, 126, 155

Kieffer, Townsend, 328n13

Kilgore, Michael L., 263

King, David, 85

King's Point Yacht Club and Marina, 144

Kiraly, John, 123

Kirk, Claude, 88

Kirkwood, James, Jr., 126, 144, 260

Klein, Calvin, 141, 144, 227

Knight, Ed, 143, 207, 218

Kress Building, 163

Kroll, Bill, 101, 102

Ku Klux Klan, 33, 306n3

Kuralt, Charles, 195–96

Laber, Austin, 202, 203, 204

Labombard, Paul Arthur, Jr. *See* Singh, Pritam

La Brisa: condominiums, 207; resort, 28

Ladd, Frank H., 34

Laissez-faire attitude, 89, 252, 287. *See also* Live-and-let-live attitude

Lambda Democrats, 172

Lang, Victor, 105

Langley, Wright, 151

La Semana Alegre, 50

Las Salinas, 236

Last Stand, 166, 200, 212–15, 243–44, 248, 250, 251, 279

Lathum, Victor, 121

Latin American Chamber of Commerce, 175

Lear, Liz, 112

Legal Services of the Florida Keys, 242

Leibovitz, Annie, 155

Lesbian population, 7, 159, 161, 162, 165, 172, 183–84, 249, 256, 264, 270, 325n4. *See also* Gay population

Lewin, Kermit, 107

Lewis, Sally, 191, 203, 204, 245

Lighthouse museum, 101, 112, 147, 329n45. *See also* Key West Lighthouse & Keepers Quarters Museum

Lincoln Theater, 80

Lions Club, 79, 102

Liszka, Joe, 148, 151, 163

Little, Ed, 148, 211

Little White House. *See* Harry S. Truman Little White House

Liveaboards, 216, 237, 271, 272, 340n20

Live-and-let-live attitude, 4, 77, 92, 145, 154, 172, 257, 286–87. *See also* Laissez-faire attitude

Logan, Molly, 215

Long Key Fishing Camp, 30

Lopez, Placeres, 87

Lower Keys, 87, 176, 278, 281

Lower Matecumbe, 39, 43, 49, 52

Lurie, Alison, 128

Lyon, Eugene, 122

Mack, Connie, 215–16

Magliola, John, 328n13

Major, Charles, 80

Major, Emery, 170

Mallory Square, 104–6, 108, 109, 112, 123, 140, 145–47, 148, 169, 172, 189–91, 192, 193, 194–96, 211, 213–14, 248, 260. *See also* Cruise ships

Mallory Steamship Company, 26, 33

Malone, William H., 45, 48

Manville, Bill, 285, 318n42

Mardi Gras, 7, 148, 180

"Margaritaville" (Buffett), 120, 187

Mariel boatlift, 174–75

Market Share Company, 259

Marks, Larry, 207, 208, 209

Marlowe, Walt, 159–60, 163

Marmorstein, Max, 110

Martello Towers development, 42

Martí, José, 162

Martínez Ybor, Vicente, 22

Martini, John, 122–23, 237, 241

McCarthyism, 89

McCoy, Sonny, 141, 152, 166, 169, 171, 202, 231

McCullers, Carson, 90

McDaniel, Steve, 238–39

McDonald, Jill, 162

McGuane, Tom, 126–27, 144, 155

McLernan, James, 165, 166

McPherson, Morgan, 273

Meacham, Malcolm, 40, 41, 42, 93, 95

Meacham Field, 42–43, 93, 95. *See also* Key West International Airport
Meeting of the Minds, 187
Meinster, Jordan, 228
Meisel Capital Partners, 264, 265
Mel Fisher Maritime Heritage Society, 188, 329n45
Meredith, Burgess, 155
Merlo, Frank, 90, 108
Merrill, James, 186
Mertz, John, 276
Metropolitan Community Church (MCC), 164, 171, 172
Miami, 22, 26, 29, 36, 280, 326n30
Miami Daily News: on gambling in Key West, 53
Miami Herald, 46–47, 85, 118
Middle Keys, 39, 49
Midtown, 227, 270
Milian, Lang, 170
Military, U.S., 16–17, 20–21, 61–64, 79, 81–82, 99, 112, 114–16, 148, 189, 214–16, 315n53. *See also* Boca Chica Field; Key West Naval Station; Naval Air Station at Trumbo Point; Naval Operating Base; Truman Annex
Military Affairs Committee (MAC), 214–15
Milk, Harvey, 167
Mira, George, 78
Mira, James, 167, 203, 210, 239
Monroe County: Land Authority, 200, 209, 232, 281. *See also* Board of County Commissioners (BOCC); Tourist Development Council (TDC)
Monroe theater, 80, 161
Morales, Antonio Pena, 48. *See also* Bars and restaurants: Pena's Garden of Roses
Morgan, Marcella, 291; *When Paradise Was Ours*, 291
Morgan, F. Townsend, 45
Morgenstern, Henry Lee, 202, 323n29
Morris, James (Jan), 91; *Coast to Coast*, 91
Mosher, Gerald ("Moe"), 142, 189, 190
Mullins, Sheila, 217, 244, 245
Murphy, George, 180, 181
National Association for the Advancement of Colored People (NAACP), 80–81, 170, 210
National Coalition for the Homeless, 280, 282
National Register of Historic Places, 140, 189, 228
Native Americans, 14
Nature Conservancy, 209
Naval Air Station at Trumbo Point, 33, 62, 81

Naval Operating Base, 61–62
Neblett, William, 152
Needham, Greg, 263
Nesbitt, Bobby, 161
Newbury, Mickey, 188
Newman, Stuart, 177–78. *See also* Stuart Newman and Associates
New Orleans, 3, 14, 33, 35, 60, 148, 309n7
New Town, 92–95, 109, 139, 140, 141, 151–53, 227, 240, 279
New York Times, 13, 47, 64, 92, 98, 144–45, 240, 249, 280
Niles, "Woodsie," 258
No Name Key, 39, 43
Nu Age Construction Company, 93
Nuestra Señora de Atocha, 121–22, 189, 239. *See also* Fisher, Mel
Nutz, Eleanor, 183

Oates, Warren, 155
Ocala, Florida, 199, 232, 233, 263
Ocean Properties, 241, 271, 273. *See also* Walsh family
Oceanside Marina, 144
Ocean View Boulevard, 40
Ocean Walk apartments, 236, 332n32. *See also* Affordable housing; SeaSide development
Oldest House, 112, 147, 329n45
Old Island Days, 102–3, 179
Old Island Restoration Commission (OIRC), 104, 203, 228
Old Island Restoration Foundation (OIRF), 102–6, 142, 147, 152, 166
Old Town, 10, 139, 140–41, 154–55, 166, 169, 250, 260. *See also* Duval Street; Gay population; Guesthouses; Historic Architectural Review Commission (HARC); Historic District; Old Island Restoration Commission (OIRC); Old Island Restoration Foundation (OIRF)
Old Town Key West Development, 142, 189, 190, 204. *See also* Belland, Christopher; Historic Tours of America (HTA); Mosher, Gerald; Swift, Edwin, III
Old Town Merchants Association, 210
Old Town Trolley, 190–91, 194, 212. *See also* Historic Tours of America (HTA); Old Town Key West Development
Olson, Charles, 111
One Human Family, 267–70, 271–74, 274–79, 280–84, 291
Oosterhoudt, Tom, 245, 256, 257, 269

Open container ordinance, 254, 280
Outer Mole dock, 190, 192, 193, 213–14, 248.
　　See also Cruise ships
Overseas Highway, 38–40, 41, 43, 49, 52, 62
OverSeas Railway, 29, 34. See also Florida East
　　Coast Railway
Overseas Road and Toll Bridge Commission,
　　52

Paige, Claire and Marvin, 161
Pais, Joe, 215
Panama Canal, 29
Pan American Airways, 41, 42, 43
Panhandling, 36, 146, 280
Panico, Virginia, 178, 243
Papy, Bernard, 51, 52, 79, 85, 87, 88, 244, 271,
　　315n34
Papy, Bernard, Jr., 88
Papy, Whitney, 85
Parra, Armando, 258–59
Parrot Heads in Paradise, Inc., 187
Parrott, Milton A., 86
Peary Court, 206, 214–16
Pell, Peter, 106, 123, 148
Peninsular and Occidental (P&O) Steamship
　　Company, 26, 33, 49, 56, 109
Perez, Armando, Jr., 323n23
Perry, Lincoln, 186
Perry, Matthew C., 16
Petronia Street, 164, 257
Pfeiffer, Pauline, 56–58, 60
Pier B, 192, 193, 203, 213, 214, 241, 248. See also
　　Cruise ships
Pier House, 108–9, 112, 121, 125, 143, 144, 148,
　　155, 203–4, 240. See also Wolkowsky, David
Pinder, Joe, 146, 154–55, 313n6; and tourist
　　tax, 149–50
Pirates, 14, 16
Pirate's Alley, 108
Planning and Restoration Commission (PRC),
　　152, 207
Plant, Henry, 26
Plant Investment Company, 26
Poinciana apartments, 278, 312n58
Pope, Tom, 237
Population of Key West, 297
Porter, David, 16, 30, 62
Porter, Jessie, 59, 102, 186–87
Porter, William R., 40, 41, 49, 59, 93
Porter Docks, 36
Port Everglades, 49
Pottinger court case, 281

Powell, Boog, 78
Powell, Harry, 204, 215–16, 235–36
PrideFest, 165, 184, 256–57, 269
Pride Follies, 165
Prohibition, 36, 37, 57, 161
Prostitution, 54, 55, 83, 85. See also Brothels
Public Works Administration (PWA), 52
Puroff, Tom, 164
Pyle, Ernie, 55
Pynchon, E. A., 51

Queen Mother Pageant, 183
Quirolo, DeeVon, 213

Racchi, Tim, 189
Ramos, Hilario, 87, 88
Ramos, Hilario (Charles), Jr., 87, 88, 168, 244
Rand, Sally, 100
Rate of Growth Ordinance (ROGO), 242–44,
　　278
Raymer, Dorothy, 77, 90
Real estate development and investment, 9,
　　10, 22, 39, 40–42, 87, 94, 110–11, 207, 227–
　　29, 261–64, 275–76, 283–84, 286, 289–90.
　　See also Affordable housing; Gentrifica-
　　tion; Old Town Key West Development;
　　Singh, Pritam; Spottswood Companies,
　　Inc.; Truman Annex; Wolkowsky, David
Reck, Herbert F. R., 51
Red Barn Theatre (formerly Red Barn Actors
　　Studio), 106, 124, 253, 260
Red light district. See Brothels
Redwine, Gary, 171
Reef Relief, 213, 248
Reflections of Key West, 202
Reid, Drew, 187–88
Reinvention of Key West, 8, 11, 287, 291
Relief rolls: during Great Depression, 45,
　　50, 59
Restaurants. See Bars and restaurants
Rest Beach, 46
Rhodes, Harrison and Mary Wolfe Dumont,
　　27
Richardson, Robert, 186
Richardson, Simon Peter, 19
Ripley's Believe It or Not, 228, 329n45. See
　　also Chain stores
Ritson, Bruce, 273
Roberts, William G., 88
Rockland Key, 258
Rodel Foundation, 262
Rodriguez, Larry, 119

ROGO. *See* Rate of Growth Ordinance
(ROGO)
Rollison, Kathy and Opie, 276
Romano, Frank, 148, 150, 163, 212
Rongo, Carl, 118
Roosevelt, Eleanor, 47
Roosevelt Gardens, 278. *See also* Affordable
housing
Rosam, Merville, 88
Rosasco, Peter, 235
Ross, Gordon, 164, 165. *See also* Gordon
Ross and Friends
Rossi, Mark, 272, 273
Russell, Jimmy, 106, 148
Russell, Joe, 36, 57, 108
Russell House, 26, 27, 28

Salt Ponds, 16, 40, 42, 81, 93, 206–9, 216,
281
San Carlos Institute, 23, 51, 140
Sanchez, Mario, 123
Sanchez, Stephanie, 123
Sands, Roosevelt, Sr., 313n11
Sands Beach Club, 202
San Francisco, 114, 159, 167, 231, 263, 269,
331n1
Saunders, J. Willard, 88
"Save Our Homes" constitutional amend-
ment, 233
Save Our Neighborhoods (SON), 202
Save Our Shorelines (SOS), 203
Save Our Waterfront, 237
Sawyer, Berlin A., 85
Sawyer, Paul, 88
Sawyer, Rita, 103
Sawyer, Tom, 204
Scales, Ed, 255, 279
Schloesser, Don, 150
Schulberg, Budd, 286
Sculpture Key West, 189
Searstown, 95, 141
SeaSide development, 208, 216, 217, 236
Secession of Key West. *See* Conch Republic
Seidenberg, Sam, 22
Seven Mile Bridge, 176
Sewage system, 50, 151, 217, 245, 324n36
Sharp, Katherine Doris, 36
Sheehan, Katha, 259
Shipwreck Historeum Museum, 190–91
Shipyard condominiums, 242. *See also* Af-
fordable housing: in Truman Annex
Sholtz, David, 44

Shrimp industry, 8, 79, 80, 82, 83, 94, 99,
115–16, 209–10. *See also* Key West Bight
Shroeder, Joe, 161–62
Sigsbee Park, 62. *See also* Dredger's Key
Silverstein, Shel, 127–28
Simonton, John W., 14
Singh, Pritam, 189, 266, 239–42
Singleton, Stephen, 97
Singleton Seafood, 209–10
Sister Season Fund, 282
Skaggs, Gene, 153
Smathers Beach, 81, 281
Smith, Eric Johan, 45
Smith, Milo, 140
Smith, Steve, 165, 183
Sociedad de Cuba, 23
Solares Hill (newspaper), 153, 243, 250
Soto, Will, 195
Southern Homeless Assistance League, 282
Southernmost House, 25, 88, 322n11
Southernmost Point, 191–92
Spalding, Ralph, 84
Spaniards: migration to Key West, 22, 79
Spanish-American War, 20
Sponge industry, 16, 47, 21
Spottswood, John, 25, 98, 110–11
Spottswood, Mary, 143
Spottswood Companies, Inc., 266, 289
Spring breakers, 155, 205, 253
Stack, Ron, 146
Starcke, Walter, 106
Stavro, John, 286
Steamships, 20, 22, 26, 33, 49
Stephenson, Charles, 254
Stevens, Marion, 92, 123, 148
Stevens, Marjorie Carr, 60
Stevens, Paul, 92
Stevens, Wallace, 57–59
Stirrup, Dan, 108
Stock Island, 50, 55, 79, 81, 86, 95, 112, 115–17,
144, 176, 209–10, 230, 262, 266, 271, 278,
281–82, 285. *See also* Tennessee Williams
Fine Arts Center
Stokes, Jim, 184
Stone, Julius, Jr., 7–8, 11, 44–45, 47–48, 50, 51,
58, 186. *See also* Federal Emergency Relief
Administration (FERA); Key West Adminis-
tration (KWA)
Stone, Robert, 186
Strand theater, 80
Strobel, Benjamin, 18
Stuart Newman and Associates, 177, 198

Studios of Key West, 262

Summers, Kelly, 163

Sunset Celebration, 112, 145–47, 194–96

Sunset Key, 241, 271, 273. *See also* Tank Island

Swanson, Gloria, 100

Swift, Edwin, III, 120, 142, 151, 178, 189, 190, 209, 249–50, 297. *See also* Historic Tours of America (HTA); Old Town Key West Development

Swinging Doors, 83

Symroski, Ty, 283

Tank Island, 238, 240, 241. *See also* Sunset Key

Tarracino, Captain Tony, 122, 204–5, 215, 217, 235, 260, 287–88. *See also* Bars and restaurants: Captain Tony's Saloon

Tea dance, 163, 265–66

Tebeau, Charlton, 20

Tennessee Williams Fine Arts Center, 123, 166, 253, 260, 261

Thielen, Benedict, 84, 96

Third District Court of Appeal, 217–18, 276

Thompson, Charlie, 56

Thompson, Hunter, 127

Thompson, J. T., 268, 282

Thompson, Norberg, 82

Thompson Company, 21, 36

Thompson Enterprises, 82, 147–48

Tift, Asa, 57, 190–91

Tinsley Advertising & Marketing, Inc., 198

Topless Fishing Charters of America, 256

Torrence, Steven, 164, 172

Tourism, 2, 3, 8, 9; before Civil War, 12–14, 17–19; from Civil War to 1920, 25–28, 29–30; devil's bargain, 9; during 1920s, 34–35, 37–39, 40–41, 43; during Great Depression, 44–49, 52–56, 58, 59; during late 1940s, 1950s, and 1960s, 79, 95, 97–100, 100–106, 107–11; during 1970s, 120, 142–43, 145–51, 155–56, 162–63; during 1980s and 1990s, 165, 175–88, 189–96, 198–202, 209–14, 229–32, 234–36, 242–44; during twenty-first century, 247–58, 259, 262–67, 277–79, 290–91

—other destinations compared to Key West: Amsterdam (The Netherlands), 331n1; Asheville, North Carolina, 233; Aspen, Colorado, 242; Jackson, Wyoming, 200; Las Vegas, 230, 255, 264, 288; Monte Carlo, 53, 54, 55; Nantucket, Massachusetts, 141; New Orleans, 3, 14, 33, 35, 60, 148, 309n7; Orlando, 200, 264 (*see also* Walt Disney World); Provincetown, 249; Vail, Colorado, 242, 263; Venice, Italy, 330n55

Tourist Development Association (TDA), 148, 179–80, 181, 259

Tourist Development Council (TDC), 8, 175, 177, 179, 183, 198–201, 246, 252–55, 260, 264, 269, 277, 290–91

Tourist development tax, 149–50, 175, 192, 199, 290, 298

Tourist impact tax, 199–200

Trade Winds, 60, 90

Trafficante criminal organization, 314n20

Transient rentals, 243–44, 263–64, 275–77

Travel writing about Key West, 24, 28–29, 144, 162, 248–49, 250, 253, 261, 266; *Charles Kuralt's America*, 195–96; *Coast to Coast* (Morris), 91; criticism of Key West, 200, 201; *Fodor's*, 201, 288; *Key West in Transition, a Guide Book for Visitors* (1934), 47; *Off to the Side* (Harrison), 127; *States of Desire: Travels in Gay America* (White), 162; *Travel Guide to Key West and the Florida Keys* (Williams), 249–50

Tropic Cinema, 260–61

Truman, Harry S., 90, 97–98, 111. *See also* Harry S. Truman Little White House

Truman Annex, 81, 115, 122–23, 141–42, 189, 236–42, 270. *See also* Key West Naval Station

Truman Avenue: renaming of, 97–98

Truman Waterfront, 213

Trumbo Point, 20, 21, 29, 33, 39, 62, 81, 108. *See also* Flagler, Henry; Naval Air Station at Trumbo Point

Trust for Public Land, 211

T-shirt shops, 3, 9, 201, 212, 288

Turner, Alice, 144

Turner, Carmen, 245, 246

Turtle industry, 21, 147–48; Turtle Kraals Museum and Educational Center, 211

Twain, Mark, 26–27

Uniqueness, 6, 9, 145, 285–89, 301n5, 302n20; and architecture, 104, 245; before Civil War, 20; and chickens, 258–59; and cruise ship passengers, 247–48; and culture, 20, 121, 139; and Elmer Davis, 11, 48; and diversity, 144–45; and George Allen England, 37; and flora, 28; and *Florida-Times Union*, 29; and generica, 257; and gentrification, 260–61; and geography, 20; and Key West Hotel and Motel Association, 245–46; and mainstream mix, 288–89; in newspaper articles 1930s, 46; and perception of the "invalid," 13; and public policy, 197, 254–57; and secession, 1, 2; and Julius Stone Jr., 11; tempered by general trends, 286; threats to, 2–3, 8, 9, 11, 30, 199–201, 218, 245, 253, 263, 265, 267; and tourism promotion, 8, 34–35, 46–47, 95, 97, 99, 100; and Tourist Development Council (TDC), 253, 260; as valued by Jimmy Buffett and others, 139; and Tennessee Williams, 60. *See also* Live-and-let-live attitude

Urban Development Action Grant (UDAG), 203

Urban renewal, 106–7

U.S. Army Corps of Engineers, 17, 207

U.S. Border Patrol: and roadblock, 1, 177–78, 179

U.S. Department of Housing and Urban Development (HUD), 142, 203

U.S. Route 1, 113, 176; roadblock on, 1, 177

Utility costs, 229, 232, 233

Vasquez, Raul, 37, 47

Verge, Bill, 272

Veterans Work Program, 49

Vidal, Gore, 90

Viele, John, 15, 16

Vinson, Fred, 98

Von Cosel, Carl, 4–5

Vonnegut, Kurt, Jr., 144

Waldron, Paul, 208

Walsh family, 272, 273. *See also* Ocean Properties

Walt Disney World, 142, 155, 179, 245

Walters, Dean, 262

Wardlow, Dennis, 1, 167–68, 172, 177–79, 181, 205, 212, 215, 216–17, 218, 244

Waterfront Playhouse, 106, 123, 124, 188, 260

Water system, 50, 62–63, 115, 140, 150–51, 176, 324n36, 327n6

Watlington House, 147. *See also* Oldest House

Weaver, Lyle, 112

Weekley, Jimmy, 172–73, 203, 215, 236, 239, 244–45, 253, 254, 279, 283

Weeks, Vicki, 183

Weiner, Arthur, 152

Weinman, Irving, 186

Wells, Sharon, 235

Welters Cornet Band (formerly Key West Cornet Band), 23–24, 78

West Indies Squadron, 16

West Martello Tower, 16, 17, 92

West Palm Beach, 29, 273

Westray, William, 152, 153, 154

Whalton, Michael, 185

Wheeler, Harold, 198, 252–53

When Paradise Was Ours (Morgan), 291

Whitehead, John, 15

Whitehead, William, 18

Whiteside, Mark, 165

Wickers, Bill, 201

Wickers Field, 81

Wilbur, Charlee, 124

Wilbur, Richard, 10, 124, 125, 186

Wilcox, J. Mark, 53

Williams, Tennessee, 6, 7, 53, 60, 89–90, 108, 112, 123, 148, 164, 172, 186; Tennessee Williams in Key West exhibit, 187. *See also* Tennessee Williams Fine Arts Center

William Street, 30, 127

Wilson, Howard E., 52

Windhorn, Stan, 151

Windsor Lane: writers' compound, 124–25, 126

Wisteria Corporation, 271

Wisteria Island. *See* Christmas Tree Island

Wisteria Island Committee, 273

Wolfson, Mitchell, 102, 190

Wolkowsky, David, 107, 108–9, 120, 143, 202

Wolkowsky, Isaac, 57, 108

WomenFest, 183

Women in Paradise Week, 183

Woods, Stanley, 45

Works Progress Administration (WPA), 50, 51, 54

World War I, 20–21, 34

World War II, 61–62, 63

Wrecking industry, 13, 14, 15, 20, 190–91

Wright, Morris, 171

Wright, William, 109

Wyndham International Corporation, 202

Yglesias, Jose, 111

Zoning variance, 243–43

Zorskey, Joe, 258

Zuelch, Kirk, 119

Robert Kerstein is professor of government
at the University of Tampa and the author of
Politics and Growth in Twentieth-Century Tampa.

THE FLORIDA HISTORY AND CULTURE SERIES
Edited by Raymond Arsenault and Gary R. Mormino

Al Burt's Florida: Snowbirds, Sand Castles, and Self-Rising Crackers, by Al Burt (1997)

Black Miami in the Twentieth Century, by Marvin Dunn (1997)

Gladesmen: Gator Hunters, Moonshiners, and Skiffers, by Glen Simmons and Laura Ogden (1998)

"Come to My Sunland": Letters of Julia Daniels Moseley from the Florida Frontier, 1882–1886, edited by Julia Winifred Moseley and Betty Powers Crislip (1998)

The Enduring Seminoles: From Alligator Wrestling to Ecotourism, by Patsy West (1998; first paperback edition, 2008)

Government in the Sunshine State: Florida Since Statehood, by David R. Colburn and Lance deHaven-Smith (1999)

The Everglades: An Environmental History, by David McCally (1999; first paperback edition, 2001)

Beechers, Stowes, and Yankee Strangers: The Transformation of Florida, by John T. Foster Jr. and Sarah Whitmer Foster (1999)

The Tropic of Cracker, by Al Burt (1999)

Balancing Evils Judiciously: The Proslavery Writings of Zephaniah Kingsley, edited and annotated by Daniel W. Stowell (1999)

Hitler's Soldiers in the Sunshine State: German POWs in Florida, by Robert D. Billinger Jr. (2000)

Cassadaga: The South's Oldest Spiritualist Community, edited by John J. Guthrie, Phillip Charles Lucas, and Gary Monroe (2000)

Claude Pepper and Ed Ball: Politics, Purpose, and Power, by Tracy E. Danese (2000)

Pensacola during the Civil War: A Thorn in the Side of the Confederacy, by George F. Pearce (2000)

Castles in the Sand: The Life and Times of Carl Graham Fisher, by Mark S. Foster (2000)

Miami, U.S.A., by Helen Muir (2000)

Politics and Growth in Twentieth-Century Tampa, by Robert Kerstein (2001)

The Invisible Empire: The Ku Klux Klan in Florida, by Michael Newton (2001)

The Wide Brim: Early Poems and Ponderings of Marjory Stoneman Douglas, edited by Jack E. Davis (2002)

The Architecture of Leisure: The Florida Resort Hotels of Henry Flagler and Henry Plant, by Susan R. Braden (2002)

Florida's Space Coast: The Impact of NASA on the Sunshine State, by William Barnaby Faherty, S.J. (2002)

In the Eye of Hurricane Andrew, by Eugene F. Provenzo Jr. and Asterie Baker Provenzo (2002)

Florida's Farmworkers in the Twenty-first Century, text by Nano Riley and photographs by Davida Johns (2003)

Making Waves: Female Activists in Twentieth-Century Florida, edited by Jack E. Davis and Kari Frederickson (2003)

Orange Journalism: Voices from Florida Newspapers, by Julian M. Pleasants (2003)

The Stranahans of Ft. Lauderdale: A Pioneer Family of New River, by Harry A. Kersey Jr. (2003)

Death in the Everglades: The Murder of Guy Bradley, America's First Martyr to Environmentalism, by Stuart B. McIver (2003)

Jacksonville: The Consolidation Story, from Civil Rights to the Jaguars, by James B. Crooks (2004)

The Seminole Wars: America's Longest Indian Conflict, by John and Mary Lou Missall (2004)

The Mosquito Wars: A History of Mosquito Control in Florida, by Gordon Patterson (2004)

Seasons of Real Florida, by Jeff Klinkenberg (2004; first paperback edition, 2009)

Land of Sunshine, State of Dreams: A Social History of Modern Florida, by Gary R. Mormino (2005; first paperback edition, 2008)

Paradise Lost? The Environmental History of Florida, edited by Jack E. Davis and Raymond Arsenault (2005)

Frolicking Bears, Wet Vultures, and Other Oddities: A New York City Journalist in Nineteenth-Century Florida, edited by Jerald T. Milanich (2005)

Waters Less Traveled: Exploring Florida's Big Bend Coast, by Doug Alderson (2005)

Saving South Beach, by M. Barron Stofik (2005)

Losing It All to Sprawl: How Progress Ate My Cracker Landscape, by Bill Belleville (2006; first paperback edition, 2010)

Voices of the Apalachicola, compiled and edited by Faith Eidse (2006)

Floridian of His Century: The Courage of Governor LeRoy Collins, by Martin A. Dyckman (2006)

America's Fortress: A History of Fort Jefferson, Dry Tortugas, Florida, by Thomas Reid (2006)

Weeki Wachee, City of Mermaids: A History of One of Florida's Oldest Roadside Attractions, by Lu Vickers (2007)

City of Intrigue, Nest of Revolution: A Documentary History of Key West in the Nineteenth Century, by Consuelo E. Stebbins (2007)

The New Deal in South Florida: Design, Policy, and Community Building, 1933–1940, edited by John A. Stuart and John F. Stack Jr. (2008)

Pilgrim in the Land of Alligators: More Stories about Real Florida, by Jeff Klinkenberg (2008; first paperback edition, 2011)

A Most Disorderly Court: Scandal and Reform in the Florida Judiciary, by Martin A. Dyckman (2008)

A Journey into Florida Railroad History, by Gregg M. Turner (2008)

Sandspurs: Notes from a Coastal Columnist, by Mark Lane (2008)

Paving Paradise: Florida's Vanishing Wetlands and the Failure of No Net Loss, by Craig Pittman and Matthew Waite (2009; first paperback edition, 2010)

Embry-Riddle at War: Aviation Training during World War II, by Stephen G. Craft (2009)

The Columbia Restaurant: Celebrating a Century of History, Culture, and Cuisine, by Andrew T. Huse, with recipes and memories from Richard Gonzmart and the Columbia restaurant family (2009)

Ditch of Dreams: The Cross Florida Barge Canal and the Struggle for Florida's Future, by Steven Noll and David Tegeder (2009)

Manatee Insanity: Inside the War over Florida's Most Famous Endangered Species, by Craig Pittman (2010)

Frank Lloyd Wright's Florida Southern College, by Dale Allen Gyure (2010)

Sunshine Paradise: A History of Florida Tourism, by Tracy J. Revels (2011)

Hidden Seminoles: Julian Dimock's Historic Florida Photographs, by Jerald T. Milanich and Nina J. Root (2011)

Key West on the Edge: Inventing the Conch Republic, by Robert Kerstein (2012)

The Scent of Scandal: Greed, Betrayal, and the World's Most Beautiful Orchid, by Craig Pittman (2012)